Beyond HTML

Beyond HTML

Richard Karpinski

Osborne **McGraw-Hill**

Berkeley New York St. Louis San Francisco
Auckland Bogotá Hamburg London Madrid
Mexico City Milan Montreal New Delhi Panama City
Paris São Paulo Singapore Sydney
Tokyo Toronto

Osborne **McGraw-Hill**
2600 Tenth Street
Berkeley, California 94710
U.S.A.

For information on translations or book distributors outside the U.S.A., or to arrange bulk purchase discounts for sales promotions, premiums, or fundraisers, please contact Osborne **McGraw-Hill** at the above address.

Beyond HTML

1234567890 DOC 99876

ISBN 0-07-882198-3

Acquisitions Editor Scott Rogers	**Computer Designer** Richard Whitaker
Project Editor Emily Rader	**Illustrator** Roberta Steele
Copy Editors Kathryn Hashimoto Cathy Baehler	**Cover Design** Ted Mader Associates, Inc.
Proofreader Rhonda Holmes	**Quality Control Specialist** Joe Scuderi

To Raquel and Emily,
with love and thanks for your
endless patience and support

About the Author

Richard Karpinski is currently Online Editor for *Communications Week* and *Interactive Age* magazines, both in print and on the Web. He is also the Webmaster of the Communications Week Interactive and Interactive Age Digital Web sites. He has degrees from the University of Illinois and Syracuse University.

Contents

Acknowledgments xv
Introduction xvii

Part 1

HTML Alternatives: Adobe Acrobat and More

‖‖‖ 1 Welcome to the World of Electronic
　　　Paper . . . .　3
　　Adobe Acrobat Basics . . . .　4
　　　Portable Document Format . . . .　8
　　　The Acrobat Product Family . . . .　9
　　Acrobat and the Web 10
　　How Acrobat Is Used Today 12
　　　Newspapers and Magazines 12
　　　Marketing and Technical Support 15
　　　Specialty Publishing 17
　　Summary 22

‖‖‖ 2 Creating Documents with Acrobat 23
　　Acrobat Reader 24
　　　Acrobat Reader 2.1 25
　　　Viewing Documents with Reader 26
　　　Navigating a PDF File 26
　　Creating PDF Files 31
　　　Creating Files with PDF Writer 32
　　　Creating Files with Acrobat Distiller 38
　　　Using Acrobat Exchange 42
　　　Some Acrobat Loose Ends 49

Acrobat and the Web 51
   PDF Design and the Web 51
   WebLink 52
   Serving up PDF 55
   The Future of Acrobat on the Web 55
Summary 60

3 Acrobat Applications 63
TimesFax 64
Voyager 66
Axcess 68
Dial-A-Book 70
Magnetic Press 71
Summary 73

Part 2

Multimedia and Interactivity: Java and More

4 Introduction to the "Programmable Web" 77
A Look at What's Possible 78
The Interactive Web: Today and Tomorrow 82
The New Web Toolbox 83
   Sun's Java 84
   Microsoft's Internet Studio and More 86
   The Netscape OS 87
   Multimedia Plug-Ins: Shockwave and More 87
Summary 89

5 Java for the Rest of Us: Tips for Nonprogrammers 91
Java-Capable Browsers 92
Working with Java Applets 94
   Java Applet Basics 95
   The Intersection of Java and HTML 96
   More HTML Tricks: Passing Parameters 96
   Some Examples 99
   Where to Find Java Applets 108
   Final Considerations: Speed, Security, and Compatibility 111
Will Java Get Simpler to Use? 112

Java Authoring Tools (for Nonprogrammers) . . 114
JavaScript and Java 115
Summary 116

6 A Crash Course in Java Programming . . . 117

Your First Swig of Java 118
The Java Coding Environment 118
Writing a Simple Applet 122
HelloWorld: A Sample Applet 122
How the HelloWorld Applet Works 123
Diving Deeper into Java 124
What is OOP? 125
The Nuts and Bolts of Java 127
Java Syntax 127
A Simple Math Program: A+B+C 129
Java Control Flow 130
Understanding and Working with Classes 133
Another Run at a Java Applet 135
Java Class Packages 137
What's Next for Java 139
The Emerging Java Toolbox 140
Summary 144

7 Java in Action 145

Java "Ground Zero": Gamelan 146
The Sports Network and Wall Street Web 147
C/Net's PC Scoreboard 149
Fun and Games 150
Dimension X: Java and VRML 151
Java on the Intranet 152
Summary 153

8 Microsoft's Internet Platform 155

Microsoft Internet Platform Overview 158
Internet Explorer 2.0 159
HTML Extensions 159
Internet Assistant 164
Creating Documents 165
Other Office Tools 172
Microsoft's FrontPage 173
Using FrontPage 174

Where FrontPage is headed 186
Internet Studio 186
Inside Blackbird 187
What to Expect of Internet Studio 189
What's Next: Internet Add-On and More 190
VB Script: What Is It? 191
Summary 193

‖‖‖‖ 9 The Netscape Internet OS 195
The Netscape Difference 197
Frames 197
Working with Frames 198
Netscape's Support for Java 205
JavaScript 205
What Is JavaScript? 207
Using JavaScript 209
What You Can Do with JavaScript 221
Plug-ins 227
Plug-ins and HTML 231
The Future of Plug-ins 232
Netscape Navigator Gold 233
Working with Gold 234
Netscape Helper Pages 240
Netscape Page Wizard 240
Summary 244

‖‖‖‖ 10 Macromedia Shockwave 245
Working with Director 247
Setting the Stage 247
Creating Animations 252
Adding Effects: Transitions and Sound 256
Adding Interactivity with Lingo 258
Building a Shockwave Movie 262
Beyond HTML: the Shocked Version 263
Preparing a Movie for the Web 267
Shockwave Player: Viewing the Movie 269
A "Shocked" Tour of the Web 269
Summary 276

Part 3

VRML: Virtual Reality Meets the Web

|||||| 11 Introduction to VRML 279

The Sixty-Second History of VRML 282
What's Possible with VRML? 283
Where to Find VRML Viewers 285
What Is VRML and How Does It Work? 287
   Close-Up on VRML 288
   VRML Authoring Tools 295
Where Is VRML Headed Next? 296
Summary 301

|||||| 12 Building Worlds with VRML Tools 303

ParaGraph's Virtual Home Space Builder 304
Using VHSB 305
   The VHSB User Interface 306
   Building VRML Worlds in VHSB 311
   Exit Thoughts: Virtual Home Space Builder . . . 317
Virtus WalkThrough Pro 318
Using WalkThrough Pro 318
   WalkThrough Pro's User Interface 319
   Building a World in WalkThrough Pro 319
Exit Thoughts: Virtus WalkThrough Pro 328
Caligari's Fountain 329
   Fountain's Browsing Mode 329
   Fountain's Building Mode 330
   Exit Thoughts: Fountain 339
Summary 342

|||||| 13 A Virtual Tour of the 3-D Web 343

Finding VRML Worlds 344
Cybertown 345
Market Central 348
Planet 9 Studios 349
   Interview with Planet 9's David Colleen 349
VRML 2.0—Moving Worlds Beta 353
AlphaWorld 353
Summary 356

Part 4

Real-Time Multimedia

||||| 14 Introduction to the Real-Time Web 359

The Streaming Audio Technology Leaders 360

VoxWare's ToolVox 361

DSP Group's TrueSpeech 362

VocalTec's Internet Wave 363

Progressive Networks' RealAudio 365

The Next Wave: High-Quality
Audio and Video 367

Xing StreamWorks 368

VDONet's VDOLive 370

The Netscape Wild Card 371

Summary 372

||||| 15 Hands-on Real-Time Audio 373

Audio-on-the-Web Primer 374

Recording Tips 375

Hands-on: ToolVox, TrueSpeech, Iwave, and
RealAudio 376

Using VoxWare's ToolVox 376

Using DSP Group's TrueSpeech 380

Using VocalTec's Internet Wave 384

Using Progressive Networks' RealAudio 388

Summary 394

||||| 16 A Real-Time Tour of the Web 395

Where to Find the Real-Time Pioneers 398

RealAudio 398

Xing StreamWorks 401

TrueSpeech 402

Internet Wave 402

Real-Time Closeup 402

AudioNet 402

CBS Up to the Minute 405

Summary 407

A Web Resource Guide 409

    HTML Alternatives: Adobe and More 410

    Java Resources 412

    The Microsoft Internet Platform 420

    Netscape Internet OS 421

    Netscape Plug-Ins 422

    VRML Resources 432

        Real-time Audio and Video 436

Index .439

Acknowledgments

I could not have written this book without the help of many key individuals. Above all, I'd like to thank the staff at Osborne/McGraw-Hill. I like to think this book was fate. Executive Editor, Scott Rogers phoned me the week that Interactive Age, the magazine I worked for, was shutting down its print side. It was a traumatic time. He wanted to pitch me on a job as a book editor, but I wasn't willing to move to California, nor to leave the magazine world. Before we said good-bye, I got my thoughts together quickly and pitched him on a book I'd been thinking about, called *Beyond HTML*. Seems he had been trying to place a book with just that title. As it turned out, he got the idea for his *Beyond HTML* from a magazine story I had written that had those words in its title. I had forgotten all about it. It was a twist of fate at a difficult moment. Scott has gently pushed and prodded this book through from start to finish. It wouldn't have gotten done without him.

Others at OMH deserve thanks as well. Daniela Dell'Orco, Scott's assistant, helped me out in countless ways and developed a strong personal relationship with my voice mail and e-mail. Vicki Van Ausdall and Emily Rader worked as project editors on the project and guided the book into its final form. Thomas Powell, of Powell Internet Consulting, San Diego, provided an invaluable technical edit on the book.

A thanks also needs to go out to my co-workers and bosses at CMP Publications, *Communications Week* and *Interactive Age,* for their help and support. Finally, I'd like to thank all the people I have met and talked with in the Web community, both for this book and in my career as a journalist. There's no greater buzz you can get as a reporter than talking with people who are truly excited about what they do. The Web is all about chasing that buzz. Thanks to everyone who has shared their time, knowledge, expertise, excitement, and enthusiasm.

Introduction

L ike most Webmasters, you probably have a shelf of books you keep handy to help you do your job. You know the type: "Learn HTML Overnight," "Running a Great Web Site," "CGI Scripts for the Programming-Impaired." It's often been said that no one is making money yet on the Internet. Well, maybe the bookstores are.

The Web is becoming more challenging, more complex, and infinitely more interesting as time flies by. And that bookshelf of yours continues to bow under the weight of your accumulating library. The aim of this book is to offer a one-stop resource that will help guide your next major step into new Web technologies. The book will assist you in moving "beyond HTML," which you probably already know about—and may be tired of working with—and lets you catch the wave of new design and authoring technologies sweeping over the Web, including Adobe Acrobat, Sun's Java, Netscape's JavaScript, Microsoft's Internet Studio and FrontPage, Macromedia's Shockwave, the Virtual Reality Modeling Language (VRML), real-time audio technologies like RealAudio, and much more.

We won't just tell you about these amazing new tools—we'll show you how they work with real-world examples and working code. We'll tell you how to download the software you need and how to get it running. We'll provide tips and advice on how to start working with these new technologies, whether you are a novice or an expert. We'll examine how leading-edge Web sites are already using these technologies to add sizzle and substance to their offerings. And we'll point you to additional Web resources to help you keep up to date with these constantly evolving technologies.

As a Webmaster, your job has never been more challenging, or more exciting. You need to keep up with the developments detailed in this book, or risk getting left behind. But more importantly, you need to keep up to speed, because it is just these sorts of technologies—such as Java, VRML, or Shockwave—that make Webmastering so exciting and your friends working in ho-hum jobs so jealous.

Keeping Up with the Web

Information overload is a common malady these days, and the Web contributes to it mightily. As a Webmaster, you are at a severe risk of being completely overwhelmed by new technologies and developments. The Web is moving so quickly these days that in the blink of a Netscape beta cycle it often seems the whole world has changed. During the creation of this book, for example, several major land shifts occurred—along with countless additional tremors—that set the stage for the next generation of the Web. You can read about all of these in more detail inside, but let's offer a tease of what I believe are the most important themes that have guided—and will continue to guide—the development of the World Wide Web.

The Netscape Revolution

Through the fall and winter of 1995, Netscape Navigator 2.0 was launched, bringing Java, JavaScript, and countless Netscape plug-ins to the Web. The introduction of Navigator 2.0 is arguably one of the most significant events in the Web's young lifetime. It turned the Web from a static repository of mainly text and graphics to a living, breathing, interactive multimedia environment.

With Java, the Web gains the ability to deliver executable programs that can run on local machines and *do* things: run an animation, play a game, create an interactive application, and much more. JavaScript offers much of the same interactivity, but on a much easier learning curve. And the plug-in architecture brings an endless variety of multimedia to the Web by letting any application vendor plug its run-time technology directly into Navigator 2.0.

Netscape 2.0 is literally changing the face of the Web. It even changed Netscape's Web site, which, at more than 40 million estimated hits per day, is one of the Internet's most popular destinations. Netscape changed its Web site in early 1996 to take advantage of JavaScript and another Navigator 2.0 enhancement called *frames*. The site, shown in the following illustration, provides users with a dynamically changing table of contents and offers us a good preview of how the next generation of Web sites will shape up.

You can learn how to take advantage of Navigator 2.0 in Chapter 9. Also, be sure to check out the detailed run down of two of the Web's most popular plug-ins, Adobe Acrobat (Chapters 1, 2, and 3) and Macromedia Shockwave (Chapter 10).

Plenty of space and time are also given to Sun's Java programming environment (Chapters 5, 6, and 7). Included is an extensive hands-on look at Java from a non-technical Webmasters point of view (Chapter 5), a tutorial on the language itself (Chapter 6), and a tour of Java-powered Web sites (Chapter 7).

Netscape and Friends vs. Microsoft

In a single week in early December, Sun and Netscape unveiled the JavaScript programming language, along with dozens of supporting partners, while Microsoft rolled out a slew of new Internet technologies and directions, including an expected license of Sun's Java, a new Web language called Visual Basic Script, a mid-year rollout of its newly-named Internet Studio (formerly Blackbird) authoring tool, as well as plans to integrate Web browser functionality directly into Windows 95.

Thus, in the span of a single week, the entire Web landscape changed, and even more important, the lines were drawn up in the battle that will determine the future of the Web: Netscape and its friends vs. Microsoft. At stake are the soup-to-nuts underpinnings of tomorrow's Web, including browser, authoring, development tool, server, and secure payment technologies. We have seen how Netscape is supercharging the Web, but Microsoft has equal, if not greater, ambitions. The following illustration shows the Microsoft Internet Development Toolbox Web site, which, as you can see, is overflowing with new technologies and hot ideas.

Check out Chapters 8 and 9 for the scoop on the Netscape/Microsoft wars, and a hands-on view of the technologies those companies will use to wage their fight.

Virtual Reality and the Web

In mid-January, the future of the 3-D Web began to take focus almost overnight. The VRML Architecture Group received a handful of proposals for VRML 2.0, which will add interactivity and behaviors to VRML.

For those who haven't experienced it yet, VRML lets you enter and navigate three-dimensional worlds on the Internet. It is a fascinating experience, though so far somewhat constrained by the limitations of the technology. The following illustration shows the VRML Museum, a 3-D world created by one of VRML's pioneers, Silicon Graphic's Chris Marrin.

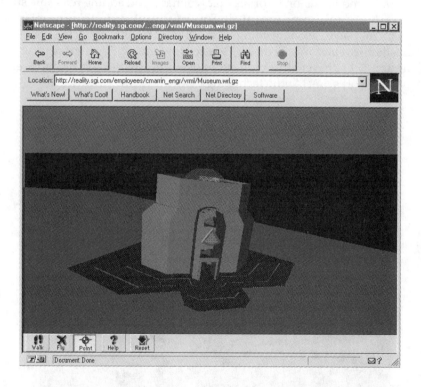

VRML 2.0 will expand VRML technology by adding support for scripting languages and advanced capabilities that literally will let 3-D Web worlds spring to life. In a single week in January, the major players drew up sides. Netscape, Silicon Graphics, and a slew of partners came out in support of SGI's Moving Worlds proposal. On the other side, once again, was Microsoft, this time with its ActiveVRML proposal.

You can learn all about VRML 1.0, including some innovative authoring tools, in Chapters 11, 12, and 13, along with a sneak preview of VRML 2.0.

Real-Time Audio and Video

In early February, Netscape (again!) announced major new plans, this time in the form of its proposed LiveMedia architecture, which will integrate real-time audio, video, telephony, and videoconferencing directly into the Netscape browser.

The real-time multimedia market was already exploding on the Web, but the Netscape move guarantees waves of new and innovative real-time technologies. For a look at the pioneers of real-time audio and video—including Progressive Networks' RealAudio, Xing Technologies' StreamWorks, VDONet's VDOLive, VocalTec's Internet Wave, VoxWare's ToolVox, and DSP Group's TrueSpeech—turn to Chapters 14, 15, and 16. There, you'll find hands-on tutorials that will have you adding real-time streaming audio to your home page in no time at all. For the adventurous, these chapters also point the way for you to add streaming video (think of it as Web TV) to your site.

Web businesses, such as MCI's 1-800 Music Now, are building entire businesses around the ability to deliver streaming audio over the Internet—in MCI's case, using Progressive Networks' RealAudio technology.

Web Resource Guide

Appendix A provides a Web resource guide, which will point you to the company and industry home pages you'll need to keep up with the rapidly evolving Web. From obvious sites, such as Sun's Java page, shown here, to more esoteric but indispensable pages, such as BrowserWatch and JavaScript Index, Appendix A tells you how to reach Web resources and what to expect when you get there.

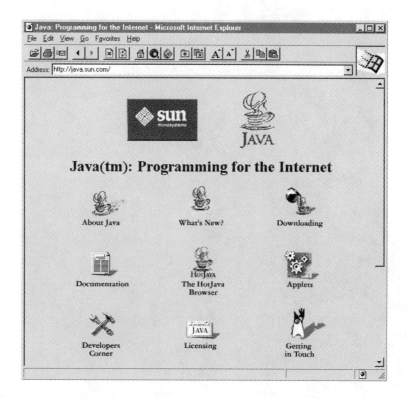

Contacting the Author

If you have a question or would like to share your experiences with the tools and technologies outlined in this book, feel free to drop me an e-mail message at **rjkarp@ix.netcom.com**. I look forward to hearing from you. I hope you enjoy this book and can share the excitement I felt in learning about and working with these next-generation Web tools.

PART ONE

HTML Alternatives: Adobe Acrobat and More

Roadmap ▶

We will focus on Adobe Acrobat, probably the most advanced electronic publishing system and the one currently moving fastest toward linking itself completely and seamlessly to the World Wide Web. Chapter 2 is a comprehensive walk-through on creating documents with Acrobat, including how to work with Acrobat on the Web. Chapter 3 offers case studies and tips from leading-edge Acrobat developers. We will also take sneak peeks at Novell's Envoy and Common Ground's Web Publisher, which are alternatives to Acrobat. (These can be found at the end of this chapter.)

Chapter One

Welcome
to the World of
Electronic Paper

Wouldn't it be great if you could avoid the intricacies of hypertext markup language (HTML) yet still deliver documents on the World Wide Web that would rival the flashiest of magazine layouts? What if instead of learning a difficult tagged language like HTML, you could create those documents using software including word processors, spreadsheets, and desktop publishing programs that you already work with and have on your desktop? And finally, what if you no longer had to worry—as is too often the case with today's Web browsers—that the page you so painstakingly designed would appear garbled on the other end due to inconsistent implementations of HTML extensions? Content providers are growing tired of different Web browsers displaying HTML pages in varied fashions, at times breaking down altogether, as shown in Figure 1-1.

An emerging category of electronic publishing tools—including Adobe Systems' Acrobat, Novell's Envoy, and Common Ground's Web Publisher—promises a solution. Each of these takes documents that are created on computer but are ultimately headed for printout on paper and preserves them in their original electronic format. Sounds simple enough. But the problem with the electronic distribution of documents in their native form is that not everyone uses the same computer software. Take word processors: some people use Microsoft Word, while others use WordPerfect. Each program formats text and embedded images in a different way. More complex is desktop publishing. Many folks use QuarkXPress, while others rely on Adobe PageMaker or other applications. Each of these very powerful packages has its own way of creating and viewing documents.

In electronic publishing systems like Acrobat, Envoy, and Web Publisher, content creators work with their existing tools and then "convert" the document to a standard file format that preserves the document's original fonts, graphics, and layouts. All an end user needs to see the document in all its original glory is the corresponding viewer, which in most cases today is available for free and is increasingly integrated right into the most popular browsers, including Netscape Navigator and Spyglass Mosaic. For instance, rather than code a complex HTML table for its Fortune 500 listings, *Fortune* magazine turned to Adobe Acrobat (see Figure 1-2).

In short, what you have is *electronic paper*: instead of printing a document out on paper, the results are preserved in digital form and are viewable on any computer, regardless of the operating system it is running or the application software residing on its hard drive. Add the Internet and the World Wide Web as the ultimate, global vehicles for distributing these documents online, and all the pieces fall into place. Electronic publishing systems promise to transform the Web into a much more dynamic, graphically rich publishing environment while relieving Web designers of the complexities and limitations of HTML.

Adobe Acrobat Basics

Acrobat software is based on Adobe's PostScript page description language, the de facto industry standard for desktop publishing and printing. It is not a single piece of software, but rather a family of tools and features that greatly simplifies the creation of

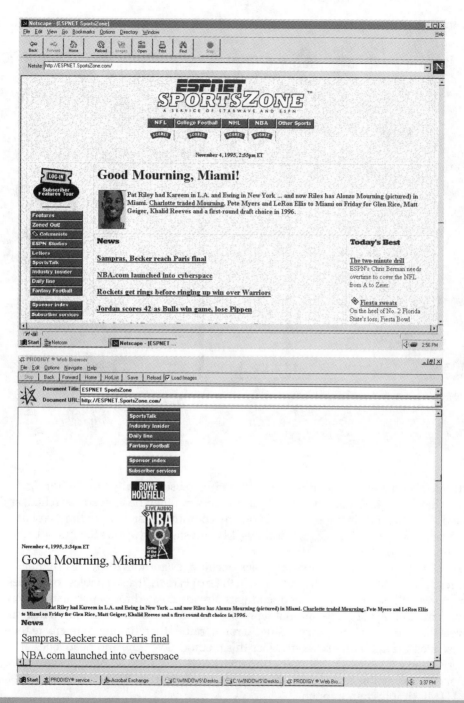

Figure 1-1. *ESPNET uses tables to good effect in Netscape, but they break down in Prodigy's browser*

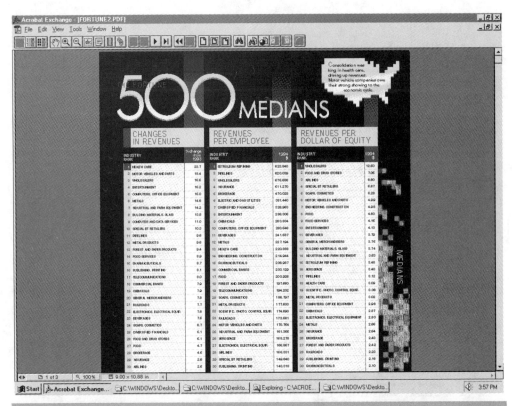

Figure 1-2. *Adobe Acrobat preserves the look and feel of highly graphical documents on the World Wide Web*

electronic documents by enabling content creators to use virtually any authoring application to create documents. Those documents can then be viewed, searched, and printed with their original look and feel on any computer that can run the Acrobat viewer software, including DOS, Windows, Macintosh, and various flavors of Unix operating systems.

Acrobat's use-your-own-tools approach encourages authors to create original, Web-ready documents in Acrobat rather than to learn HTML. It also enables companies or individuals with large numbers of documents already created for paper distribution (such as marketing materials, annual reports, or technical documentation) to instantly convert them into electronic form using Acrobat, rather than having to re-create them from scratch using HTML. Not only does this method save time and headaches, it preserves the valuable—and at times trademarked—look and feel of important corporate information across the paper and electronic worlds. These are advantages that HTML simply cannot touch.

Adobe Acrobat

▶ VS ◀

HTML

The Good, the Bad, and the Fuzzy

ADVANTAGES

- ■ Acrobat lets content creators maintain firm design control; the pages they design are exactly the same documents that users will view on the other end. HTML code gets interpreted differently by different Web browsers, and is at times rendered unreadable. Also, Acrobat PDF files can be saved with all their formatting and can be viewed offline; most Web browsers save only the text of HTML documents, not the inline graphics.

- ■ With Acrobat, authors can use tools with which they are already comfortable—from word processors to desktop publishing tools to spreadsheets—to build their Web content. With HTML, authors must learn a complicated tagged language or rely on just-emerging WYSIWYG tools.

- ■ Acrobat is becoming increasingly integrated with the Web. Acrobat Weblink lets PDF files link out to the Web. New APIs, already in beta, display PDF files directly within Web browsers and allow page-at-a-time delivery, enabling Acrobat to become a better browsing tool.

- ■ Acrobat's built-in compression shrinks highly graphical files for delivery over the Web, which is often accessed by users with low-speed modems. A compressed Acrobat document—fonts, graphics, layout, and all—may often not be any larger than a good-sized GIF image.

DISADVANTAGES

- ■ Acrobat assumes users are already fluent in electronic document creation. If you aren't already a wizard with Quark, for example, Acrobat isn't going to make you one. Garbage in, garbage out.

- ■ Adobe Acrobat is not cheap. High-end, desktop publishing-level capabilities require Acrobat Distiller (about $600) plus the DTP package itself (about the same if not more). Powerful HTML authoring packages can now be had for less than $100 (and often for free).

- Acrobat is based on paper publishing technologies. Although the Web today looks like an online publishing environment, at its core it is a platform for distributed computing and two-way communications. If what you want is simple, powerful electronic publishing, Acrobat may be your tool. But if you want interactive capabilities, you may have to look elsewhere. Existing Web technologies, like Common Gateway Interface (CGI) scripts and emerging capabilities like inline, real-time audio, video, and virtual reality, Netscape's "frames," and Sun's interactive Java, are making the Web a moving target possibly heading well beyond Acrobat's reach.

- Acrobat is a "closed" environment. Its development is controlled and guided by Adobe. While third parties can build plug-ins to extend its features, doing so is often a lengthy process. On the Web, by comparison, new features and capabilities appear almost weekly, in large part because no one "owns" the Web and its key protocols are open to all.

Portable Document Format

At the core of Acrobat is Adobe's Portable Document Format (PDF), a portable, platform-independent, and fully extensible electronic document environment. PDF files preserve the fonts, graphics, and layout used to create the original document. In essence, Acrobat takes a snapshot of the document, capturing the document electronically just as it appears onscreen. That's a big advantage over the HTML world, where different Web browsers display HTML pages in different ways. Some browsers support advanced HTML tags, and some don't. What the user sees is at times a crap shoot, which is not great for Web authors, who often end up building multiple versions of HTML code suited to individual browsers—again, more work and more headaches.

PDF is a powerful and flexible document-creation environment. Because it has evolved from the print world, PDF continues to use the "page" as its core building block. Each page in an original document gets its own page description in PDF written in PostScript format. PDF deals with the building blocks of an electronic document (text, fonts, and graphics) in very creative ways. For example, one of the major challenges in preserving the appearance of documents is in preserving fonts. Not every computer has the same fonts. Acrobat and PDF deal with this challenge by including standard fonts like Times Roman in every copy of Acrobat. PDF will also emulate fonts that aren't on a viewer's computer, as well as enable authors to embed unusual fonts directly into their PDF files so they are shipped along with the document. PDF also has strong support for images, including compression options that make PDF files smaller so they can be more quickly transmitted online.

Creating a PDF file is just the start. Once the electronic document is created, Acrobat can be used to add navigation features to complicated, multipage documents. Examples include bookmarks and cross-document links, features that add dynamic hypertext capabilities to documents that previously would have been simply printed out and laid flat on the page. Acrobat also enables full-text searching of PDF files, allowing users to quickly scan through documents to find the information they need. And recently added multimedia capabilities bring pages to life through the addition of QuickTime or AVI movie clips and sound bites. For more sophisticated users, Acrobat also includes an application programming interface (API) that lets developers customize the viewer's user interface, integrate Acrobat with other products, or create plug-in modules for adding new features and capabilities.

Most importantly, PDF files are not meant to die on the desktop; Acrobat is all about sharing electronic documents. PDF files can be distributed across a wide range of media including CD-ROM, electronic mail, Lotus Notes, corporate networks, and, of course, the World Wide Web.

The Acrobat Product Family

Adobe offers a full line of products in Acrobat, for everyone from office workers to high-end publishing professionals. The products—and this is key if Acrobat is to mimic the universality of HTML—are available on a wide variety of computer platforms. The tools for creating PDF files run on Windows, Macintosh, and Unix (including SunOS, Sun Solaris, and HP-UX) systems. The Acrobat reader runs on even more platforms, thus ensuring a universal audience, including Windows 3.1, Windows NT, Windows 95, native Power Macintosh, Macintosh, SunOS 4.1.3 and higher, Sun Solaris 2.3 and 2.4, HP-UX 9.0.3, and Silicon Graphics' IRIX 5.3-5.X.

The individual components that make up Adobe Acrobat include the following:

- **Acrobat Exchange** lets you view and work with PDF files. It is best thought of as a management tool that lets you work with and add value to PDF documents. Authors use Acrobat Exchange to add features like bookmarks, links, notes, and security controls to PDF files, as well as add, move, or delete individual pages from a larger PDF document.

- **Acrobat PDF Writer** is a driver that lets you automatically "print" or create an electronic PDF file from common applications such as word processors or spreadsheets. Just like a printer driver, which enables an application to send a document to a paper printer, Acrobat PDF Writer resides within an application and with a single click automatically creates an electronic PDF file. PDF Writer is suited for less-intensive PDF creation, for instance, if you have only a couple of fairly simple pages to create.

- **Acrobat Distiller** takes the concept of the driver to a higher level. Instead of simple word processing documents, Acrobat Distiller instantly converts any document in Adobe's PostScript language into PDF. Acrobat Distiller is used mainly for converting files created in professional, high-end publishing tools including drawing, page layout, and image editing programs. The key is that Distiller maintains the high-resolution graphics and layout complexity made possible by Adobe's PostScript, resulting in a very high-quality PDF document.

- **Acrobat Catalog/Acrobat Search** creates searchable indexes of PDF files. Acrobat Catalog creates the full-text PDF database; Acrobat Search provides for full searching capabilities.

- **Adobe Type Manager** is a utility that provides sharp, clear text onscreen or in print at any size or resolution.

- **Acrobat Reader** enables Macintosh, Windows, DOS, and Unix users to view, navigate, and print any PDF files they receive. It is free for downloading on online services as well as Adobe's home page, **http://www.adobe.com**. The idea in making the Acrobat Reader free is to create a wide audience of Acrobat-capable users, thus encouraging more content providers to work in the Acrobat environment. It also can be licensed for distribution with your documents.

- **Acrobat Capture** fully extends the power of Acrobat into the paper world by converting existing paper documents into PDF files. You simply scan a collection of pages into your computer and drop them into the Acrobat Capture folder. Using a combination of technologies including optical character recognition, font recognition, bitmap imaging, and page decomposition, Acrobat Capture ensures that it can accurately replicate the original document. Once converted, the new electronic files are virtually indistinguishable from other PDF files, and they can be searched, amended, and published to the Web like any other Acrobat document. Adobe Capture is sold separately from other Acrobat products. It runs on Microsoft Windows 3.1 or later.

The cost of Acrobat (see the "Tech Resources" box) may be a sticking point for some Web authors. Getting started with HTML costs next to nothing. Very strong HTML editors are available for download on the Web as freeware (i.e., at no cost). But again, no HTML tool offers the ease of authoring or preserves the look and feel of documents the way Acrobat can.

Acrobat and the Web

Adobe has made Acrobat an even more appealing technology for Web developers by continually adding new capabilities specifically targeted at improving Acrobat's performance on the Web. Acrobat could always be used on the Web as a so-called *helper application*, a program that could be invoked by a Web browser and used to display formats not supported by the browser. But this scenario is limiting. It requires

Acrobat Packaging and Pricing

Adobe offers the Acrobat programs in four versions to meet the needs of different types of users:

ADOBE ACROBAT EXCHANGE   Includes Acrobat Exchange, Acrobat PDF Writer, Acrobat Reader (one for each platform supported), and Adobe Type Manager. It costs about $200 for the Macintosh and Windows versions, and about $300 for the Unix version.

ADOBE ACROBAT PRO   Includes everything in Exchange plus Acrobat Distiller. It costs about $600 for Macintosh and Windows, and about $1,900 for Unix.

ADOBE ACROBAT FOR WORKGROUPS   A ten-user license for everything in Acrobat Exchange, plus Acrobat Distiller and Acrobat Catalog. It costs about $1,600 for Macintosh and Windows, and about $3,300 for Unix.

ADOBE ACROBAT CAPTURE   Total package costs about $3000. Capture is only available in a Windows version.

end users to configure their browsers—a step that may perplex novice users—and forces Web surfers to disrupt the flow of their browsing and work in two completely separate applications simultaneously.

The answer, which Adobe has vigorously pursued, is to more fully integrate Acrobat and the Web. One part of the equation is in cutting deals with major industry players to support Acrobat. Among the companies that have announced support for integrating Acrobat into their browsers, online services, servers, and search engines are Apple Computer, AT&T, Fulcrum Technologies, Microsoft, Netscape, Open Market, Personal Library Software, Spyglass, and Verity. Most of these deals are agreements that ensure that Acrobat will work seamlessly with other products. But Adobe made one other smart move as well: it bought a 5 percent stake in Netscape, a deal that later turned to gold when Netscape's initial public offering (IPO) flew through the roof. Besides adding millions to Adobe's coffers, the deal ensured that Acrobat would always have the ear of Web leader Netscape.

With support from industry partners in place, Adobe has turned its attention to improving Acrobat. The first Web capabilities came in Acrobat 2.1, which added Weblink, a plug-in application that lets authors embed a Uniform Resource Locator (URL) within a PDF file. This lets users jump from Acrobat out to other HTML pages and goes a long way toward breaking down the barriers between PDF and Web/HTML content.

The next step for Acrobat comes in early 1996, with the expected release of a new version of the product that will give Acrobat new levels of integration with other software applications, including Web browsers, online services, and workgroup applications. The new version (code-named Amber in its early stages) will enable the viewing of PDF documents directly within an application's window—for instance, a browser screen—without having to launch Acrobat as a separate helper application. The new version will also allow Web-based search and indexing tools to include PDF files in their databases, enabling Web surfers to find PDF files alongside HTML documents when they conduct a search of the Web.

The new version will also optimize the delivery of PDF on the Web, allowing users to download a single page of a PDF file at a time rather than the entire, bulky PDF file. Users can then browse PDF files much like they browse the Web. Rather than wait for large PDF files to download, users can deal with smaller chunks of PDF data that download quickly and are rendered progressively on their screen, with text flowing in first, followed by higher-bandwidth graphics.

Initially, Amber is slated to work with Netscape Navigator 2.0, which also has extended its APIs to reach out and accept inline multimedia formats like PDF. But Adobe is working with other vendors to incorporate Amber—and thus inline Acrobat—into a variety of software applications.

Although the release of Amber brings Acrobat fully inline with the Web, it does not represent the final evolution of Acrobat. Adobe has licensed Sun's Java programming language. The integration of Java applets will add executable code to Acrobat, enabling PDF documents to literally spring to life (see the "Inside Spin" box).

How Acrobat Is Used Today

The best way to understand the promise of Acrobat on the Web is with some examples (a more detailed look at some of these snapshots will follow in Chapter 4). From color brochures and technical documentation to online magazines and government forms, a wide variety of individuals and businesses are using Acrobat to liven up their Web presence.

Newspapers and Magazines

Axcess is a magazine covering (in its own words) art, cyberculture, music, and style. You can pick it up on the newsstand, or you can see a version of the magazine in HTML form on the Web. Or, using Acrobat, you can enjoy the best of both worlds—online delivery and the original graphics and layout (see Figure 1-3). You can find *Axcess* at **http://www.internex.net/axcess**.

INSIDE **Spin**

What Adobe Says About Acrobat

"We see two big advantages with Adobe Acrobat," says Pam Deziel, product manager for Adobe Acrobat. "The first is design control. PDF is derived from PostScript, and nobody has gotten close to how we do page description. The second is we let you use the tools you already have today. If you are an Illustrator user, a Quark user, a Microsoft Excel user, it doesn't matter. You'll be able to create [electronic] documents using those tools."

Deziel notes that with the advent of the Web there is finally a global network that "lets us truly take advantage of electronic tools. And Acrobat is probably best positioned to let you take corporate information and make it available on the infrastructure of the Web."

With a new set of APIs and features linking Acrobat closer than ever to the Web, authors now have tools in their hands with Acrobat that offer a real alternative to HTML, says Deziel, adding that she sees Acrobat not as a replacement for HTML but rather as a complement to it. According to Deziel, the challenge now for designers is to author in Acrobat in a way that takes full advantage—and recognizes the limitations—of the Web.

"The design principles for online viewing and distribution are different than for print documents." For example, she says, some fonts that work well on paper are hard to view onscreen. In addition, Web-minded Acrobat authors might also want to create more Web-like documents, with an overview home page and a series of short, interlinked pages following. Such a design will best take advantage of Amber's page-at-a-time download capabilities.

While Amber fulfills the Web vision Adobe has long laid out for Acrobat, the company is already working on keeping Acrobat up to date as the Web moves forward in typical blinding speed. Looming largest on the radar screen is the integration of Sun's Java technology, which promises to bring the Web to life with executable content and animations.

"We see something like Java or a scripting language adding interactive functionality to PDF documents and other Adobe products," says Deziel. "We definitely have things going on in those areas. But it took [Adobe] 15 years to evolve the set of content creation tools the industry has today, and it's going to take a whole lot of work to create a whole new set of completely interactive authoring tools."

Figure 1-3. AXcess *magazine uses Acrobat to publish its complete print magazines on the Web, with all layouts, graphics, and fonts intact*

Perhaps the best-known use of PDF on the Web is by the *New York Times*. The New York Times Fax is an eight-page daily news summary (see Figure 1-4), with the traditional layout and features (even a crossword puzzle) of the paperbound *Times*. Find it at **http://nytimesfax.com**.

The Times' use of Acrobat demonstrates the high value of a publication's graphical look and design. The *New York Times* is arguably the most respected newspaper in the world, and its page layout, fonts, and graphic design are a major part of its image. The newspaper did not want to abandon these important elements, and thus publishes the New York Times Fax with Acrobat, which lets them keep their design elements and also speeds production by allowing them to reuse existing Quark-based layouts rather than starting from scratch each afternoon.

For an in-depth examination of the New York Times Fax and a discussion with its editors, see Chapter 3.

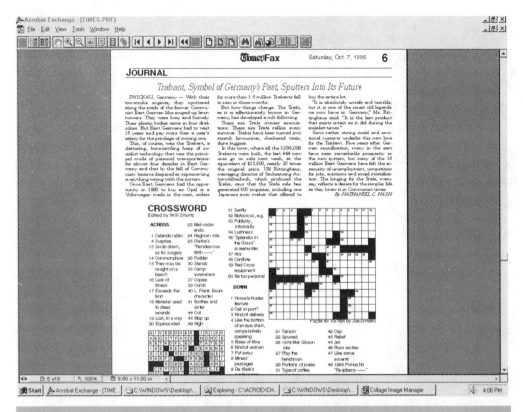

Figure 1-4.   *Acrobat lets the* New York Times *retain its well-known look and feel*

Marketing and Technical Support

The financial services firm J. P. Morgan uses Acrobat to deliver high-quality versions of company brochures, newsletters, and more (see Figure 1-5). Clearly, image means a lot in the financial world, and Acrobat lets J. P. Morgan maintain a first-class look on the Web. Find them on the Web at **http://www.jpmorgan.com**.

Acrobat is a good solution for taking existing materials such as brochures and putting them up on the Web. For starters, these materials already exist on paper and most likely in digital form. Companies prefer that their corporate publications look consistent, and Acrobat lets them extend that consistency to the Web.

Another great advantage is that companies can take the files used to create their paper publicity materials, run the files through Acrobat Distiller, and almost instantly create new files ready to be published in Acrobat format on the Web. This saves both time and money. These documents can also be transmitted digitally via e-mail, computer disk, or CD-ROM, giving a company great flexibility in its distribution of important company documents.

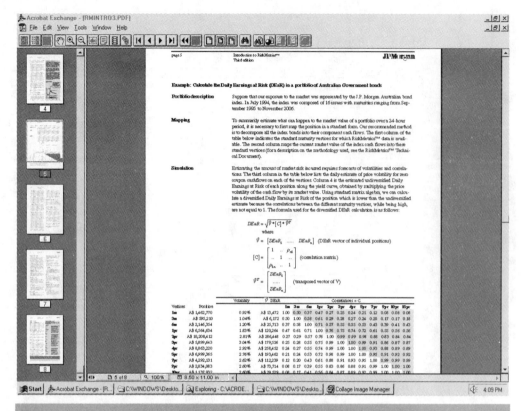

Figure 1-5.   *Repurposing brochures to the Web is an obvious use of Acrobat*

The computer networking company Bay Networks provides customer support in PDF format, including versions of all of its technical support documentation in PDF form (see Figure 1-6). This is a good example of repurposing existing paper products for the Web while retaining complex graphics such as diagrams of computer networks. See Bay Networks at **http://support.baynetworks.com/marcom.htm**.

In general, technical publishing is a very popular use of Acrobat on the Web. The sheer amount of technical documentation that some companies generate makes it unrealistic to rework such documents into HTML form.

Intel, for example, offers a PDF version of a white paper providing a detailed statistical analysis of the recent flaw in its Pentium processor (see **http://www.intel.com/ product/pentium/fdiv.html**). Intel's need to get accurate information to customers in an easily readable form led the company to turn to Acrobat. Interestingly, Intel posted the white paper in two forms, Acrobat and native PostScript format. The Acrobat file checked in at 204K; the PostScript version was 1751K. Not a tough decision if you are a Web surfer on a slow modem connection.

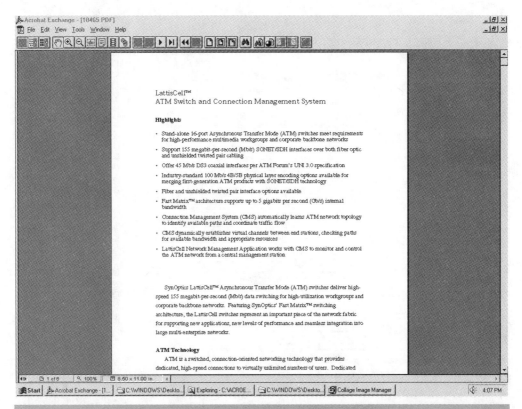

Figure 1-6.   *It may not look flashy, but the ability to instantly prepare technical documentation for the Web is a huge time- and money-saver*

Specialty Publishing

Uncle Sam can't be wrong, especially when it comes to taxes. The Internal Revenue Service uses Acrobat to distribute copies of tax forms and publications, maintaining the well-known look and feel of the 1040 and other documents (see Figure 1-7). Get your forms early at **http://www.ustreas.gov/treasury/bureaus/irs/taxforms.html**.

This use of Acrobat shows the true power of electronic paper. Though the IRS forms are being distributed in digital PDF format, they will ultimately be printed out and distributed via paper. Just because a file is in digital form doesn't mean it has to stay that way. Indeed, Acrobat can serve as a replacement for fax machines, overnight mail, photocopying, and other standard ways of duplicating and distributing documents.

Put a document in PDF format up on a Web server—either on the Internet or on a corporate network—and encourage the people who need the document to come and get it. We all are bombarded by unsolicited mail, e-mail, and fax documents every day. Wouldn't it be better to get a one-line e-mail saying a high-quality PDF document is available on the Web? Then, at your own convenience, you can retrieve the document for yourself.

Figure 1-7. *Building HTML tables and forms is a pain—imagine trying to build an accurate 1040 form*

ALTERNATIVE Technologies

ENVOY Envoy for Windows or Macintosh is an electronic publishing technology that promises most of the same features as Acrobat: it lets users exchange, distribute, manipulate, and view portable compound documents across different computers and different operating systems independent of the application and fonts that created the documents. Envoy was created by Tumbleweed Software but was acquired and has been marketed by Novell Corp.

As this book was being written, Novell had placed its applications business, including Envoy, up for sale. Another company will likely be supporting Envoy by early 1996. Tumbleweed Software, the original creator of Envoy, is continuing to develop new Envoy products, including a Netscape plug-in for Envoy.

Indeed, if Acrobat has its roots in high-end publishing, then by comparison Envoy can be viewed much more as a mainstream business tool. The Envoy reader runs on just 500K of RAM for Windows and takes just 1MB of disk storage space (compared to 2MB RAM and 3–4MB of disk space for Acrobat), thus making it possible to attach an Envoy reader to a document and send it over a network. Another attraction is that the ability to create and view Envoy files ships with Novell's WordPerfect word processor and PerfectOffice suite. Envoy can perhaps best be viewed as enabling workgroup collaboration among business users. But like Acrobat, the Web beckons for Envoy as well. Both Netscape and Spyglass have committed to integrating Envoy support into their Web browsers.

Envoy consists of Envoy Publisher (a printer driver) and the Envoy Viewer (see Figure 1-8). Envoy Publisher works with any application that prints and also has the

Figure 1-8. *Novell's Envoy Viewer has a look and feel very similar to Acrobat but is targeted at corporate applications*

ability to produce run-time files that embed the Envoy Viewer with the document. The Viewer is freely distributable without additional licensing. Envoy Publisher is priced at around $200.

The Envoy Publisher has a number of features to keep files small for online delivery and to make them visually appealing onscreen, including the following:

- Built-in compression of text and graphics
- Custom page sizes
- User-definable down sampling of bitmap resolution
- Optional dithering of color for bitmap images
- Line art always supported at 24-bit color
- Selective TrueType font embedding
- Built-in intelligent font substitution for ATM Type 1 and TrueType fonts

The Viewer also has some powerful capabilities, most notably strong annotation features. This makes sense, given that Envoy is probably best viewed as a workgroup tool for colleagues to mark up and comment on distributed files. You can easily add comments to an Envoy file with sticky notes, highlighter pens, hypertext links, and bookmarks.

In addition to these core capabilities, Envoy creator Tumbleweed Software continues to add value to the product. Tumbleweed has released Tumbleweed Publishing Essentials (about $700). The product provides advanced font embedding technology, full-text indexed search, batch conversion of complex PostScript documents, and automated tools for generating hypertext links between Envoy documents.

COMMON GROUND   Less well known than Adobe or Novell, Common Ground Software nonetheless has a powerful electronic publishing technology—and one that was linked closely to the Web well before Acrobat. Based on a platform-independent technology called DigitalPaper, Common Ground's Web Publisher ensures that documents appear onscreen and print exactly the way they were intended, regardless of the application or fonts you use. The Windows-based Common Ground software also includes search, indexing, and hyperlinking capabilities.

Common Ground arguably has a couple of key benefits over the better-known Acrobat, including a much smaller (just over 200K) viewer and better font control; see Figure 1-9. Common Ground also beat Adobe Acrobat to market with a complete Web-ready publishing system featuring page-at-a-time download capabilities, which is a great time-saver for Web surfers. Common Ground's Web Publisher is priced at about $200.

One of the most unique aspects of the Common Ground system is its Page-on-Demand technology, which lets users download and view a single page of a Web

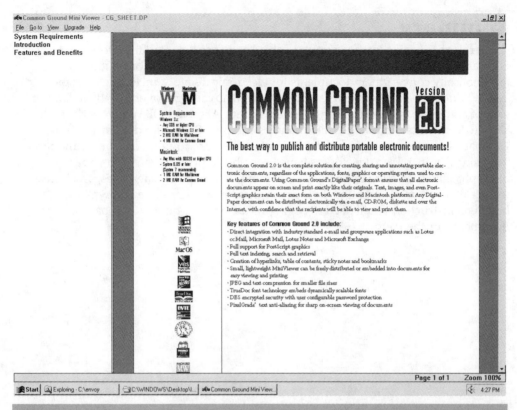

Figure 1-9.   *The Common Ground viewer is much smaller (200K) but offers many features similar to Acrobat*

document. The software automatically creates an HTML cover page that acts as a table of contents for the DigitalPaper document. Users can then pick the pages they want and download them one at a time.

Web Publisher also handles fonts in a unique way, incorporating Bitstream's TrueDoc and Common Ground's own PixelGrade technology to improve the fidelity of fonts onscreen. Fonts are also automatically anti-aliased to avoid jagged lettering.

An upgrade released at the end of 1996 brings new capabilities to the system, including new Web features such as the ability to embed Web URLs into Common Ground documents and automatically create a menu of all URLs contained in a DigitalPaper document. The new version also includes added PostScript support, improving the speed and reliability of converting PostScript files to DigitalPaper.

Summary

In this chapter, we learned about Adobe Acrobat and its Portable Document Format, which enables Web developers to use their existing authoring tools and automatically convert their documents for electronic delivery, including over the World Wide Web. Acrobat holds some significant advantages over HTML, including ease of authoring and greater control over layouts. Acrobat PDF Writer works with simple documents, Acrobat Distiller handles complex PostScript documents, and Acrobat Exchange adds value in the form of bookmarks, annotations, links, and more.

Using Acrobat, Web developers have been able to post to the Web a wide variety of graphically interesting documents, including newspapers, magazines, brochures, technical documents, and more. In the next chapter, we'll provide you with the hands-on instruction you'll need to begin producing high-quality Acrobat documents for the Web.

Chapter Two

Creating Documents with Acrobat

Now that you've been introduced to the power of electronic paper, it's time to create some documents for the Web using Adobe Acrobat.

There are a variety of ways to create PDF files. At minimum, you need Acrobat Exchange, which acts as a PDF document editor, and PDF Writer, a printer driver that lets you create PDF files directly from Windows or Macintosh applications. If you want to set your sights higher—and you aren't against spending a little more money—you can create PDF files that look just like your high-end PostScript documents. For that, you'll need Acrobat Distiller, part of the Acrobat Pro package.

As we noted in Chapter 1, Acrobat itself won't help you build an impressive electronic document. You have to already be skilled in your document creation tools, whether they are word processors, desktop publishing packages, or some other tool. But once you've built that prized document, Acrobat can almost instantly convert it to a form that is ready for electronic distribution on the Web.

Before we begin creating PDF files, let's take a brief look at Acrobat Reader, the tool that the people visiting your Web site will use to view your PDF content. You cannot build good PDF documents without fully understanding the platform to which you are writing.

Acrobat Reader

Acrobat Reader is a royalty-free tool used to view PDF content, as shown in Figure 2-1. The free Acrobat Reader is available in a variety of ways:

- It can be downloaded from Adobe's Web site (**http://www.adobe.com/Software/Acrobat**).

- It is available at many sites that offer PDF content.

- It can be found on most online services.

- It can be distributed directly to customers on disk, CD-ROM, via e-mail, or in any number of other ways.

Reader allows users to view the pages of a PDF document as well as any features added using Acrobat Exchange, including bookmarks, notes, annotations, hypertext links, or thumbnails of PDF pages. Remember, the free Reader can only view PDF files; to make any changes, you'll need Acrobat Exchange.

Note ▶ *If you are using Exchange, that program can also be used to view PDF files. You don't need a separate read-only Reader.*

As this book is being written, the latest version of Acrobat available is 2.1. We will concentrate on that version, which includes everything you'll need to create PDF files ready for the Web. Adobe plans to roll out a new version of Acrobat in the first half of 1996, including many new features for more closely linking and improving the

Figure 2-1.   *Acrobat Reader in page-only view*

performance of Acrobat Reader on the Web. We'll deal with those new capabilities later in this chapter.

Acrobat Reader 2.1

Acrobat Reader 2.1 offers a number of advantages over earlier versions, including the following features:

- Additional operating system platform support
- Greater embedded font support
- MovieLink, which enables the playback of multimedia files, including QuickTime movies and AVI files
- A plug-in application called WebLink for using links that can be embedded into PDF documents and reach out to the Web

Perhaps most important for Web authors are the new platforms. Acrobat Reader 2.1 runs not only on the expected Windows and Macintosh platforms but also on

OS/2, Windows NT, Sun Solaris and SunOS, Hewlett-Packard HP-UX, and Silicon Graphics IRIX. One of the World Wide Web's greatest strengths is the fact that it is multiplatform: any computer user, regardless of the platform, can find a Mosaic-compatible browser to view HTML content on the Web. With a version of Acrobat Reader now available for most major operating systems, Acrobat authors can be assured of an equally large audience of users that can view their PDF content.

Viewing Documents with Reader

Acrobat Reader offers some flexibility in how users view and navigate PDF files. With HTML, authors are constantly struggling to build more intuitive user interfaces to help users better navigate a site. Acrobat, in comparison, not only offers three built-in viewing options to aid navigation but also lets users choose which view they like best. Three view options are available:

- Page-only view displays the entire document in the main window all by itself (see Figure 2-1).

- Bookmarks view splits the screen in two. The main page is displayed alongside a list of hotlinked bookmarks, which are clicked to take the user to the page associated with that bookmark (see Figure 2-2). This is a capability that is just now coming to the Web. It is similar to Netscape's "frames" feature in its Navigator 2.0 browser.

- Thumbnails view is similar to bookmarks, but instead of a text index the user gets thumbnail views of all the pages in a document (see Figure 2-3). Again, the instant (and in this case graphical) overview of a PDF file is a great improvement over the often confusing and hard to navigate HTML pages.

As noted above, the person reading a PDF file gets to choose the best view for any document—it's as easy as the click of a button (see Table 2-1).

Navigating a PDF File

If you think of Acrobat as electronic paper, then not surprisingly the methods for browsing a PDF document are similar to paging through a book. You can move through a document a page at a time (forward and backward) or use the bookmarks or thumbnails views as an electronic table of contents that leads directly to a page within a document. The most basic page-turning commands can be found on the Reader toolbar (see Table 2-2).

You can also use the scroll bar located to the right of the main window to move up and down through a document. It is important to note, however, that scrolling a document with Acrobat Reader is a little bit different than with a Web browser. For instance, with a Web browser, you can scroll smoothly down a long page without a break, pausing at any part of the document. Acrobat Reader, on the other hand, adheres tightly to its page-oriented paradigm. When you reach the end of a PDF

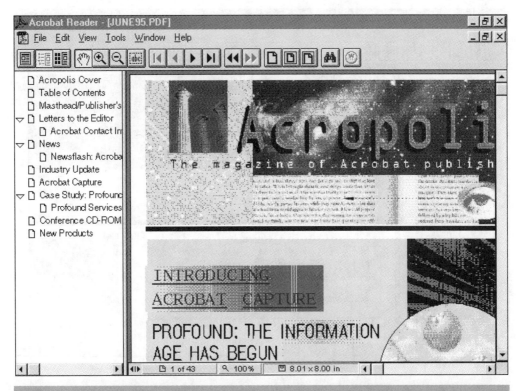

Figure 2-2.   *Acrobat Reader in bookmarks view*

View	Menu Command	Button	Keyboard Shortcuts	
			Windows	**Macintosh**
Page-only	View/Page Only		CTRL-6	COMMAND-6
Bookmarks	View/Bookmarks and page		CTRL-7	COMMAND-7
Thumbnails	View/Thumbnails and page		CTRL-8	COMMAND-8

Table 2-1.   *Acrobat Reader View Modes*

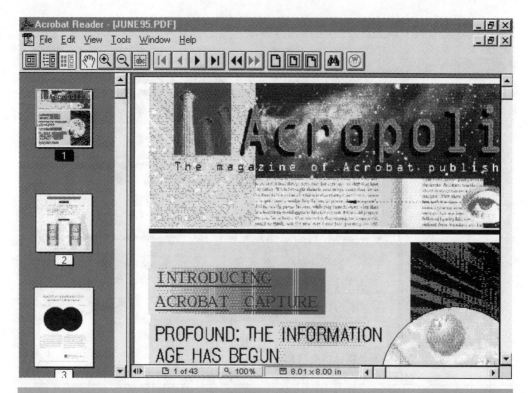

Figure 2-3.   *Acrobat Reader in thumbnails view*

"page," the Reader automatically jump-scrolls the top of the next page. Thus the top of one page and the bottom of the next cannot be on the screen at the same time. This can be somewhat disorienting for someone accustomed to working with a Web browser; authors need to think about building their PDF files as a series of discrete pages and not as a long, single file as in an HTML document.

Indeed, that is just one example of how using Acrobat Reader to view documents onscreen—rather than printing them out—is often not as friendly as using a Web browser. HTML pages almost always fit perfectly in a Web browser window (you simply scroll up and down to see the rest of a page; rarely do you need to scroll left or right), with onscreen readable font types and sizes. PDF documents, in comparison, are often not designed with onscreen viewing in mind. For instance, many PDF documents at a readable onscreen resolution are much larger than can fit in the Acrobat Reader window, as demonstrated in Figure 2-4. That forces the viewer to either scroll the document left to right (a very unnatural way to view a document on the screen) or shrink the size of the document to fit in the main window, which usually lowers the resolution and makes it impossible to read (see Figure 2-5.)

Acrobat Reader offers a variety of options for changing the size of a displayed PDF document onscreen. One set of options resizes the document within the Reader's main window (see Table 2-3).

Page-Turning Command	Menu Command	Button	Keyboard Shortcuts Windows	Macintosh
Next page	View/Next Page	▶	CTRL-3	COMMAND-3
Previous page	View/Previous Page	◀	CTRL-2	COMMAND-2
Go to the first page	View/First Page	◀	CTRL-1	COMMAND-1
Go to the last page	View/Last Page	▶	CTRL-4	COMMAND-4

Table 2-2.   *Navigating PDF Documents*

Page-Scale Command	Menu Command	Button	Keyboard Shortcuts Windows	Macintosh
Display the page at its actual size	View/Actual Size		CTRL-H	COMMAND-H
Display a full page in the window	View/Fit Page		CTRL-J	COMMAND-J
Display the page width in the window	View/Fit Width		CTRL-K	COMMAND-K

Table 2-3.   *PDF Document Sizes*

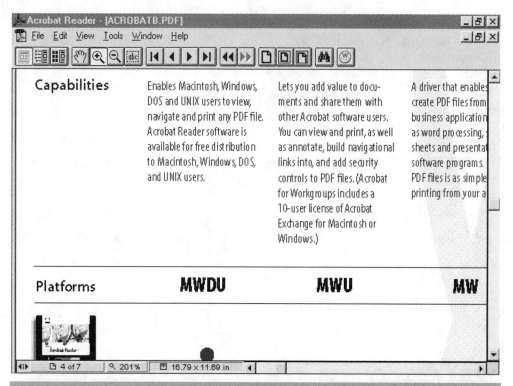

Figure 2-4. *An Acrobat brochure in PDF format is readable using the zoom function, but you can only see a small portion of the entire document at one time*

If these commands don't make a document readable, you can also zoom in to magnify the document even further (as we did in Figure 2-5, which was magnified at just over 200 percent). That enables you to take a close-in look at a particular part of the page. The toolbar buttons for zooming in and out are shown in Table 2-4.

Zoom Command	Menu Command	Button
Enlarge a part of the document	Tools/Zoom In	
above Reduce the magnification	Tools/Zoom Out	

Table 2-4. *PDF Document Zoom Commands*

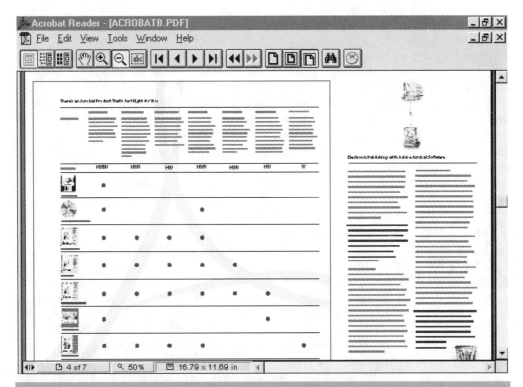

Figure 2-5. *When viewed in its entirety on screen, the same brochure is unreadable*

The size and fit of PDF files onscreen—and how much work that causes the people viewing your content online—are important issues to keep in mind when creating PDF files for the Web. We will deal with Web-specific design issues in greater detail in coming chapters.

That is just a taste of some of the more important features of Acrobat Reader and a quick overview of how it works. Now, we'll take a look at how to create and modify PDF files using Acrobat PDF Writer, Acrobat Distiller, and Acrobat Exchange.

Creating PDF Files

There are two main ways to create PDF files: you can use the PDF Writer driver included in Acrobat Exchange, or you can use Acrobat Distiller, which comes as part of the more expensive Acrobat Pro package. Whether you use one or the other of these approaches depends mainly on the quality of publishing you want to do. In many cases, your publishing tools will dictate the answer. For instance, if you work mainly with word processors or presentation programs, then using the PDF Writer driver is sufficient to meet your needs; using Acrobat Distiller would be pure overkill.

However, if you use high-end publishing and graphics tools and typically print the files you create to Adobe's PostScript format, then Acrobat Distiller is the tool for you. It retains the high-level page description of PostScript and ensures that the PDF files you create are of the same quality as the PostScript-driven print products you created in the first place.

While the PDF Writer versus Distiller choice may seem cut and dried, here's a trick from veteran Acrobat users: when prototyping a page—in other words, making frequent changes and seeing how Acrobat deals with them—use PDF Writer. It is a quicker tool and does the job well enough for prototyping purposes. When you finally have your original document locked down, run it through Distiller for a final version. For more about PDF Writer and Distiller read the following tips and tricks.

Using Distiller

Use Acrobat Distiller in the following situations:

Your document contains Encapsulated PostScript (EPS) artwork or images.

You are using an application that generates its own PostScript language files when printing or produces the highest quality output on a PostScript printer. Examples include Adobe Illustrator, QuarkXPress, Harvard Graphics, Harvard Draw, or CorelDRAW.

Your document contains high-resolution images that you want to downsample, or compress, for faster delivery online.

PDF Writer produces poor quality or too large files. This often happens when a document contains complex blends, gradient fills, or EPS artwork or images.

You are working in an environment—for instance, Unix or DOS—that does not support PDF Writer but allows the creation of PostScript files.

Creating Files with PDF Writer

Creating PDF files using PDF Writer isn't much more difficult than printing out a hard copy of a document. When you install Acrobat Exchange, the program installs PDF Writer as one of the available printer drivers on your machine. Instead of printing out to paper, this driver prints to disk, preserving the document in electronic form. For purposes of our demonstration of PDF Writer, we will use Acrobat running on a Windows machine. The steps on the Macintosh are very similar and just as easy.

To start, open an application (for our example we'll use Microsoft Word for Windows) and create a document. Once you have your original document in the form you want, the process of creating a PDF document begins:

1. Print the document by choosing Print from the File menu.

2. In the Print dialog box, click on Printer to open the Print Setup dialog box, shown in the following illustration. Specify the PDF Writer driver as your driver of choice and select Set as Default Printer. Close the dialog box.

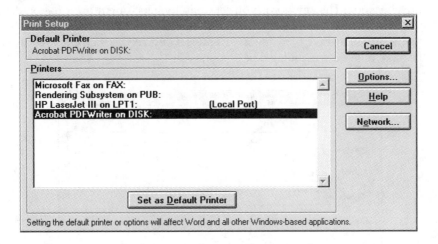

3. Now that the PDF Writer driver has been set as the default, click OK in the Print dialog box.

4. Name the PDF file and select a destination drive and folder, as shown in the following illustration. Be careful when naming the file: Macintosh users and, to some extent, Windows 95 users can use long file names; MS-DOS and Windows 3.1 users cannot. Since PDF files are inherently multiplatform, it is probably best to use the standard MS-DOS file naming convention of eight uppercase letters followed by a period and a three letter extension, in this case, PDF.

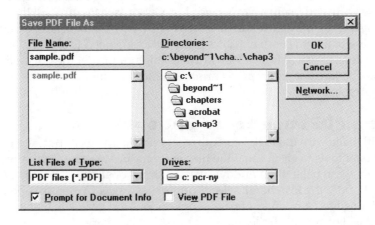

5. In the Save PDF File As dialog box, you have two additional options. If you want to immediately view the PDF File in Acrobat Exchange, select the View PDF File checkbox. If you want to enter more information about the file (for instance, subject, author, keyword, or date), select the Prompt for Document Info checkbox. The keywords you set up in the Document Information dialog box, shown below, can be used later by Acrobat as search criteria for tracking down particular PDF files. If you've entered keywords, click OK to return to the Save PDF File As dialog box.

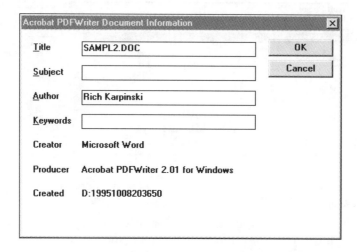

6. Click OK. The PDF file is then generated and, if you clicked the View PDF File option, appears onscreen in the Exchange window.

That's it. You've created a PDF file that now can be hosted on your Web page, downloaded by others across the Internet, and viewed using Acrobat Reader. Our sample file was created using a simple word processor (see Figure 2-6); the output in Acrobat looks for the most part the same (see Figure 2-7). Unlike HTML, there was no tedious tagging to do, no complex tables to construct, no need to worry about what HTML extensions to use or how a Web browser might interpret the document. Creating the document is as simple as printing a file; viewing the document is as easy as firing up Acrobat Reader.

Choosing PDF Page Setup Options

Creating a PDF file with the PDF Writer driver is simplicity itself. But Acrobat offers some additional tools to ensure that the files you produce are as graphically rich and compact as they can be. In the Windows version of Acrobat, the PDF Writer options can be found under the File menu: select Printer, then select Options to open the following dialog box. A number of page setup options are available that can change the look and feel of your PDF files, and they're described here.

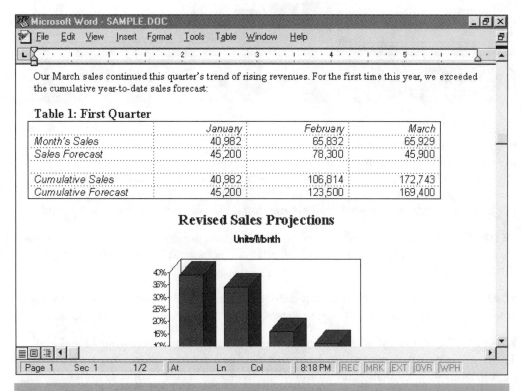

PAGE SIZE AND ORIENTATION   You can choose from a variety of standard page sizes, plus a screen option (6.5 × 5.18 inches, 72 dots per inch) that is optimized for online viewing on a computer monitor. This is a very important decision if you are using PDF on the Web. If you are distributing documents on the Web but ultimately expect users to print and distribute them on paper, then a PDF page size matching the

Figure 2-6.   *The original document created in Microsoft Word for Windows*

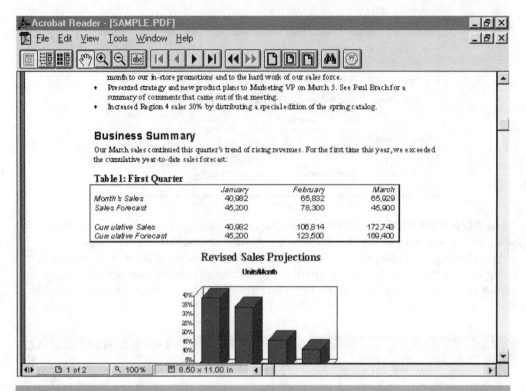

Figure 2-7.   *The PDF version of the same document, now viewable by any Acrobat Reader*

original document (for instance, 8.5 × 11) makes sense. But if you are expecting users to read your PDF files on the Web, then use the screen option.

You also can select either portrait or landscape, depending on the type of document you are creating. Portrait works best for a report done in a word processor; landscape might be the choice if you are making a PDF file out of a presentation slide.

RESOLUTION   The PDF Writer driver—like a regular printer—offers options on how many dots per inch (dpi) it can print. PDF offers choices including screen, 150 dpi, 300 dpi, or 600 dpi.

SCALING   Selecting scaling does not change the page size of your document but the scale on which it prints. For instance, at 50 percent, the page prints at half the original size.

FONTS   PDF Writer gives you options on how to deal with fonts in your PDF files. The decision on whether or not to embed fonts comes down to preserving the fidelity of your original document versus minimizing the PDF file size. Acrobat Reader reproduces fonts in one of three ways:

- By using the same font installed on the viewing computer. In this scenario, the font name is placed in the PDF file upon creation, and when viewed by another user the Acrobat Reader simply calls the fonts installed on that computer. This works with so-called Base 14 fonts that are standard on every PostScript printer, including Helvetica, Times, and Courier fonts.

- By creating a substitute font using information in the PDF file. Here, Acrobat's multiple master font technology re-creates the font on the viewer's machine. Results vary on a font-by-font basis. Generally, it works well with simple fonts and less well with very fancy fonts.

- By displaying a font that has been embedded in the PDF file. With this option, the creator of the PDF document explicitly embeds all of the fonts used as part of the PDF file. This increases the size of the PDF file anywhere from 10K to 25K per font, but it ensures that the document is viewed just the way it was created.

The Font Embedding dialog box offers options on how to deal with fonts. You can access the dialog by clicking on the Fonts… button shown in the previous illustration. Select the Embed All Fonts checkbox to ensure all fonts used in the source document are embedded in the PDF file. Alternatively, you can check Always Embed List, as shown in the following illustration, or Never Embed List and choose precisely which fonts to embed or not to embed in a PDF file.

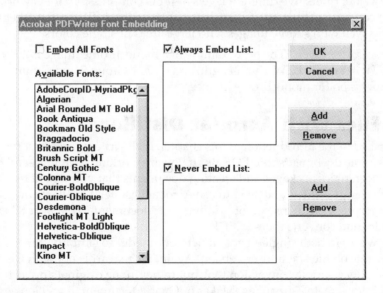

COMPRESSION Acrobat lets you compress the text, line art, and graphics in your PDF files to make them smaller for online delivery. Press on the Compression… button in the Page Setup dialog box to access three options for compressing PDF files, as shown in the following illustration:

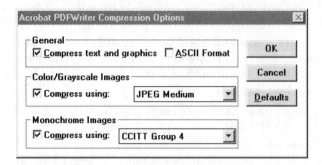

- *General*   This compresses text and images with the Lempel-Ziv-Welch (LZW) compression algorithm. If you also choose ASCII format, the LZW compression will be encoded in Adobe's ASCII Base 85 format.

- *Color/grayscale images*   This includes options for LZW compression of images as well as Joint Photographic Experts Group, or JPEG, compression. The trade-off here is fidelity versus file size. Of the two methods, JPEG achieves the higher level of compression, but it does so by "losing" some data in the process. PDF Writer offers five different levels of JPEG compression. JPEG works best with continuous-tone images, such as photographs. LZW, on the other hand, works well with simple images with large areas of single colors.

- *Monochrome images*   The best example of a monochrome image is a fax image. PDF Writer offers LZW, Run Length, and CCITT Group 3 and Group 4 compression for monochrome images.

Creating Files with Acrobat Distiller

As we described in the introduction to this chapter, PDF Writer works best for converting simple documents into PDF. But if you are working with high-end desktop publishing or graphics packages and creating documents that you would traditionally print to a PostScript printer, you need to use Acrobat Distiller. Distiller is in essence a PostScript interpreter—but instead of printing your document to paper, it takes your PostScript files and converts them to PDF.

Distiller works in both single-user and network mode. To simplify things here, we'll concentrate on the single-user version. Again, the real art is not with Distiller, which is in reality a simple conversion tool, but rather in the original applications themselves. If you create a great PageMaker or Quark document, it will look great when it is converted to PDF. The good news is that desktop publishing tools are fairly easy to use these days and are very powerful (although they can run a pretty penny for high-end software).

Getting Started with Distiller

First thing you'll need is a PostScript file in electronic form. The beauty of this process is that while you need an application capable of outputting a PostScript file, you don't even need a printer—just a PostScript-capable file driver. When you go to print the document you have created, simply print it to file rather than to the printer (for our purposes, we chose the QMS ColorPrint 100 from the Windows 95 Printers folder).

Once you have a PostScript file in hand, converting it to PDF using Distiller is a fairly simple matter. The interface for Distiller is even simpler than Exchange, as shown in Figure 2-8: it's not much more than a status bar and a couple of buttons to stop or pause the current job.

You have several options for bringing a PostScript file into Distiller. You can start Acrobat Distiller and open a PostScript file using menu commands; drag a PostScript file onto the Distiller icon that appears when you open Distiller; or drag a PostScript file into a Watched In folder on your hard drive or on a local area network (see Figure 2-9). Another alternative is to use Distiller Assistant, which lets you print a file directly to Distiller from your original application, thus creating a PDF file in a single step. When Acrobat Distiller is installed, Distiller Assistant installs a printer driver (distasst.ps) in your list of installed printer drivers, and a Distiller Assistant icon is added to the Acrobat program group.

 **Note** ▶ *Distiller Assistant does not work with Windows 95.*

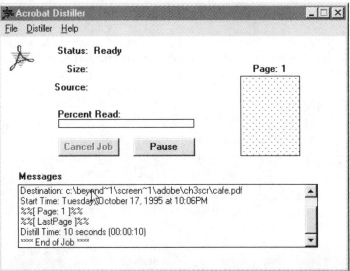

Figure 2-8. *The Distiller user interface*

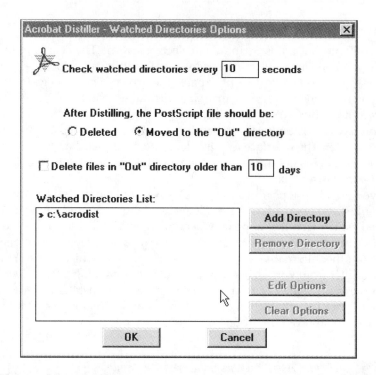

Figure 2-9.   *The Watched Directory option lets you set up In and Out directories that perform PS-to-PDF conversions automatically*

Once the file is brought into Distiller, it is instantly converted in PDF form. It can then be worked on using Acrobat Exchange.

Distiller Options

The art of Distiller is in the setup. You'll have a number of options for compression, font embedding, and more that affect the ultimate look of your document. To access your choices, open the Distiller menu on the Distiller menu bar and select Job Options to see the dialog box in the following illustration. The options for Distiller are similar to but slightly more expansive than the options for PDF Writer. All of the options discussed below can be accessed from the Job Options dialog.

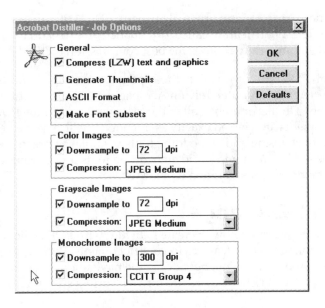

GENERAL OPTIONS   The first option allows you to compress text and graphics (the same as in PDF Writer), and it is recommended for most jobs. You can also automatically create thumbnails for the distilled document, which is a good idea unless the added size—about 2,000 or so bytes per page—is a factor. Another option enables you to embed just a subset of a font group—i.e., the characters you actually use in your document. This can help cut down on the size of your PDF file.

DOWNSAMPLING   Distiller has the option of *downsampling,* or reducing the (byte) size and resolution of an image. If a PDF file is to be viewed only onscreen—such as on the Web—then downsampling can be used to create a much smaller file (important to speed online delivery) with very little loss of resolution, since a computer monitor typically has a resolution topping out at no more than 96 dpi and typically coming in at 72 dpi. The best advice here is to experiment with your images. For the Web—especially as low-speed (14.4 kb/s modems or less) continue to predominate—it may be best to sacrifice image resolution for smaller PDF files.

COMPRESSION   Distiller offers the same options for image compression as PDF Writer: LZW and JPEG. One difference with Distiller is that it lets you specify separate compression options for color and grayscale images; PDF Writer does not. Acrobat version 2.1 also offers a new feature called Automatic Filter selection, which examines your images and automatically chooses the best compression method.

FONTS   As with PDF Writer, you have three options: use simple fonts that will likely be found on the viewing computer; rely on Acrobat to create a substitute font using information in the PDF file; or embed all of the fonts used within the PDF file to ensure your documents are viewed exactly as intended. We'll skip the details here, since the process of choosing and embedding fonts is similar in practice and in spirit to PDF Writer. In general, you should avoid embedding fonts if you want to keep your files small—an important consideration on the Web.

Using Acrobat Exchange

Now that we've demonstrated how to create PDF files with PDF Writer and Distiller, it's time to use Exchange to add features to your documents. Putting converted documents on the Web is one thing, but adding the navigation features Exchange enables makes for a much richer experience for Web surfers encountering your documents.

Among the features you can add using Exchange:

- Links
- Bookmarks
- Thumbnails
- Notes
- Multimedia files
- Security

For the most part, Exchange uses the same user interface as the Acrobat Reader. It just has additional content creation capabilities and buttons (see Table 2-5).

Adding Hypertext to PDF Files

The World Wide Web's key feature is that it lets users click a hotlink to instantly transport to a new document, whether it's an adjacent page on the same server or a related document stored halfway around the world. Acrobat has similar hypertext capabilities. In this section, we'll examine how to add links between pages of your own PDF files. Later on in this chapter we'll take a closer look at Acrobat and the Web.

Exchange Command	Menu Command	Button
Create a link	Tools/Link	
Add multimedia files	Tools/Movie	
Add a note	Tools/Note	

Table 2-5. *Exchange Menu Commands and Buttons*

At that time, we'll examine how you can link from a PDF document out to the HTML documents on the Web, integrating PDF seamlessly into the rest of the Web.

There are many uses for local PDF links. You can use links so your readers can jump to definitions of unfamiliar terms, get more detailed information on complex subjects, or jump to pages with related information, among other examples. A link can also lead a reader to an embedded multimedia file, for instance, a QuickTime movie.

To create a link, click on the Link tool button. That turns the Acrobat cursor into a cross-hair pointer, which you can then move down into the document to indicate the source of the link. The source can be as small or large as you like (for instance, a single word or an entire sentence), and it can be graphics as well as text (just as in HTML documents, you can hotlink an image).

Next, simply move the cross hair to the place where you want to create the link and drag a rectangle around the appropriate word or image. When you release the mouse, the Create Link dialog box appears (as shown in the following illustration) offering options for the hotlink's appearance (you can change the color, width, and style of the hotlink) and action (you can link to another spot in the document, to a new file, or out onto the Web).

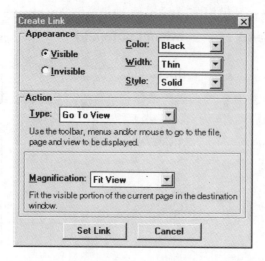

If you are linking to another spot in the same PDF document, simply use Exchange to scroll down to the link destination (the dialog box stays displayed, but it won't be affected). When you get to the right spot, click OK, and the link from your original mark to the new destination is made. The hotlink is indicated in the PDF file by a box around the linked word or image, as demonstrated in Figure 2-10.

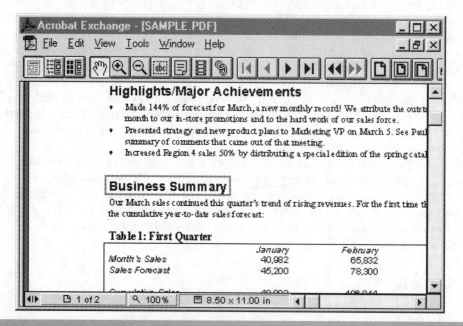

Figure 2-10.   *In this document, the heading "Business Summary" is hotlinked*

Hypertext can be a curse as well as a blessing. It's nice to be able to drill down into a document for more information or jump to an area of related interest. But it can also detract from the flow of a reading experience. In all cases, give the reader the option of whether or not to jump out of a document at a given time. Don't force a reader to jump when he or she doesn't want to. Indeed, perhaps the best use of hyperlinks may be in creating a table of contents or index that is hotlinked while keeping the number of links within the text of a document to a minimum.

One final note on links: when a reader is sent off on a link, the only way to get back to the original document is to use the View/Previous Page menu item or the Previous Page button on the toolbar. If possible, give your readers some instruction on how to get back to where they started after they hit a hotlink.

Using Links in Acrobat

The World Wide Web already has some conventions regarding hotlinks. In an HTML document, a hotlinked word is typically underlined and highlighted in a color. Clicking anywhere on the word initiates the link.

Hotlinking a word in PDF is a bit different. In our earlier example, we built a box around the hotlinked word. That lets the viewer click anywhere on the word. If we were simply to underline the word using the Exchange Link tool, the only part hotlinked would be the line (not the word itself), making it difficult for the viewer to initiate the link. The same would hold for a graphical PDF link. To make the image hot, we would need to draw a link box around the entire image. Adding such a box clearly detracts from the layout.

There are some solutions. One idea is to use Exchange's Invisible option for creating links. This lets you hotlink a part of a PDF document without leaving a visible box around it. This works especially well if you create the original document with the idea that it will eventually be turned into PDF. For instance, in the original document, you could put words you later want to hotlink in italics, bold, or colored fonts. Later, using Exchange, you could add Invisible links but still have the words stand out for the reader. That may be the cleanest way to create links.

Since you won't always have control of a document from start to finish, this may not always work. So be sure to make your links visible. A clean document is nice, but not giving clear indication of the links on a PDF page shortchanges the reader.

Adding Bookmarks

As we saw when we examined Acrobat Reader earlier in the chapter, the bookmarks view can give readers of your PDF documents a table of contents snapshot of your PDF file. The bookmarks view is a standard feature of Acrobat Reader, but you have to build the bookmark contents yourself manually. Typically, you'll want the bookmarks to provide a navigation guide to your PDF document, but an individual bookmark could also leap to another PDF document or open a separate application altogether.

The process of creating bookmarks is very similar to creating links:

1. Call up your document into the exchange window and click on the bookmarks view.

2. Since you haven't created any bookmarks yet, the bookmark window is blank.

3. Set the main page view window to exactly where you want the bookmark to jump to.

4. Then, create a bookmark by selecting the menu item Edit/Bookmarks/New.

5. A bookmark with the name Untitled is created. Type in a name or copy and paste a name from your PDF document.

You can create as many additional bookmarks as needed (see Figure 2-2, shown earlier in this chapter, for an example). For instance, you can set a bookmark for all of a document's headings and subheadings. You can also build a more hierarchical view of your bookmarks, for instance, setting the chapters of a book on one level and setting subordinate bookmarks within each chapter for each subheading within a chapter.

Creating Thumbnails

The counterpart to bookmarks is thumbnails (see Figure 2-3, earlier in this chapter). The thumbnails view lets a user browse a PDF file by looking at small thumbnail views of all the pages in a document. Creating the thumbnails view is extremely simple: select the menu option Edit/Thumbnails/Create All. That's all there is to it. Thumbnails are a potentially useful navigation tool, since they give users a snapshot of a page including any text, graphics, or charts. If you choose not to create a thumbnails view, Reader will show blank thumbnail pages when user clicks on Thumbnail view.

Adding Notes

Another useful feature of Exchange annotates PDF files with text notes that the user can open up on demand. This is perhaps most useful as a collaborative tool: an author creates a PDF file, and the readers reply back with comments embedded in the document as notes. Since most Web developers are looking to Acrobat to simply publish documents to the Web, two-way collaboration may not be a major priority (though it could potentially be used to some interesting ends on the Web, especially for corporate training or academic applications).

To create a note, you simply press on the Notes tool button. As when we created links, the cursor changes into a cross-hair pointer. Move it into your document, click, and you've created a note. When the note is opened, it is in its display view (see Figure 2-11). When you close the note, it is in icon view.

Drag the cursor to create a bigger textbox for your note.

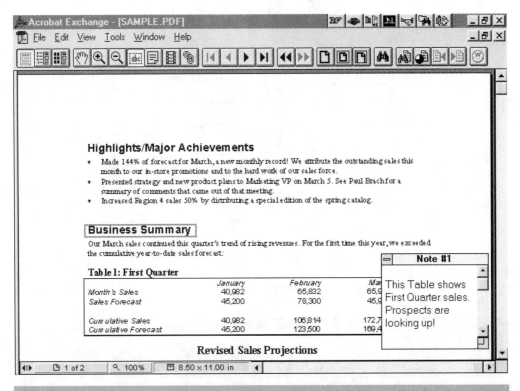

Figure 2-11. *A note is displayed*

Adding Multimedia Files

Another feature available starting in Acrobat 2.1 is the ability to embed multimedia files into your PDF documents and have them played back automatically by Acrobat Reader. This is made possible by the MovieLink plug-in, which now ships as a standard part of Acrobat Exchange. Windows platforms can playback both QuickTime and Microsoft's Video for Windows files; Apple platforms can only playback QuickTime files.

To embed a multimedia file, click on the MovieLink button. Again, the cursor turns to a cross-hair pointer. Click on the point in the PDF document where you want to embed the file. If you click once, the movie appears at its full size. Alternatively, you can drag the cursor to create a box in which the movie plays. When you release the mouse, you see a dialog box that lets you choose the desired multimedia file. Next, a Movie Properties dialog box appears that lets you choose some options for the Movie, including whether or not to include a control panel with the video file and whether to have your file run "inline" within the predefined box or in a *floating window* that disappears after the movie plays, as shown in the following illustration.

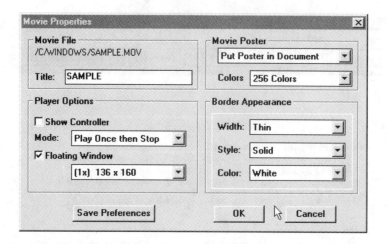

Click OK, and the multimedia file is embedded. All a user has to do to play back the file is click on the small icon, or *poster*, and the movie runs automatically. In Figure 2-12, we set MovieLink to play back the embedded QuickTime file in a floating

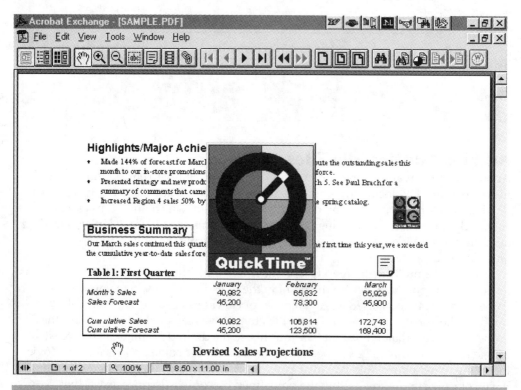

Figure 2-12.   *MovieLink plays back the embedded QuickTime file in a floating window*

window in the middle of the screen, which disappears after it plays. The poster stays visible to guide viewers to the link for the movie.

Adding multimedia—especially video—to Acrobat files is obviously very exciting. But if you are developing PDF for the Web, beware. Video and audio files are bandwidth hogs and can take many minutes to download. Most Web page developers don't offer QuickTime or AVI files for just this reason; Acrobat authors should be just as cautious.

Adding Security to PDF Files

With Exchange, you can control access to your PDF documents. Security is added when you save the file. From the Save As dialog box, you can click on the Security... button. That will access the dialog box shown here:

Among the options available are

- Requiring a password to open and view a document

- Disallowing printing, changing, copying to a clipboard, or changing notes

The security options at first glance appear best suited for use in workgroups or other corporate situations. But they could be applied in some interesting ways on the Web as well. For instance, setting password protection could be a good way to sell PDF documents on the Web. Only when you have received payment do you give the viewer the access to open a particular PDF file. A password also could stop users from freely distributing downloaded PDF files. Similarly, by disallowing printing, you can ensure that your for-pay Web content isn't printed and widely distributed.

Some Acrobat Loose Ends

Acrobat is a powerful family of publishing tools. We've hit the highlights of creating and viewing documents with Acrobat, but a few other capabilities are also worth noting, namely plug-ins and Acrobat Capture.

A Word About Plug-Ins

One of the most unique features of Acrobat is its plug-in architecture, a feature available in other Adobe products as well, notably Adobe PhotoShop. Plug-ins allow the addition of new capabilities to Acrobat. MovieLink, which we discussed, and WebLink, which we will look at in more detail later in this chapter, are examples of Acrobat plug-ins. Another important plug-in is Acrobat Search, which is a standard feature of Exchange.

Late last year, Adobe began posting free Acrobat plug-ins on its Web page, at **http://www.adobe.com/Acrobat/Plug-Ins**. In addition to the WebLink plug-in, the site also included the following plug-ins.

SUPERPREFS PLUG-IN   Adds an extended list of features to the Acrobat Exchange Preferences dialog box.

SUPERCROP PLUG-IN   Adds the ability to crop pages in Exchange, similar to the cropping function in Adobe PhotoShop.

AUTOINDEX PLUG-IN   For adding automatic search and indexing capabilities to a PDF file.

OLE SERVER PLUG-IN   Enables Acrobat Exchange and Reader to act as an OLE server to view PDF documents embedded in other OLE-enabled container applications.

MONITOR SETUP PLUG-IN   Allows creators of PDF documents to specify the color of objects in a page description independent of the color characteristics of the destination device, for example, a monitor or printer.

Overall, the plug-in architecture ensures that Exchange and Reader will always be able to grow to support new capabilities.

Using Acrobat Capture

Acrobat Capture is a Windows-based product that takes the idea of electronic paper to a higher level. Acrobat Capture lets you scan in documents using a digital scanner and have them converted into PDF format. Acrobat Capture preserves all of the fonts, graphics, and multiple columns of the original. For content creators with documents in paper form but with no corresponding computer-based files, Acrobat Capture is a godsend.

Acrobat Capture employs a variety of technologies—including optical character recognition, font recognition, bitmap imaging, and page decomposition—to ensure that PDF files match the original document. If Acrobat Capture is unsure of a word, it places a bitmapped image of the word in the PDF file. It will even place a best-guess text version of the suspect word behind the bitmap image, so the entire file remains searchable. Users can also work with a simple editor to clean up the captured text.

Though expensive at around $3,000, Acrobat Capture offers even paper-only users the ability to create PDF documents and deliver them online.

Acrobat and the Web

Acrobat is a very flexible publishing technology: PDF documents can be distributed via e-mail, CD-ROM, Lotus Notes, and many other ways. But our focus here is on the World Wide Web, and the Web is its own unique publishing environment with a very specific catalog of do's and don'ts. So before we wrap up our look at Acrobat, we need to answer a few key questions about how best to work with PDF on the Web:

- How can you design Acrobat and PDF documents optimized for the Web?
- How do you link your readers from the Web to Acrobat, and from Acrobat out onto the Web?
- How do you integrate PDF documents into your hypertext markup language (HTML) files and deliver them from a Web server?
- What are the future prospects for Acrobat and the Web?

PDF Design and the Web

Every artist should take measure of their canvas before they begin to create. How can you make PDF and the Web mesh as artfully as possible? In broad strokes, here's what you need to keep in mind:

- Always optimize your PDF files for download over the Web—and the slow modems that are the norm there.
- Guide Web surfers to your PDF files as skillfully as possible, and hold their hands to get them started using Acrobat and PDF.
- Don't create PDF islands. The Web is a hypertext environment where "everything is intermingled," as hypertext creator Ted Nelson has described it. Link your PDF files out to the Web, and they become a part of a truly global information infrastructure.

Optimizing PDF for the Web

When creating PDF files earlier in this chapter, we tried to keep an eye on creating PDF for the Web. Here are some of the things we learned:

- *Page vs. screen*   Acrobat lets you choose to output your PDF files to a particular page size and orientation. If you expect your readers to view your PDF files on the Web, consider choosing printing to screen size (6.5 × 5.18 inches). It is very difficult to navigate an oversized PDF layout on an undersized monitor screen. If, however, you figure most of your readers will end up printing out your PDF files, go ahead and choose page size (8.5 × 11).

- *Fonts*   Use standard fonts, and you will be rewarded with smaller files, which will speed up download over the Web. Use fancy fonts, and most likely you will be forced to embed the fonts with your PDF files, bulking up your file size.

- *Compression*   Don't be afraid to compress graphics. In most cases, a computer monitor has nowhere near the resolution of a PostScript printer. Smaller graphics mean smaller files—and little loss of resolution onscreen.

- *Downsample*   One of the best ways to shrink your file size is to use Acrobat Distiller's downsample capability. Lowering graphics resolution for fewer bytes is a good trade-off on the Web.

- *Think Web from the start*   If you have the luxury of knowing in advance you will be creating documents that will ultimately be turned into PDF files, consider that in your design. Create short (screen-length) pages and plan out a structure and flow for your document that can ultimately be implemented using Acrobat's Bookmarks and Links features. Even little things like setting words that you plan to hotlink in bold or italics will help the eventual look of your document when converted to PDF.

WebLink

The best way to make your PDF files an integral part of the Web is to link directly from your files out to HTML documents on the Web. This capability, added in version 2.1 of Acrobat as a standard plug-in feature, is called WebLink.

Start by setting the preferences for WebLink, found on the Edit menu under Preferences. Select WWW Link to open the dialog box shown here:

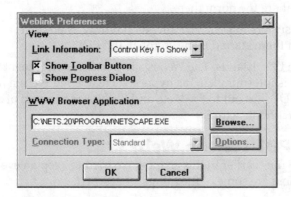

The dialog box for WebLink offers a number of options:

- The Link Information option determines whether or not Acrobat Reader will show the WWW Uniform Resource Locator (URL) when the cursor passes over the WebLink hotlink.

■ The Show Toolbar Button option allows you to add a button on the Acrobat Reader toolbar that automatically starts your Web browser.

■ The Show Progress dialog lets you display the progress of the WebLink download in a dialog box within Acrobat Reader.

■ The WWW Browser Application option lets you choose a Web browser to work with Exchange. Use the browse feature to find and select the browser you wish to use. WebLink works with most major browsers.

Once you have WebLink configured, creating a World Wide Web link is very similar to creating a regular link within Exchange. Click on the Link button in the toolbar and drag the cursor (now a cross-hair pointer) around the word you wish to link, creating a box. That action calls up the Link Properties dialog box, as shown in Figure 2-13. Instead of choosing Go To View or Open File under Action Type, choose World Wide Web Link. Click the Edit URL button, which opens another dialog box; in the textbox, enter the URL you want the link to jump to. Click OK to return to the Link Properties dialog box, and then click on Set Link.

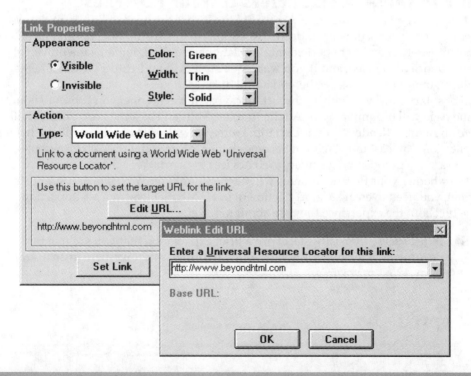

Figure 2-13. *The Link Properties dialog box lets you select a URL that the user can reach when they hit on a WebLink*

Now, when a user clinks on your WebLink, Acrobat Reader will automatically fire up a Web browser and call down the page corresponding to the URL.

The degree to which you will need to use WebLink depends, of course, on the type of PDF document you have created. Many times, PDF documents are islands onto themselves (for example, brochures, customer support documents, magazine pages). And many times they should stay that way. But WebLink, like the Web itself, opens up new vistas of possibilities for presenting information. Consider adding a page to your PDF file that contains some URL links to relevant information on the Web. Or comb through your document and hotlink certain words—for instance, company names—to give the person viewing your PDF document the opportunity to instantly hotlink via the Web to more information. WebLink becomes even more powerful and even more closely integrated with the Web when the next generation of Acrobat arrives, which will let PDF documents open directly in a browser window. Then, there is almost no practical difference between an Acrobat WebLink and a Web URL.

In short, always remember that in posting PDF on the Web you are part of a universe of information—take advantage of it.

How to Guide Web Surfers to Your PDF Files

Just as important as linking from Acrobat to the Web is the need to link from the Web over to your PDF documents. Indeed, just because you're using PDF doesn't mean you can completely abandon hypertext markup language. HTML remains the universal lingua franca of the Web, and if you want Web surfers to find your PDF documents, you are going to have to leave behind a trail of HTML tags.

Let's start, however, with an important caveat: not everyone who comes to your home page will be familiar with Adobe Acrobat. You can't assume your visitors will have an Acrobat Reader on their desktop. Worse, downloading and installing a helper application—at least until Acrobat becomes better integrated with Web browsers—can be a scary proposition for many Web novices.

So whether your PDF documents will be the star of your Web site or a supporting format, you need to create a short document in HTML that lets your visitors know a little bit about the experience they are about to have:

■ *Introduction*   Typically, start with a brief explanation that you are making documents available in Adobe's Acrobat format, as shown here in an example from *Axcess* magazine:

New at Axcess On-line

Axcess is now also availble for download in Adobe's Portable Document Format (PDF) viewable using Adobe Acrobat. Download a 2.5MB sample of Axcess in full graphic glory by clicking here. The Electronic Axcess sampler contains 100 pages of Axcess articles, so it's worth the wait. If you would like to see more articles in PDF format please e-mail us at *acrobat-request@axcess.com*

If you are going to make your visitors jump through some hoops (download a Reader, deal with a new format), then give them some idea of the benefits (richness of layout, portability, etc.) as well.

■ *Pointers* Give a pointer to the Adobe Acrobat home page, and explain clearly that visitors will need a Reader to view your PDF documents. If you have the resources, you may also offer the Reader directly for download from your own FTP site. With the popularity of Acrobat increasing, and the bundling of the Reader with browsers growing, this may soon be a nonevent. But until PDF is as common as HTML, give your visitors every guidance they might need.

■ *Make it clear* It is very important to clearly label and identify PDF documents. Adobe offers three sizes of icons in GIF format, downloadable from its Web site, to indicate PDF documents. Use them. A standard identifier for PDF documents helps not only your site but others publishing with Acrobat. In addition, give a very clear description of the document, including the size (in bytes), as shown in the following illustration. Don't waste your visitors' time. PDF files can be big at times, and if users are going to take the time to download one, they should know exactly what they are getting and how long it is going to take.

> (7 pages / 1 MB) Click on this PDF document icon to download the Adobe Acrobat 2.1 product brochure for viewing with Adobe Acrobat.
> **First**, make sure you've downloaded a **Free Adobe Acrobat Reader** for your platform, and configured it for use with the World Wide Web. **Here's How!**

Serving up PDF

Delivering PDF files on the Web is fairly pain-free, but there are a few technical issues of which you need to take note.

For starters, you'll have to deal with PDF within your HTML files. This is fairly straightforward for anyone already familiar with HTML. You simply "reference" the directory where you have the PDF file stored using the HTML tag "HREF." The HTML hotlink itself can be a PDF icon, an underlined text description of the file, or both (see Figure 2-14.)

You also need to reconfigure your Web server slightly so that it knows how to deal with the PDF file type. The specifics will vary depending on what sort of server you are using, but in general your server must know about the PDF MIME type (application/pdf), how to identify PDF documents on your server (.pdf extension), and, in some cases, how to treat a PDF data stream (binary data).

The Future of Acrobat on the Web

The latest version of Acrobat Exchange (due out in beta in early 1996) represents a quantum leap for Acrobat on the Web. Among the important new authoring and viewing capabilities scheduled to appear:

- The ability for PDF files to open up directly within a browser—initially Netscape Navigator, but eventually others as well—without the need for a separate helper application

- The ability for Acrobat to deliver large PDF files a page at a time, which is a feature that will greatly improve Acrobat's performance over slow Web links

The new capabilities will be implemented in an Application Programming Interface (API) from Adobe. That API, coupled with APIs from browser vendors, will tightly couple Acrobat Reader with a Web browser, enabling Acrobat to pass data directly to the browser screen.

While the formal version of Exchange containing these new authoring features is due in 1996, Adobe in December of 1995 released Amber, a new (initially Windows-only) version of Acrobat Reader that includes the ability to display the new features (see Figure 2-15). Amber's first appearance was as a plug-in for Netscape Navigator 2.0. Other browser vendors that have said they will support inline PDF include Microsoft, AOL, Spyglass, and Spry.

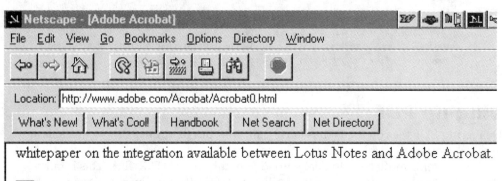

Figure 2-14.   *In this Web browser, the PDF icon is an HTML hotlink*

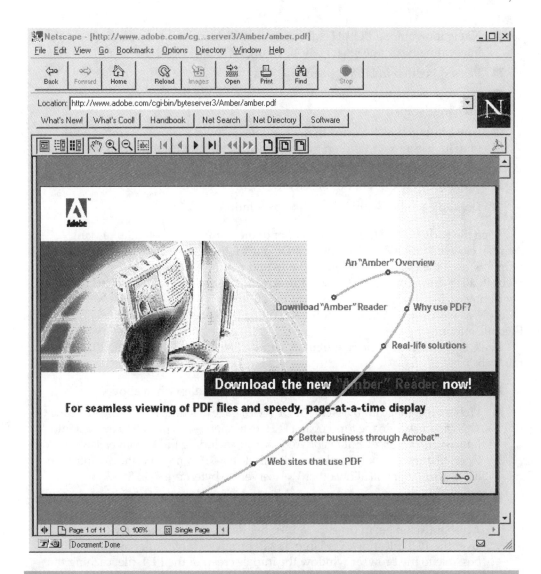

Figure 2-15.   *The Amber reader places PDF files within the Netscape browser landscape*

The features available in the Amber Reader beta include:

■ The ability to view PDF files seamlessly within the same window as the browser page

■ The somewhat limited ability (mainly because the Exchange part of Amber was not yet available) to deliver page-at-a-time downloads

- Navigation among PDF, HTML, and other Web content transparently by integrating Netscape's navigation features (Go Back, etc.)

- PDF embedded in HTML pages

- Progressive display of the PDF file (also somewhat limited until the new Exchange ships).

- Font blitting, which means that when viewed over the Web, Acrobat will initially use a font found on the user's system until the embedded fonts are retrieved and then are "blitted" onscreen for full fidelity.

- Anti-aliased text for better onscreen viewing

- Dockable toolbar within the Netscape window

Even the early beta of the Amber Reader demonstrates the potential of tying Acrobat closely to the Web. The flow of PDF date in the browser window is extremely seamless, as is the linking between PDF files and other HTML-based Web pages. The Web site PDF Zone, for instance, takes full advantage of the hybrid Acrobat/HTML environment. Notice, in Figure 2-16, the PDF annotation displayed in the Netscape window, as well as the Web-links at the top of the page that jump seamlessly from the PDF file out onto the Web.

In all, there are four basic requirements for delivering fully integrated PDF files on the Web:

- The Amber Reader, for integrated file viewing, as described above.

- Web servers that can "byteserve" PDF files a page at a time to the Amber Reader. This capability—in the form of an HTTP extension—is expected to be built into future versions of several major Web servers, including those from Netscape and Open Market. Adobe also plans to distribute a free Common Gateway Interface (CGI) script that will allow other Web servers to byteserve PDF files.

- Optimized PDF files for progressive display and maximum file compression. These capabilities will be built into the next version as standard features of Acrobat Exchange. In practice, an Amber Reader will initially try to download an entire PDF file, however large. It will progressively render as quickly as possible to the browser window the initial screen of the PDF file, caching the rest of the file as it comes in. If the viewer requests a specific page deeper in the file before it is entirely downloaded, Amber will break off the initial connection and immediately retrieve the requested pages. While it is obviously preferable to have your PDF files optimized for delivery to an Amber Reader, it is not a requirement. Amber can read any PDF file created with current versions of Acrobat Exchange, 2.1 or earlier. However, the Web-optimized features will not be delivered. Building small, easily downloadable PDF files would be a simple way to take advantage of the Amber Reader until you upgrade to full Amber Exchange capabilities.

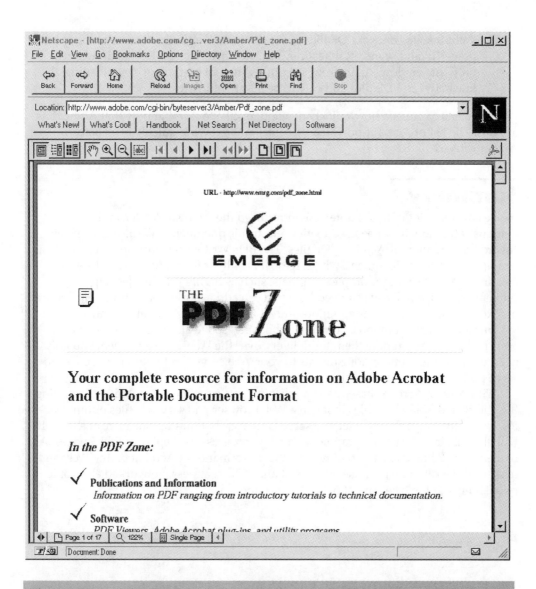

Figure 2-16.   *The PDF Zone demonstrates how to integrate PDF features and the Web*

Although Acrobat retained the code name Amber for the beta release of the Reader, it may not keep the name for long. Most likely, the next version of Acrobat will simply be called 3.0.

■ WebLinks to connect PDF files out to the Web. WebLinks become much more powerful and seamless when they are launched from a PDF file drawn in a browser window. Apart from a slightly different method of downloading, the line between PDF files and HTML pages are blurring.

It remains to be seen how quickly developers take to Acrobat now that Amber has arrived. The list of Acrobat-powered Web sites was growing quickly even before Amber arrived.

Summary

We've covered a lot in this chapter. We introduced the Acrobat Reader, and demonstrated how it can be used to view electronic documents. We also extensively covered the creation of Acrobat PDF files. The PDF Writer makes creating a PDF file as simple as printing a document, while Acrobat Distiller offers advanced features for creating PDF out of more complex originals, such as highly graphic desktop publishing files. Finally, we showed how you can add a variety of features—including indexes, links, notes, movies and more—to a PDF file using Acrobat Exchange.

Our focus here is obviously on Web publishing, so we also showed how to take your PDF files and prepare them for delivery over the Web. As we've seen, you only need to make a few minor adjustments to your Web server and your HTML pages to serve up PDF from your Web site.

With Amber, Acrobat-based Web publishing gets even more capabilities, including the ability to display PDF files inline in a Web browser and serve up files optimized for Web delivery. Amber will let you serve large Acrobat files up one page at a time. It will also display text before graphics and allow progressive display of PDF images. All of these capabilities will greatly improve the performance of Acrobat on the Web, and make real the ultimate promise of Acrobat and PDF: seamless, networked electronic publishing and the true advent of electronic paper.

System Requirements for Acrobat Exchange

FOR MICROSOFT WINDOWS

- A 386-, 486-, or Pentium-based personal computer
- Microsoft Windows 3.1 or 3.11, Windows 95, Windows NT 3.5 or 3.51, or OS/2 running in Windows compatibility mode
- A minimum of 4MB of RAM

FOR APPLE MACINTOSH

- A Macintosh computer (68020 or later) or Power Macintosh
- Apple System 7.0 or later
- 2MB of application RAM (for 68020 to 68040) or 4MB of application RAM (for Power Macintosh)

Where to Find More Information on Acrobat

ADOBE ACROBAT WEB PAGE
http://www.adobe.com/Acrobat

EXAMPLES OF PDF ON THE WEB
http://www.adobe.com/Acrobat/PDFsites.html

OTHER WEB SITES DEVOTED TO ACROBAT
Acrobat Reader tutorial at **http://w3.ag.uiuc.edu/AIM/SLOAN/tutorials/Acrobat/index.html**

NEWSGROUP
comp.text.pdf

LISTSERVS
Acrobat: send e-mail to **acrobat-request@blueworld.com**
In message: subscribe
PDF: send e-mail to **majordomo@binc.net**
In message: SUBSCRIBE PDF-L YOUR NAME <Your ID@Domain>

MAGAZINES

Adobe magazine (paper product): (206) 628-2321

Acrobatics (Web-zine, in PDF):
http://www.ep.cs.nott.ac.uk/~dre/merlin/acrobatics.html

Acropolis (Web-zine, in PDF): **http://www.acropolis.com/acropolis/**

FAX SUPPORT

Call (206) 628-5737 from your fax machine for technical documents.

COMPUSERVE FORUMS

GO ADOBEAPP is for end user questions, including Acrobat. GO ADOBESYS is for developer questions.

Chapter Three

Acrobat Applications

So what sorts of things can you do with Acrobat? The obvious kinds of applications—publishing marketing brochures and technical documents, repurposing newsletters or magazines to the Web—are just the start. With a little creativity, individuals and companies are building entire online businesses around Acrobat that take advantage of the software's key attributes: ease of use and strong graphical layout capabilities. As we'll see, many of these applications would not be possible, or would be much more limited, if they used HTML rather than Acrobat.

Some common threads run through the discussions with Web developers in this section:

■ For high-end publishers with a branded graphical identity, only Acrobat can let them fully retain their brand online.

■ Next-generation Acrobat capabilities like page-at-a-time viewing and progressive rendering are key if Acrobat is to be more widely used on the Web.

■ For serious publishers, Acrobat Distiller—not PDF Writer—is the product of choice. It is simple to use, they say, but for best results on the Web, you should go easy on the fonts and colors, design to a computer screen if you expect to be viewed online, and experiment with compression until you find the fit that's best for your project.

Let's dive in and see how Acrobat is being used on the Web.

TimesFax

Perhaps the best known and probably the first truly commercial Acrobat-based service is TimesFax, a daily, condensed version of the *New York Times*. Introduced originally in 1989 as a fax-only service, TimesFax has been published using Acrobat since May 1993, and it has been freely available for download on the Web since February 1995 from **http://www.nytimesfax.com** (see Figure 3-1).

TimesFax distributes two PDF versions per day. One goes to the U.S. Navy and is then distributed via satellite and printed out on every ship in the Navy; the second goes out on the Web. TimesFax has about 180,000 registered users on the Web and gets about 10,000 downloads of TimesFax per day.

"The reason why we settled on Acrobat is to preserve the look and feel of the newspaper, right down to the fonts we use, the amount of air around the headlines, and the way we lay pages out," says Jaime Greene, editor of TimesFax. "For a newspaper, that is part of the information we provide to our readers. An important story runs on the top of the page, has a bigger headline, maybe a bold headline. We can't control those kinds of things in HTML like we can in Acrobat."

The TimesFax operation runs in parallel with the *New York Times*, using the same reporters and edited copy as the newspaper. A four-person TimesFax staff picks the stories to run, edits them down to fit the much smaller eight-page PDF version, and does the layouts. The result is a product that very strongly reflects the print version of

Figure 3-1. *The HTML front end to TimesFax includes several advertisers, which helps keep the service free*

the *New York Times* (see Figure 3-2). The staff creates TimesFax on a network of high-end Macintosh Quadras running QuarkXPress. They use Acrobat Distiller to do the conversions to PDF. The Quadras can do the conversions in "about two minutes," whereas when TimesFax first started using Acrobat on slower computers, it would "take 25 to 30 minutes to distill a file," according to Greene.

"The way Acrobat handles fonts and compresses text and graphics is very helpful to us," says Greene, who says he tries to keep the Internet edition of TimesFax down to 100K or less. Even at that size, he is able to deliver a couple of graphic-intensive ads, some different fonts, and some relatively complex photos, he says.

"The ads are the real killer. The body and headline copy [of the news stories] we can control. We can control our own graphics as well, compress them down. But from advertisers we get very high-quality, camera-ready copy and we have to explain to them that our readers, if they are lucky, will only have a 300 dpi printer, and it's worse if they are reading onscreen. You have to design down more or less so you know everyone will be able to process and print the file."

Because they do such a high-volume business on the Web, Greene says they run into complaints from readers who must first download and install Acrobat before they

Figure 3-2. *The front page of TimesFax*

can view TimesFax. "We are hoping Acrobat becomes more of a standard," he says. "When Netscape makes Acrobat standard in its next version, that's a good thing for us."

Voyager

CD-ROM publisher Voyager Company is one of the more creative users of Acrobat on the Web. To dip its toes in the water, Voyager initially developed a PDF-based site for 3Sixty, its full-color source catalog for its CD-ROMs, shown in Figure 3-3. Acrobat let the company maintain the attractive layouts and graphics of its catalog as it moved from print to the Web.

"The look and feel of our catalog is very important to us. We've done a lot of brand identity and direct mail work with it. So we put the catalog up in Acrobat. It was easier to distribute and worked so well that we scaled back the print catalog and began working on direct marketing through the Web," says Trevor Kaufman, Voyager's online director.

Voyager next turned its attention to more elaborate Acrobat products. The company had developed a very interesting technology called CD-Link, which initially worked as a helper application to Web browsers. CD-Link opens up a line of

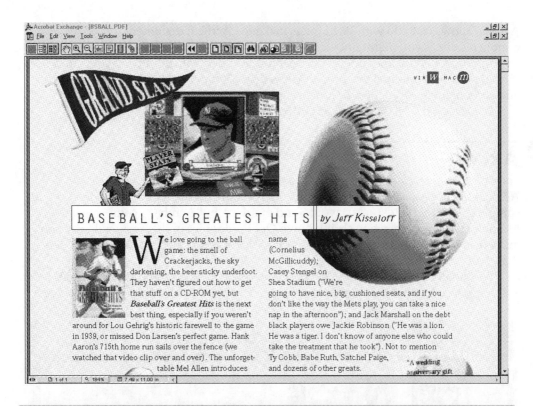

Figure 3-3. *Voyager highlights its CD-ROM titles using Acrobat*

communication between an audio CD player and a Web browser. Voyager used that link to create interactive, Web-based liner notes. The liner notes, created initially in rather sparse HTML, let readers click on a hotlink in the text and automatically play the corresponding passage on audio CD. Voyager and third-party developers have used CD-Link to create interactive liner notes for everything from jazz to rock to rap albums.

As this book is being written, the company had begun work on its first PDF liner note (for a new Brian Eno album), which sets up CD-Link as an Acrobat plug-in and includes Exchange-created hotlinks within the document. Voyager also is working on a similar project with a sheet music publisher, using Acrobat to post sheet music to the Web and CD-Link to let users click on a passage and hear it played automatically, according to Kaufman.

While Voyager is a PDF enthusiast, the company "right now is concentrating on HTML and Java versions of our pages, using Acrobat as a downloadable deliverable" rather than as an onscreen Web format, reports Kaufman. In that scenario, users download a relatively compact PDF file and use Acrobat's WebLink feature to retrieve additional remote resources—for instance, RealAudio versions of songs. "One thing

Acrobat allows us to do with WebLink is make the Acrobat document the key to remote resources you might not want to download right then," says Kaufman.

For now, CD-Link liner notes are free, but the added value of PDF layouts may let Voyager charge a minimal fee, probably less than $5, for access to the PDF document and accompanying Web files, Kaufman says.

Voyager's CD-Link home page is **http://www.voyager.com**.

Axcess

For a magazine as graphically rich as Axcess (**http://www.internex.net/axcess/**), Acrobat is a perfect solution (see Figure 3-4). Not only does it let the magazine keep its complex background textures, layouts, and graphics, but Acrobat's compression technology lets the magazine shrink down Quark files that in their original form run more than 9GB. A single article that may run 8MB in print can be compressed to less than 100K, the magazine has found.

"We initially approached the Web in the pre-Netscape days, and we didn't get anything close to what we wanted to do," says Thomas Powell, who consulted Axcess

Figure 3-4. *Axcess magazine uses Acrobat to retain the rich graphics of its print version on the Web*

on how to get up on the Web and writes for the magazine as well. "These days theoretically you can do anything with HTML," says Powell, "but is it worth the trouble and is it the most efficient way to do it?"

Axcess turned to Acrobat, but it wasn't content to just run pages through Distiller. Instead, the magazine's editors resized every article and feature "around the Internet and screen delivery," says Powell. "We reduce everything as small as possible. We resize everything. Sometimes we have to reedit things."

Powell says he uses Exchange and PDF Writer more as a prototyping device and uses Distiller to fine-tune his PDF files.

Like Voyager, Axcess is considering working with Java to make its Web presence come alive with animations. But it continues to believe Acrobat is a strong alternative for publishers who come from a print medium and want to move their publications to the Web. "What we really want to see is Netscape progressively render an Acrobat page within its window," says Powell. "If you could do that you'd see a lot of magazines working with PDF for its 2-D (nonanimated) Web work."

Developer Tips, Tricks, and Complaints

Don't embed fonts for Web delivery. If you need a fancy font for a headline, rasterize it and make a small JPEG out of it in PhotoShop and include that in your PDF file.

—Thomas Powell, Axcess

It's possible to use Acrobat Capture to turn paper documents into PDF, but it can be time consuming fixing up where the Optical Character Recognition (OCR) technology misses. Use the original digital files, Quark or PageMaker, for instance, whenever possible.

—Stanley Greenfield, Dial-A-Book

One frustration with Acrobat is that Adobe was not responsive in the early days to developer requests. Things are getting better, but given the "closed" nature of the Acrobat environment, Acrobat may always be slow to implement new features.

—Trevor Kaufman, Voyager

Try to stick to files of 100K or less. Any more, and users become impatient waiting for the download. Even at 100K, TimesFax can deliver eight pages of highly compressed news, graphics, and ads.

—Jaime Greene, TimesFax

If you expect the readers to view PDF on their computer monitors, optimize the files for onscreen delivery. Make each page no bigger than a single screen, even if it means reediting original documents.

—Thomas Powell, Axcess

Dial-A-Book

While there is a lot of talk of keeping PDF files small for delivery over the Web, Dial-A-Book, Inc. (**http://dab.psi.net/DialABook/index.html**)has gone in the other direction: letting users download complete books over the Internet in PDF format. The company uses Acrobat to retain the original look and feel of the books.

Dial-A-Book was established in 1994 by Stanley Greenfield, former senior vice president of Ziff-Davis Publishing, to develop applications for the sale and delivery of digital products over digital networks. The concept was tested on the ZiffNet online service in 1993, and it moved to the Web and PDF in 1995.

Since then, the company's business plan has gone through several evolutions, but late last year it settled on a unique idea: users pay full list price for hard copies of a book, and as a bonus they can download a free, fully indexed and searchable PDF version of the book (see Figure 3-5). The first books up on the site were some engineering titles from the IEEE, available at $5 plus shipping and handling.

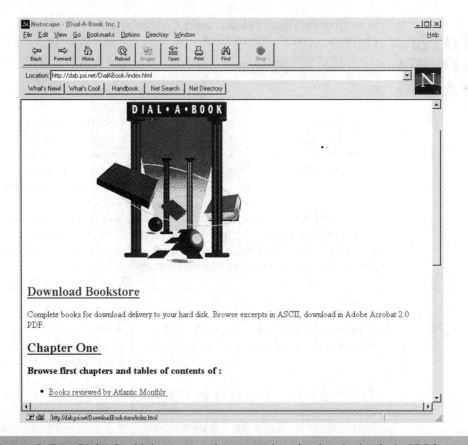

Figure 3-5. *Dial-A-Book's home page lets users download entire books in PDF form*

One of the more unique aspects of the effort is a custom-developed plug-in that adds RSA Data Security RC4 encryption to the PDF files. The plug-in "registers" the paid user of each book and gives that person access to its encrypted contents. In addition, it "buries" the registration number in the reader's hard drive, making it possible to read the document only on the PC where it was downloaded. The plug-in also disables the print and save as functions of Acrobat, providing further copyright protection.

A separate Dial-A-Book effort, dubbed Chapter One, puts the first chapters of books up in HTML format on the Web. Readers can browse more than 250 books and buy any they choose in hard copy. Eventually, Chapter One may put its samples in PDF format as well, according to Greenfield.

"There aren't a lot of people that want to download books right now," admitted Greenfield. "But there's a revolution coming. The economics of book distribution are going to change radically. The 40 percent cut that goes to the bookseller goes away, the 25 percent the wholesaler gets goes away, and the 15 percent spent on paper and binding goes away. When I sell a book by downloading, 70 percent of the current list price goes away."

The final piece of Greenfield's plan is a flat-screen reader—essentially a luggable computer monitor—which he says will cost less than $300 by 1998. That will let him reach people who read books in the three "Bs," Greenfield says, which are "the bathroom, the bedroom, and the bus."

Magnetic Press

From New York City's SoHo district, Magnetic Press runs its own Acrobat "printing plant." The systems integrator and consulting firm takes in major PDF projects (including Dial-A-Book's Download Bookstore) and also publishes Acropolis (**http://www.acropolis.com/acropolis/**), a Web-zine done entirely in PDF that tracks the development of the Acrobat market (see Figure 3-6).

Much of the company's work today, says company president Sanford Bingham, is what he calls "digital printing and binding," or taking in digital documents and converting them to PDF for distribution on CD-ROM, disks, or on the Web. The company also builds custom Acrobat plug-ins, including Dial-A-Book's encryption plug-in and a second tool called Acro-Bot that helps automate the production of PDF files.

"The fundamental insight of PDF is that it's about documents, it's not about networks or media," says Bingham. "This I think in time will assert itself in the minds of publishers. You want to have only two processes, an authoring process and a distribution process. The distribution process might involve any number of media: CompuServe, Prodigy, the Web. But you couldn't possibly agree as a publisher to a

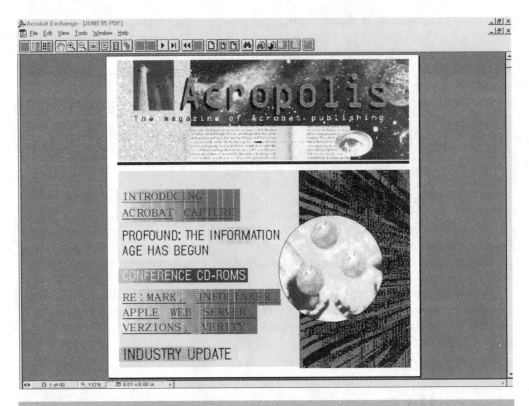

Figure 3-6. *Magnetic Press publishes Acropolis, a Web-zine in PDF format covering developments in the Acrobat market*

situation where you had to author differently for each distribution channel. That would be completely backward. Every tool that tries to impose a format standard based on distribution technology—whether it's Blackbird, AOL, whatever—will all fail in the end."

Bingham says his fear for Acrobat is that (rather ironically) HTML will become the de facto publishing standard for highly graphic Web publishing and that companies will use Acrobat only as an easy method to crank out and convert reams of more basic documents—say, technical catalogs—to electronic form. But Acrobat has significant advantages as well, he says.

"There is already an authoring process in place, people know how to do it, and the output of it is in almost all cases PostScript," according to Bingham. "With minimal additional effort it is possible to create from that electronic products. The efficiencies are pretty significant there."

Summary

We've seen five strong examples of PDF publishing on the Web. The themes running through this chapter are consistent. Acrobat provides greater layout control, graphic richness, and ease of use than HTML. And the reasons for using Acrobat and PDF will only grow as the technology becomes a standard feature in Web browsers and online services, and as new features (including page-at-a-time viewing and progressive rendering) come online.

We've discovered that the business opportunities for using Acrobat are diverse, but they generally spring from traditional print medium: newspapers, magazines, books, interactive liner notes, etc. The strong print bias is not surprising. As we noted at the start, Acrobat is perhaps best described as electronic paper. And it is an important emerging technology for the World Wide Web.

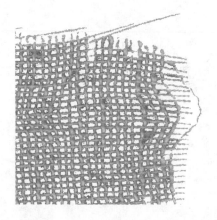

PART TWO

Multimedia and Interactivity: Java and More

Roadmap ▶

We'll start Part II with an in-depth look at Sun's Java: the language, emerging Java tools, and cool Java applets. Chapter 5 will introduce Java and show how non-programmers can take advantage of its powerful capabilities. Chapter 6 offers a crash course in the language itself. In Chapter 7, we'll take a tour of Java applets on the Web. We'll move in Chapter 8 to take a look at Microsoft's Internet Platform. Chapter 9 will discuss the Netscape juggernaut, focusing on its Web authoring tools. And finally, in Chapter 10, we'll take a hands-on look at Macromedia Shockwave for the Web.

Chapter Four

Introduction to the "Programmable Web"

Microsoft's Bill Gates calls the Internet and the World Wide Web the "greatest opportunity since the IBM PC"—the box upon which he launched his fortune. Sun Microsystem's chief technology officer Eric Schmidt sees the Web as the fulfillment of Sun's vision of "The Network is the Computer," and he wonders if "maybe we aren't *under*estimating the Web's potential." Oracle chairman Larry Ellison has shunted aside his company's lofty interactive TV plans and turned full attention to the Web, predicting a $500 diskless PC that will be driven at its core by an intelligent Web browser and Net access.

These computer industry titans see the Web not only for what it is today—a repository of mostly text-and-graphics hypertext information—but for what it can become: a global computing platform. Forget your hard drive. Forget that CD-ROM. In the future, all you'll need is a reasonably fast (the faster the better) Net connection and software intelligent enough to reach out onto the Internet and on the fly grab whatever it needs—not only text, graphics, sound, and video, but executable programs as well.

In short, what you have is a "programmable Web": able to deliver via the Internet the same multimedia and interactive experience users have come to expect from their desktop PCs.

The Web is just now entering the cusp of this revolution. The tools that will drive this change began appearing late last year (1995): Sun's Java programming language; Netscape's Navigator 2.0 application platform and JavaScript scripting language; Microsoft's Internet Explorer and Internet Studio; Macromedia's Shockwave; and much, much more. Even as these tools trickled out in beta form, Web developers and end users flocked to them enthusiastically, driven by the vision of a truly multimedia, interactive, and programmable World Wide Web.

A Look at What's Possible

The implications of this revolution for the Web are staggering. No longer do pages just *sit* there. They spring into action with: live animations; forms with instant feedback; real-time data feeds; and applications with local processing and computation. As this book was being written, Web developers were making some of their first stabs at a programmable Web. The results will only get better, but here's a quick look at what's possible:

■ *The animated Web* Java animations are showing up everywhere on the Web. Start on Sun's Web site, where the friendly Java "mascot" Duke gives a wave or tumbles across the page while steam swirls and rises from the Java logo. Java animations pale somewhat compared to what is possible with Macromedia's Shockwave technology (see Figure 4-1), which was released late last year and almost instantly brought to the Web waves of animations and multimedia titles created by newbies and seasoned multimedia developers alike using Macromedia's widely used Director authoring software. "Until Shockwave came out, we had no interest in the Internet whatever," says Aaron Singer,

Figure 4-1.   *The animated Shockwave logo spins on its axis*

president of a multimedia design house, ad hoc Interactive, which is developing a CD-ROM and companion animated Web site using Macromedia Director and Shockwave. "The interesting thing that Shockwave allows us to do is blur the edges between what a CD can do and what the Internet can do."

■ *Local processing and computation*   By now, every experienced Web surfer has filled out dozens of questionnaires or registration forms on the Web. But how about a form that reacts immediately to your input—perhaps telling you an answer is not valid or leading you to the next step? Or consider a real-time adding machine or mortgage calculator that automatically responds to your input, such as the one in Figure 4-2, which was created using JavaScript. All of these, and more, are possible with downloadable, executable content.

■ *Fun and games*   The Web's killer app? Initially, client-side processing will bring relatively simple games like crossword puzzles, solitaire, or even Missile Command to the Web (see Figure 4-3). But marry full multimedia and local processing with the Web, and the result could be some fantastic networked, multiplayer games.

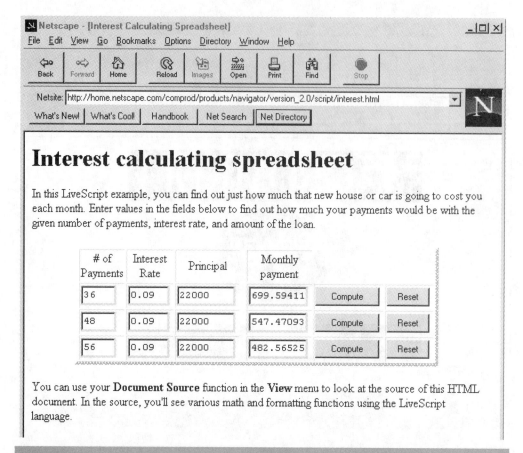

Figure 4-2. *JavaScript was used to create this live spreadsheet, on which you click a button and the outputs are rendered instantly—and locally*

■ *The end of the helper application* Everyone who has spent time downloading and configuring helper applications knows it can be a pain. And what happens when you stumble upon a new data type? Well, you head off to find the correct helper app to download. Even when you get it working, you are still dealing with content delivered to a separate window. The programmable Web promises to end all that. First, browsers like Netscape (with its new plug-in architecture) has exposed browser-level application programming interfaces that let third parties integrate their players directly into the browser, making it possible to deliver inline multimedia content, such as animations, audio, video, and more. In an even more hands-free fashion, technologies like Sun's Java and Microsoft's Object Linking and Embedding (OLE) will check your hard drive to see if you have the helper application you need and if not, download and configure it automatically.

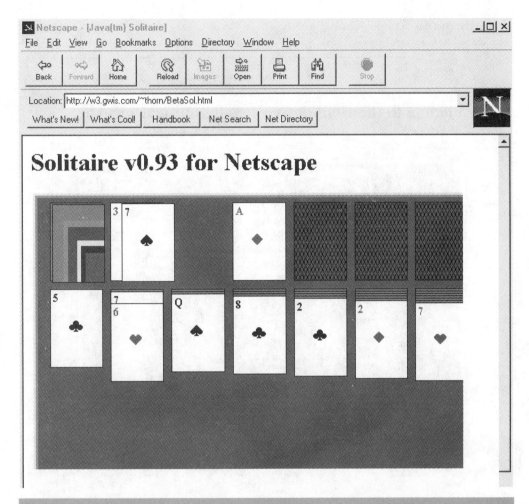

Figure 4-3. *Solitaire is a standard on Windows machines, but this version is Java-ized, executable content downloaded over the Net*

■ *Serious business applications* The programmable Web isn't just fun and games. Big business will take advantage of it as well. In some cases, it will mean a friendlier face for marketing purposes, such as BellSouth Telecommunications Java-ized home page shown in Figure 4-4. In other cases, companies will build heavy-duty distributed applications. At a Java Day held on Sun's campus late last year, two of the first large-scale applications were publicly demonstrated: National Semiconductor showed an interactive, Web-based ordering system that will let its customers search its 30,000-product catalog, while Applix Inc. showed a Net-based spreadsheet with an interactive, Java-based client tied via the Internet to a back-end computation engine running Java. "Without a

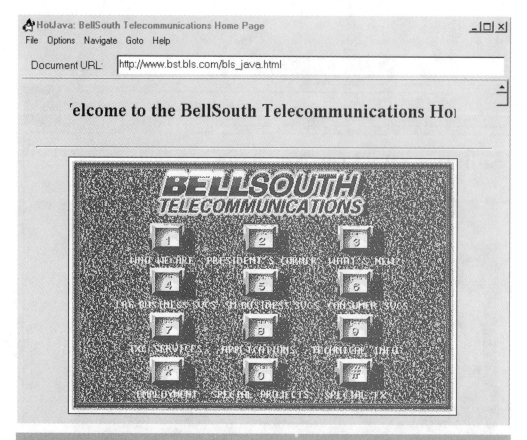

Figure 4-4.   *BellSouth was one of the first mainstream business sites to use Java—move your cursor over any of the buttons, and an audio clip plays*

well-designed, machine-independent, open language [like Java], this kind of application just couldn't happen," said Barry Zane, vice president of technology for Applix.

The Interactive Web: Today and Tomorrow

Amazing stuff, no doubt. But isn't the Web already interactive? Isn't it possible to fill out and submit forms, perform calculations, view animations, and more? Yes. But there's a key difference between the way Web interactivity has been done up to now, and how it will be done in the future. Up to now, scripts have run on the server side of the equation, spitting back information in response to a browser's request. This multiple-step process goes something like this:

1. The user clicks on a URL that calls a script.
2. The request is sent back over the network to the server.
3. The server executes the script.
4. The output from the script is sent back over the network for display on the user's browser.

Enabling the server-side script is the Common Gateway Interface (CGI), which defines how the browser, server, and script communicate. Almost all Web servers and browsers are equipped to handle CGI scripts, and the scripts themselves can be written in almost any language, ranging from Perl to Basic to C++. Server-side scripts have added a powerful interactive element to the Web. Among the now practically ubiquitous features that take advantage of CGI scripts are: data request forms, password checks, search engines, image maps, and database queries.

In the cases described above, the "engine" that reads and processes the CGI scripts is located at the server. Shift that capability into the browser, and you've moved the intelligence down the network, from the server into the client machine. That's the key difference between first-generation Web browsers and more intelligent browsers like Sun's Hot Java, Netscape's Navigator 2.0, and Oracle's PowerBrowser. No longer does a dumb client have to reach out over the network to a smart server every time some processing needs to be done. These browsers have the smarts to do it themselves. For Web developers, it means you can view a formerly static HTML page as a canvas on which to paint all sorts of interactive features, including animations, interactivity, and local data processing.

The New Web Toolbox

These tools and capabilities add powerful weapons to the arsenal of every Web developer. Yet even as new technologies emerge to leapfrog over HTML, it is important to remember that HTML has two fundamental strengths that helped build the Web into the juggernaut it has become:

- It has an incredibly low barrier to entry. It is easy to use, enabling anyone to build his or her own home page.
- It is cross-platform, able to be displayed in a similar fashion on browsers running on Windows, Mac, and Unix machines.

As the Web is driven forward by the powerful new technologies we describe in this chapter, these two core tenets will at times find themselves under attack. Not everyone can write Java code, program in Visual Basic, or create a Director movie. The challenge will be to develop new easy-to-use tools, and in some cases new business models, that will let nonprogrammers either build or be able to buy and customize sophisticated Web applications. If not, the Web will splinter into two groups: technology haves and have-nots.

There will also be some challenges to the inherent multiplatform nature of the Web. One of Java's greatest strengths is its ability to run the same code on different computer platforms. This capability takes the Web's cross-platform text-and-graphics capabilities and extends it to executable content. Hard-core developers cheer the fact that they don't have to compile and debug their code again and again for different platforms. But there will also be a strong Windows-only thrust to next-generation tools as Microsoft discovers and tries to conquer the Web. Internet Studio will initially be a Windows-only technology, as will early versions of OLE. How will the Internet community view such developments? The answer is that many will resist, but many others will see the masses of Windows users storming the Web and not be able to turn away. Microsoft has great tools, a huge developer base, and an even larger user base, none of which can be ignored.

In short, as the Web gets more interactive and programmable, it will also become undeniably more complex. It will be a difficult challenge for Webmasters to brave these new waters. They will need to wear many hats—networking guru, graphics artist, programmer. The likely result will be the end of the Webmaster and the creation of the Web-Team, a group of people with diverse, specialized skills working together to deliver a compelling interactive, online experience.

So as we dive in for a closer look at some of the tools we'll cover in this chapter, we do so with the understanding that not every Webmaster will work hands-on with all of these tools. But it is vital you understand them and know how they work and what they will mean for the Web. And keep an open mind. Because if the Web has proven anything, it's that anyone—marketers, designers, writers, engineers, software developers, students, home users—may find himself or herself one day building a Web site. You can never be sure what hat you might be wearing—and what Web tool you may need to learn how to use—as the Web hurtles toward its interactive, multimedia future.

Sun's Java

The Web technology grabbing the most attention is undoubtedly Sun Microsystem's Java programming language and Hot Java browser. The history of Java is an interesting one, and it demonstrates the amazing overnight development of the Internet. Java (then known as Oak) began as a project to build an advanced programming language for consumer-oriented devices, most notably set-top boxes and personal digital assistants. The Sun team developed the language, lost a few key early ITV contracts, and then saw the whole world of interactive TV crumble all around them.

Fortuitously, the Web, spurred on by the development of the Mosaic graphical interface, had just began to boom. So Sun turned its attention to the Web, and Java was born—the first programming language specifically tailored to deliver small, executable bits of code (which Sun calls applets) over the Internet.

What exactly is Java? Sun, with its tongue slightly in cheek, calls upon a long list of buzzwords to explain Java: a simple, object-oriented, distributed, interpreted, robust, secure, architecture-neutral, portable, high-performance, multithreaded, and dynamic language. Yet the buzzwords fit, and a closer look at a few of them go a long way toward explaining the power of Java:

- *Simple*   At its core, Java is a programming language. It is patterned after C++, the language most programmers use today to do object-oriented software development. But Sun engineers had grown tired of bloated, hard-to-understand software. So with Java, they stripped away many of the most difficult and less useful parts of C++, including operator overloading, multiple inheritance, and extensive automatic coercions, while adding some new features of its own—most notably, garbage collection, which deals with memory allocation and helps cut down on bugs. Sun also kept Java small. The core of Java is just 40 kilobytes.

- *Object-oriented*   Java is an object-oriented language, which describes a method of building software that focuses on creating reusable data objects that can be linked together to create programs.

- *Distributed*   Java is specifically designed to work in a networked environment like the Internet. The language has built-in routines for communicating via TCP/IP protocols like HTTP and FTP. In addition, Java applets can go out over the Net to access needed objects as easily as accessing them from a local hard drive.

- *Secure*   Sun has paid a lot of attention to security issues with Java. Since Java applets are downloaded and run on a user's local machine, there needs to be a way to ensure that what is being downloaded is not a virus or bug. Java accomplishes this in several ways, including running applets in a restricted, software-based "virtual machine" and limiting low-level machine access. Longer term, Java will also get public key encryption and other methods to ensure it keeps the bugs out.

- *Architecture-neutral and portable*   One of Java's greatest strengths is its ability to run the exact same bytecode on different computer platforms. Developers don't have to code, compile, and debug for every platform under the sun—they just do it once. As long as the computer is running the Java interpreter, the Java applet will run. This is most clearly a shot across the bow of Microsoft, which has gained control of the desktop PC market on the strength of its Windows operating system (and the Intel processor) and at the expense of other OSs like Apple Macintosh. Java doesn't care what the OS is; in a sense, Java itself is an "online OS," a platform on which a developer can write applications.

■ *Multithreaded* Java is able to perform multiple tasks simultaneously. This is vital for a language targeted at the Web, because it offers better interactive response and real-time performance.

All of these features make Java an ideal language for the Web. And Java is becoming widely adopted. Browser vendors including Netscape, Spyglass, Oracle, and others have licensed Java, while Java tools are in development by Sun, Borland, Macromedia, Metrowerks, and others.

Microsoft's Internet Studio and More

The Internet community has been holding its breath in anticipation of Microsoft's entry onto the World Wide Web. Microsoft was a latecomer to the Web, but by the end of 1995 had clearly committed major resources to tie practically all of its products to the Internet, as well as develop new products specifically aimed at the Web.

At the heart of Microsoft's Web authoring strategy is Internet Studio, its online application development platform. Internet Studio is the successor to Blackbird, Microsoft's long-in-development on-line authoring tool. Because of the blockbuster success of the Web and the proliferation of HTML, Microsoft killed Blackbird completely earlier this year. Microsoft took its work on Blackbird and shifted it over to Internet Studio, which it says will offer the same powerful yet easy-to-use authoring environment of Blackbird but will output Web standard HTML rather than Blackbird's proprietary file formats.

As promised by Microsoft, Internet Studio aims to make HTML authoring a much easier task than ever before. At its core, Internet Studio offers a "frame-based" layout environment, very similar to today's desktop publishing software. Layout is handled by simple drag-and-drop commands as well as templates that let designers add features to a title with a single click. Pictures, text, sound, and video can be easily added to an application. No programming is required, though the environment supports custom Object Linking and Embedding controls written in C and Visual Basic. Developers can use these controls to add almost any imaginable feature to an Internet Studio page. Using OLE controls, third parties ranging from Macromedia (multimedia), InterVista (Virtual Reality Programming Language) and Adobe (Acrobat) are working to integrate their media types into Internet Studio.

Internet Studio has the potential to become a powerful online authoring solution, but it has some high hurdles to overcome. At a minimum, there is significant resistance among Web developers in backing a completely new set of HTML extensions that will be developed largely under Microsoft's control, regardless of how powerful that product is. And on a more cynical note, many Web watchers wonder if the product formerly called Blackbird will ever see the light of day or whether it is total "vaporware."

As if to hedge its bets on Internet Studio, Microsoft acquired Vermeer Technologies, whose FrontPage application already does a lot of what Internet Studio promises to do: offer users a simple way to build and manage interactive Web sites.

We will take a look at all of these platforms in Chapter 8, as well as at Microsoft's Internet Explorer browser. Like Netscape Navigator, Internet Explorer is much less a browser and more like an online OS (operating system) or platform. Microsoft's current browser, Internet Explorer 2.0, is a strong platform, but Microsoft has promised to build even more powerful new capabilities into the 3.0 version of Internet Explorer.

The Netscape OS

Remember when Netscape was a cash-poor startup with a simple browser as its main product? It wasn't too long ago (fall of 1994). Now Netscape has a valuation in the billions and a client product that can no longer be viewed as just a browser but as a total Web operating system (OS). Indeed, the most recent commercial release of Netscape Navigator, version 2.0, contains enough features aimed solely at developers that it merits individual attention in this part of the book. With 75 percent or more market share, most Web developers already customize their pages for viewing by Netscape browsers; that will only likely accelerate as Netscape Navigator 2.0 features take hold.

What has Netscape added? A lot more than mere HTML extensions (although they've got a few cool extensions in there too), including:

- *Java support* Netscape was the first browser vendor to implement Java.

- *JavaScript scripting language* A higher-level language than Java, JavaScript lets Web authors embed executable scripts directly into their HTML pages, enabling live Web content.

- *Frames* This new HTML extension lets Web developers break up and divide a page into different sections. One section could include static information, such as navigation bars, banners, or advertising, while a separate window contains scrollable information (see Figure 4 -5).

- *Plug-ins* The Navigator 2.0 architecture lets helper applications display directly in the browser window, giving Web authors a whole new range of file formats they can work with. Existing technologies including Adobe Acrobat PDF documents, Apple QuickTime movies, and Macromedia Director titles can be viewed directly in the Netscape browser.

Together, the features of Navigator 2.0 offer Web developers the opportunity to create a completely new experience for Web surfers, complete with multimedia, live content, and interactivity.

Multimedia Plug-Ins: Shockwave and More

We talked a little bit about plug-ins in our discussion of Netscape. But Netscape (and other browser vendors like Spyglass) simply provide the enabling technology for plug-ins. The real action is with the makers of these Web multimedia plug-ins themselves. Many companies are working on linking their technologies closer to the Web, including Macromedia Director (Shockwave), Apple Computer (QuickTime), and others. In addition, many of the technologies we discuss in other chapters—including Acrobat, VRML, and real-time audio and video applications—also are being positioned as plug-ins.

The power of inline plug-ins is that they let Web browsers deal with major new media types the same way they deal with text and graphics: bringing video, animations, sound, and more to the Web. These plug-ins are made possible by the development of powerful Application Programming Interfaces now a part of most major browsers. Makers of third-party applications link their players to the browser over these APIs, allowing the multimedia content to be displayed within the browser window.

This emerging browser plug-in architecture represents a powerful new paradigm for the Web, placing virtually no limit on what can be integrated into an HTML page. In Chapter 11, we'll take an extended look at one of the most popular plug-ins—Macromedia's Shockwave—which brings multimedia and interactivity to the Web in an unprecedented fashion. Netscape is way ahead in pioneering the use of plug-ins, but other browser vendors are likely to follow as well.

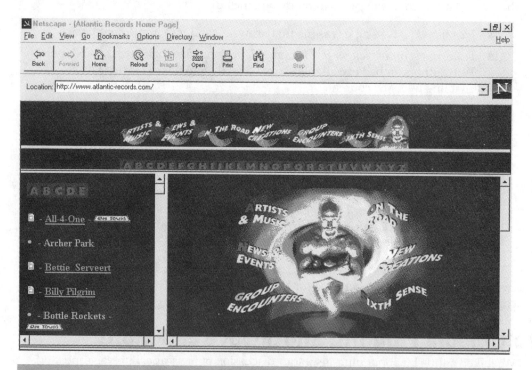

Figure 4-5. *Here's an innovative use of Netscape frames by Atlantic Records*

Summary

Web authoring is headed for a revolution. No longer limited by the basic inline data types (text and graphics mainly) supported by HTML, the Web has already begun to spring to life with a variety of multimedia and interactive content. Even more revolutionary is the emergence of executable content, which will let Web browsers download and run small applications, called applets, that spring to life and run locally on the desktop.

The implications of these developments are tremendous. The already graphically oriented Web will get a major new infusion of multimedia and interactivity. In addition, Web developers will be able to design Web pages that look more like desktop programs, including games, animations, financial applications, and more.

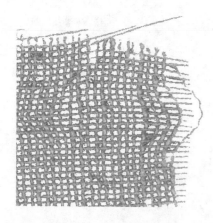

Chapter Five

Java for the Rest of Us: Tips for Nonprogrammers

So you've become fluent in HTML, served up a few pretty complex tables, played with server push animations, and tested the waters with some Common Gateway Interface (CGI) scripts. Are you ready to take the next step and dive headfirst into the hottest thing on the Web today—Sun's Java programming language?

How you answer this question—and the realistic consequences of your answer—depends on your background. If you are a hard-core programmer used to dealing with C code and the like, answer yes and you'll find yourself on new but somewhat familiar ground. But if you are a typical Webmaster, answer yes and your first reaction upon diving deeper into Java may be that you've gotten yourself in over your head. Java coding is a far cry from HTML tagging, and despite the new language's elegance and power, it is not something picked up easily.

Yet there is no denying Java's potential impact on the Web. As we saw in Chapter 4, Java and similar Web development environments bring amazing new capabilities to the Web, including interactivity, multimedia, and localized processing. No Webmaster can afford to get left behind.

Don't worry. There are myriad ways to take advantage of the power of Java without doing any bare-bones Java coding at all. We'll provide you with all the skills you need to acquire, manipulate, and deliver Java applets from your HTML pages without writing a single line of code.

So right off the bat, let's set our agenda. This is not a Java programming manifesto. It is a hands-on look at Java in a way designed to meet the needs of a typical Webmaster. In this chapter, we'll provide Java tips and tricks for Webmasters, including how to acquire, modify, and use Java applets on your Web pages. We will demonstrate how to feed basic parameters to a Java applet via HTML, instantly customizing the applet for your site. A variety of freely available applets are already posted on the Web, mainly in the areas of animation and audio engines and various special effects generators. More will come. We'll also examine the emerging buy-sell-and-trade market for Java applets on the Web and give you some tips on navigating the next-generation software distribution landscape.

For the adventuresome, Chapter 6 will offer a hands-on introduction to the Java language and get you started on writing your own applets. We'll also introduce some emerging Java development environments and authoring tools that will move programming in Java beyond the rather bare-bones programming environment provided by the Java Software Development Kit (SDK). And Chapter 7 takes a look at how Java is being used on the Web and talk to some Web developers building and deploying leading-edge Java applets.

Java-Capable Browsers

To start working with Java, you'll need to get your hands on a Java-capable browser. The obvious place to start is with Sun's own Hot Java browser. But beware. As of the beginning of this year, Hot Java was still capable of running only applets written to the alpha version of the Java Application Programming Interface (API). The other browsers available at the time—including Netscape Navigator 2.0 and the Oracle PowerBrowser—were built to run beta API Java applets. As the Java programming language moves out of beta and into 1.0 early in 1996, vendors will have to upgrade their browsers to work with the latest version of the Java API.

At the beginning of 1996, the following browsers supported or were expected to support Java:

- **Sun's Hot Java** Alpha API applets only. Available at **http://java.sun.com**. Sun also provides an "appletviewer" with the Java Software Development Kit (SDK). The version demonstrated in Chapters 5, 6, and 7 runs beta API applets. The applet viewer is a good way to run Java applets locally without having to serve them from an HTTP server.

- **Netscape Navigator 2.0** Beta API applets. Available at **http://www.netscape.com**.

- **Oracle PowerBrowser 1.0** Beta API applets, as shown in Figure 5-1. Available at **http://www.oracle.com**.

- **Spyglass Mosaic** Spyglass, which OEMs its Web technology to leading browser vendors including Spry, Quarterdeck, and many more, has licensed Java. It will incorporate the technology sometime in early 1996. For updates, see **http://www.spyglass.com**.

- **Microsoft** The software giant shocked the Net community late last year by licensing Java and promising to integrate it into versions of its Internet Explorer browser. Check **http://www.microsoft.com** for details.

The bells and whistles of these browsers will vary. But at the core they will include the interpreter and virtual machine engine needed to execute Java applets on a local computer. They will all support a base level of classes, ensuring that Java applets will operate on any platform. The interesting thing to watch will be the extent to which some or all of these vendors add support for additional Java classes.

And even though Java is inherently multiplatform, it is also unlikely that Java browsers will appear at the same time on all platforms. As will likely be the case in all areas as the Web moves forward, all of these vendors have shown an early favoritism toward Windows (95 and NT) platforms. Market share rules, not just for Microsoft but Netscape as well, which concentrated its early work with Java on the Windows environment. But as 1996 dawns, additional platforms, most notably Macintosh and possibly even Windows 3.1, are expected to be served by Java-capable browsers.

The Netscape beta browser did not allow the calling of a Java applet from a local file. The applets had to be served from a Web server. So for purposes of our demonstrations here, we show the Java applets running in the Java appletviewer.

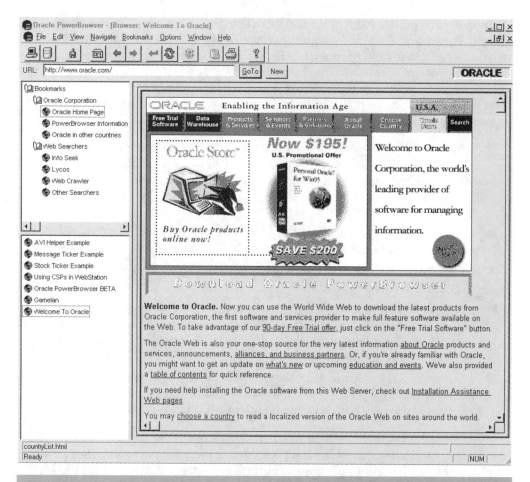

Figure 5-1. *The Oracle PowerBrowser.*

Working with Java Applets

As we noted earlier, you don't necessarily have to know how to code in Java to use Java applets. Many applets are already available on the Web, and they can be reused and modified on your Web site. Most often, the original applet designer will let you freely use the applets; at a minimum, an e-mail seeking permission and maybe a nod of thanks on your page will keep most applet authors happy. In addition, Java applets shops soon will be opening upon the Web, offering a wide variety of customizable applets for download—for a fee.

To deal with these acquired applets, you'll need to know a little bit about the files that make up a Java applet and some basic HTML tagging tricks.

Java Applet Basics

What is a Java applet? An applet is a small program written in the Java programming language. The HTML tags to invoke an applet are written directly into an HTML page. The code for the applet itself resides in a separate file on your Web server. Web browsers deal with Java applets just as they do any other media type, such as graphics, audio, or video files. When a user reaches a page that includes a Java applet, the browser reaches out over the Net for the appropriate applet—consisting of the applet's machine-neutral bytecodes and any supporting files, such as graphics or audio files—and downloads them to the local machine. The applet is downloaded into the local browser, verified as legitimate, and executed. A Java applet (for instance, an animation) can appear anywhere on the page as an inline feature, or it can literally take up the entire page, as in the case of a Java-powered game.

As you learned in Chapter 4, a Java applet can also be an interactive element on a Web page. A Java applet will take a variety of user input, including data entered via the keyboard, a mouse, or by pushing onscreen buttons or scroll bars. All of the interaction is done locally—the browser does not need to call back to the server for more data.

Another important point: using a Java applet on an HTML page will not exclude users of non-Java-enabled browsers from visiting your page. Their browsers won't crash, and if you are careful, they may not even realize the difference. Savvy HTML authors will put a backup text file or GIF image that can display in place of the applet for users running browsers without Java support.

Dissecting a Java Applet

Java applets are made up of several different files. It is important to understand these files before we discuss how to add an applet to your HTML page:

- *Java class files (.class)*   These files contain the compiled bytecode for the Java applet. The bytecode is created when a Java program is run through the Java compiler. You will need the class files if you want to run an applet on your Web page.

- *Java source code (.java)*   These files are the applet's source code, before it is run through the compiler. You don't need these files to run an applet, but you will need them if you want to modify the applet's code.

- *Data files (.gif, .jpeg, .au, etc.)*   These files are used by the Java applet as it is loading. For instance, an animation applet will also include along with it a series of images that the applet will flip through.

In the best case scenario, you will only have to deal with Java class files when adding an applet to your HTML page. If you have the class files, all you will need to do is write an HTML page that invokes the Java class and feeds it the appropriate parameters. That is all it will take to add an applet to your Web page.

In some cases, you won't have the class files, but you will have access to the Java source code (.java files) for a particular applet. This is often the case when you try to download an applet from the Web—applet authors usually provide source code on their pages but not always the class files. If you have the source code but not the class files themselves, you can run the source code through the Java compiler to create a class file, and then use that to add the applet to your Web page. We will discuss how to download and use the Java compiler in more detail in Chapter 6. In this chapter, we will concentrate on working with class files.

As the market for Java applets matures, as a Webmaster you will in most cases be dealing with prebuilt applets and already have the class files on hand. So implementing an applet on your Web page will simply be a matter of writing an HTML page that calls the applet and feeds it the appropriate parameters.

The Intersection of Java and HTML

Applets are added to Web pages using the <APPLET> tag. Not all browsers will understand this tag. However, most browser vendors are moving to include Java support, so that will change shortly. When a browser encounters this tag, it downloads a Java applet and executes it. The tag includes the following information about the applet:

- Location
- Name
- Width and height of the display place
- A variety of parameters, or values, that need to be passed onto the applet
- Alternate data to display for browsers that cannot run Java applets

Here's the syntax for a simple Java call in HTML:

```
<APPLET CODE="SampleApplet.class" width=100 height=150></APPLET>
```

This code tells the browser to load an applet whose compiled code is SampleApplet.class—which should be stored in the same directory as the HTML document—and to set the initial size of the applet to 100 pixels by 150 pixels.

 **Note** ▶ *The HTML tag in the alpha release of Java was <APP>, replaced in the beta release and continued in Release 1.0 with <APPLET>.*

More HTML Tricks: Passing Parameters

You can do much more in HTML to customize an applet than just set its height and width. Applets have parameters that you can specify in the HTML file that is used to deliver the applet. In this way, you can do some very powerful customization of Java applets without ever having to write a line of Java code. All you need to do is some

ADVANTAGES

- Java takes the Web to a whole new level of programmability. Suddenly, whole new classes of applications—including animations, games, and a variety of new forms of interactivity—are possible with Java. And Java provides methods for Webmasters to manipulate Java applets without any coding.

- Java has quickly been adopted by a wide array of industry vendors as the de facto standard for Web programming. Sun is aggressively licensing the language and working to keep it open.

- Java is built from the ground up to be secure—a key element for the Internet. While Webmasters worry that Java applets could send local computers crashing down, Sun has built in a number of security measures to ensure that downloaded Java code is safe and secure.

DISADVANTAGES

- Java is several orders of magnitude more complex than HTML. The danger is the Web will split into technology haves and have-nots. Everyone can learn HTML and build a Web page; Java is clearly not for everyone.

- Java could be superseded by other Web languages. In particular, Microsoft is making a major push on the Web with its Visual Basic language, which already has a massive developer base.

- At least initially, Java runs only on the latest, most expensive computers. It is a great challenge to port the Java run-time engine to operating systems such as Windows 3.1 and Apple Macintosh. So while HTML works on every platform, Java shows a prejudice for high-end computers, including Windows 95 and NT and Unix systems.

basic HTML tagging. Here's the basic syntax for the applet tag, shown in appropriate order of appearance on an HTML page. Tags in brackets [ ] are optional.

```
<APPLET
    [Codebase="codebaseURL"]
    Code=appletFile
    [Alt=alternateText]
    [Name=appletInstanceName]
    Width=pixels Height=pixels
    [Align=alignment]
    [Vspace=pixels] [Hspace=pixels]
>
[<Param Name=appletAttribute Value=value>]
    [alternateHTML]
</APPLET>
```

So what does each of these tags mean, and how do they work? Here's the rundown:

■ Codebase=*codebaseURL*   An optional attribute that specifies the base URL of the applet. Used when the applet is not in the same file as the HTML document that is calling the applet. You can write an HTML page that calls a Java applet from a server anywhere in the world; all you need to know is the applet's URL. If this attribute is not specified, then the base document's URL is used.

■ Code=*appletFile*   This is a required attribute. It gives the name of the file that contains the applet's compiled Applet subclass.

■ Alt=*alternateText*   This optional attribute is one of two ways to specify what should appear in case a browser can't display a Java applet. This tag supports text only. In addition, you can include other sorts of HTML, including graphics, right before the closing </Applet> tag. Java-enabled browsers will ignore this HTML and play the applet instead.

■ Name=*appletInstanceName*   This optional attribute tag specifies a name for the applet instance, which lets applets on the same page find each other and pass information back and forth if needed.

■ Width=*pixels* and Height=*pixels*   Required attributes that give the initial width and height of the applet display area.

■ Align=*alignment*   This is an optional attribute that specifies the alignment of the applet on the page. The values are the same as for the IMG tag: left, right, top, texttop, middle, absmiddle, baseline, bottom, absbottom.

■ Vspace=*pixels* and Hspace=*pixels*   Optional attributes that specify the number of pixels above and below and on each side of the applet. Ensures that text or other elements wrapping around a Java applet are spaced properly.

■ Param Name=*appletAttribute* Value=*value*   This optional but very important tag lets the HTML author input key information directly into a running applet.

Some Examples

So now, let's play around a little with our newly learned parameters and see how we can use them to customize Java applets. In each of the examples, we'll use a graphical-oriented applet so we can see the results of our efforts. We'll take a look at three different scenarios:

- Accessing a Java applet that is stored on a server other than your own. A Java applet doesn't even need to be stored on your own server to run on your HTML page.

- Using a public domain applet that you can download for free and customize for your Web page. We'll look at two applets provided by the Sun Java team: an applet for creating animations and a second for creating a scrolling billboard.

- Acquiring one of the very first supported—for a price—applets on the Web, a streaming animation player from DimensionX. This example will help demonstrate the fact that as Java matures, it will become even easier for Webmasters to acquire applets that include all the documentation you need to get them running. DimensionX offers a free version of its streaming animation applet and a $195 supported version that gives the user access to improvements in the player's compression engine as they are developed—an interesting example of how applet distribution will be handled in the not-too-distant future.

Nervous Text Across the Net

First, we'll examine how you can include a Java applet on your page without even having a trace of the applet on your local server. Open a text editor or HTML authoring program and type in the following. Save it under the name nervous.html:

```
<HTML>
<HEAD>
<TITLE>Remote applet</TITLE>
</HEAD>
<BODY>
<APPLET  CODEBASE="http://java.sun.com/JDK-prebeta1/applets/NervousText"
    Code="NervousText.class" Width=400 Height=100 Align=center >
<Param Name="text" Value="Beyond HTML by Richard Karpinski">
</APPLET>
</BODY>
</HTML>
```

What this short HTML page will do is run an applet residing not on the server delivering the HTML page but on a server located elsewhere, in this case, a server at

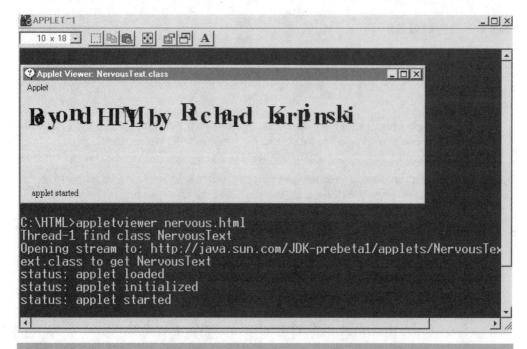

Figure 5-2. *The nervous text applet runs with our specified input*

java.sun.com. By changing the parameter settings, we can include any string of text we'd like. The output of our work is displayed in the Java applet viewer (see Figure 5-2).

Note ▶ *If you want to test these examples yourself using the applet viewer, see Chapter 6 for instructions on how to download and use the appletviewer, which is downloaded as part of the Java Developer's Kit.*

We didn't write a line of code, or for that matter, even lay our hands at all on the Java applet we used. We simply referred to its location on a remote server and fed in our own parameters. The result: a customized Java applet running on our own Web page.

A Look at Two Java Team Applets

Downloading Java applets from all over the Web on the fly is probably not the most efficient way to Java-ize your HTML pages. What you'll want to do is have the Java applets residing on the same server that serves up your HTML pages.

THE ANIMATOR APPLET For demonstration's sake, let's take apart and examine another Sun-created demo applet, the animator. The class files for the animator applet are included with the Java SDK. If you haven't downloaded the SDK, you can also find the source files for the animator at **http://java.sun.com/applets**. The Sun Java site includes a bunch of Java applets and in many cases includes detailed descriptions of how to add them to your Web pages.

The animator applet is made up of a number of files, each of which is necessary for the animation engine to function (see Figure 5-3):

- A folder containing image files (GIF)

- A folder containing audio files (AU)

- Animator.java (the source code), Animator.class (the main class for the animator), and several other supporting class files

- Several HTML pages used to call the animator applet (i.e., example3.html)

All of these different parts are needed to make up the complete applet of a waving Duke animation with background sound, which we'll discuss below.

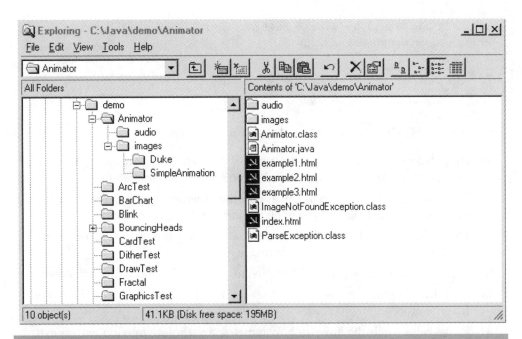

Figure 5-3. *Contents of the demo directory in Windows 95 Explorer*

We won't bother with the Java code itself, which is rather lengthy; you can examine it in depth on your own if you'd like. Simply open the file Animator.java in a text editor to see the Java code. What is of interest to us are the HTML files, because it is here that we can see how the parameters get fed into the Java applet. We will also examine the two folders—one for images and one for audio clips—to see how you can easily feed any sort of pictures or sounds into the generic Animator applet.

First, the HTML code for example3.html:

```
<HTML>
<HEAD>
<TITLE>The Animator Applet</TITLE>
</HEAD>
<BODY>
<HR>
<applet code=Animator.class width=200 height=200>
<param name=imagesource value="images/Duke">
<param name=endimage value=10>
<param name=soundsource value="audio">
<param name=soundtrack value=spacemusic.au>
<param name=sounds
value="1.au|2.au|3.au|4.au|5.au|6.au|7.au|8.au|9.au|0.au">
<param name=pause value=200>
</APPLET>
</BODY>
</HTML>
```

What is this HTML code doing? We'll take it step by step:

■ Appletcode= tells the browser or appletviewer where to find the applet and the size of the display window. Next come a series of parameters.

■ Imagesource value="images/Duke" tells the browser to look in the named directory for the images that will be fed into the animation engine.

■ Endimage value = 10 tells the browser that there are ten images in total that will be used. The default start is at image number 1.

■ Soundsource value = points to the directory where the audio files are stored.

■ Soundtrack value= and Sounds value= defines the sound files as AU files and tells the browser in what order to play the files.

■ Pause value= tells the browser how long to pause before moving to the next image file; in other words, it controls the speed of the animation.

If you've ever watched a cartoonist at work, you know that there's no trick to animation, just a lot of drawing and a little bit of simulated movement. It's the same with the Duke applet. It consists of ten separate images (see Figure 5-4), which when run in succession through the Animation applet and displayed in the browser show the little guy waving from the screen (see Figure 5-5).

The Animation applet is a breeze to customize. All you need is your own sound and graphics files, which you can store in a local directory and reference as parameters from your HTML page. And presto, you have a Java animation without having to write a single line of Java code.

SCROLLING IMAGES APPLET Another interesting applet that can be found on Sun's applet page is the scrolling images applet. Think of it as a scrolling billboard, with a series of images moving across the screen at a set pace. The example that Sun provides shows photos of the Java team and one interloper (see if you can spot him in Figure 5-6).

Let's customize this applet. Instead of photos of the Java team, let's build a scrolling billboard for a potential Web site supporting this book, using some of the logos of the companies and technologies we'll talk about in the book.

Figure 5-4. *The Duke animation is a series of ten illustrations, each with a slightly different position*

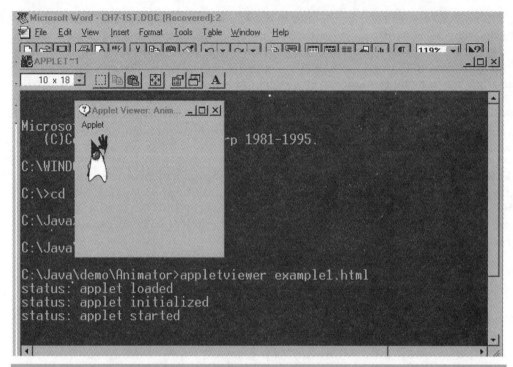

Figure 5-5. *Here's the final Duke animation running in the appletviewer (a simple string of sounds plays in the background)*

First, we'll place the source code file (ImageTape.java) and the two class files (ImageTape.class and ImageTapeLoader.class) for the scrolling images applet into a separate directory. Let's also build a subdirectory called "images" to hold the .gif files

Figure 5-6. *Sun's scrolling images applet*

that will make up our billboard. We'll rename the five files T1.gif through T5.gif.
Finally, we'll write the HTML page to invoke our applet:

```
<HTML>
<HEAD>
<TITLE>Image Tape</TITLE>
<HEAD>
<BODY>
<HR>
<applet code="ImageTape.class" width=550 height=100>
<param name=speed value="5">
<param name=img value="images ">
<param name=nimgs value="5">
</APPLET>
</BODY>
</HTML>
```

The parameters for this applet are somewhat similar to the animator applet: width
and height set the size of the applet; speed sets the rate at which the images scroll
across the screen; img tells the applet where to find the images to scroll; and nimgs
tells the applet how many images to include. The results of our scrolling images applet
can be seen in Figure 5-7).

The Future: Java Applets for Sale
The early days of Java are like the old Wild West—there aren't many rules and you're
never sure what you are going to find over the next plain. While the numbers of applets
available on the Web are growing every day, the quality is mixed, and you are never

Figure 5-7. *The customized scrolling images applet*

sure if you are going to find class files to download or just source code. And even if you download source code, you can't be sure it will compile and run correctly. Nobody makes any promises with beta code.

But a more mature market for Java applets will begin to emerge later this year. In this new marketplace, you'll be able to acquire Java applets from vendors you know and trust—not leading-edge Java hacks developing code on the weekend. You'll be able to download classes—not source code—all ready to go. You'll get detailed instructions on how to feed parameters to the applet. And depending on the vendor, you'll probably pay a fee, ranging anywhere from pennies for one-time use of an applet to hundreds of dollars for a very sophisticated applet.

We found one of the earliest examples of a for-pay Java applet from DimensionX, a San Francisco-based Web design house that has done some of the best early work with Java and is now turning its attention to building—and selling—Java applets and tools. DimensionX has built a streaming animation player applet that solves two of the biggest problems with early animation players (such as the one we examined earlier in this chapter): the built-in animation capabilities of Java are actually pretty poor, and waiting for a series of .gif images to download before an animation runs can be a very slow process. DimensionX offers an intriguing alternative with its streaming animation player, written by Kurt Jacob. The applet has a built-in compression and playback engine that runs FLC files—a standard animation format. FLC encoders are available from AutoDesk and other vendors (including DimensionX).

The streaming animation applet—and other Java projects built by the DimensionX team—can be found at **http://www.dimensionx.com/dnx/java.html**. When you get to the site, you have the option of downloading and using the beta version of the streaming animation player for free (which we'll do for our example). But the page also offers an option to buy a licensed version of the applet for $195 that includes the current version of the decoder, e-mail support, and a DimensionX-supported FLC encoder to create the animations.

Before we can download the player, we have to agree to a lengthy licensing agreement (a standard procedure for most software, coming shortly to downloadable Java applets). Then we download the files we need in .zip format. Unzipping the file, we see all of the files we need to run the applet, including a Readme.txt file that provides instructions on how to run the applet (see Figure 5-8). This is a nice bonus. Often, with early Java applets, you'll need to figure out on your own how to run the applet.

Per the instructions provided, we'll build an HTML page that calls the applet and loads the FLC file—which, for this example, we obtained from the sample page of another encoder vendor, AniCom. Here's what the HTML to run the applet looks like:

```
<HTML>
<HEAD>
<TITLE>Streaming animation player</TITLE>
</HEAD>
```

```
<BODY>
<APPLET CODE="dnx.StrAnimItem.class" CODEBASE="./" WIDTH=320 HEIGHT=220>
<PARAM NAME="stranim" VALUE="josh.flc">
<PARAM NAME="dither" VALUE="better">
</APPLET>
</BODY>
</HTML>
```

The output—an animated stork making his delivery—can be seen in Figure 5-9. The streaming animation player offers a quicker playback and smoother playback than typical Java animation applets. In addition to being a good example of a customizable applet, the player also shows how Java can be used to replace helper applications and plug-ins on the Web. In the past, in order to view a special media type such as an FLC file, a user would have had to download and install a helper app or plug-in. With Java, the entire process is seamless: the applet downloads both the player and the file to be viewed. You don't have to worry if visitors to your site are

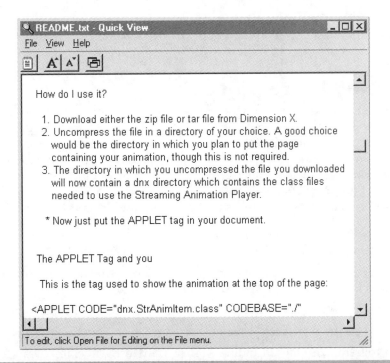

Figure 5-8. *DimensionX provides detailed instructions along with the applet*

Figure 5-9. *DimensionX's streaming animation player*

equipped with the latest, esoteric plug-in. All you need to know is that they have a Java-equipped browser.

Where to Find Java Applets

As we have seen, you don't need to write Java applets to add them to your pages, but you will need to find them. So a key skill for Webmasters will be tracking down the best Java applets. Where are the best hot spots on the Web for Java applets?

A good place to start is at the Java home page. A supply of Java applets have been produced by the Sun Java team (see Figure 5-10). Many of the applets can be found as part of the Java SDK, or alternatively, on the Sun Java Web page, at **http://java.sun.com/applets**. Sun breaks the applets up into several categories, including:

- ■ Games and Other Diversions, including Hangman and Tic-Tac-Toe
- ■ Applets to Spice up a Page, including Image Loop, Animator, Blinking Text, Sound Player, Live Image Feedback Map, and more
- ■ Educational Applets, including 3-D Chemical Models and Fractal Figures
- ■ Utilities, including a clock, a spreadsheet, and several graphing applets
- ■ For Programmers Only, including ArcTest, CardTest, DitherTest, DrawTest, GraphicsTest, and more

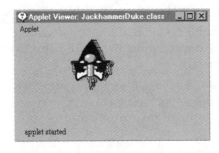

Figure 5-10.   *Several simple applets from the Sun Java page, including Clock, UnderConstruction, and Tic-Tac-Toe*

Another great place to find applets is the Gamelan page, **http://www.gamelan.com**, which has emerged as the first official directory and registry of Java applets (see Figure 5-11). Backed by Sun and built by EarthWeb, a high-end design house, the page is a good all-purpose resource to all sorts of Java information. But it is most exhaustive in the area of applets, where it has hundreds of listings for Java applets all over the Web. EarthWeb hopes to turn its registry into an applet marketplace later this year, with users able to download applets and pay for them with a Net-based transaction or electronic cash system.

Another site worth mentioning is the Java Applet Rating Service (JARS), which has created a panel of judges that separates the innovative Java applications from the me-too animations. Sponsored by Web Creations, a Blue Spring, Missouri-based Web development house, JARS consists of a panel of judges that rank applets based on how useful, well-written, and unique they are. Check out JARS at **http://www.surinam.net/ java/jars** (see Figure 5-12).

Many developers of early Java applets will let you freely reuse their source code with no restrictions at all. Sun's Java team, for instance, has put out a wide variety of free applets to help seed the Web with Java. However, as Java progresses, many developers will want to be paid for their efforts or will not want to have their work taken and modified. Check the source code for an applet or contact the applet author if you're not sure whether you can reuse the code. The Sun applets we've used in this chapter, for instance, include wording in the applet that declares "Permission to use, copy, modify, and distribute this software and its documentation for NON-COMMERCIAL or COMMERCIAL purposes and without fee is hereby granted."

Also likely to emerge are Web-based "storefronts" selling Java applets that can be downloaded for a small fee. As this book was being written, no specific Java store had yet emerged, but it is almost certain such places will emerge in early 1996. Indeed, object code is already being bought and sold on the Web. For instance, check out:

- OLEBroker, at **http://www.olebroker.com**, which offers OLE components for sale

- Cybersource's Resusable Software Component Market, at **http://www.software.net/components**, which delivers a variety of object components over the Net

- IBM's evolving infoMarket Search service, at **http://www.infomkt.ibm.com**, which will let publishers—including Java applet creators—distribute and sell their content with full copyright protection

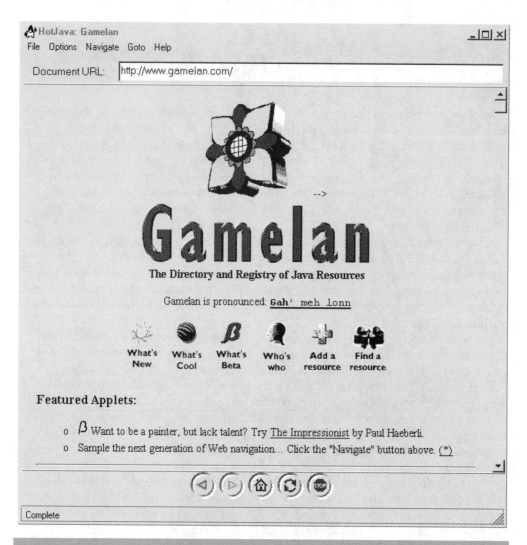

Figure 5-11. *The Gamelan home page, a one-stop directory and registry for Java applets.*

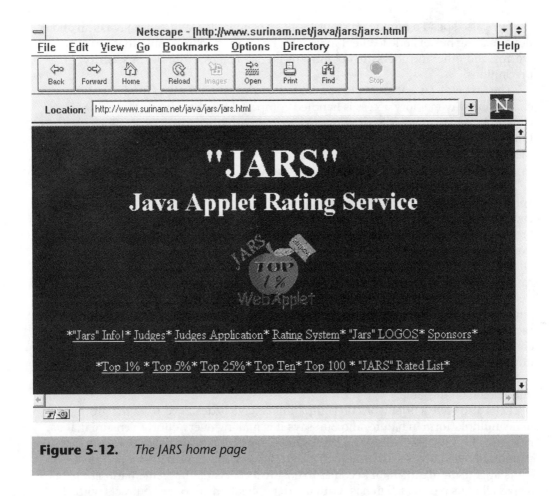

Figure 5-12. *The JARS home page*

It doesn't take much of a stretch to imagine these sites and others selling Java applets as well.

Final Considerations: Speed, Security, and Compatibility

Java applets are a great addition to any Web site. But there are a few additional issues Webmasters should keep in mind when dealing with this new technology.

For starters, while Java applets are optimized for delivery over the Web, they can become fairly large in size, especially if they are delivering not only code but also graphics and audio files. So, keep in mind the same download rules of thumb for Java applets that you do today for graphics files. Anything more than 100K and you need to realize the folks visiting your newly Java-powered Web site will be doing more waiting than interacting.

Let's also spend a minute on security, a key element for Java. Since Java is all about downloading bits of code to client machines, it is important to ensure that viruses, worms, and other intruders are not introduced. Java takes a number of security precautions.

The first way Java attempts to eliminate security problems is to fundamentally change the way memory access is handled compared to other languages such as C or C++. In those languages, programmers can access arbitrary memory locations on a local computer using pointers. Java eliminates the use of pointers and thus eliminates the chance that a faulty Java applet will try to overwrite memory areas and perhaps cause major damage—for instance, erase your hard drive.

In addition to eliminating pointers, the Java interpreter includes a bytecode verifier that makes sure there are no major problems with the incoming Java code that could harm the local computer. In particular, the verifier ensures the code doesn't break the basic rules of the Java language. Once the Java applet code is verified, it is executed in a restricted—also known as a trusted—environment. A Java applet is not allowed to read or write any local files. It also is limited to accessing additional data from only the host computer and URL from which the applet originated.

All of these restrictions place some limitations on what a Java applet can do. But Sun believes it is important to ensure above anything else that an applet is not a security threat. In future versions of Java, Sun plans to implement public key encryption technology that will provide a more seamless way to verify that downloaded code is safe. But until that security add-on arrives (probably late 1996 at the earliest), the issue of security and the limits it places on the capabilities of applets will remain on the table.

Let's also have a brief word on compatibility. Java is designed from the ground up to be multiplatform in nature, and Sun says it is making every effort to ensure that as it licenses Java to other vendors, a stable and consistent API and class library is supported by all licensees. For Sun, this area is a classic catch-22: the more licensees its signs up, the more difficult it becomes to ensure a consistent implementation of Java across all of its partners. Sun has written strict obligations into the contracts with all of its licensees that they cannot change the source code. Sun also plans to have a Java compatibility test available in early 1996. Those vendors that pass the test will get to use a "Java Compatible" logo that ensures its tools pass the muster.

Finally, while we're on the subject of logos, note that Sun's two popular animated logos, "Duke" and the "steaming coffee cup," are trademarks and are reserved for Sun's use only. You can't use them on your Web pages. Sun instead plans to develop a free Java-Powered logo—which had not yet appeared as this book was being written—for Webmasters to use on their pages.

Will Java Get Simpler to Use?

What does the future hold for Java? In many ways, it will become even more powerful, gaining new features, capabilities, and run-time speed. Even more important is that we can also expect to see the emergence of authoring tools that

INSIDE *Spin*

What Sun Says About Java

Sun Microsystems has a lot riding on Java, and it has thus far successfully driven the still-evolving programming language straight to the top of the Internet.

A major player in computer workstations and hardware—including a leading position in the Web server market—Sun has never been able to crack Microsoft's software empire. But with Java, Sun may at last have the technology to turn the tables. Discussions with top Sun executives and lead members of the Java team demonstrate that Sun does indeed have big plans for Java.

"Our over-arching goal is to make Java ubiquitous. We want Java everywhere," says Kim Polese, the lead product manager for Java. "So far people have been thinking about Java in a really narrow sense. They see some animations transmitted across a Web page and they think that's pretty cool. But if you look under the hood, there's a very powerful programming language in there. That's the message that needs to come out next."

James Gosling, inventor of the language that eventually became Java and currently a Sun Fellow, says the priorities for the Java team going forward are building a consistent security policy among its browser licensees; building new class libraries supporting multimedia, video, and 3-D; speeding up the run-time performance of Java; and developing a much-improved next version of the Hot Java browser.

Another challenge will be to keep Java open and consistent as more and more vendors license it, says Polese. "One of the things that we have agreement with all of the vendors on is that there's a core API that they've all agreed to support. As the API grows and acquires new capabilities, they've all agreed to adopt them."

If Java continues to grow and evolve at its present pace, it will spell big changes not only for the Web but for the entire software industry, claims Geoffrey Baehr, Sun's chief networking officer.

"We are trying to architect a franchise that will enable a whole new model of software development and a new mechanism for software distribution. Java is really a technology designed to lower the barrier of entry to software developers. That, in turn, will be liberating to consumers of applications. The monolithic software application will be replaced by the applet."

output Java code but do not require the user to do the coding themselves. Sun and its partners are promising such tools, but so far the promises outnumber the realities.

In addition, Webmasters should keep tabs on the evolution of Sun and Netscape's JavaScript scripting language, which promises to provide a new way to script Web objects, including Java applets.

Java Authoring Tools (for Nonprogrammers)

What Webmasters and nontechnical Web designers really need are Java authoring tools that require little or no programming experience whatsoever. Sun has promised that such tools will eventually appear, but in the early days of 1996, the promises clearly outnumbered the realities.

One good place to look for very easy-to-use Java tools in the future may be from two of Java's most notable licensees: Macromedia and Adobe. Macromedia has promised to build Java into future versions of Macromedia Director, and it appears likely that it will include a simple way to author Java applets without programming. But details are scarce so far. Adobe also would seem a likely candidate to take advantage of Java while shielding most of its complexities from its users, who are typically graphics artists or publishers, not programmers. But again, Adobe's support of Java is still in its early stages.

One interesting Java authoring tool that we were able to uncover in these early days comes from DimensionX, the company that also built the animation player we examined earlier. The tool—which has gone through a series of name changes but was first known as JAM for Java Animation Machine—should be available on their Web site, **http://www.dimensionx.com**, by the time this book appears (see Figure 5-13).

JAM holds a lot of promise, and is a good demonstration of the type of authoring tools possible with Java. JAM is a drag-and-drop tool that lets you create animated scenes with backgrounds and soundtracks, sprites with different behaviors, drawn paths, and more. When you click Save, JAM outputs a set of class files that make up a new java applet you can immediately incorporate into a page for Java-capable browsers. There's no need to write a single line of Java code unless you want to modify JAM and create your own behaviors.

Scott Fraize, developer of JAM, points out that while it is impossible to hide the complexity of Java code in a general purpose coding environment, if a toolmaker sticks to a specific application—for example, animations—all sorts of drag-and-drop Java tools become possible.

Another intriguing Java-based authoring tool slated to appear is Texture, from FutureTense Inc. Texture is a Java-based authoring environment that gives authors complete control over the layout and appearance of their documents. Texture documents also can contain interactive elements such as pop-up windows, scrolling text and time-based content. Authors work in an authoring environment similar to most desktop publishing applications and with the push of a single button output a fully-coded Java applet. Texture authors do no coding themselves.

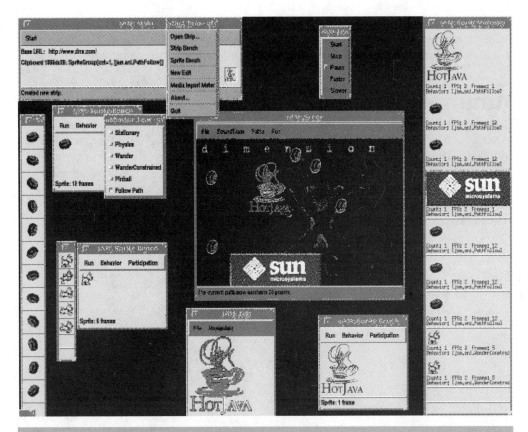

Figure 5-13. *DimensionX's JAM lets nonprogrammers build Java animations*

FutureTense Texture had just been announced as this book was written. For an update, visit **http://www.futuretense.com**.

JavaScript and Java

Passing parameters via HTML tags is an easy way to deal with Java applets, but Sun, Netscape, and a long list of more than 25 partners are also backing JavaScript, a scripting language designed to be simple enough for most Webmasters to use. JavaScript is in its early stages right now and in the version available as this book was being written lacked some key features—including applet scripting. But as envisioned, JavaScript will eventually be used by HTML authors to dynamically script the properties and behavior of objects including Java applets. It can also be used to do some simple client-side processing, such as local forms or calculations, as we'll examine in more depth in Chapter 9.

Though still in its infancy, JavaScript looks like a winner. In addition to broad industry support, Netscape and Sun plan to propose JavaScript to the W3 Consortium and Internet Engineering Task Force as an open Internet scripting language standard.

Summary

This chapter demonstrated everything you need to know to deliver Java applets on your Web site without doing any programming whatsoever. All that is needed is knowledge of some new HTML tags and a basic understanding of what a Java applet is and how it works. You learned how to use a basic HTML page to feed parameters to a Java applet, instantly customizing it for your own home pages. You can add a wide array of animations, special effects, and more to your Web site just by learning these basic HTML skills—you'll never even have to write a line of Java code to bring the power of Java to your Web site.

Chapter Six

A Crash Course in Java Programming

Now that you know how to work with Java applets on your Web pages, you may be curious to try your hand at some Java coding. Be warned, Java is not for the faint of heart. But neither is it an impossible language to learn. If you have some programming experience, that would be a good head start—especially if you have C or C++ experience, since Java is based on the syntax of these familiar programming languages.

But even if you are coming at Java and programming for the very first time, this chapter may well be worth a trip. It will help you understand how Java applets work, what to expect when you add them to your Web pages, and exactly what kinds of applications are possible with Java. Indeed, by the time you're done with this chapter, you'll have a number of feathers in your cap:

- A jump start on learning the key concepts of object-oriented programming, especially as they apply to the Java language

- A solid understanding of Java and how this programming language will bring new power and flexibility to Web pages

- The ability to write and manipulate some simple Java applets and the know-how to dive deeper into this powerful language

Consider this your first morning cup of Java. If you want to delve even deeper into this emerging standard language for Web programming, we'll also point you to a wealth of additional Java resources available on the Web (see the "Tech Resources" box at the end of this chapter).

Your First Swig of Java

Let's start at the beginning: getting your hands on Java. You'll need two things to get started with Java: a browser capable of running Java applets and an environment for creating and compiling Java code. We outlined where to find Java browsers in the last chapter. Here, we'll concentrate on the Java coding environment.

The good news in both cases is that it most likely won't cost you a penny to get started with Java. It should always be possible to find a free Java-capable browser, and Sun has pledged to keep the basic code and tools to create Java applets free to developers as well. As Sun has seen with close ally Netscape, nothing sells on the Web like free technology, and the most important thing for Sun is to make Java as ubiquitous as possible as quickly as possible.

The Java Coding Environment

Toward the end of 1995, Sun released the pre-beta 1.0 version of the Java Developers Kit (JDK). All of our work here will be done with the beta JDK, which was not expected to change significantly as Java moved out of beta and into final 1.0 form. Before getting started writing Java applets, we will quickly run down how to get and what to expect with the JDK.

Note ▶ *Version 1.0 of Java appeared in early 1996; JDK. No major changes were made from the beta to the 1.0 release, so this run-through of the beta JDK should serve as a good illustration of the Java coding environment.*

The Java Developers Kit can be downloaded from Sun's Java home page, **http://java.sun.com**. The 1.0 pre-beta release runs on SPARC Solaris (2.3 or higher) and Windows NT/95 (Intel x86). A version for Apple Macintosh became available with Java's 1.0 release. For our examples here, we will work with the Windows 95 version of the JDK.

The JDK installation page includes detailed instructions on how to download and install the developers kit, but there a few things you should be aware of. The JDK is downloaded as a self-extracting archive file (.zip for Windows and .tar for Solaris). Once you have downloaded the JDK archive file, execute the self-extracting archive to unpack the individual JDK files. Unpack the files in the root directory of your C drive to create C:\Java. Unpacking the archive will also create a number of subdirectories in the Java directory.

Before you can use the JDK, you'll have to take one more step and add the Java\bin directory onto your computer's PATH statement. In Windows, you do this by editing the Autoexec.bat file and making the change to the PATH statement there. Reboot your computer for the change to take effect.

Once you get it installed, you'll see that the Java JDK contains the following elements:

JAVA APPLETVIEWER This is a viewer for testing newly written beta applets on a local machine. The beta versions of Netscape Navigator 2.0 would only load Java applets from an HTTP server and not from a local file. So for testing applets you've just written, use the appletviewer.

To invoke the appletviewer (for instance, to run the Tumbling Duke demo included in the Java SDK), exit out to a DOS prompt and move to the C:\Java\demo\TumblingDuke directory. There you'll find class files for the applet plus an HTML page that calls the applet. To play the animation, launch the appletviewer from the command line like this:

```
appletviewer example1.html
```

And watch Duke tumble across the Applet Viewer window (see Figure 6-1).

The appletviewer also can be used to look at the Java applets on remote Web pages. For instance, by typing in the following at the DOS command line, you will see the Java applet—but not the HTML content—contained on that page (assuming you are connected to the Internet):

```
appletviewer "http://www.javasoft.com"
```

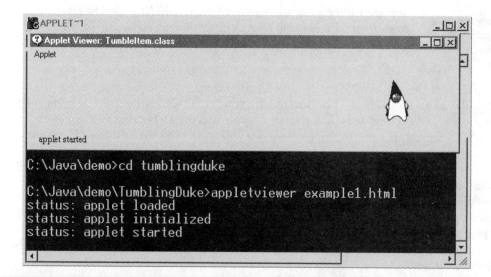

Figure 6-1. *Sun mascot Duke goes tumbling in the JDK appletviewer*

JAVA DEBUGGER API AND PROTOTYPE DEBUGGER   These are very early and somewhat rudimentary tools for debugging Java applets.

JAVA COMPILER   This is the tool for turning raw code into Java classes and applets. The Java compiler doesn't produce a native executable but rather builds bytecode that is executed on the Java "virtual machine," the mechanism for ensuring that Java applets can be written once yet run on a variety of computer platforms.

To run the Java compiler, go to a directory that includes the Java source code (a file that ends in .java, for instance example.java) and type in

```
javac example.java
```

If the Java source code is correct, the compiler will create a new file with a .class extension, for instance, example.class.

If a mistake has been made in the Java code, the compiler will instead spit back a descriptive error message. You will then have to go back into the source code and fix the problem. If you are lucky, the problem will be a typo. If you are unlucky, the program might have more serious problems.

JAVA INTERPRETER   This is the piece of software needed to view Java applets. It can be ported to a variety of hardware platforms. The key is that it is small (about

40K), which makes it portable not only to $3,000 PCs but in the future to inexpensive consumer electronics devices such as Portable Digital Assistants or a scaled-down, diskless "Net station."

JAVA PACKAGES   The final applet API consists of the following class packages: java.lang, java.util, java.io, java.net, java.awt, java.awt.peer, java.awt.image, and java.applet. See Table 6-1 for additional details. The Java class packages are collections of predeveloped code that provide core functionality for a Java program. Java programmers can tap into these capabilities and build upon them. Sun and its partners say they will support the classes in this API moving forward, an important commitment for consistency of Java applets across different vendor platforms. We'll take a closer look at the Java packages later, when we've learned a little more about the language itself.

The 1.0 pre-beta JDK is a significant milestone in Java's overall development. But it is still a rather crude development environment and one that is likely to be quickly superseded by more sophisticated and easy-to-use development and authoring tools, which we will explore later in this chapter. But the pre-beta JDK does give us a good platform to begin exploring the ins and outs of Java.

Library	Description
java.lang	The language foundation provides the basic classes for strings and arrays, the fundamental structure of the Java language.
java.util	Provides utilities including encoding/decoding, hash tables, vectors, and stacks.
java.io	The java.io package contains classes for handling the input and output of data.
java.net	Provides tools for accessing network protocols such as telnet, FTP, and HTTP.
java.awt, java.awt.peer, java.awt.image	AWT stands for Abstract Window Toolkit and provides graphical interface tools such as fonts, controls, buttons, and scrollbars.
java.applet	Defines the core capabilities and features of Java applets, which developers can then build upon.

Table 6-1.   *Java Class Libraries*

Writing a Simple Applet

To get our feet wet with Java, let's spend a few minutes building a very simple applet. This process will familiarize you with the basics of creating and compiling a Java applet and serving it up from an HTML page. The example is the programming standard "HelloWorld" program. We'll run through the process of creating this applet step by step—it serves as a good introduction to not only the Java programming language but the JDK as well.

One final note: Java can be used to create both applets and applications. An applet is intended to be compiled and interpreted by a Web browser. A Java application is a stand-alone program written in Java. Sun's Hot Java browser, for instance, is an application written in Java. Given our focus on the Web, we will concentrate our efforts on Java applets, which are small programs that can be downloaded across the Internet and run inside a browser to enliven Web pages.

HelloWorld: A Sample Applet

To begin, let's create a directory to store the HTML file and Java applet you are about to create. For this example, call the directory C:\HTML.

Next, we'll write some simple Java code. To write Java code, you'll need a text editor of some sort—for instance, Windows' NotePad works just fine. Type in the following sample Java source code (don't worry for now what it all means):

```
import java.awt.Graphics;
public class HelloWorld extends java.applet.Applet {
  public void init() {
    resize(150,25);
  }
  public void paint(Graphics g) {
    g.drawString("Hello world!", 50, 25);
  }
}
```

Once the code is written in exactly as shown here, save the file by the name HelloWorld.java into the HTML directory you created. With that, you have created a Java source code file.

Next, you must compile the file. If you are working in Windows, as we are in this example, you'll need to exit out to a DOS prompt—the JDK runs only from the command line. Run the Java code through the compiler using the command "javac" we demonstrated earlier:

```
javac HelloWorld.java
```

If everything works—and it should—the compiler will create a new file in the same directory called HelloWorld.class containing the bytecodes for the HelloWorld applet.

Java is case-sensitive. So watch where you capitalize letters. For instance, if a class is called HelloWorld.class, the applet viewer won't run helloworldclass.

Finally, you'll need to create an HTML file to deliver the Java applet. Still using your text editor, create a new file called Hello.html and enter the following HTML code:

```
<HTML>
<HEAD>
<TITLE> A Simple Program </TITLE>
</HEAD>
<BODY>
<APPLET CODE="HelloWorld.class" WIDTH=150 HEIGHT=25>
</APPLET>
</BODY>
</HTML>
```

Notice the HTML tag <APPLET>. As we saw in Chapter 5, it is with this simple tag that the Web browser knows to invoke and execute the Java applet.

You now have three files in the HTML directory: HelloWorld.java, HelloWorld.class, and Hello.html. From the DOS prompt again, invoke the Java appletviewer to run the applet (as shown in Figure 6-2):

```
appletviewer Hello.html
```

How the HelloWorld Applet Works

Before diving more deeply into Java, let's take a quick look at the components of the HelloWorld applet. You won't understand all of this quite yet, but by the end of the chapter it will all make better sense.

- import java.awt.Graphics: This step identifies the preestablished class this applet will draw on and includes the class with the source code you have written. The class java.awt.Graphics is one of the package of classes that ships as part of the Java API.

- public class HelloWorld extends java.applet.Applet: This step declares HelloWorld as class, more specifically as a subclass of the java.applet.Applet class. This is a shorthand method for giving HelloWorld access to the built-in features of all Java applets, a concept known as *inheritance* (more on inheritance later).

- public void init() { resize(150,25): This tells the browser—or in this case the appletviewer—to size the window to 150 by 25.

- public void paint(Graphics g) {g.drawString("Hello world!", 50, 25): This "paints" the string "Hello world!" at the given coordinates.

Diving Deeper into Java

You've now seen the (very) basics of Java, enough to give you some idea of how the Java SDK works, how the Java programming language is structured, and how Java applets can be used on the Web. But already we've run into some concepts—such as classes, methods, and inheritances—that may not be familiar to you. So before we try our hand at any more Java programming, let's delve a little deeper into the Java programming language, beginning with a brief primer on object-oriented programming concepts.

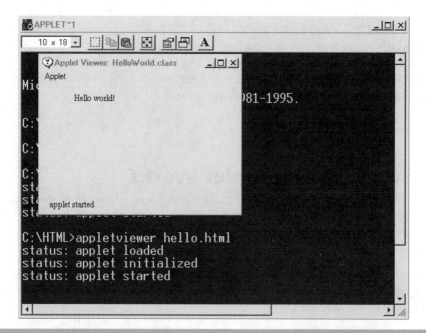

Figure 6-2. *The appletviewer displays the executed "HelloWorld" applet*

What is OOP?

To understand object-oriented programming (OOP), we'll start with an even more basic question: what is an object? Like objects in the real world, software objects have two common characteristics: a state and a behavior. In the real world, for example, bicycles can have a state (current gear, current pedal, number of gears) and a behavior (changing gears, accelerating, slowing down).

Software objects are ruled by similar concepts. A class is a software object defined by a state, called an *instance variable,* and a behavior, called a *method.* Still using the bicycle metaphor, objects can be visually represented as in the following:

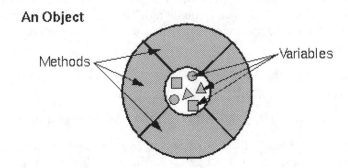

Everything that an object knows (its state) and can do (its behavior) can be represented by the variables and methods within that object. So, a software object that modeled a real-world bicycle would have variables that indicated the bicycle's current state (moving at 10 mph, its pedal cadence is 90 rpm, and it's in fifth gear) and its behavior (brake, change gears, change pedal cadence), as shown here:

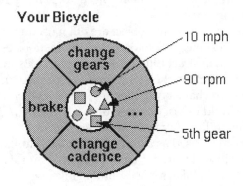

The illustrations, which we've borrowed from Sun's white paper on Java, demonstrate another important concept of objects, called *encapsulation*. In the above illustration, the methods literally "surround" or encapsulate the variables, shielding them from interaction with other objects. This keeps an object's core details (its variables)—for instance, how a bike's gears work—hidden behind the scenes, while exposing the ways to manipulate those variables (its methods)—for instance, pushing this lever changes gears—to other objects. Thus the core details of an object can change (in this example, a bike's precise gear assembly) without changing an object's methods or how those methods interact with other objects in a program.

Indeed, a single object in isolation is not a very useful thing. Only when individual objects interact or pass information back and forth do things get interesting. Extending the bicycle analogy yet again, the object of a bicycle is only really useful when another object (a person) starts interacting with it (pedaling). Thus in the object software world, objects are able to send messages to one another. *Messages* can comprise three bits of information:

- The object to which the message is addressed (the bicycle)
- The name of the method to perform (change gears)
- More specific parameters to guide the method (make the gear lower)

The power of messaging in a distributed, secure environment like Java is that any object can send a message to any other object, regardless of whether it is part of the same program located on the same computer or if it is located on another system located across the world.

Another important concept in object-oriented programming—particularly in the Java language—is classes. A class is a template that defines the variables and the methods common to all objects of a certain kind. For instance, all bicycles have a certain number of things in common: they have two wheels, a seat, handlebars, etc. A particular bike, in object terms, is simply a particular *instance* of the class of objects known as bicycles. By defining the core characteristics of a specific class, it is much easier to build a unique instance of an object. You simply flow the unique information into the template for that class.

Although the terms class and object are often used interchangeably, when dealing with Java that is a mistake. Java makes clear distinctions between class and object. Think of a class as an abstract blueprint for an object; its methods and variables have no real values. An object, on the other hand, is a particular instance of a class; its variables and methods have been filled in. Just as a bike manufacturer uses the same basic blueprint to build lots of bikes, so does a software programmer use the same class over again to build many individual objects.

While a class can be used as a blueprint to make similar objects, a class can also be extended with additional features, creating a *subclass* of the original class. In the bike world, a specific type of bike, say a mountain bike, would be a subclass of the bike class. In the object world, subclasses inherit the core variables and methods of the main class, also called the *superclass*. The subclasses can add additional variables and methods or even override certain aspects of the original class and implement new methods altogether. It is possible to create many generations of subclasses, each having an additional or different subset of methods and variables than the original class, yet still retaining some set of consistent features. Inheritance gives a glimpse at the real power of object-oriented programming. By building on well-defined original classes, software can be reused again and again, built up and stripped down. Yet a commonality remains: the original class structure.

Java maintains strict adherence to all of these object-oriented concepts. With the exception of only its most primitive data types, everything in Java is an object, and even the primitive types can be encapsulated within objects if the need arises. Java's strict object-oriented paradigm meshes well with the needs of client-server, distributed software environments, of which the Internet is the best example.

The Nuts and Bolts of Java

With a working knowledge of the JDK and the basic concepts of object-oriented software in hand, let's turn now to the Java programming language itself: what it is, how it works, and how to use it. We'll satisfy ourselves with an overview of the basics, which should be enough to give you a taste the fundamentals of Java programming. Even as we take this mini-tour, the complexity—and power—of Java should become clear to readers unfamiliar with hard-core object-oriented programming languages. Yet even if you are not a programmer and do not have plans to become one, an understanding of the makeup of Java can be a big help if you want to be able to work with and, especially, customize Java applets.

To program in Java or any object-oriented programming language, you need to have a firm grip on two basic areas:

- *The basic structure or syntax of the language:* This includes such things as the fundamental types and flow control of the language.

- *The concept of classes:* Learning the basics of classes—what they are, how they work, and how to extend them—is fundamental to programming in Java.

We will tackle these subjects one at a time, giving an overview of the basics and counting on interested readers to delve even deeper into the subjects on their own.

Java Syntax

While Java breaks away from traditional programming languages in some important ways, it also mirrors C and C++ in key areas. For programmers, that means they do not have to learn an entirely new language from the ground up but can instead build on their basic knowledge of C programming. In its basic syntax most of all, Java follows most closely to C and C++.

Any computer language needs a way to name things and represent data. Java has five core data types: identifiers, keywords, literals, operators, and separators.

Identifiers are the names given to variables, classes, and methods. The Java compiler understands code written in the Unicode format, which among other things expands beyond ASCII to support non-Latin characters. The simple rule of thumb in naming in Java is this: all identifiers must begin with a letter (uppercase or lowercase), an underscore (_), or the dollar sign ($). Subsequent characters can also include digits (0-9). A good tip is to give your identifiers simple yet descriptive names. Classes typically have a capitalized first letter with all other letters lowercase. In addition, the first letter of words that appear in the middle of an identifier are usually capitalized. For instance, the class we worked with in the earlier applet was identified as HelloWorld.

Keywords are identifiers reserved by the Java language itself. We won't go through the whole list of 50 words here, but they include words such as class, else, false, package, void, and other such words used by Java to name data types and control program flow. You cannot use Java-reserved keywords as identifiers.

Literals are real values that variables can have. In Java, literals can be represented as either numbers or characters. Literal types include integers (a number, represented in decimal, hexadecimal, or octal format), floating points (used to represent decimals), characters (a single character), strings (collections of characters enclosed in quotation marks), and booleans (represented by keywords true or false). It is also possible to declare a variable to be an array, for instance a series of numbers or characters.

Operators can be used to perform some sort of computation, such as addition (+), subtraction (-), multiplication (*), and division (/), or a comparison of objects, such as less than (<), less than or equal to (<=), and not equal to (!=), and a full suite of additional functions.

Separators break up and organize Java code. As we saw in the HelloWorld applet earlier, Java programmers use symbols to logically break up their code, making it easier to arrange and view raw code. Some common separators include ( ), { }, and ; .

In addition, Java, like any computer language, allows for the addition of comments to the code, an important feature in object-oriented programming, because as object code is reused, a plain-language translation of exactly what a program is trying to do can be a big help to decipher Java code. Comments in Java can be done in several styles:

/* comment */	/*Comments can be written across several lines as shown here.*/
// comment	// Comments can start after the double slash and go to the end of a line.
/** comment */	/** Comments in this format are used by the javadoc tool to automatically create documentation to support Java programs.*/

A Simple Math Program: A+B+C

Let's play around with some simple math to get a feel for the basic structure of the Java language and how to use identifiers, literals, and operators.

In the examples in this part of the chapter, we will be dealing more with Java's basic syntax than with its object-oriented nature. The fact is, Java is in some ways very similar to a procedural language like C, but it also has some very strict object-oriented features. As we discuss the syntax of Java in this section, we will be looking at the more procedural features of the language. Later, we'll discuss Java objects and classes in more detail.

Here's one other explanatory note: As we run through the examples here, the code provided is for illustrating the examples, not to produce working applets. Later on in the chapter we'll investigate further how to build applets for the Web.

On to our math example. To give real values to our variables, we declare them, for instance, int a = 1. In addition to declaring variables in our code, we'll set it up so we can also let the user declare some variables on his or her own before the program runs. Type the following code into your text editor:

```
// This is a simple math program in Java
class MathLesson {
  public static void main (String args[]) {
    // Lets define some integers and character strings here
    String name = "A simple math program";
    int a = 5;
    int b = 6;
    int c = 7;
    int array[] = {10,20,30};
    // Now let's run the math and print it out
    System.out.println(name);
    System.out.println(args[0]);
    System.out.println(a+b+c);
    System.out.println(args[1]);
    System.out.println(a*b*c);
    System.out.println(args[2]);
    System.out.println(array[2]);
    }
  }
```

Save the code with the name MathLesson.java into the same HTML directory we set up earlier. Run the code through the Java compiler. For this example, we'll run this class directly into the interpreter straight from the DOS command line. At the C prompt, type in the following:

```
C:\java MathLesson Add Multiply Array
```

The input "Java MathLesson" will run the code through the Java interpreter. The input "Add Multiply Array" is called a command line argument (args), and lets the user assign values to variables at run time. In this case, we add the strings "Add," "Multiply," and "Array" to the program, all of which will print out in our program. The program will also do the calculations we defined and print out the results. See the results of our simple Java math lesson in Figure 6-3.

One final note on this example: Notice how the line "System.out.println(array[2]);" prints out the third—not the second—value in the array. An array starts counting at zero, not one.

Our "Simple Math Lesson" program was easy to put together, and it gives a good, basic illustration of how to give values to variables and how to run through some basic calculations with them. As with anything, the devil is in the details, and there is much more for the interested programmer to learn about the finer details of Java syntax, such as diving deeper into operators, dealing with more complex integers, understanding how and when to use boolean literals, and more. We'll leave that for your own explorations.

Java Control Flow

Our Simple Math Lesson had a simple logical flow: the program ran a top-to-bottom pass over our code. You'll want to provide your program with more direction than

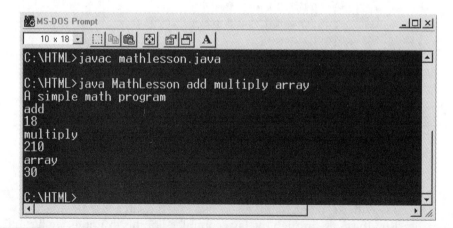

Figure 6-3. *The applet spits back the input parameters and does the simple math equations*

that. Program control flow lets a program react to calculations and jump to different spots in the code depending on the results. It can also make it easy to repeat a run of code many times. These and other situations are easy to code using Java's control flow methods (see Table 6-2).

The most widely used control flow requirements are for branching and looping. Branching takes a program in one of several directions, depending on program inputs. Branching can be handled in Java in several ways, most simply using an "if-else" expression, as in "if the stoplight is red, stop; else go." Looping too can be expressed in several ways, including using a "for" expression. The for loop compares variables to a specific limit. When the variable reaches the limit, the loop is broken.

Here's a very simple example of if-else flow:

```
// If Then logic flow
class IfThen {
  public static void main (String args[]) {
  int a = 5;
  if(a == 4)
  System.out.println("a = 5");
  else System.out.println("a does not equal 5");
  }
}
```

The output of this bit of code is "a does not equal 5."

And here's an example of a for loop, demonstrating a classic entry-level programming challenge: creating a Celsius-to-Fahrenheit conversion table. The for

Statement	Keyword
Decisionmaking	if-else, switch
Loops	for, while, do-while
Exceptions	try-catch-throw
Miscellaneous	break, continue, label, return

Table 6-2. *Control Flow Keywords*

loop instructs the program to do the Celsius-to-Fahrenheit conversions for Celsius 0 degrees to Celsius 50 degrees. Type in the Java code and compile it.

```
// A temperature conversion program
class TempConversion {
  public static void main (String args[]) {
    int fahrenheit, celsius;
    System.out.println("Temperature Conversion Chart");
    System.out.println("");
    System.out.println("Celsius Fahrenheit");
      for(celsius = 0; celsius <= 50; celsius +=10) {
      fahrenheit = celsius * 9 / 5 + 32;
      System.out.println(celsius + "\t" + fahrenheit);
    }
  }
}
```

To run the program, type at the command line:

```
java TempConversion
```

The output of the program is in Figure 6-4.

Figure 6-4. *Here's the output of our for loop*

We'll end our look at control flow here. Programmers need to have a firm grip on program control flow to write powerful programs with the least amount of code and the most logical, elegant design.

Understanding and Working with Classes

Learning the procedural syntax of Java only gives the slightest hint of the power of this new programming language. As we observed earlier, Java is designed from the ground up as an object-oriented environment. Java positions classes as the basic unit of all programming efforts. Earlier, we discussed the concepts of classes (remember the bicycle example?). And in writing the small bits of code so far, each time we've defined classes and methods—the core engines of Java. Now let's take a more hands-on look at classes.

Defining a Class

The basic method for declaring a class in Java is as follows, where class is a keyword and *name* is an identifier for the class:

```
class name {
\\variables and methods of a class go between the curly brackets
}
```

The block of code above is called the class definition block. The class is named, and the variables and methods for that particular class are contained within the curly brackets. To recall our earlier discussion, a class is a template that describes the data (variables) and behavior (methods) associated with the instances of that class.

As an example, consider a class that represents a rectangle. First, we define the class. Then we define some variables for the class, for instance its height and width. Finally, we include a method that calculates the area of the rectangle. See the code below, but realize this is just a theoretical example (no need to compile the code).

```
class Rectangle {
int width, height //define variables here
int area(int w, int h){
  int a;
  a=w * h; //here is the engine for the method that computes the rectangle's area
  return a;
  }
}
```

Before we move off our rectangle program completely, let's briefly discuss another concept that is part of Java: packages. A *package* is a collection of classes that all belong together. Java itself includes some packages, such as java.lang and java.util, as we outlined earlier. You can also define your own packages. For instance, the rectangle might be part of a package called shapes, which would also include triangles and circles.

Extending a Class

In addition to defining a class or package from scratch, you can create a subclass that extends an already created class, or even more powerfully, that extends one of the comprehensive class packages that ships as part of Java. The ability of a subclass to inherit characteristics from another class is one of the most powerful features of object-oriented programming. It helps significantly in the reuse of code and makes it easy for one programmer to build on the work of another.

To build upon the work of a previously built class, you need to "import" that class into your program. Here, let's import some data from the java.util class. If you type in the code below, run it through the compiler, and then call it from the command line, this program will spit out the current day, time, date, and year:

```
import java.util.Date;
class Date {
  public static void main(String args[]) {
    Date today = new Date();
    System.out.println(today);
  }
}
```

The Date program is a simple example of making use of data that is part of an existing class. More often, you'll want to take an existing class and build upon it. This is the concept of class inheritance that we discussed earlier. Here's the basic syntax for extending a preexisting class:

```
import name;
class newname extends name; {
  //add the code to add new capabilities to the name class here
}
```

Just because you import and extend a class, it does not mean you need to keep all of the previous class's code. By using a concept called "method overriding"—which in Java is implemented using the keyword void—you can override certain methods in a class while retaining the rest of the code in the parent class. By using the same method name and arguments in the new extended class as in the old class, you replace the old method with the new method. This lets you extend the functionality for a class while at the same time reusing the bulk of the code in the parent class.

We've now covered the basics of classes and packages, including advanced concepts like inheritance. There's more to learn for would-be Java programmers, but with what we've run through so far you should have a good understanding of Java classes.

Another Run at a Java Applet

Let's use what we've learned about Java's syntax and class structure and build an applet with a little more going on than our original stab at HelloWorld. We'll also pick up a few more nuances specifically relating to the creation of Java applets, which is after all the main reason Webmasters are interested in Java.

Our goal with this applet will be to write a "self-conscious" program that outputs a descriptive string whenever it reaches a milestone in its life—for instance, when it is loaded—as well as when the end user performs some predefined actions.

Below you'll find the code for the applet. Type in the program exactly as it appears and save it to a file called Simple.java. Then compile the program and include it in an HTML page. We'll then run the applet in the appletviewer and see the results.

To examine more closely what this program is doing step by step, see the comments included along with the code. That is the best way to get a feel for what each part of the program is doing. But in terms of output, here's what we should see (as shown in Figure 6-5):

■ The program will print a descriptive string detailing each stage of its "life," for instance when initializing or starting.

■ The program will print a descriptive string in response to certain user actions, for instance a mouse click or drag.

Here's the code:

```
// simple event driven applet
import java.awt.Graphics; //bring in the Graphics class to draw on-screen
public class Simple extends java.applet.Applet { //calling the applet class is required
  StringBuffer buffer = new StringBuffer();
  public void init() {  //here, we are resizing the applet area
    resize(500, 100);
    addItem("initializing... "); // the applet is defining outputs for several milestones
  }
  public void start() {
    addItem("starting... ");
  }
  public void stop() {
    addItem("stopping... ");
  }
  public void destroy() {
    addItem("preparing for unloading...");
```

```
    }
  public void addItem(String newWord) {  //the applet prints to screen each
milestone
     System.out.println(newWord);
     buffer.append(newWord);
     repaint();
  }
  public void paint(Graphics g) {  //a simple rectangle is drawn to frame the
action
     g.clearRect(0, 0, size().width - 1, size().height - 1);
     g.drawRect(0, 0, size().width - 1, size().height - 1);
     g.drawString(buffer.toString(), 5, 15);
  }
  public boolean mouseEnter(java.awt.Event event, int x, int y) {
     addItem("here comes the mouse!"); // reacting to the mouse entering the
field
     return true;
  }
  public boolean mouseDown(java.awt.Event event, int x, int y) {
     addItem("click!... "); //reacting to the mouse button being clicked
     return true;
  }
}
```

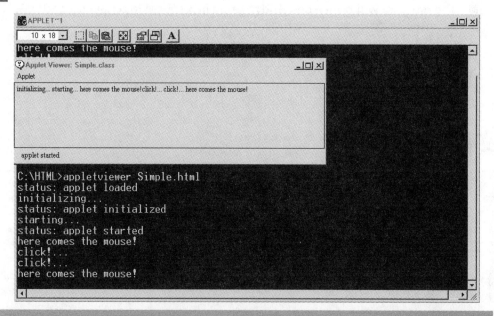

Figure 6-5. *The output for the Simple applet*

Java Class Packages

While relatively simplistic (pun intended), the Simple applet draws together everything we've learned about Java syntax and classes and demonstrates it in the context of a working applet. If you can understand how the Simple applet works, you've gone a long way towards getting a solid handle on the Java programming language.

Without a doubt, you'll want to continue to expand your working understanding of classes and packages. The real power of Java comes into play when you can take Java classes and tap into and extend the power of those classes. The ability to reuse preexisting code and objects is one of Java's major strengths.

In particular, you'll want to have a very strong working knowledge of the Java class packages that ship with the JDK: java.lang, java.util, java.net, java.awt, and java.applet. This is no simple task; the Java APIs detail the Java packages across literally hundreds of pages of text. But in light of all we've learned thus far in this chapter, let's expand on our earlier look at the Java packages (refer back to Table 6-1), taking a little extra time to detail some of the jazzier elements (graphics and sound, for instance).

JAVA.LANG This package provides classes that are core to the Java language, including some key capabilities we've passed over up to now:

- *Object:* The king of all classes, from which all other classes derive.
- *Data Type Wrappers:* A collection of classes used to wrap variables of a simple data type: Boolean, Character, Double, Float, Integer, and Long.
- *Strings:* Java provides two classes that store and manipulate character data: String, for strings that won't be changing, and StringBuffer, for when you know the value of a character will change.
- *System and Runtime:* These two classes let your programs use system resources. System provides a system-independent programming interface to system resources, and Runtime gives you direct system-specific access to the run-time environment.
- *Threads:* This group of classes lets you implement the multithreading capabilities of Java, which lets you run multiple executions at the same time. This is a vital capability and deserves a much deeper look if you want to do sophisticated Java programming.
- *Classes:* This provides a run-time description of a class as well as a ClassLoader class that allows you to load classes into your program during run time.
- *Math:* A library of math routines and values.
- *Exceptions, Errors, and Throwable:* Another area that deserves a deeper look by serious Java programmers. A good understanding of the Exception class will allow you to build programs that won't cause major crashes if a coding error sneaks through.

JAVA.IO   The java.io package contains classes for handling the input and output of data. Input streams read data from an input source, which can be a file, a string, or memory—anything that can contain data. Output streams write data to an output source, again including a file, a string, or memory. The java.io package is important for adding interactivity to a Java program.

JAVA.UTIL   The Java utilities package provides basic low-level utilities, most of which are a little beyond our needs here. We saw the Date class in use earlier in the chapter.

JAVA.NET   The Java networking package is an important behind-the-scenes class for Web applets. This package extends the input/output capabilities of Java to include key network protocols such as sockets, telnet, FTP, , and the Web. By taking advantage of these protocols, the distributed nature of Java extends across networks, enabling applets to tap into resources anywhere in the world via the Internet.

JAVA.APPLET   This package contains the applet class, which is obviously key for writing Web-ready applets. As we've seen in some of the programs we've already written, you must extend this class whenever you are writing an applet, for instance:

```
public class Simple extends java.applet.Applet {
```

The applet packages supports a number of important methods, including:

- init( ): Whenever an applet is loaded into a browser, the init( ) method is called. You will likely resize the window in which your applet runs whenever you call the init( ) method, as we did in the HelloWorld applet:

```
public void init() {
  resize(150,25);
}
```

- getAttributes: This is the method for getting attributes from an HTML page that feeds into a Java applet. It is one of the easiest ways to customize a Java applet.

- getImages: For Java-fueled animations such as Tumbling Duke, you use the getImage method for loading a series of images, which when run in succession produces the animation.

- paint, repaint: The run( ) method runs through the series of animations, painting and repainting the screen with the supplied images. The paint( ) method itself is closely linked to the java.awt's Graphics class, which has the functions for drawing all of the basic graphics types, such as lines, rectangles, and strings. In the Simple applet, we used these methods to paint a rectangle inside of which all the action took place:

```
public void paint(Graphics g) {
  g.clearRect(0, 0, size().width - 1, size().height - 1);
  g.drawRect(0, 0, size().width - 1, size().height - 1);
  g.drawString(buffer.toString(), 5, 15);
```

■ mouse, keystroke: These methods enable a level of user feedback through mouse and keyboard actions. Again, recall the Simple applet, where the Java program responded to mouse actions:

```
public boolean mouseDown(java.awt.Event event, int x, int y) {
  addItem("click!... ");
  return true;
```

■ getAudioData: Java handles streaming audio very well, and sound adds a nice element to many applets. The getAudioData( ) method retrieves an .au file for playback, and the play( ) method runs the file.

JAVA.AWT   The Java Abstract Window Toolkit package provides graphical user interface elements used to get input from and display information to the user such as windows, buttons, fonts, images, scrollbars, and text items. The class provides more than 60 predefined classes and interfaces, some of which are demonstrated in the applet shown in Figure 6-6.

■ Graphics: We saw a demo of the graphics class just above. We can draw rectangles, strings, and lines, as well as set colors and fonts with this class.

■ Color: The color class lets you specify the color for use by the graphics class.

■ Controls: This allows for the easy creation of control elements, such as dialog boxes, scroll bars, buttons, menus, and more.

■ Buttons: Once you've created a button, this class lets it react as expected: push the button, and something happens.

What's Next for Java

Pinning down Java is next to impossible—the language is evolving too quickly. It's important to remember that even with all the hype surrounding Java, it is still in its very early days. The language at the beginning of 1996 will just enter its first release, having gone through half a year of public alpha and beta cycles.

Even as the basic structure of the language is settled and bugs get cleaned up, there will be plenty of action in the area of class packages. New classes have been proposed by Sun and its partners, including graphical packages from Silicon Graphics and Macromedia. One challenge for Sun will be to keep all of its licensees committed to at least a base level of class packages. If not, Java could splinter just like HTML. Microsoft, with its "embrace and extend" Internet strategy, could be a particular challenge to this consensus. It could possibly "extend" Java in ways optimized for its Windows-using masses that competitors might be loath to adopt.

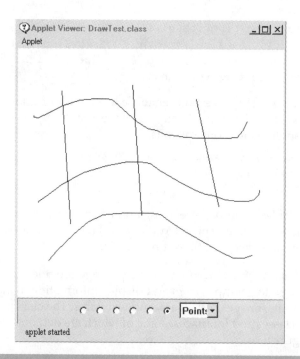

Figure 6-6.　*Here's a drawing applet that shows some simple user interface elements drawn from the AWT class*

Just as significantly, new Java development tools are promised from a wide variety of vendors, including traditional programming tool vendors such as Borland, Symantec, and Metrowerks and more multimedia-oriented tool vendors such as Macromedia and SGI. These new tools will make it easier for developers to work with Java.

The Emerging Java Toolbox

Java is taking the same growth path of any other programming language (although it is moving undeniably more quickly). First comes the programming language itself, then some basic coding, compiling, and debugging tools, and finally an advanced set of visually oriented development tools. As this book was being written, the number of companies licensing Java was skyrocketing (see Table 6-3).

Many of these companies aim to produce Java development and authoring tools. There are sure to be many more (at least until witty, coffee-inspired code names like Latte and Espresso run out). Most are scheduled for a mid-1996 delivery.

New development tools should give another major boost to Java. Indeed, one of the main things that Java programmers today crave is a more elegant programming environment. Dealing with DOS command lines and text editors is fine, but a completely integrated, visually oriented programming environment will make it much more enjoyable to work with Java. As you see in Table 6-3, most of the major

Companies Licensing Java (as of early 1996)	Plans for Java
Adobe (http://www.adobe.com)	Will incorporate Java support into its Acrobat and PageMill products
Borland (http://www.borland.com)	Will build rapid visual development environment for Java programmers, code-named Latte
IBM (http://www.ibm.com)	Will include Java support with its browser and server platforms, as well as handle Java ports to OS/2, AIX and Windows 3.1 platforms
Macromedia (http://www.macromedia.com)	Include Java support in multimedia authoring tools including Director and Authorware; build easy-to-use Java authoring tools; codevelop graphics class libraries with Sun
Metrowerks (http://www.metrowerks.com)	Will integrate Java programming tools into its Macintosh-based Code Warrior platform
Microsoft (http://www.microsoft.com)	Signed letter of intent in late 1995; part of its "embrace and extend" Internet strategy
Natural Intelligence (http://www.natural.com)	Has built Roaster, a Mac-based development environment, including one of the first third-party Java compilers
Netscape (http://www.netscape.com)	Java interpreter in both browser and server; codevelop JavaScript with Sun
Oracle (http://www.oracle.com)	Java support part of its Network Loadable Objects architecture, more specifically, supported in the Oracle PowerBrowser
Silicon Graphics (http://www.sgi.com)	Will build Java support into its Cosmo development environment and work with Sun on graphical and 3-D class libraries and Java/VRML integration
Spyglass (http://www.spyglass.com)	Largest OEM browser vendor will make Java available to its long list of browser customers including Quarterdeck, Spry, and others.
Symantec (http://www.symantec.com)	Building Java development environment code-named Espresso

Table 6-3.   *A Sampling of Java Licensees*

programming tool vendors—including Sun's own SunSoft division, Borland, Symantec, Metrowerks, and Natural Intelligence—have committed to building Java programming environments.

SunSoft's Workshop Java, for example, will include a fully visual programming environment, a WYSIWYG HTML page editor and a unique feature called an applet portfolio, which will let developers include documentation and other supporting data along with an applet.

Delivering one of the earliest Java development environments was Symantec, which built Java capabilities—code-named Espresso—as a free add-on sitting on top of its Symantec C++ 7.2 development environment for Windows platforms. Espresso features included a complete visual development environment (see Figure 6-7), including a class editor that allows the browsing and editing of methods, data, classes, and two "wizard"-like tools (ProjectExpress and AppExpress) that speed the creation of Java applets.

As you can see, these new development environments are a major improvement over working with the Sun JDK and will encourage even more developers to work with Java and build a whole new class of applications for the Web.

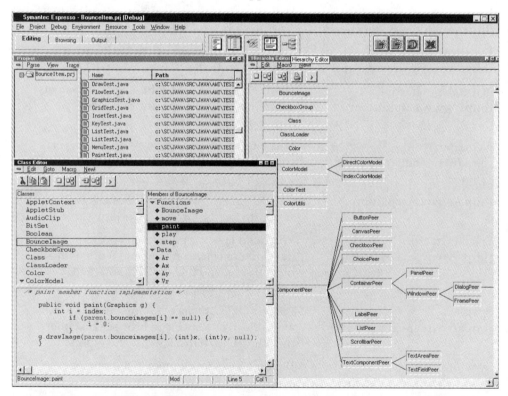

Figure 6-7. *Symantec Espresso's ProjectExpress lets programmers quickly get a Java applet off the ground*

TECH
RESOURCES

System Requirements for Java*

FOR THE JAVA DEVELOPERS KIT

- 1.0 Beta 2 Kit for Sun Solaris 2.3, 2.4 and 2.5
- 1.0 Beta 2 Kit for Windows NT or 95

FOR HOT JAVA BROWSER

- 1.0 Alpha3 for Windows NT and 95
- 1.0 Alpha3 for Solaris 2.3, 2.4, 2.5

FOR NETSCAPE NAVIGATOR 2.0 BETA 5 (WITH JAVA SUPPORT)

- Windows 95 and NT
- HP-UX
- SGI IRIX
- SunOS 4.1
- Sun Solaris 2.3 and 2.4

* This information valid as of 1/96.

Where to Find More Information About Java

SUN'S JAVA WEB PAGES
Main page: **http://www.javasoft.com**
Trail Guide Tutorial: **http://www.javasoft.com/tutorial/**
Java Starter Kit: **http://www.javasoft.com/starter.html**
Documentation: **http://www.javasoft.com/doc.html**

WHERE TO FIND JAVA APPLETS
Sun's Java applet page: **http://www.javasoft.com/applets**
Gamelan: **http://www.gamelan.com**
Java Applet Rating Service: **http://www.surinam.net/java/jars/jars.html**

OTHER WEB SITES DEVOTED TO JAVA
Digital Espresso (summary of Java newsgroups):
http://www.io.org/~mentor/DigitalEspresso.html
Java FAQ: http://sunsite.unc.edu/javafaq/javafaq.html
Java Tutorial: http://sunsite.unc.edu/javafaq/javatutorial.html
Java Developer/Java Store:
http://www.digitalfocus.com/digitalfocus/faq/index.html
A Guide to Java: http://www.surinam.net/java/java.html

JAVA USERS GROUPS AND TRAINING
SunSite User Group List: http://sunsite.unc.edu/javafaq/usergroups.html
Sun User Group List: http://www.javasoft.com/Mail/usrgrp.html
SunService Training:
http://www.sun.com/sunservice/suned/catalog/java_sched.html

NEWSGROUPS
Java: **comp.lang.java**
Hot Java: **alt.www.hotjava**

Summary

In this chapter, we've provided a good, introductory overview of the Java programming language that can start you down the path of writing Java applets. Even if you never write a Java applet, you'll understand how they work, what kinds of things can be done with Java, and what to expect when you add them to your Web pages. We also examined the next generation of Java programming tools. If you want to take the next step and delve deeper into Java, there is no end to the Java books, tutorials, and training programs that can help you take a bigger swig of Java. Happy coding.

Chapter Seven

Java in Action

Java is a very new technology, but even in beta form developers all over the world picked up the Java Developers Kit and started cranking out Java applets. We've seen a few of these applets in previous chapters, but now let's take a tour of the Web in search of the most innovative uses of Java.

As we take our tour, we'll talk with some leading-edge Java developers and get some insight into how they view the language, how they are using it today, and where they see it heading. In addition, we'll chat with some Webmasters to see how they are working with and using Java applets on their site. Together, these two groups will give us a good feel for what Java is capable of from both a technical and creative perspective. Their thoughts may spur your own thinking about how you could use Java on your Web site.

Some common threads run through the discussions with Web developers in this section:

- One of Java's greatest strengths is its multiplatform nature, which lets developers build an applet once and offer it to all sorts of users.

- Java applets delivered over the Web heralds a new age of software distribution—and potentially an end to floppy disks.

- Java will work its magic both on the public Internet, with games, services, and features targeted at mainstream users, and on the private Intranet with corporate-grade applications.

Let's dive in and see how Java is being used on the Web.

Java "Ground Zero": Gamelan

Any tour of the Java-powered Web should obviously start with Sun's Java page. The second stop: Gamelan, the directory and registry of Java resources run by Web development company EarthWeb. The site is an essential outlet for all things Java: applets, source code, class packages, Java news, and more. It can be accessed at **http://www.gamelan.com**; you can find EarthWeb at **http://www.earthweb.com**.

The Gamelan site includes an interesting Java applet in its own right: the Navigator, which serves as a point-and-click table of contents for the Gamelan site (see Figure 7-1).

The folks behind Gamelan, EarthWeb Inc., have some intriguing plans for moving Java to the next level. EarthWeb's plans start with Gamelan, which it envisions as evolving into one of the Web's first storefronts for online software distribution, ranging from small Java applets to more full-scale Net-based applications.

"Gamelan is poised to become the center of online software rental," says Nova Spivack, EarthWeb's senior vice president of marketing strategy and development. "We are considering and will experiment with allowing people to rent access of various programs via Gamelan. It's not really a market yet, but it will be soon."

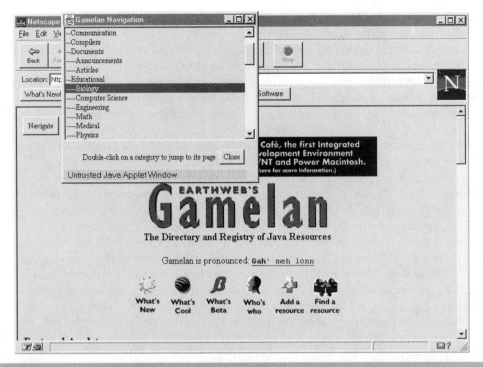

Figure 7-1. *The Gamelan Navigator*

Spivack sees the site offering Java applets and applications, object libraries, compilers, and more.

EarthWeb also is using Java to build a new class of "real-time" client and server technology that it will use to launch not Web sites but what it calls Web *channels,* which are continually refreshed streams of information that Web surfers can tap into. "Eventually, the Internet will be what people thought interactive TV would be. It's about jacking into the feed, getting information you need all the time, any way you want it," says Spivack.

Spivack says Java is perfect for the type of work EarthWeb is doing because "it is secure enough to distribute widely, fast enough to work with real-time data, and open enough to integrate seamlessly with the Web." EarthWeb has already built prototype Java-based servers and clients that can receive, stream, and visualize real-time data on the Net, according to Spivack.

The Sports Network and Wall Street Web

While EarthWeb plots a grand vision of a Java-powered, real-time Web, several companies have already begun to wade into this territory, including The Sports

Network (surf over to **http://www.sportsnetwork.com**) and Wall Street Web (**http://www.bulletproof.com**).

The Sports Network provides breaking sports scores and news. The bulk of the site is HTML-based, with scores and headlines refreshed frequently. The site has also begun using Java in the form of a scrolling ticker tape that carries the latest news directly to the user's desktop. The user interface, shown in Figure 7-2, not only displays the ticker, but lets the user control the speed of the scrolling and repeat the last headline.

An even more sophisticated real-time Java applet is BulletProof.com's Wall Street Web. The Java-based service lets users get instant stock quotes, search for stocks based on a variety of parameters, dynamically build stock charts, and manage their portfolios online. The service is run on a custom-built Java-based server and is fed with real-time stock information from Standard & Poor's. The client information comes in the form of a dynamically generated Java applet (see Figure 7-3).

A service like Wall Street Web benefits greatly from Java, says Scott Milener, BulletProof.com co-founder. "You get platform independence, which is phenomenal itself," Milener says. "But one of the biggest advantages is centralized distribution. The applet sits on our server and everyone instantly has the latest version of the applet. If a bug crops up, boom, we fix it, and everyone instantly has the fix. This is software distribution at its best. I don't think people even realize the potential of Java yet."

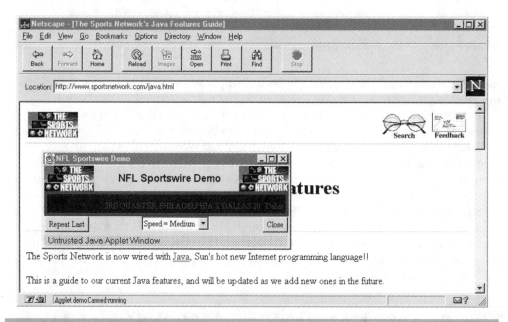

Figure 7-2.   *The Sports Network sports wire*

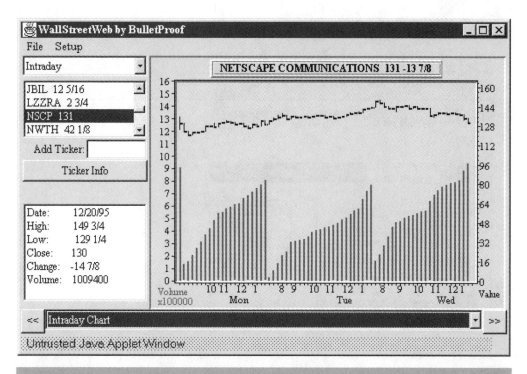

Figure 7-3. *BulletProof.com's Wall Street Web*

C/Net's PC Scoreboard

One of the coolest early applets is from C/Net, the television show/Web site that chronicles the digital revolution for the masses (**http://www.cnet.com**). C/Net began its Java explorations with a simple scrolling news ticker, but then it quickly moved to more sophisticated applets. Its first major applet was the PC Scoreboard, a graphical, interactive guide to PC shopping (see Figure 7-4).

To use the PC Scoreboard, you first drag the feature "sliders" on the left side of the screen. Options include performance; software bundle; setup and ergonomics; components and features; and price. Move the sliders to the left if these factors aren't important, or shift them to the right if they are vital. Once the settings are in place, you click on Submit and the applet spits back the computers that best match your needs, charted on a graph. Pass the mouse over the graph, and the applet provides more details on the PCs.

PC Scoreboard demonstrates a good, mainstream use of Java. All of the complexity is shielded from the end users—they simply move slider buttons. And each time, a result is dynamically generated, making the applet customizable for each end user.

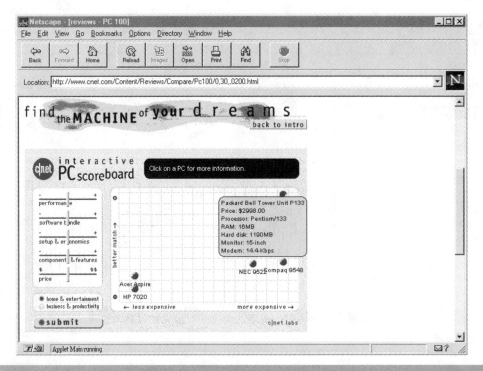

Figure 7-4. *C-Net's PC Scoreboard*

Fun and Games

If you're looking to have a little fun with Java, you don't have to look far. Developers have used Java to build interactive games that look and feel like the arcade originals, including Asteroids (**http://www.mediascience.no/nms/asteroids**) and Pacman (**http://www.csd.uu.se/~alexb**). These games were built by individual developers playing around with Java. But major game companies are discovering Java as well. For instance, Viacom New Media released a demonstration version of its game Zoop, built with Java (**http://www.zoop.com/vnm/zoop/java-game**).

The Zoop demo, shown in Figure 7-5, could give the gaming industry a whole new way to publicize upcoming games. But it also points out how Java can change the dynamics of software distribution. When software companies want to release a new version of a game—or indeed any piece of software—all they need to do is post a new applet on their Web server. There is no legacy user base to deal with and no floppy disks to send out. Upgrades are instant and universal. Software developers also don't have to worry about building different versions for different computer platforms. A single Java applet serves users on all types of systems. Economic advantages like that will go a long way toward convincing the mainstream software industry to adopt Java.

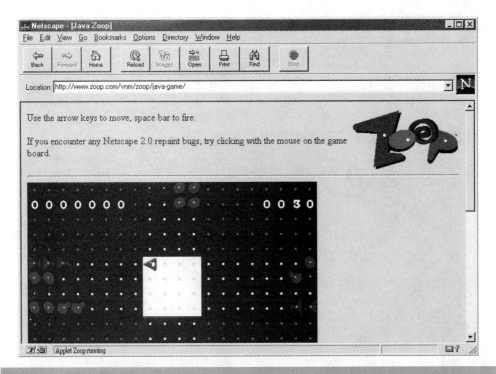

Figure 7-5. *The Java Version of Zoop*

Dimension X: Java and VRML

We've talked about Dimension X (**http://www.dimensionx.com**) in previous chapters, but the company's most interesting contribution to the Java community may be Liquid Reality, a Java-based authoring kit and viewer for interactive 3-D worlds, and ICE, a Java class library for 3-D graphics rendering.

As we'll see in Chapter 13, Java will very likely be integrated into the next version of Virtual Reality Modeling Language (VRML), the standard for creating 3-D worlds on the Web. Liquid Reality offers a sneak preview of what is to come. For instance, in Figure 7-6, the VRML file features a flowing brook, flying birds, and a spider that scurries away when the viewer gets too close to it. All of these interactions, or behaviors, are made possible through Java scripts, according to Scott Fraize, Dimension X's chief technical officer.

Most of the VRML 2.0 specifications, as described in Chapter 13, in some way add scripting capabilities to VRML. Java's security and cross-platform capabilities make it a strong contender to be the scripting/programming language of choice for interactive, 3-D worlds.

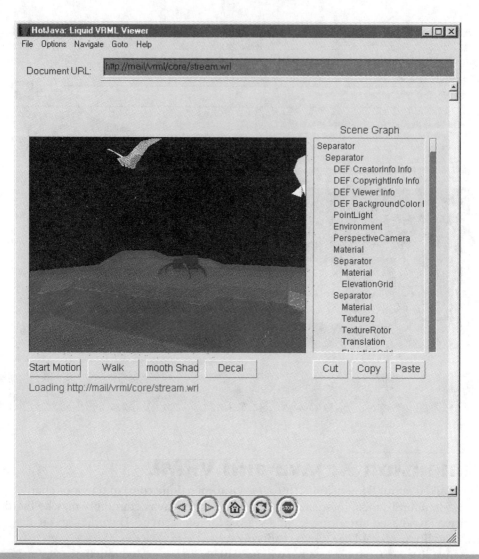

Figure 7-6. *Liquid Reality, a Java-powered VRML viewer*

Java on the Intranet

Some of the most powerful applications of Java will never see the light of day on the Internet. Instead, they'll work behind corporate firewalls over corporate Intranets, the name for private networks running over TCP/IP protocols.

One company that has made a big splash on the Intranet is NeoGlyphics Media Corp. At a Java Day earlier this year, company president Alex Zoghlin showed a couple of innovative Intranet applications, including a Java-based application designed to search the entire Internet in response to a user request, for instance, a price quote on a particular product. Such an exhaustive search over a 14.4 kb/s modem would take 12 hours, Zoghlin said, but by building a dynamic Java applet that automatically off-loads processing onto other Java-enabled servers, the search time was cut to 12 minutes.

Zoghlin also showed a Java-based Intranet application his company built for CSX Transportation, a nationwide railroad company. The application called up mapping data from a database and in real-time displayed in a Netscape browser the location and contents of trains running across the country. CSX had tried to write the application using traditional client-server tools but couldn't; using Java, NeoGlyphics wrote the application from scratch in three months.

"We do Internet applications for the exposure, but the real action is on the corporate Intranet," says Zoghlin. "Java gives companies a way to completely reinvent the way they do business, replacing private networks and proprietary protocols with open standards and the Internet. It is a powerful combination."

Java within a corporation offers many of the same advantages we discussed earlier: cross-platform functionality, instant and coordinated upgrades to new versions of applications, and the power of networked applications.

Summary

We've seen a good representation of Java applets in this chapter, ranging from serious business to sports to gaming applications. Practically anything is possible with Java. While we are seeing just the first wave of applets hit the Web today, increasingly sophisticated applets will be surfacing soon that will tap into the true power of the secure, cross-platform, networked Java programming environment.

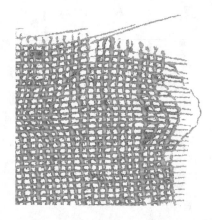

Chapter Eight

Microsoft's Internet Platform

It was touted as the technology battle of the century: Microsoft versus the Web. Windows 95, the Microsoft Network, and a slew of Microsoft-specific technology on the one hand; the juggernaut of Web technologies from Netscape, Sun, and other companies on the other. Which side would hold the winning formula? Would Microsoft roll over the Web, or would the Web bring Microsoft's software empire crashing down?

The computer industry thrives on such intrigue. But in the end, pitting Microsoft against the Internet has proven to be a non-issue, for two major reasons:

- Microsoft is a company; the Internet is a collection of physical networks, protocols, and standards. Microsoft Chairman Bill Gates loves to point this simple fact out. He also enjoys detailing how Microsoft from the start has been involved in some of the most important Internet developments. There never was anything stopping Microsoft from more widely adopting and supporting Internet and Web technologies, which leads to our second point below.

- Microsoft made an abrupt and rather far-reaching decision late last year to "embrace and extend" Web protocols rather than try to compete with its own proprietary platforms and technologies. Maybe Microsoft was never competing with the Internet per se, but they clearly were competing with companies—Netscape, Oracle, Sun, and others—that adopted the Web as the cornerstone of their networked futures. Rather than fight the trend, Microsoft chose to fully embrace the Web and Web technologies like Java, casting aside proprietary services and tools such as the Microsoft Network and its Blackbird design tool.

So the "battle" for online supremacy is over, right? Wrong. It's just heating up. Microsoft's decision to "embrace" the Web was applauded by all. But its strategy—some say threat—to "extend" key Web technologies shows the software giant is ready for a fight. Already, Microsoft has mimicked Netscape and introduced some basic HTML extensions for inline sound, video, VRML, and text marquees. Next step: continue to optimize key Web technologies—even Sun's cross-platform Java—for its Windows OS, which continues to hold dominant market share.

Microsoft can probably honestly say it has always had the Internet in its sights. But with the explosion of the Web, the software giant clearly looked in its rearview mirror and saw the incredible momentum building behind companies like Netscape and Sun and took to heart that sage advice, "Objects in mirror may be closer than they appear."

Webmasters will need to follow Microsoft's moves closely—they could have a big impact on the future of the Web. This chapter will provide a hands-on look at the tools Microsoft is shipping today and provide a glimpse at what the company has in store for tomorrow.

INSIDE Spin

The Inside Spin

No company spins faster—or better—than Microsoft. With their stock falling on analyst claims that the company lacked a coherent Internet strategy, the Redmond, Washington–based giant assembled press and financial types in early December, 1995 to prove the world wrong. It was an intriguing event. Microsoft obviously had plenty of ammunition, but was finalizing demos and strategies even the night before the event. For instance, the company reportedly agonized over decisions on the new WebView for Windows 95 and the licensing of Java and JavaScript (which at the time was no more than a letter of intent) up to the last minute. "Microsoft is hard-core about the Internet," said Microsoft Chairman Bill Gates, and just like that, hot Internet stocks like Netscape dropped tens of percentage points. The highlights of Gates' remarks:

- On introducing new HTML extensions: "It's not as simple a question as you might think because the rate at which publishers are willing to embrace new extensions is finite. You can't have, year after year, 20 new extensions and such a variety of browsers out there that people don't really even know what to test against, what they can expect. However, at the same time, the richness of Web pages today is not high enough, and given the intense competition between people with similar types of content, they're always looking for something that can make their pages more effective and appealing."

- On Web programming languages: "When we talk about developers, a key distinction is between content developers and programmers. There will be far more content developers, but they won't be doing programming. They'll be using rich sets of controls that they plug into the active pages they create and those will be made very easy for them to take. And so people have a choice. They can use Visual Basic, C++, Java, Java Script, however they want to do that, and the browser will browse those pages."

- On competing with Netscape: "They've got their very high browser share, and they've got the attention of the world. Very important for us in competing with them will be growing our browser share. That's a metric that I will look at on a very regular basis and see what it is that we need to do."

Microsoft Internet Platform Overview

Microsoft's plans for the Net are anything but small. Microsoft is extending support for the Internet and the Web to all corners of its software universe, including operating systems, software applications, servers, transaction technologies, programming languages and tools, and more. We'll focus on the company's authoring and programming tools, including:

- **Internet Explorer**, Microsoft's free Web browser, which is already emerging as a viable competitor to Netscape Navigator. The browser follows Netscape's lead of supporting varied media formats, scripting languages, and programming environments. The most important of those will be Microsoft's Object Linking and Embedding (OLE) environment. Microsoft envisions that small bits of OLE code, called OLE Controls (OCXs), will be downloaded to a browser and executed locally, much like Java applets. Internet Explorer is even more important since Microsoft has abandoned its own proprietary Blackbird Data Format (BDF) online file format.

- **Internet Assistant**, Microsoft's free HTML authoring environment, which the company is using to help drive its new HTML extensions and other Web development technologies to the masses.

- **Internet Studio** (formerly Blackbird), Microsoft's online design environment that is being completely reworked to output a newly extended version of HTML. Internet Studio is perhaps the most advanced effort to hide all the complexities of online design from authors, but Microsoft faces a major challenge in reworking it for the Web.

- **Microsoft FrontPage**, a full-featured Web creation and management platform, which Microsoft acquired from Vermeer Technologies. We'll do a hands-on examination of FrontPage.

- Microsoft's next-generation **Internet Platform**, which will fully integrate Web capabilities with Windows 95 and include support for a variety of tools and scripting languages, including the new Visual Basic (VB) Script. VB will compete with JavaScript for the attention of Webmasters with little or no programming experience.

Clearly, Microsoft has a lot of dollars, programmers, and software to throw at the Web. The key question Microsoft asks when it comes to the Internet is this: "Does everything have to be reinvented as the Web evolves towards applications?" The answer, it believes, is no. Instead, the Web can be built on the back of existing users, platforms, and technologies, including:

- One hundred fifty million-plus users of Windows
- Tens of millions of Office productivity tools users
- Five million developers with three million using Visual Basic

■   One thousand-plus suppliers of OLE Controls (OCXs)

This represents a wave that Microsoft hopes it can surf right to the top of the Web.

Internet Explorer 2.0

As Microsoft embraces Web technologies, its Internet Explorer browsers grow in importance. The name of the browser gives some indication of its direction. "Explorer" is the name of the Windows 95 combination of File Manager and Program Manager, i.e., the way that users of Windows 95 find files. Microsoft's Web browser is headed on a collision course with the Explorer. Eventually, Internet Explorer will become an integrated part of the Windows operating system, and users will take advantage of a single interface to find files, whether they are on their hard drive or on the Internet. That day is coming quickly—probably by mid-1996.

But for the foreseeable future, Internet Explorer is important enough as a stand-alone Web browser. Microsoft has promised to always give the browser away for free and to always continue upgrading its capabilities. The version we'll discuss here is Internet Explorer 2.0, which was available initially for Windows 95 and NT and later for Windows 3.1 and Apple Macintosh platforms.

Internet Explorer 2.0 is by all accounts a very solid Web browser—it's fast, seldom crashes, and has a lot of nice features. It also represents Microsoft's initial attempt at playing the Netscape game: winning market share and mind share through significant additions to HTML standards. Internet Explorer 2.0 supports a number of innovative additions to standard HTML, including inline sound, video, animated text (marquees), and VRML.

We will outline the new extensions here, but it is important to note that the extensions have not been widely used, mainly because Internet Explorer continues to lag far, far behind Netscape in browser market share.

For Web designers, the equation is simple: only use extensions when a large number of browsers support them. It is possible that Microsoft will pick up greater market share in 1996, or that other browser vendors—most likely Microsoft's increasingly close ally, Spyglass, but maybe even Netscape—will pick up some of the more interesting extensions. But for now, view these extensions with a caveat: many Web browsers may not be able to view them at all.

HTML Extensions

Internet Explorer 2.0 includes several innovative HTML extensions designed to bring new multimedia capabilities to the Web with a very minimal learning curve for Web designers. We will highlight both the raw HTML tags here as well as demonstrate Microsoft Internet Assistant's built-in support for the new extensions via a simple, template-based approach.

The extensions do indeed add a lot of life to an HTML page. For example, the Microsoft demo page (**http://www.microsoft.com/windows/ie/iedemo.htm**) shown in

Figure 8-1 includes a scrolling text marquee ("Get on the Great Taste Tour"), an animated .avi video clip (the coffee cup spins and smokes), and a background sound file of beating drums.

Following are some of the Internet Explorer 2.0 extensions that make these and other notable Microsoft HTML hacks possible.

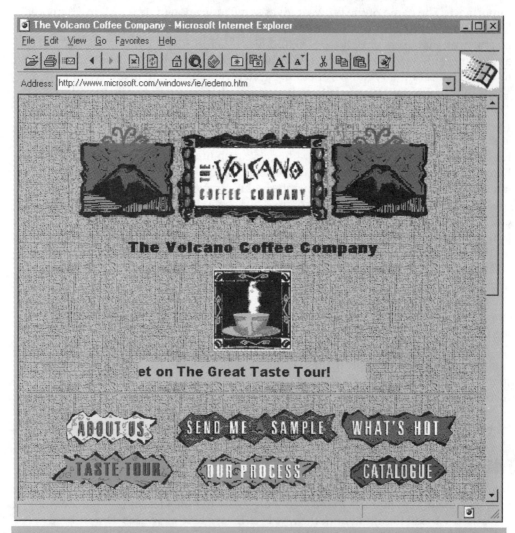

Figure 8-1. *The fictitious Volcano Coffee Company page shows off Microsoft's HTML extensions*

BGSOUND   This tag lets you create pages with background sounds that play when the page is opened up. Sounds can be samples (.wav or .au) or MIDI (.mid). Using the Loop tag, you can specify how many times the file will play from one time to "Infinite," meaning as long as the page is open. Here's the correct syntax:

```
<BGSOUND SRC="start.wav">
Loop=Infinite
```

BGPROPERTIES=FIXED   This tag creates a watermark: an image that does not move even when the user scrolls down the page. Several uses spring to mind. You could use it to simulate the sorts of watermarks you see on stationery (background logos that you can write on top of). Another use might be a small advertisement or logo that stays in place on the page even as the user scrolls down. The correct syntax is:

```
<BODY BACKGROUND="image.gif"
BGPROPERTIES=FIXED>
</BODY>
```

IMG DYNSRC   This tag stands for image, dynamic source, and it lets the Internet Explorer display both video clips and VRML files inline. You can also loop the video (as we did with sound files), embed a standard control bar (start, stop, rewind, fast forward) onto the page, and designate when the file should play (at the start, when the mouse touches it, or both). Here's a generic example showing the proper way to use these tags.

```
<IMG SRC="sample.gif" DYNSRC="test.avi"
LOOP=INFINITE
CONTROLS
START=MOUSEOVER,FILEOPEN>
```

You can also use all the standard image tags you already use (ALIGN, BORDER, VSPACE, HSPACE) to set the image where you want on the page and wrap text or other elements around the file. Also notice how you can set up a placeholder image using the tag IMG SRC that will display until the .avi file is loaded.

MARQUEE   This tag implements in simple HTML the same text marquees that first popped up on the Web as Java applets. Internet Explorer allows a page author to define a marquee with a number of attributes, including behavior (SCROLL, SLIDE, or ALTERNATE); background color; marquee box width and height; scrolling direction (LEFT or RIGHT); number of loops; and how fast the marquee will run (SCROLLAMOUNT or SCROLLDELAY). Here's an example of a marquee with real attributes included:

```
<FONT FACE="Times New Roman" SIZE="5">
<MARQUEE BEHAVIOR="ALTERNATE"
BGCOLOR="WHITE"
LOOP=INFINITE
HEIGHT="50"  WIDTH="500"
SCROLLDELAY="5" >
Here is the text for our marquee!
</MARQUEE>
</FONT>
```

And here is how it looks:

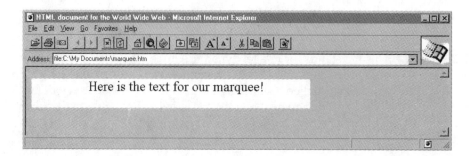

FONT COLOR, FONT FACE   As you may have noticed in the marquee example, Internet Explorer lets you specify the color and type style of the font to be used by a browser when viewing your page, overriding any choices made by the individual accessing the page. This returns to Web page designers an element of typeface style control that has been lost on the Web. The correct uses of the tags are:

```
<FONT COLOR=BLUE>
<FONT FACE="Arial,Lucida Sans,Times Roman">
```

The first tag changes the color of the typeface; the second tag changes the type style. The tag lets you list several fonts as backup in case an individual user does not have a particular font stored locally on the computer. Here's an example:

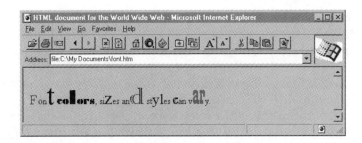

NEW TABLE TAGS   Internet Explorer supports tables based on the HTML 3.0 draft specification, but it also adds three new extensions. Tables can be left- or right-aligned using the ALIGN tag; each individual cell can be colorized using BGCOLOR=NAME; and a caption can be added using the CAPTION tag. The syntax for a simple table is as follows:

```
<TABLE
ALIGN=RIGHT BORDER=1 WIDTH=20%>
<CAPTION CENTER> Example Table<CAPTION>
 <TR><TD BGCOLOR=#ffdddd>Cell 1</TD></TR>
<TR><TD BGCOLOR=#ccffff>Cell 2</TD></TR>
</TABLE>
```

Here's the output of our simple table, right-aligned, with colored cells and a centered caption:

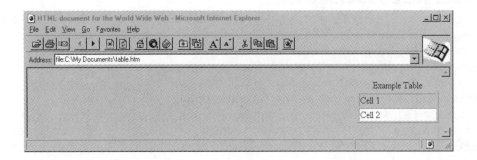

As we'll see later in this chapter, the Internet Assistant add-on to Microsoft Word lets you build HTML tables as easily as building a table in Microsoft Word, which is quite a feat for Webmasters accustomed to the elaborate coding that goes into building a table in HTML. We'll take a more extended look at these and other Microsoft-supported HTML tags when we take a closer look at Internet Assistant later in this chapter.

Several Microsoft extensions support the use of color names rather than the standard RGB HEX codes used by Netscape. Supported color names in Internet Explorer include black, maroon, green, olive, navy, purple, teal, gray, silver, red, lime, yellow, blue, fuchsia, aqua, and white. The color feature is not compatible with Netscape and can result in inaccurate colors in the Netscape browser.

Why Microsoft Is Doing Extensions

As we bring our look at Internet Explorer to a close, let's emphasize the reason why we spent time detailing the Internet Explorer's HTML extensions: as Microsoft embraces the Web and discards its own proprietary formats like Blackbird, HTML will become increasingly important to the company. Microsoft will continue to push new extensions that will make the Web both a more interesting and a more fractured place.

We'll examine just how far Microsoft plans to extend HTML later in this chapter when we examine Internet Studio (formerly Blackbird). Microsoft is in the process of converting the former Blackbird design tool to output a brand new, Microsoft-enhanced flavor of HTML. Exactly what HTML tags will be needed to make this transformation a reality wasn't being disclosed by Microsoft as this book was being written. But our look at Microsoft's initial HTML extensions gives us some feel for Microsoft's vision for the future of HTML.

Internet Assistant

Microsoft's strategy is not just to dump some HTML extensions on the market and see if they fly. The company is crafting a tools strategy to ensure that every extension and technology they bring forth for the Web can be easily implemented by Web page designers using simple authoring tools. These tools feature drag-and-drop, style sheets, and, in the case of Internet Studio, full frame-based layout, which gives an author control over every inch and aspect of the design.

Microsoft's first HTML authoring tool was Internet Assistant, which runs as an add-on to Microsoft Word. The 1.0 version of Internet Assistant was a bit buggy, slow, and under-featured. But the Windows 95-based Internet Assistant 2.0 features better performance and support for a slate of new features, including all of Internet Explorer's extensions and a simplified method for creating tables. What started as an afterthought became (with a little Microsoft elbow grease) a tool capable of building very sophisticated, well-designed Web pages. Microsoft Word is the market-leading word processor, so Microsoft's move puts powerful HTML authoring tools into the hands of the average computer user.

Creating Documents

Let's create an HTML page using Internet Assistant 2.0 that includes the HTML tags we discussed above. If you haven't done so already, download Internet Assistant from the Microsoft Web site. You can find it at **http://www.microsoft.com/internet/ products.htm**. Remember, version 2.0 works only with Word for Windows 95 (version 7.0).

To start, pull down the File menu and click on New. You will see a series of icons (see Figure 8-2). Click on HTML.dot, which is the template for building HTML pages. After you've clicked on it, the Microsoft Word toolbar will change, adding icons and menus to help you create HTML pages. Yet the toolbar also retains some of Word's familiar buttons and menus, making it a comfortable environment to work in.

You are now looking at a blank page, so let's begin:

1. First add a head to the document by typing **Sample Internet Assistant Page**. Then highlight the phrase and add the Head1 style using the Style drop-down menu on the toolbar and then center the title using Word's familiar Center icon on the toolbar. The <HEAD> and <CENTER> tags will not show, but in true WYSIWYG fashion, the head will change typestyles and become centered.

2. Next type a few lines of normal formatted text describing the page. Center that text as well. Steps 1 and 2 can be seen in Figure 8-3.

3. Then add a background color. Under the Format menu, click on Backgrounds and Links. Notice the options, which include the ability to choose background color or images, make an image a watermark, and choose text and link color.

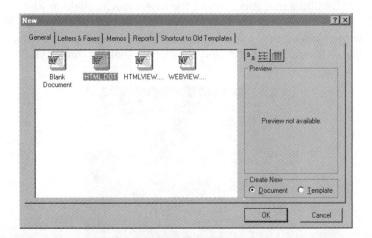

Figure 8-2.   *Setting the HTML template*

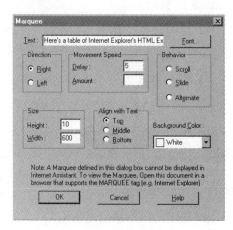

4. We'll also add a simple horizontal rule, found under the Insert menu.

Now, let's dive into some of Internet Assistant's more innovative extensions and capabilities.

5. First, we'll add a background sound. Under the Format menu, we'll click on Background Sounds to call up the Background Sound dialog box (see Figure 8-3). We'll add a .wav file that welcomes users to our page (obviously background sounds are hard to demonstrate in a book, but take our word for it—it sounds great).

6. Next, we'll build a marquee. Under the Insert menu, click on Marquee to bring up the dialog box. All of the marquee options described earlier are available in the Marquee dialog box. We'll input some text, select a background color and size, choose a scrolling speed, and change the font size and style:

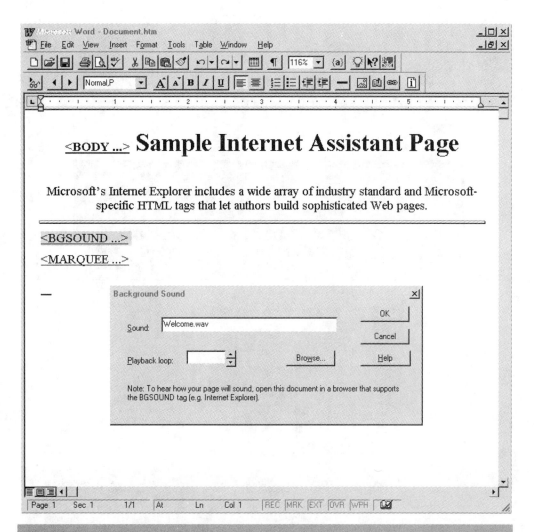

Figure 8-3. *The Background Sounds dialog box*

7. Finally, build a table using the familiar table tools on the Microsoft Word menu. Click on the Table menu and then click on Insert Table. Choose a table of three columns and three rows. Then take advantage of some of the other options on the Table drop-down menu, including Borders (build a border around our table), Align (center the table), and Background Colors (change the color of individual cells, as demonstrated in Figure 8-4).

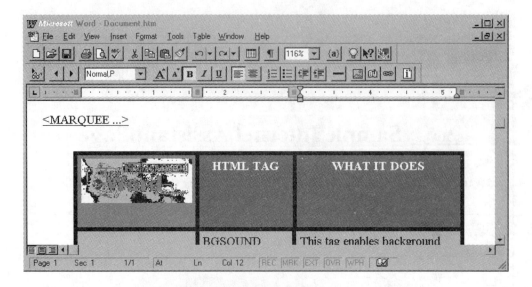

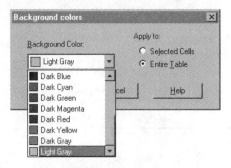

Figure 8-4. *Add background colors to individual table cells using a simple drop-down menu*

8. Within the table cells, input typical text fields as well as an image, in this case, a JPG image of the Internet Assistant logo.

Now let's take a look at our work both in the Internet Assistant edit window (see Figure 8-5) and as it will be displayed in the Internet Explorer browser window (see Figure 8-6).

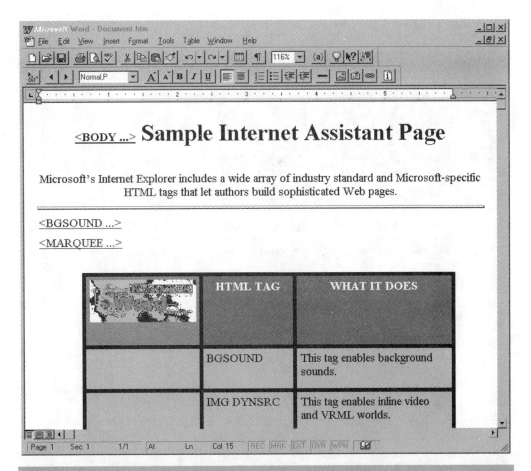

Figure 8-5. *Our project displayed in the Internet Assistant edit window*

While we built this page without writing a single word of HTML, let's close this section on Internet Explorer with a look at the HTML behind the page. Most of the tags can be displayed by browsers other than Microsoft Internet Explorer with no problems, and the ones that don't—most notably MARQUEE—are displayed in a way that doesn't wreck the page.

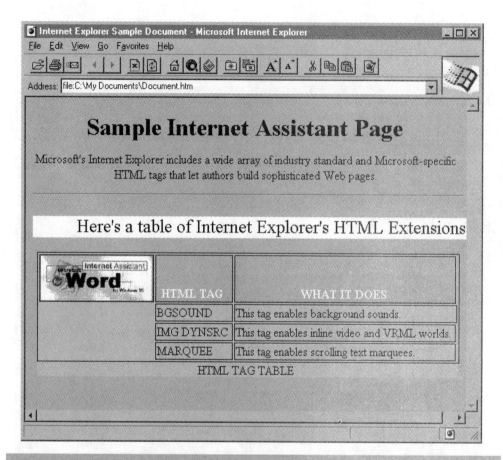

Figure 8-6. *Our project displayed in the Internet Explorer browser window*

And for those readers interested in the raw HTML code for our example, here it is:

```
<HTML>
<HEAD>
<TITLE>Internet Explorer Sample Document</TITLE>
<META NAME="GENERATOR" CONTENT="Internet Assistant for Microsoft
Word 2.0z Beta">
</HEAD>
<BODY BGCOLOR="#808000" TEXT="#000000" LINK="#000080" VLINK="#00ff00">
<H1>
<CENTER>
<FONT SIZE=6 COLOR=#000000>Sample Internet Assistant Page</FONT>
```

```
</CENTER>
</H1>
<P>
<CENTER>
<FONT COLOR=#000000>Microsoft's Internet Explorer includes a wide
array of industry standard and Microsoft-specific HTML tags that
let authors build sophisticated Web pages.</FONT>
</CENTER>
<HR>
<P>
<BGSOUND SRC="Welcome.wav">
<P>
<FONT COLOR="#000080" FACE="Helvetica Regular Bold Italic"
SIZE="5"><MARQUEE BGCOLOR="#ffffff" ALIGN="TOP" DIRECTION="LEFT"
HEIGHT="10" WIDTH="600" SCROLLDELAY="5">Here's a table of Internet
Explorer's HTML Extensions</MARQUEE></FONT>
<P>
<CENTER>
<TABLE BORDER="5"COLOR="#ff0000" ALIGN="CENTER" BGCOLOR="#c0c0c0"
BORDERCOLOR="#000000">
<TR><TD BGCOLOR="#00ff00"><A NAME="UQHTML12"><IMG SRC="ialogo.JPG"></A>
</TD><TH ALIGN="CENTER" VALIGN="BOTTOM" BGCOLOR="#808000">
<CENTER>
<B><FONT COLOR=#FFFFFF>HTML TAG</FONT></B>
</CENTER>
</TH><TD ALIGN="CENTER" VALIGN="BOTTOM" BGCOLOR="#808000">
<CENTER>
<B><FONT COLOR=#FFFFFF>WHAT IT DOES</FONT></B>
</CENTER>
</TD></TR>
<TR><TD BGCOLOR="#c0c0c0"></TD><TD BGCOLOR="#c0c0c0">BGSOU<A
NAME="UQHTML31">ND</A>
/TD><TD BGCOLOR="#c0c0c0" COLSPAN=2>This tag enables background sounds.
</TD></TR>
<TR><TD BGCOLOR="#c0c0c0"></TD><TD BGCOLOR="#c0c0c0">IMG DYNSRC
</TD><TD BGCOLOR="#c0c0c0">This tag enables inline video and VRML
worlds.
</TD></TR>
<TR><TD BGCOLOR="#c0c0c0"></TD><TD BGCOLOR="#c0c0c0">MARQUEE
</TD><TD BGCOLOR="#c0c0c0">This tag enables scrolling text
marquees.
</TD><TD BGCOLOR="#c0c0c0"><CAPTION ALIGN="BOTTOM">
```

```
<CENTER>
<A NAME="UQHTML21">HTML TAG TABLE</A>
</CENTER>
</CAPTION></TR>
</TABLE>
</CENTER>
<P>
</BODY>
</HTML>
```

Other Office Tools

The real power of Internet Assistant is that it is not a separate application at all but simply an extension of Microsoft Word, a program that millions of people use on a daily basis. Microsoft's plan is to make all of its Office applications—Word, Excel, and PowerPoint—fully Internet-enabled. Look for the evolution to take place in two steps:

- All three programs will be able to output HTML as a standard format. Word has this already; PowerPoint (presentation program) and Excel (spreadsheet) will gain this in early 1996.

- Free Web viewers will be made available for all three Office programs. These viewers will initially work as helper applications but will eventually work as plug-ins to the Internet Explorer. This has some interesting implications. For instance, Office viewers may soon make the easiest way to do simple animations—including screen swipes, animated text, and more—over the Internet.

The first viewer to become available was for Microsoft Word. Word Viewer 7.1 gives users the flexibility to view page layout, zoom, outline, headers/footers, footnotes, and annotations (see Figure 8-7). It also allows users to follow hyperlinks embedded within Word documents, a new Word capability that is made possible via Internet Assistant. This capability allows individuals—most likely on internal corporate networks rather than on the Internet—to create "Webs" of interlinked Word documents.

The Office viewers are just the start. Microsoft promises that Internet capabilities will be a major theme of the next full release of Microsoft Office. Expect a fully integrated environment where applications can both seamlessly output Web-ready content as well as reach out over the Net to pull down information that can be fed into Microsoft word processors, spreadsheets, and presentation programs.

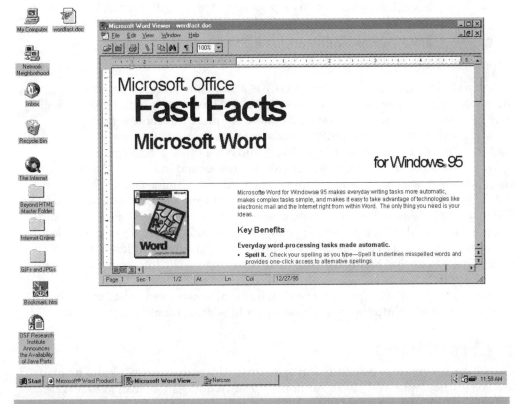

Figure 8-7. *Here's the Microsoft Word Viewer working as a helper application to a Web browser*

Microsoft's FrontPage

The newest addition to Microsoft's Office family is FrontPage, a Web site editor and management tool. FrontPage, which was already available in version 1.0 before Microsoft bought the product from Vermeer Technologies, is a very comprehensive tool, yet it is designed to make Web publishing as simple as possible. The client-server platform consists of:

■ FrontPage Editor, a WYSIWYG HTML editor for creating Web pages

■ FrontPage Explorer, a tool for creating, viewing, and maintaining Web sites

■ To-Do List, a tool that lets Webmasters keep track of what needs to be done on a site, and distribute chores among a variety of people

■ WebBots, drop-in bits of code that enable advanced features like threaded discussion groups without the need for programming

- Wizards and templates, which help speed the process of creating Web sites by providing pre-built blueprints for individual HTML pages

- Personal Web server, a fully-functioning Web server, plus separate server extensions to make FrontPage work with other Web servers

As you can see, FrontPage, version 1.0, has a lot to offer. It received a lot of attention when Vermeer originally rolled it out, and having Microsoft behind it will only help sales and future developments (more on future directions later).

Microsoft plans to offer FrontPage from its Office Products Group—which also markets Microsoft Word, PowerPoint, Excel, and other office productivity software—and position it as a tool to enable businesses and individuals to author Web sites. Microsoft says that Internet Studio, which we will examine later in this chapter, will be positioned as a high-end tool for the development of larger, more sophisticated Web sites. To be honest, it is hard to imagine how the two products—FrontPage and Internet Studio—will differ in the long-run. They are both designed to make it easy for users to build and maintain rich Web sites. Indeed, the major difference in the early days may be that FrontPage exists and is shipping while Internet Studio is still being invented.

Microsoft FrontPage is priced at $695. A free trial version was available when this book was written at **http://www.microsoft.com/MSOffice/FrontPage/fs_fp.htm**.

Using FrontPage

One of the key concepts behind FrontPage is that Web authors are not building just Web pages, but entire Web sites. "Authoring" a site requires more than just an HTML editor. You need site management tools that let you visualize your site as it grows. Most Webmasters today sketch site blueprints out on paper; FrontPage gives you the tools to visualize your site onscreen and watch it grow as you add pages to it. This capability not only lets you build your site, but it helps you maintain and update it as time goes by.

To demonstrate the power of FrontPage, we will build a hypothetical site for this book. We won't dwell on the installation issues surrounding FrontPage—suffice it to say that the product runs on Windows machines only and requires a healthy amount of RAM (16 megabytes minimum for good performance) plus a TCP/IP stack to operate. We also won't spend much time here discussing how to use the Personal Web server or the server extensions. Instead, we'll focus mainly on authoring issues. But enough preliminaries, let's dive in.

FrontPage Explorer

The place to start with FrontPage is with the Explorer, which lets us view and administer a web site. FrontPage Explorer includes three views:

1. Outline View shows a hierarchical view that can be expanded or collapsed to display a full outline of your Web site. In Outline View, the home page appears at the top of the view and has an icon of a house beside it. When the view is collapsed, any page with a link to another page displays a plus sign next to it and a red arrow on the page icon.

2. Link View displays a graphical representation of the site that lets you visualize the links between pages. In Link View, pages are displayed as page icons, with lines indicating the links between Web pages. The selected page or file in Link View sits at the center of the screen, and all of its links are displayed. You can change which page is at the center of the screen by clicking on an icon. In this way, you can instantly view your Web site from any vantage point.

3. Summary View provides information about the pages and files that make up a Web site, including the file's name, size, type, modified date, and page URL.

The FrontPage Explorer, with Outline and Link Views showing, can be seen in Figure 8-8.

Rather than build on an existing Web as shown in Figure 8-8, let's start a new one from scratch. To do so, click on File/New Web from the Front Page Explorer menu.

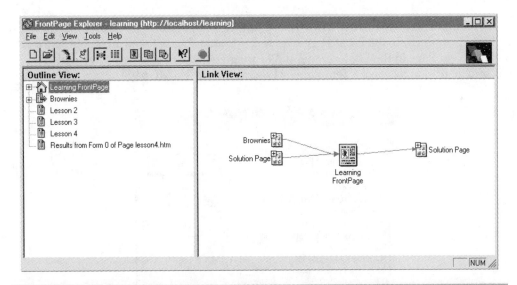

Figure 8-8.   *The FrontPage Explorer*

That calls up the New Web dialog box that will let us use a site template (for instance, Corporate Presence Wizard) or start a new project (Empty Web) as shown here.

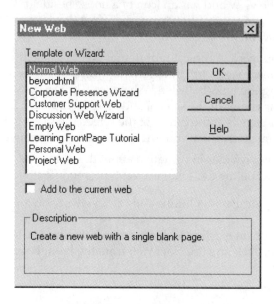

For the purposes of this exercise, choose Empty Web. Since we are building a new Web site from scratch, the Front Page Explorer is blank. To create our first page, click on File/New Page in the Explorer menu. We are greeted with the New Page dialog box and an option to select a Template or Wizard for our HTML page.

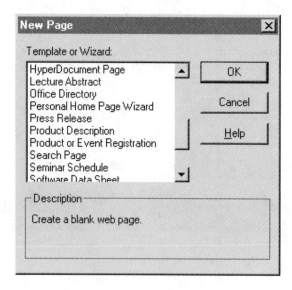

Some of the other choices in the New Page dialog box include Employee Directory, Feedback Form, Frequently Asked Questions, Personal Home Page Wizard and more than two dozen more. The Wizards make it easy to build a page, setting in place some basic HTML tags and features upon which you can build a page. We'll examine Wizards and Bots in more detail later, but for now, choose Normal Page, which will give us a blank slate to work from. The Explorer, with our new page, looks like this:

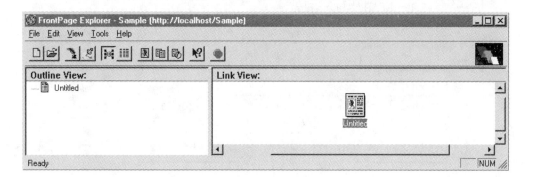

Now that we have created our first page in the Explorer, we can begin editing the page in FrontPage Editor. To do this, in Link View, simply double-click on the icon of the page. This launches FrontPage Editor. You can also use FrontPage Editor as a standalone tool—without Explorer—to create and save individual Web pages.

FrontPage Editor

FrontPage Editor is a very strong WYSIWYG HTML editor. It lets you work as you would in a word processor, using toolbars and drop menus, to change the style of text, headings and other elements on a page. All of the changes are tagged in HTML, but you don't have to write any of the tags yourself. In addition to basic formatting, FrontPage lets you create forms, threaded discussion groups, live image-maps and other advanced features directly without doing any coding or programming at all.

Now that we've created the first page for our sample Web site in FrontPage Explorer and fired-up FrontPage Editor, our next step will be to name the page and give it some basic settings. To do this, click on Edit/Page Settings in the FrontPage Editor menu. This calls up the Page Settings dialog box, as shown in Figure 8-9. Here, we can set a background image or color for our page, as well as customize the color of our text and links. Turn ahead to Figure 8-10 if you want to see the image and text options we have chosen.

Before we build the body of our page, let's take a brief look at the four toolbars used in the FrontPage Editor. This introduction will give you a good idea of what FrontPage is capable of as a page editor.

Page Settings ✕

Page title:

Home Page

URL:

File: C:\VERMEER\BIN\home.htm

Customize Appearance

☑ Background Image
   Source:
   C:\WINDOWS\Desktop\GIFs and JPGs\c   Browse...   Properties...

☐ Use Custom Background Color   ☑ Use Custom Link Color
   Choose...   Choose...

☑ Use Custom Text Color   ☑ Use Custom Visited Link Color
   Choose...   Choose...

Base URL (optional):

OK   Cancel   Help

Figure 8-9. *The Page Settings dialog box*

The Standard toolbar, shown below, includes the basic buttons for creating and saving pages; cutting and pasting text and images; inserting hot-links; and toggling between FrontPage Editor and the Explorer and To-Do Lists.

The Image toolbar includes simple drawing tools for creating image-maps in WYSIWYG fashion.

The Format toolbar is for creating bold, italic and underlined text; building bullet and numbered lists; and increasing and decreasing indents.

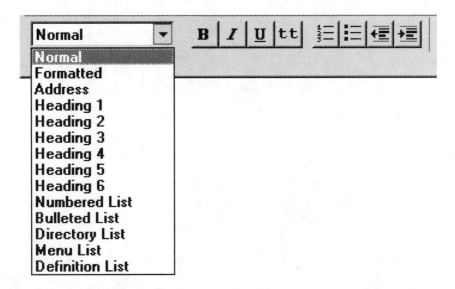

The Forms toolbar lets you add a variety of forms, menus and buttons to a Web page.

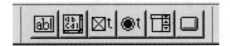

Now, let's build a basic page in a few steps:

1. First, we'll add a header to the page, and center it. To do so, simply type the text "Beyond HTML: Weaving a New Web" directly in the FrontPage Editor window. Then highlight the text and apply the Head1 style to the text. We'll follow that by adding a horizontal line. Click on Insert/Horizontal Line from the Editor menu.

2. Next, we'll add the text for what will eventually become links to other pages on our site, for instance, "Adobe Acrobat," "Netscape Navigator," and "Microsoft Internet Platform."

   Then, we'll turn the text references into hotlinks. To do so, individually highlight each of the text elements, such as "Adobe Acrobat," and click on the

Link button on the Standard toolbar. Clicking on the button calls up the Create Link dialog box shown below, which lets us fill in the target URL or Web page for our hotlink.

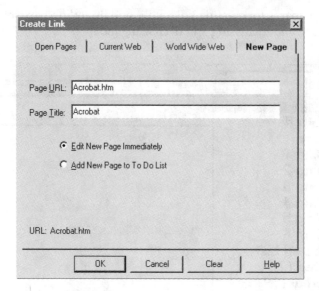

Next, click on the New Page tab to send each of these hotlinks to other pages on our site. By clicking on New Page, we are creating new pages within FrontPage Explorer at the same time as we create the links. In addition, as we create the pages, we can either edit them immediately or add them to the To Do List. We'll add two of our pages to the To Do List for further editing later.

3. To keep things simple, let's end our page here. Press the Save button to store the work we have generated so far.

It might not seem like much, but FrontPage has actually done a lot of work, much of it behind the scenes. The HTML page we created can be seen in Figure 8-10.

As we were building our pages and links in the FrontPage Editor, FrontPage Explorer was busy keeping the view of our expanded site up-to-date. Remember, that each time we created a link, we sent that link to a new page on our Web site. So while our site started with a single page, it is now made up of four pages—the "home" page plus three pages that are linked to that page. You can see the results of this in Figure 8-11.

Finally, remember we decided to send two of the new pages directly to the To Do List so we could assign the work later. The To Do List is automatically updated to reflect these additions in Figure 8-12.

As you can see, FrontPage is more about site authoring than page authoring. As we build new pages, the graphical view of our site is continually updated, ensuring

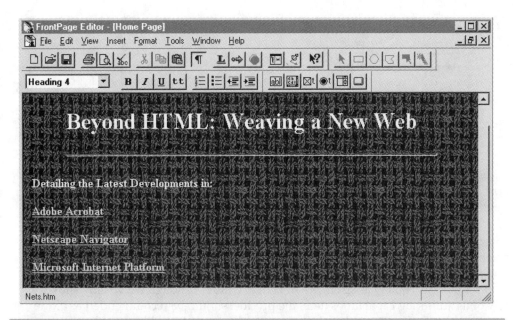

Figure 8-10. *Our sample page in FrontPage Editor*

that we don't lose track of how the site is growing. We can also use FrontPage Explorer to keep the links on our pages fresh, and to update and maintain content on individual pages. At the same time, we can use the To Do List to schedule the ongoing

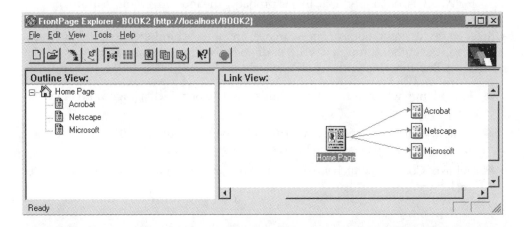

Figure 8-11. *FrontPage Explorer keeps our graphical view up-to-date*

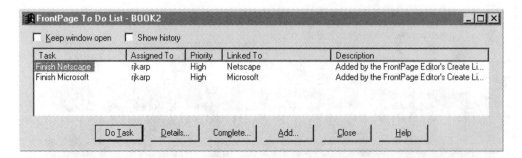

Figure 8-12.   *The To Do List updates our work-list*

construction and maintenance of our site. Since FrontPage is a client-server tool, we can have client machines spread out across a building or a country to share the To Do List—and thus the work—in building and maintaining our site.

FrontPage is equally as strong as an HTML editor. Although we've only shown a few of its authoring capabilities here, the product should be recommended as a true WYSIWYG HTML editor, able to handle not only simple tasks like font changes but also links, forms, and more in very simple template-based manner.

Forms and WebBots

One of FrontPage's most powerful capabilities is its ability to add forms and simple Common Gateway Interface scripts to a Web site without requiring any programming on the part of the author. We discussed forms briefly when we introduced the Forms toolbar. We'll create a form in this section.

As for WebBots, or simply Bots, this is probably the most ingenious feature of FrontPage. With Bots, all of the complex scripting and coding to create features, such as threaded discussion groups or site-searches, are done behind the scenes. FrontPage simply leads the author through a series of dialog boxes to customize the Bot. A partial listing of the Bots that ship with FrontPage include:

- TimeStamp, which automatically adds the date on which a page was created to the page at run-time.

- Search, which creates a search form on the page. At runtime, the form lets users search for pages in the Web containing specified text.

- Table of Contents, which creates a table of contents for a Web site, with links to each page.

- Discussion, which collects information from a form, formats it into HTML and adds the page to a table of contents.

- Registration, which allows users to register for a service on your server.

To demonstrate how easy it is to work with Forms and Bots, we'll add a simple feedback form to our sample site. Such a form consists of two main elements, an HTML form and a Common Gateway Interface (CGI) script running on the server. FrontPage will create this feature in a few simple steps:

1. First, we'll add the following text to our HTML page to describe this feature to our visitors:

   Please send your comments and suggestions:

2. To give our visitors plenty of space to comment, we'll add a scrolling text box to the page. We can do this by clicking on the Scrolling Text Box button on the Forms toolbar, or by clicking Insert/Form Field/Scrolling Text Box on the FrontPage Editor menu.

3. When we click on OK to create the box, we'll see the Scrolling Text Box Properties dialog box, as shown here.

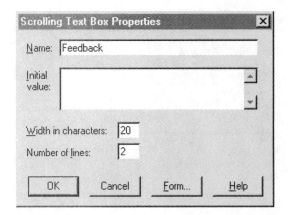

This is where we define the function of the Scrolling Text Box. To give the box a Name, type **Feedback**.

4. Click on the Form... button to call up the Form Properties dialog box. Click on Form Handler and choose Save Results Bot. This will provide the script necessary to retrieve and store user-provided feedback on our Web server.

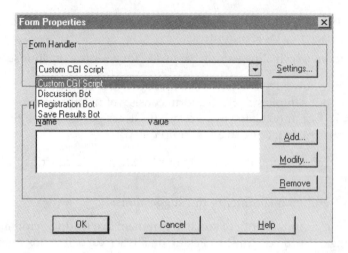

5. Next, let's configure the Save Results Bot to meet our needs. The Settings for Saving Results of Form dialog box allows us to choose a File name (or "File for results" on the dialog box), where the feedback information will be stored and to add the Time, Date, User name and Browser type to our server log file, as shown here.

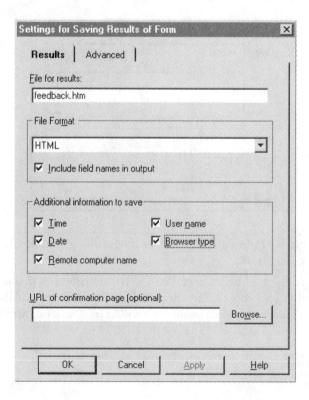

6. Click on OK to close the dialog box and we're done. We've created a feedback form and script. The final step is to create a push button on our HTML page that users can click on to submit their comments. We can do this using the Forms toolbar, which has an icon for creating Push Buttons. Click on the icon and we are greeted with a dialog box that asks us to give the button a name and a value, which we should enter as "Submit Feedback" (see the button in Figure 8-13).

That's it; the job is done. FrontPage's Bots make it very easy to add advanced functionality to a Web site with no scripting or coding required at all. The Feedback form we created, running on our page in a Netscape browser, is shown in Figure 8-13. If this were a live page, users could enter a comment into the Scrolling Text Box, click on the Submit Feedback button and the comments would be stored for us in a file on our Web server.

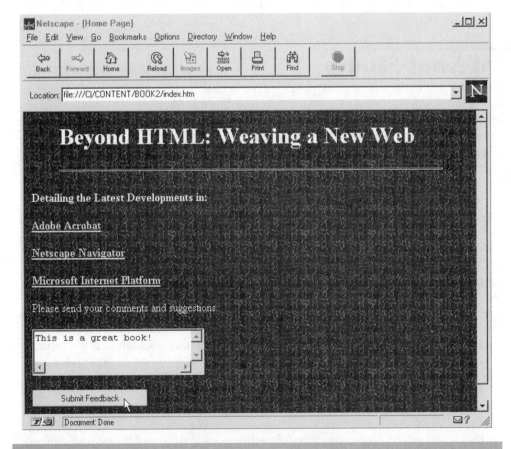

Figure 8-13.   *The final page, Bot and all*

Where FrontPage is headed

Microsoft picked up a leading-edge Web tool when it acquired FrontPage. Their decision to place FrontPage in the Office Products Group seems peculiar, though the company says it is a good tool to build department-level Web sites within companies. FrontPage could eventually have much broader appeal than that, although the initial price ($695) is very high for most mainstream tastes. It will be interesting to see how Microsoft manages the ongoing development of both FrontPage and Internet Studio—the two products really do seem to be similar in many ways.

As for FrontPage itself, Microsoft's next goal is to add support for more advanced HTML tags, including tables and possibly frames. Also important is support for scripting languages such as Microsoft's Visual Basic Script, Netscape's JavaScript and Sun's Java. The Vermeer team and their new bosses at Microsoft promise that support for these new capabilities will be handled using WebBots, which as we've seen, enable the addition of very sophisticated features to a Web site with very little programming knowledge required.

Internet Studio

The wild card in Microsoft's Internet plans is Internet Studio, formerly known as Blackbird. The renaming and repositioning took place at Microsoft's highly publicized Internet briefing last December, and the change in strategy seemingly occurred overnight. Just weeks before, Microsoft was trumpeting the imminent arrival of proprietary Blackbird viewers and titles designed for the Web. The next moment, they were outlining plans to abandon Blackbird's proprietary Blackbird Data Format (BDF) and embracing HTML.

Why the change of heart? Content developers, as much as they liked Blackbird's ease of use and powerful toolset, were unwilling to commit to a platform on the Web that many users would be unable to view. Already struggling with different flavors of HTML, another completely new file format for the Web was less than welcome. And with the Microsoft Network (MSN) itself moving completely to HTML form and opening up to non-MSN subscribers, Microsoft clearly felt it was fighting a losing battle with Blackbird's proprietary data formats. By reworking Blackbird to output an extended version of HTML, Microsoft can ensure that even those Web surfers who don't have an Internet Studio-enabled HTML browser will still be able to see the page. It will only be laid out with a little less flash—a not unfamiliar situation in the world of HTML, where browsers that don't support tables, backgrounds, or other advanced tags are still able to view Web content.

Indeed, the greatest irony is that for all its hype, most Webmasters won't even get to see what Blackbird was supposed to be. Well, let's fix that. What follows is a very brief tour of Blackbird, based on a beta version we reviewed.

Given that Microsoft promises that the editing environment of Internet Studio will remain the same—it will simply output HTML instead of proprietary Blackbird titles—you will not only get a sneak peak of what Blackbird looked like, you'll be able to judge for yourself whether the Internet Studio, when it is ultimately released, falls short or meets the same standards as Blackbird.

Inside Blackbird

Blackbird consisted of several different pieces, most of which should remain in about the same form as part of Internet Studio. A Project Editor modeled on Windows 95's Explorer organized titles and files:

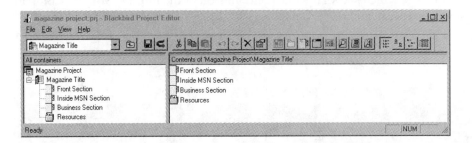

A separate Page Editor provided the working space for building new titles. If you have used a WYSIWYG HTML editor, the Page Editor, shown in Figure 8-14, was somewhat similar, but it offered an even greater level of control. Every effect can be delivered via a menu or simple drag-and-drop operation, and the editor features full frame-based layout, meaning you have precise control over where every element goes on the page.

Blackbird worked through the use of controls—the OCXs, or OLE Controls, we mentioned earlier—which were used to add pictures, sound, text, and other features

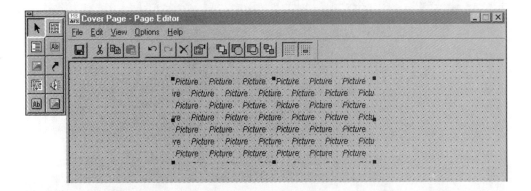

Figure 8-14. *Blackbird page editor*

to a title. Each control has a set of properties that can be changed and customized. With text, for instance, you can change font or color.

A group of prepackaged controls were included with Blackbird and were accessible via the Toolbox. New controls could be built or acquired by a Blackbird user and added to the Toolbox, including controls that added third-party tools such Adobe Acrobat or Macromedia Director files to the Blackbird mix.

Blackbird enabled the creation of content that looked more like a CD-ROM title than a Web page. Content was viewed in a separate Blackbird viewer. As an example, see Figure 8-15, which shows the Blackbird version of the Internet Volcano Company site shown earlier in an HTML version.

Figure 8-15.   *A Blackbird title*

What to Expect of Internet Studio

Much of what Blackbird was able to do will evolve very easily into the new Internet Studio. Indeed, even as Microsoft moves away from its proprietary formats and embraces HTML, the product managers in charge of Internet Studio claim that the tool will retain all its former features and ease of use. As this book was being written, Microsoft was hard at work on the first beta release of the retooled Internet Studio. Official descriptions of Internet Studio from Microsoft's Web site describes Internet Studio as having many of the features we saw earlier with Blackbird:

- The creation of multimedia Web pages incorporating hypertext documents, rich graphics, real-time sound, and animations, all within a drag-and-drop edit environment with no need for any programming or HTML coding.

- It can include content from any OLE-enabled application, including Internet Assistant for Word, which will be bundled with it. Also, it is fully extensible via OLE Controls and a published Software Developer Kit. Relationships with software tool vendors Adobe (PDF), Macromedia (Director and Shockwave), and Caligari (VRML) have already been announced.

- Support for open HTML extensions that Microsoft plans to propose to the Internet Engineering Task Force. Microsoft will also provide a free viewer application that will let other existing browsers view the Internet Studio extensions. For browsers that do not have this viewer, users will still be able to view the HTML content in a less highly stylized format.

- Native support for scripting languages including Visual Basic, VB Script, and C++. Microsoft has also agreed to license Sun's Java and JavaScript technologies, so support for those languages can also be expected. Any scripting language can be supported via a custom OLE control.

- Built-in support for electronic forms and secure transactions: Secure Sockets Layer (SSL) and Private Communications Technology (PCT) for secure communications; Secure Transaction Technology (STT) for financial transactions.

There's the promise. We'll see how well Microsoft delivers. The software giant is somewhat vague on the delivery date for Internet Studio; all it will say is that Version 1.0 of Internet Studio for publishing on the World Wide Web will be released sometime in 1996, most likely by midyear. Pricing and packaging also had not been set at press time.

What's Next: Internet Add-On and More

Internet Explorer, Internet Assistant, and Internet Studio are important steps on the way to Microsoft's ultimate goal: the evolution of Windows 95 into a fully integrated Internet platform. The time frame for this goal is sooner than you might think (mid-1996). By that time, Microsoft promises it will ship what for now it is calling an Internet Add-on to Windows 95. These technologies will also be a standard part of the next release of the Windows platform. They include:

- *WebView*   This will let Windows 95 users choose to view the contents of their hard drive as HTML documents. The implications are interesting. Instead of drilling down folders and subfolders, contents can be displayed as a hypertext Web page. It will even be possible to add live applications to the WebView using OLE Controls.

- *A single Explorer for Windows PCs and the Internet*   While Microsoft will continue to ship a stand-alone browser, the Internet Add-on will integrate the Internet Explorer and the Explorer file finder in Windows 95. The result is that users will have an integrated interface to all information, whether it is on their hard drive or on the Web.

- *Active pages via OLE Controls*   The Internet Add-on will add support for OCXs to the Internet Explorer browser, enabling Web developers to add active content to their Web pages.

- *VB Script*   The Internet Add-on will provide the first run-time engine for VB Script, Microsoft's new scripting language especially designed for the Web (more on that below).

- *Java and JavaScript support*   The Internet Add-on will also likely have run-time support for Java and JavaScript, which Microsoft announced its intention to license.

- *Internet Studio HTML extensions*   The release will also likely support the HTML extensions that will make Internet Studio Web-enabled.

- *PC collaboration/sharing over the Internet*   The Internet Explorer will turn into a basic groupware tool, running on Web protocols. Users will be able to share screens and applications—such as working together on a spreadsheet or word processing document—over the Internet. In addition, Microsoft will offer support for Internet telephony.

VB Script: What Is It?

The Microsoft Internet client platform is a very powerful, integrated set of technologies. One capability we haven't discussed yet in much detail—but which is extremely important for Web developers—is VB (Visual Basic) Script, Microsoft's answer to Sun and Netscape's JavaScript.

As this book was being written, VB Script was still in the early design stages at Microsoft. The company describes it as a small, cross-platform, lightweight scripting language that, among other uses, will be used for inline scripting of HTML pages. It can also be used for simple server-side scripting as well. The language is a subset of the popular Visual Basic for Applications programming environment. Whereas JavaScript uses the syntax of Java as its base, VB Script represents a dialect of Visual Basic.

VB Script will be licensed to application and browser vendors at no cost. Microsoft is also proposing VB Script as an Internet standard scripting language.

Microsoft envisions VB Script being used to link and automate objects in Web pages, including OLE objects and applets written in Java. It can also be used to do client-side information processing, such as validating forms data or performing small client-side calculations.

A key concern for VB Script will be security. Microsoft will address these concerns in two ways. First, it will offer a restricted run-time engine for VB Script that will allow the downloaded code to do only a limited number of things on your machine. This "sandbox" approach will keep the VB Script code from causing any harm to your system. Second, Microsoft is working on a digital signature mechanism that will let your machine know that downloaded code has not been tampered with. Even with these precautions, security will continue to be a major concern for users downloading OCXs and VB Script applets.

VB Script Sneak Preview

The language itself is a strict subset of Visual Basic for Applications, albeit significantly scaled back for simplicity's sake. As this book was being written, an early version of the basic syntax of VB Script was released as a trial balloon. The evolution of VB Script can be charted on Microsoft's Developer page (**http://www.microsoft.com/devonly/**).

VB Script will let Web developers write Visual Basic code that lives and works within an HTML document. For page designers, using VB Script is a simple matter of writing VB Script code in ASCII text from right within an HTML document. There is no need to compile the code in advance, as we did with Java. VB Script is interpreted on download. On the end user side, of course, the Web browser must include support for VB Script as well as the ability to integrate scripting with controls or applets embedded in the HTML stream.

As VB Script was being finalized, Microsoft provided several examples of how it might be used on a Web page. Here's a simple calculation script. Note the basic syntax and how it fits within an HTML page:

```
<Script>
  Sub Command_click
    Dim FlowerCount
    For x = 1 to 10
      FlowerCount = FlowerCount + 2
    Next
    MyHTMLListBox.Text = FlowerCount
  End Sub
</Script>
```

How does this code work? When the Web browser hits the <Script> tag, it calls the VB Script interpreter to compile and run the code. In this case, the code is tied to the click event on a button named "Command," with the output written in a text box called "MyHTMLListBox".

Note ▶ *Microsoft says the <Script> tag is a proposed name, pending approval from Web standard bodies.*

Another important use of VB Script will be to set properties and methods on OLE Controls and Java applets that are called within an HTML page. For example, the VB Script code for this might look like:

```
<Insert>
  clsid = {"insert class ID here"}
  OLEcontrol.forecolor = true
  OLEcontrol.animate
  javaapplet.forecolor = olecontrol.forecolor
<\Insert>
```

Again, this is more an example of the possible syntax of VB Script than a real working bit of code. But it does give some idea of how VB Script could be used to feed attributes to Web applets. The <Insert> tag, like the <Script> tag before it, is a proposed tag, pending standards approval. It will be interesting to see how <Insert> competes with Netscape's <Embed> tag, which proposes to do much the same thing.

TECH
RESOURCES

System Requirements
The following information is valid as of January, 1996.

INTERNET EXPLORER 2.0   Runs on Windows 95, NT, 3.1, and Mac OS.

INTERNET ASSISTANT ADD-ON   Works with Microsoft Word, both Windows 95 and latest Macintosh versions.

MICROSOFT FRONTPAGE   Runs on Windows-based platforms.

Where to Find More Information about Microsoft's Internet Platform

MICROSOFT'S NET-RELATED PAGES
Internet Resource Center: **http://www.microsoft.com/internet/irc.htm**
Internet Development Toolbox: **http://www.microsoft.com/intdev/default.htm**
Download Internet tools: **http://www.microsoft.com/intdev/download.htm**
Internet Explorer: **http://www.microsoft.com/windows/ie/ieexplorer.htm**
Internet Studio: **http://www.microsoft.com/istudio**

Summary

Don't count Microsoft out. That is probably the best summary that we can give of this chapter. Though a latecomer to the Web, Microsoft has the installed base of user and ability to Internet-enable all of its software in a way that will no doubt make it a major player on the Web.

For Webmasters and developers, a few key points stand out. Windows 95 (and future versions of the operating system) will gain even greater integrated support for the Internet, ensuring an ever-growing base of potential users. Internet Explorer will likely grow to be a very important platform supporting enhanced HTML, live software applications—including OLE Controls as well as Java applets—and a variety of scripting languages. Internet Studio holds great potential as a Web design tool, though it remains to be seen if Microsoft can execute its bold strategy of replacing its proprietary Blackbird data formats with a new flavor of HTML.

Bill Gates said it best himself: "Microsoft is hard-core about the Internet." That alone should be enough for Webmasters to stand up and take notice.

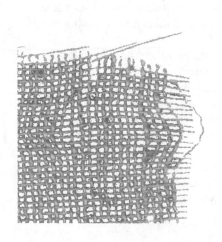

Chapter Nine

The Netscape Internet OS

The story of Netscape's rise to fame, fortune, and (at least for now) Internet dominance is by now a familiar one. Called upon by ex-Silicon Graphics chief Jim Clark to build a better browser, Mosaic creator Marc Andreessen and a team of his former University of Illinois colleagues set up shop in Silicon Valley. In a few a short months, they emerged with the first beta of a speedy new Web browser and a plan to give it away for free until it became the World Wide Web standard. It's always instructive to remember that the birth of Netscape came only in the spring of 1994—it seems a world ago but is really just the blink of an eye.

Jump to 1995: Netscape is working hard to stay out in front as the Web speeds to new heights, fueled in large part by Netscape extensions to hypertext markup language (HTML) that bring new life and vitality to Web page layouts. What would Netscape's next step be?

The answer came with Navigator 2.0, which Netscape claimed was less a traditional Web browser and more an entirely new platform for live, online applications. No longer would the Web be a static repository of hyperlinked text and graphics. Instead, we would enter an era of live applications, unlimited media types, and instant interactivity. Even now, as Netscape delivers on its promises, it is hard to even remember what radical concepts these were when they first appeared: at the time, Sun's Java programming language had been announced but was still not much more than a vague notion among Internet watchers—with Netscape as the only licensee. Helper applications were proliferating, but as they became more common they were becoming unwieldy to deal with. And many leading Web developers began to feel that their future on the Web—if they chose to accept it—would be in hacking Perl code to make server-side Common Gateway Interface (CGI) scripts run a little faster, do a little more.

Netscape Navigator 2.0 helped change all that. It may not be the only platform supporting interactivity and real-time applications today, but it was the first—and remains the most widely used. In addition to such features as integrated e-mail and newsgroup access, encryption, and digital signatures, 2.0 included the first support for new Web design features that are becoming a standard part of the Web:

- *Frames*   Lauded by some, laughed at by others, frames nonetheless offer savvy Web designers an interesting new way to organize their pages. Used right, frames could usher in a completely new look for Web user interfaces.

- *Java support*   Even as 1996 dawned, Netscape Navigator 2.0 was the only option for most users wanting to run the most up-to-date Java applets. Sun introduced Java, but Netscape, with its huge embedded base of loyal users, popularized it and helped make it an industry standard.

- *JavaScript*   First called the Netscape Scripting Language, then LiveScript, and ultimately JavaScript, this simple scripting environment promises to bring a base level of client-side interactivity into the hands of nonprogrammers. In the long run, it may also be the standard way to deal with and meld together Java applets, inline plug-ins, and HTML.

■   *Plug-in architecture*   Again, other vendors are promising plug-ins, but Netscape delivered them first. Almost immediately, the Web became a more interesting place, as plug-ins enabled formerly exotic media formats such as Macromedia's Director, Adobe's Acrobat, the Virtual Reality Modeling Language, and much more to be displayed as inline features right within an HTML page.

■   *Integrated editing*   With Navigator 2.0, not only can you view Web pages, but you can create them as well. Navigator Gold 2.0, an expanded version of the standard Netscape browser, offers a fully integrated WYSIWYG HTML editor that instantly turns every Web surfer into a content provider.

In this chapter, we'll take an in-depth, hands-on look at each of these elements to see whether Netscape Navigator 2.0 lives up to its advance billing. We'll also catch an inside peak, in our "Inside Spin" feature, at where Netscape is heading next—as usual, the next generation of Netscape software will be upon you before you realize it.

The Netscape Difference

As Netscape introduces generation after generation of new Web software, it has become simultaneously loved and loathed. Loved, because it has driven the Web to new, more graphically interesting heights. Background images, more flexible page layouts, tables, and many more elements were first introduced to mainstream Web audiences via Netscape Navigator.

The problem with Netscape extensions is that—initially, at least—they were only supported by the Navigator browser. That means that if a Web page designer isn't careful with his or her work, a page optimized for Netscape Navigator may look ugly or break down altogether in other browsers. The good news is that most browser vendors are adopting HTML 3.0 and Netscape extensions in their latest releases, ensuring a growing common denominator of advanced HTML features.

But with Navigator 2.0, Netscape is jumping out ahead again. There will no doubt be a good six-month lag between the time that Netscape releases some of the 2.0 features until the rest of the browser world catches up. The good news is that Netscape is becoming better at introducing ways to keep your pages from breaking down when viewed with non-Netscape browsers. But be careful before you swallow the latest Netscape features hook, line, and sinker: at times, it's best to design for the masses rather than the leading edge, no matter how cool it may make your site look.

Frames

The most drastic pure design feature introduced in Navigator 2.0 is undoubtedly frames. This is less an incremental extension to HTML than an entirely new direction for Web page layout. Used properly, frames can be an interesting addition to a Web site's user interface. Yet frames can be tricky as well, at times leading users to make page jumps that don't quite mirror the usual navigation techniques of Web browsers. And for now, frames work only with the Netscape browser, although other vendors—including Microsoft with its Internet Explorer—have said they will pick them up. Netscape has proposed the frames feature to Web standards bodies for consideration.

What are frames, and how do they work? Frames enable a Web page designer to break up the Navigator browser window into distinct segments. Each frame can have its own scroll bar—moving horizontally or vertically—as well as its own Uniform Resource Locator (URL). Hotlinks in a framed document can update and control not just the contents of their own frames but the contents of other frames as well. For example, imagine a page that contains a main frame and a smaller frame featuring a navigation bar. Click on a hotlink in the navigation frame and the new page is called upon in the main frame, while the navigation frame stays unchanged.

The result can be improved navigation and greater flexibility in Web page design. Frames are a good way to provide visitors to your site a consistent view of elements such as a table of contents, display panel, or navigation bar. They can also let users scroll through multiple sites simultaneously or enable them to submit a database query in one frame and have the results delivered back to another frame. That can reduce the need to jump back and forth from page to page—visitors can do all their work on a single split window.

A good use of frames can be found in Figure 9-1, a page on the HotWired site. The browser window is broken up into three segments:

- The top frame contains a static headline for the page. Called a *ledge,* this design feature of frames can run either horizontally or vertically on a page.

- A navigation frame running down the left side of the window. This frame, too, stays static and gives the visitor easy access to navigation buttons to flip through several pages of related content.

- A main frame that displays the site's content. Click on a different navigation icon in the frame on the left, and a new page is shot into the main frame window. A scroll bar lets the page extend beyond the main browser window.

In their early days, frames often seemed like an extravagance: when you ran into them on the Web, they seemed nice but often didn't add enough to the page to justify their use. That will change as Web page designers become more practiced in their use of frames. Also, as the use of client-side processing accelerates, frames will be a good way to organize a site, letting a user make an input into one frame and instantly returning outputs in another frame in the same browser window.

Working with Frames

Frames are generated by a pair of new HTML tags: FRAMESET and FRAME.

Figure 9-1.   *Use of Netscape frames on the HotWired site*

The tag that enables frames and starts off and ends each frame-enabled page is FRAMESET. In an HTML page, the FRAMESET tag replaces the usual BODY tag, telling the browser that the browser window will be broken up into several frames.

Using the FRAMESET Tag

Let's take a closer look at the FRAMESET tag. FRAMESET declares the width and height of the frames in a browser window. The tag itself has two attributes: row list (ROWS) and column list (COLS). Each list consists of the values representing the dimensions of the frames we want to set, separated by a comma. The attributes—which should be contained in quotes—can be real numbers, which give the frames a specific width or height in the browser window, or you can give them the value *, which means the size of the frame will be determined as a function of the overall browser window's total size. A single '*' character is a "relative-sized" frame and is interpreted as a request to give the frame all remaining space. If multiple relative-sized frames exist, the space is divided evenly among them.

For instance, the following tag will set two vertical frames in the browser window:

```
<FRAMESET COLS="100,*">
```

The first frame will be 100 pixels in width; the frame to the right will vary in size depending on the overall size of the browser window (see Figure 9-2). The size of the second frame will get larger or smaller depending on how large the user sets the browser window.

 *Frame column and row values can be absolute pixel values (e.g., 100), percentage values between 1 and 100 (e.g., 60%), or relative scaling values (in addition to using *, we can assign a number, such as 2*, which means the frame would get two-thirds of the available browser window).*

Netscape offers several additional optional attributes for the FRAMESET tag:

- **MARGINWIDTH="value" and MARGINHEIGHT="value"** This attribute lets the page author set frame margins in pixels.
- **SCROLLING="yes | no | auto"** This attribute tells whether a frame should have a scroll bar or not. Auto can be used to let the browser decide whether a scroll bar is needed, for instance if text extends beyond the frame window.

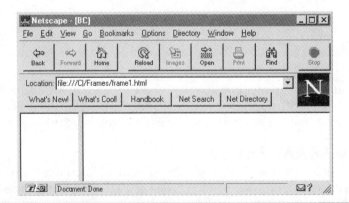

Figure 9-2. *An example of the FRAMESET tag*

- **NORESIZE** This attribute has no value. It means that the frame is not resizeable by the user. Without it, a user can take a frame border and drag the window to a new size. With this tag, the frame borders are frozen at their predetermined settings.

Using the FRAME Tag

The FRAMESET tag sets the size of the frame. But you'll also need to tell the browser what to put into each frame window. To do that, we use the FRAME tag, which appears between the opening and closing FRAMESET tags and defines the contents of each declared frame. The FRAME tag assigns a page to the frame with the property "SRC=URL." As an option, you can also give the frame a name, which is useful later when you want to target a frame to be hit with a hotlink.

We'll continue to build the page we started above, assigning a distinct URL to the two frames we declared. The output of our page can be seen in Figure 9-3. The HTML code looks like this:

```
<HTML>
  <HEAD>
  <TITLE>frame</TITLE>
  </HEAD>
  <FRAMESET COLS="100,*">
    <FRAME SRC="A.html" "name=left">
    <FRAME SRC="B.html" "name=right">
  </FRAMESET>
</HTML>
```

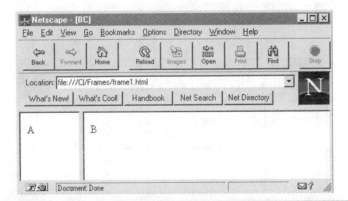

Figure 9-3.   *The two frames with URLs assigned to them*

Nesting Frames

In order to build a page with more than two frames, we'll need to nest one frame declaration within another. One way to do this is to directly nest one FRAMESET declaration inside of another. The output is shown in Figure 9-4. The HTML code looks like this:

```
<HTML>
  <HEAD>
  <TITLE>frame</TITLE>
  </HEAD>
  <FRAMESET COLS="100,*">
    <FRAME SRC="A.html" "name=A">
    <FRAMESET ROWS="*,*">
      <FRAME SRC="B.html" "name=B">
      <FRAME SRC="C.html" "name=C">
    </FRAMESET>
  </FRAMESET>
</HTML>
```

Another way to accomplish the same effect would be to first create an HTML page that would break into two vertical frames, as we did in the first example (Figure 9-2). When assigning the URLs to each of the frames, we could have the second URL refer to a page that also includes a FRAMESET command, this one breaking the page into two horizontal frames. Like two transparent templates being laid on top of one another, this would first break the page into two vertical frames and then break the

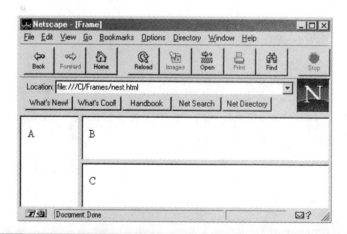

Figure 9-4. *An example of nested frames*

right frame—which is defined by a URL containing its own FRAMESET command—into two horizontal frames. The output would look the same as shown in Figure 9-4, but via a slightly different method. This technique is called indirect nesting.

Before we move on, let's take notice of one thing: we have been dealing with what amounts to two different types of HTML documents here. The documents that draw A, B, and C in the various frame windows are fairly standard HTML pages. They contain some content that is displayed in the browser window. But we have also been dealing with documents containing the FRAMESET tag. Notice that these documents do not contain any content. They simply contain information about how the HTML should be laid out—the specific size of all of the browser frames.

Thus we can now think of two kinds of HTML documents: layout documents and content documents. This distinction—between HTML pages that contain information about layout and those that contain content—is making its first appearance with Netscape's implementation of frames. This sort of distinction is also a key part of the proposed HTML 3.0 style sheets, a much more comprehensive effort to separate layout from content (see **http://www.w3.org/pub/WWW/Style/**).

Frames and Hyperlinks

Netscape offers the frame builder great control over not only how frames appear on the page but also how hyperlinks in a frame window are handled. As we saw in the earlier HotWired example, a typical use of frames is to have one window "feed" new pages into another. To accomplish this, Netscape provides a new keyword, **target**, for specifying exactly where the new URL should be displayed. The basic format for this new way of linking is as follows:

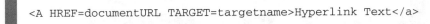

```
<A HREF=documentURL TARGET=targetname>Hyperlink Text</a>
```

The targetname can either refer to the name you give to a frame (for instance, earlier, we named our frames "top" and "bottom") or to one of several options that Netscape provides, including

- **_self** This tells the browser to display the loading URL into the same frame from which the hyperlink was launched. This is the default target if no target is specified.

- **_parent** This tells the browser to load the link in the immediate FRAMESET parent of this document.

- **_top** This tells the browser to repaint the entire window with the new URL, regardless of the current frame layout.

- **_blank** This tells the browser to launch an entirely new blank window—an entirely new browser—and display the document there.

Now for an example. We'll use the basic A, B, C pages we built earlier, but we'll add a hyperlink in frame A. When clicked on, this link will send a new page, D (containing the text "Thanks for sending me this link, frame A!" into the frame B window. The output is shown in Figure 9-5. Here's the HTML code on page A (the page containing the hyperlink) needed to accomplish this:

```
<HTML>
  <HEAD>
  <TITLE>A</TITLE>
  </HEAD>
  <BODY>
  A
  <p>
  <A HREF=D.HTML TARGET="B">Send this link to Frame B</a>
  <BODY>
</HTML>
```

Browsers without Frames Support

As we mentioned at the start of this chapter, not all users will be working with a Netscape browser. Netscape is becoming better about giving Web authors alternatives tags to include in their pages to ensure that a single page can meet every browser's capabilities.

For frames, the alternative tag is NOFRAMES. The tag is used in the layout HTML document (the page that otherwise contains no content, only information about the

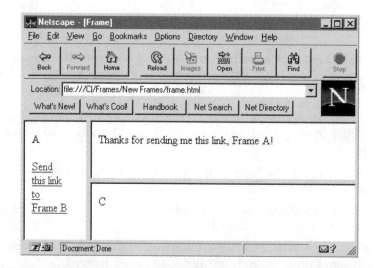

Figure 9-5. *An example of one frame targeting another*

layout of the frames themselves). It should come after the first FRAMESET tag but before the bulk of your frame tagging. Here's an example (showing just the NOFRAMES code):

```
<NOFRAMES>
These pages are made to be viewed using a frames-enabled browser
such as Netscape Navigator 2.0.
</NOFRAMES>
```

Page authors can put any content they want—literally an entirely new page if they desire—that will be seen by non-frames-capable browsers and ignored by browsers that can view frames. The typical use of the NOFRAMES tag is to create an alternative to the original, top-layer frame-based page. Since most of the other content on a site will have an original URL (pages that in a frames environment will get sucked into another frame), the NOFRAMES page can simply contain a list of links to these same URLs. For example, on the HotWired site we took a look at earlier, the original FRAMESET page contains NOFRAMES HTML code that creates a version of the page viewable by browsers without frames support (see Figure 9-6).

Netscape's Support for Java

The story goes that Marc Andreessen saw Sun's Java technology and immediately knew he had to have it inside of Navigator. Like most moves Netscape makes, it didn't take long to move from vision to reality. Netscape licensed Java, and engineers at Sun and Netscape worked night and day to bring the first implementation of beta-grade Java code into Navigator 2.0.

There's not a whole lot to say about Netscape's support of Java. It was the first browser to have support for beta applets, and it is likely to have the first support for 1.0 Java applets. For now at least, Netscape is committed to supporting the standard Java object classes and application programming interfaces. It is also working with Sun, Silicon Graphics, Macromedia, and others to introduce a standard set of object classes for supporting virtual reality and multimedia within Java. Netscape could one day take Java in some new directions, but it has committed to feeding any new work back to Sun for inclusion in Java. For more details on Java, see Chapters 5, 6, and 7.

JavaScript

JavaScript has an interesting story behind it, one that shows the fluid, breakneck pace at which the Web develops. Netscape executives say that in all of the hands-on contact they had with early customers, a common refrain they heard was that the Web needed an easy-to-use scripting language, one that could let even nonprogrammers create client- and server-side applications. Java, they heard, was great, but it was too difficult

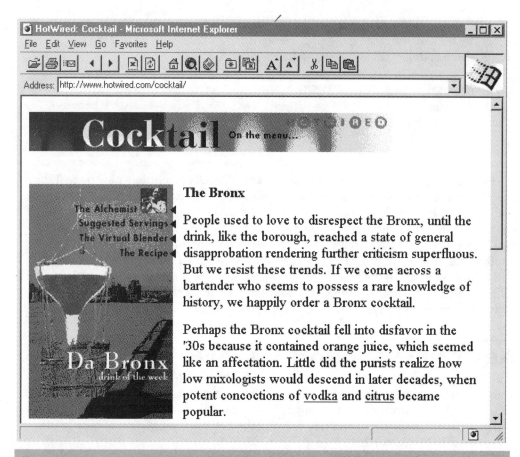

Figure 9-6. *The NOFRAMES version of the HotWired frames page*

for most Webmasters. And, customers said, they wanted Netscape to create the language. So they did, and the Netscape Scripting Language was born.

The language's first official name, LiveScript, was a reference to Netscape's LiveWire platform, an integrated server-side environment for managing Web sites, building server applications, and interfacing with databases. In the early days, Netscape executives often said LiveScript was Java-based, because it drew a lot of its basic syntax from Java. Sun executives always bristled at this comparison, mainly because Sun had no part in the creation of LiveScript and was unsure what effect the simple scripting language would have on its more complex but infinitely more powerful Java programming language.

Finally, last December, Sun and Netscape set aside any concerns and agreed to jointly develop the scripting language, renaming it JavaScript. They also gathered support from more than 25 other companies that announced they would support JavaScript, making the language instantly a de facto Web standard, and perhaps some day, an official one. Again, timing is everything. The same week that LiveScript was renamed JavaScript and was repositioned from a proprietary Netscape technology to an open, industry-wide technology, Microsoft unveiled its own Internet strategy, including a Web scripting language it called VB Script. Did the two events have any connection? Of course. Fear and Microsoft are probably the two largest motivating factors in the computer industry. But that shouldn't minimize the fact that JavaScript overnight went from being a Netscape anomaly to an almost universally accepted Web scripting language—supported even by Microsoft.

What Is JavaScript?

JavaScript is a streamlined scripting language for developing applications for both Web servers and clients. Netscape claims JavaScript is designed for nonprogrammers and HTML authors. That claim is debatable. While it is a much less rigorous environment than Java, JavaScript is nonetheless a full-featured, object-based scripting language. If you are not a programmer, you won't be able to pick it up overnight. But with a little time and work, you should be able to learn the language and add some very effective client-side programs to your HTML pages.

Here's how JavaScript works: on the client side, Netscape Navigator 2.0 interprets JavaScript statements that are embedded directly into an HTML page. That means that a script can be performed right there on the client computer; there is no need to connect back out to a server to perform the script there. By moving the ability to execute scripts from the server down to the client, the process of adding interactivity to a page is speeded up tremendously.

Meanwhile, LiveWire—Netscape's server-side development environment—includes a JavaScript interpreter that lets you create server-based applications. We will focus our attention on client-side JavaScript, which can be implemented immediately by any HTML author.

JavaScript is an interpreted language. This means JavaScript code is not compiled like C code, or even Java code, which first must run through a compiler to create interpreted byte code. Instead, you can write JavaScript code in any text editor and place it directly on an HTML page, and the JavaScript interpreter will read and interpret the code on the fly. That makes it a much simpler language than Java for simple scripting. It also enables you to view the source of an HTML page in a Web browser and see the JavaScript code right alongside the HTML tags. Indeed, while this book and various Web-based tutorials can help you learn Java code, perhaps the best way to learn about leading-edge JavaScript techniques is to View Source on innovative JavaScript pages and scour the code for tips and tricks.

Client-side JavaScript programs can do a number of interesting things:

- Locally verify form input, notifying the user with a dialog box if the input is invalid.

- Create small stand-alone applications, such as calculators, color pickers, and more (Figure 9-7 shows an innovative application that lets you choose a color in one window and instantly test it out in a second window while also providing the color's correct hexadecimal code).

- Eventually, though not in its initial form, you will be able to use JavaScript to communicate with Java applets and inline plug-ins.

How does JavaScript compare to Java? As we noted, Java is a compiled language, while JavaScript is interpreted. Yet JavaScript, as we shall see, supports much of Java's basic syntax and control flow constructs. See Table 9-1, authored by Netscape, for the full slate of differences between Java and JavaScript.

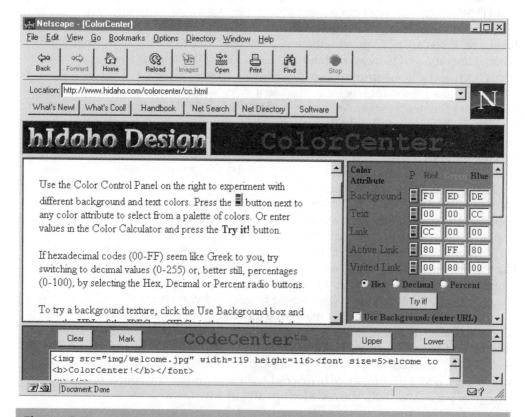

Figure 9-7. *An innovative use of both JavaScript and frames*

JavaScript	Java
Interpreted by client—not compiled.	Compiled on server before execution on client.
Object-based. No classes or inheritance; built-in, extensible objects.	Object-oriented. Programs consist of object classes, with inheritance, etc.
Integrated with/embedded in HTML.	Applets distinct from HTML (accessed from HTML pages).
Do not declare variables' data types (loose typing).	Must declare variables' data types (strong typing).
Dynamic binding; object references checked at run time.	Static binding; object references must exist at compile time.
Secure. Cannot write to hard disk.	Secure. Cannot write to hard disk.

Table 9-1. *Comparing JavaScript and Java (Courtesy of Netscape)*

Note ▶

As this book was being written, JavaScript was being written as well. As each Netscape Navigator 2.0 beta came out, changes (mostly slight) and additions (sometimes large) were introduced to the scripting language. We will work here with specifications relating to the beta 5 release, which are not expected to change drastically (though they will continue to expand as JavaScript evolves). They also were not yet complete, though the holes will likely be filled in by the time this book is published. Our lessons here obviously owe a great debt to the early release specifications Netscape posted to its Web site.

Using JavaScript

JavaScript programs are embedded directly into an HTML page. There are two ways to embed JavaScript into an HTML page. The HTML page below demonstrates the general guidelines:

```
<HTML>
<HEAD>
<SCRIPT LANGUAGE="JavaScript">
< !-- The main part of the script goes here, including all of its
functions, -- >
</SCRIPT>
</HEAD>
```

```
<BODY>
< ! --The body of the HTML document goes here, including new HTML
tags that let a //user interact with the JavaScript program
above-- >
</BODY>
</HTML>
```

As we demonstrate in the HTML code above, the main part of a JavaScript program goes between the SCRIPT tags. It is good script-writing practice to put all of a program's functions—which also must be contained within the SCRIPT tags—within the page's HEAD tags as well. That ensures they load first and are ready to be invoked as needed.

The LANGUAGE attribute of the SCRIPT tag is the usual way you will define the Web scripting language you want to use. Microsoft also uses a SCRIPT tag to invoke VB Script. The W3 Consortium is working on creating standard HTML tags for calling embedded executable content like Java applets and scripting languages.

The alternative to using the LANGUAGE attribute is to tell the SCRIPT tag to load a script from a separate file or URL (rather than including it within the HTML page). For example, this tag offers an easy way to reuse a single script across several pages. The syntax for this is

```
<SCRIPT SRC="http://myscript.js">...</SCRIPT>
```

In order to hide your JavaScript program from other browsers, you should enclose the contents of your scripts in HTML comment tags. In that way, a non-Netscape browser won't display the text of your script. You can do that like this:

```
<SCRIPT LANGUAGE="JavaScript">
<!--- begin hiding script
Script contents
// end hiding script -- >
</SCRIPT>
```

Note ▶ *To keep things simple, we won't hide our scripts in the examples that follow.*

While the main functions of your script are written high in your HTML page, you can access those functions from anywhere in a page. To do this JavaScript includes new parameter tags that let standard HTML tags such as FORM call JavaScript functions. These new attributes are called event handlers, reflecting the fact that most JavaScript programs will be invoked by user events, such as the input of data or a click on a hotlink. We'll provide more details of event handlers later, after we learn a little bit more about the JavaScript language.

The JavaScript Language

Before we write any scripts, let's get a good feel for the language itself. JavaScript was created to reflect the syntax of Java, so some of the keywords will be familiar. (If you've made it through the Java chapters.) We will give a basic rundown of the language here. If you want more detailed information, check the JavaScript tutorial on Netscape's home page, **http://www.netscape.com**, which includes a detailed introduction to JavaScript as well as a reference that provides the authoritative syntax for the language. As we noted earlier, JavaScript is an evolving language. Check Netscape's specifications for the latest changes and additions.

JavaScript is built on three basic building blocks:

- *Values* The data types supported by JavaScript, including numbers, logical, strings, and null.

- *Objects* A named container for a collection of properties (values). Can also be made up of other objects.

- *Functions* Procedures that an application can perform. The functions associated with a particular object is that object's methods.

VALUES, LITERALS, AND NAMES JavaScript recognizes a fairly small set of values, or data types. They include

- Numbers, including integers expressed in decimal, hexadecimal, or octal format, as well as floating point literals (such as 3.1415).

- Boolean values, either true or false.

- Strings, such as "Hello World". Strings are bracketed in quotes. JavaScript also includes several special string characters to indicate a backspace ("\b"), a form feed ("\f"), a new line character ("\n"), a carriage return ("\r"), and a tab character ("\t").

- Null, which is a special keyword denoting a null value.

You can also use variables to hold values in your script. The most obvious example would be something like X=5, with the variable X holding the value 5.

A variable name can include letters A through Z (uppercase and lowercase) and digits 0 through 9. A name must start with a letter or an underscore (such as _name)—it cannot start with a number.

JavaScript is case-sensitive, so be sure to note the exact case of every command and variable we discuss.

EXPRESSIONS AND OPERATORS   An expression is a set of literals (literal values), variables, operators, and expressions that evaluates to a single value. JavaScript supports the following kinds of expressions:

- Arithmetic, which evaluates to a number
- Logical, which evaluates to true or false
- String, which evaluates to a character string
- Conditional expressions, which can have one of two values based on a condition

JavaScript supports a number of operators, which effect an action upon a value or set of values. JavaScript supports arithmetic, string, logical, and comparison operators—including both binary and unary operators. This includes all of the standard arithmetic operators you would expect: addition (+), subtraction (–), multiplication (*), and division (/). Other useful arithmetic operators include increment (++), which adds one to an operand, and decrement (—), which subtracts one from an operand.

The most common string operator is (+), which concatenates two strings together. Here is an example:

"Beyond" + "HTML" returns the string "Beyond HTML"

Logical operators are used to compare and contrast values and return a value of either true or false. Examples include And (&&), which compares two values and returns true if both expressions are true; and Or (| |), which compares two logical expressions and returns true if either is true, and false if both are false.

Comparison operators compare two values and return a logical value based on whether the comparison is true or not. Comparison operators include equal to (==), not equal to (!=), greater than (>), greater than or equal to (>=), less than (<), and less than or equal to (<=).

STATEMENTS   JavaScript also includes built-in statements, which allow you to do things like set up loops in your program. One of the most important statements is the function statement, which is the keyword you will use to create JavaScript functions—a set of procedures that performs a specific task. Once defined, a function can be called from anywhere within a script. We will look at the function statement more closely later in this chapter, when we examine how to build a JavaScript object.

Most of the remaining JavaScript statements are used to build branches or loops in your JavaScript programs. Some of the most commonly used statements include

- **var** The var statement declares a variable name with its given value, for instance, var a= 1. It is good practice to use the var statement within a function to ensure that any variables of the same name elsewhere in the program do not override it. But it is not strictly necessary. For instance, you could also write a=1 in your script.

- **if…else** This is a conditional statement that executes one set of statements if a condition is true and a second set of statements if a condition is false. A simple example (note the syntax, which is consistent in all statements) is shown here:

```
var x=2
if (x==1) {
   document.write ("x=1")


} else {
   document.write ("x does not equal 1")
   }
```

The output for this script is

```
x does not equal 1
```

- **for** The for statement is used to build loops. A typical application of a for loop is a counter, as we show below. A for statement usually includes an initial expression (var a=0) that initializes the counter; a condition (a<9) that is evaluated on each pass through the for loop; an update expression (a++), which updates the counter each pass; and finally a block of statements (document.write (a)) that are performed as long as the condition remains true.

Here's a simple counter example:

```
for (var a = 0; a < 9; a++) {
   document.write (a)
   }
document.write ("Stop")
```

The output for this script is

```
012345678Stop
```

- **while**   A while loop evaluates an expression's condition, and if it is true, executes a statement. It repeats this process until the condition is no longer true. Here's a simple while loop, in proper syntax:

```
var a=0
while (a<10) {
  document.write (a); a++
}
document.write ("Stop")
```

The output for this script is

```
0123456789Stop
```

- **break**   The break statement terminates a while or for loop based on some condition, jumping the program to the statement following the loop.
- **continue**   The continue statement terminates a while or for loop, and continues execution of the loop with the next iteration. In contrast to the break statement, it does not terminate the execution of the loop entirely. Instead, in a while loop, it jumps back to the condition; in a for loop, it jumps to the update expression.
- **return**   The return statement specifies the value to be returned by a function. Here is an example:

```
function square (x) {
  return x*x
document.write(square(4))
}
```

- **with**   The with statement lets you attach multiple statements to an object. For instance, the following example attaches all of the statements to the Math object:

```
with (Math) {
  var a = PI
  var b= PI * 2
```

```
   var c= PI * 3
}
```

To do this without the with statement, you would have to attach the Math object individually to each variable:

```
var a = Math.PI
var b = Math.PI*2
var c = Math.PI*3
```

JavaScript's Object Model

Now that you have a good feel for the syntax of JavaScript, let's move on to more advanced topics. Like Java, JavaScript is based on an object-oriented paradigm, albeit a less strict one. In JavaScript, an object is a construct with properties that are variables or other objects. Functions associated with an object are known as the object's methods. JavaScript includes some built-in objects and functions, but you can define your own as well.

BUILT-IN OBJECTS   JavaScript comes with a number of predefined objects. Like Java's built-in classes, these objects make it easy to build some basic functions into a JavaScript program without having to do all the work yourself.

The first built-in object is the string object. Whenever you assign a string value to a variable or property, you've created a string object. An example is

```
samplestring = "Hello World"
```

The advantage of making a string into an object is that the object can have methods attached to it, as shown here:

```
document.write(samplestring.toUpperCase())
will return "HELLO WORLD."
```

Another built-in object is the math object, which has properties and methods for mathematical constants and functions such as pi or sin and cosine.

Another built-in object is the date object. The date objects and its methods let you use dates within your programs. The syntax for creating a date object is

```
varName = new Date(parameters)
```

You can feed a variety of parameters into the date object, including

- None, as in new Date(). This will return today's date.
- A text and number string, such as today=new Date("January 10, 1997").
- A set of integer values, such as today=new Date(97, 1, 10).

These are the main built-in objects defined in the early specifications of the JavaScript language. The specifications also detail objects that are a part of the Navigator client itself. The Navigator objects correspond to items on an HTML page, including its windows, location, history, and contents.

Whenever you load a page in Navigator, it automatically creates objects. Every page has the following objects:

- *Window* This contains properties for the main window as well as any "child" windows created with the FRAME tag.
- *Location* This contains the properties on the current URL.
- *History* This contains properties representing URLs the user has previously visited.
- *Document* This contains properties for the current document, including title, background color, links, anchors, forms, and form elements such as radio button forms and text areas.

We'll examine some uses of the Navigator objects later in this chapter.

BUILDING YOUR OWN OBJECTS In addition to the objects built into JavaScript, you can construct your own objects. If you recall our discussion of objects from Chapter 5, an object is similar to a template in that it describes the general characteristics of a thing. Once an object is defined—that is, the template is created—you can create a particular instance of the object by filling in the object template with specific values. For example, you could create an object describing a dog, with generic properties including color, family, and age. Let's create such an object in JavaScript:

```
function Dog (color, family, age) {
  this.color = color;
  this.family = family;
  this.age = age;
}
```

We use the function command to build the template for the Dog object. To give the Dog object its properties, we can use an array, an ordered set of values associated with a single variable name. The keyword **this** is used when you are feeding multiple properties to a single object.

Let's create two instances of the Dog object:

```
Waldo = new Dog ("black", "Labrador", 6)
Spot = new Dog ("brown", "Collie", 10)
```

We use the keyword **new** to create two objects, Waldo, a six-year-old black Labrador, and Spot, a 10-year-old brown Collie. We can create any number of Dog objects using **new**.

A CLOSER LOOK AT FUNCTIONS AND METHODS   So far, we've created the Dog object and defined two instances of the object. To finish our lesson, let's attempt to print out the properties for the two Dog objects we created. In doing this, we'll learn how to create several additional functions, as well as how to call the functions from within an HTML page. It is important to note that a function doesn't do anything within a page unless it is called.

What precisely is a function? It consists of the **function** keyword, followed by:

- The name of the function
- A list of parameters, enclosed in parentheses and separated by commas
- Statements that define the function, enclosed in curly brackets

Once you've created a function, you can create a method that associates the function with an object. The syntax to do this is as follows:

```
object.methodname = function_name
```

Finally, after you have defined a function and associated the function with a particular object (created a method), you will need to call the method from within your HTML script for it to execute. The syntax to call a method is as follows:

```
object.methodname (params);
```

To bring all of this together, let's go back to our Dog object, writing the entire script that will define the Dog object and then print out the parameters of two instances of the object. The script does the following (also included as comments within the script):

- Defines the Dog object, as we demonstrated earlier.
- Declares two instances of the Dog object.
- Defines a function to print a string. The document.write statement enables the printing.

- Defines a function to display the properties of the individual instances of the Dog object. Notice how we use the previous function (which we call _print) within this function.

- Calls the displayDog method to invoke the functions that print the dogs' properties to the screen.

The output of the script is in Figure 9-8. The complete script looks like this:

```
<HTML>
<HEAD>
<SCRIPT LANGUAGE="JavaScript">
< ! -- 1- Define the Dog object, and in the final line, make the
displayDog function a //method of Dog -- >
function Dog(color, family, age) {
  this.color=color
  this.family=family
  this.age=age
  this.displayDog =displayDog
}
< ! -- 2 - Declare two instances of the Dog object -- >
Waldo = new Dog ("black","Labrador",6)
Spot = new Dog ("brown", "Collie",10)
< ! -- 3 - Define a function to print a string -- >
function _print(string) {
  document.write("<HR><P>" + string)
}
< ! -- 4 - Define a function to display the properties of the Dog
object -- >
function displayDog() {
  var result = "A " + this.color + " "  this.family + ", " +
this.age + " year's old";
  _print(result)
}
< ! -- 5 - Call the displayDog method -- >
Waldo.displayDog()
Spot.displayDog()
</SCRIPT>
</HEAD>
</HTML>
```

Event Handlers

Now that you know the basic concepts behind the JavaScript language, we'll need to examine a little more closely a concept we introduced earlier: event handlers. Event

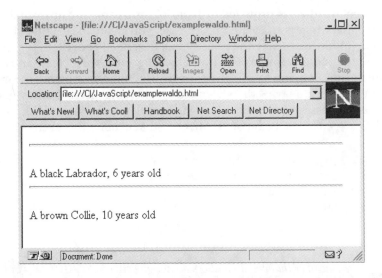

Figure 9-8. *The output of the Dog objects script*

handlers are important because nothing really happens in a JavaScript program until the user initiates an action. You use event handlers to link a user event to the execution of a JavaScript program.

Event handlers are embedded in documents as attributes of HTML tags. The tags are then associated with the JavaScript code that is executed when an event occurs. The general syntax for an event handler is

```
<TAG eventHandler="JavaScript Code">
```

TAG represents some HTML tag (for instance, INPUT), eventHandler is the name given to the particular event handler, and JavaScript Code represents the name of a function that you have written in JavaScript. For example, say you defined a function called Compute. You could have Navigator perform this function when the user clicks on a button with an HTML tag that looks like this:

```
<INPUT TYPE="button" VALUE="Calculate"
onClick="Compute(this.form)">
```

The event handler in this example is onClick, which calls the Compute function (defined earlier on the page) when the user initiates the event of clicking on a button.

A list of event handlers is provided in Table 9-2. You can build an event handler for any HTML tag that triggers an event. In each case, you create the event handler and call the JavaScript function using the basic syntax described above.

Here's an interesting example of an event handler. First, we'll create an HTML page with an anchor pointing to a fictitious page. When the user passes the mouse pointer over the anchor, a JavaScript statement is called that gives the Navigator status window a special message rather than the usual display of the target URL. See the results in Figure 9-9. Here's the bit of HTML code that enables this event:

```
<A HREF="http://www.beyondhtml.com"
  onMouseOver="window.status='Smart choice! Go to. . . Beyond HTML
Home Page'; return true">
Beyond HTML home page
</A>
```

Remember that event handlers do not go between SCRIPT tags but rather in the regular part of an HTML document. See the examples below for proper use of event handlers.

Event	Occurs When	Event Handler
blur	User removes input focus from form element	onBlur
change	User changes value of text, text area or select element	onChange
click	User clicks on form element or link	onClick
focus	User gives form element input focus	onFocus
load	User loads a page	OnLoad
mouseover	User moves mouse pointer over link or anchor	OnMouseOver
select	User submits a form	onSubmit
unload	User exits a page	unLoad

Table 9-2. *Common Event Handlers*

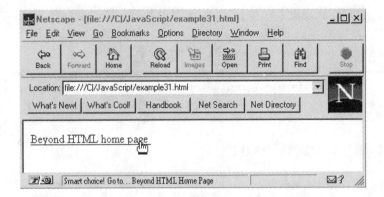

Figure 9-9. *A special message for the Navigator status window*

What You Can Do with JavaScript

As we've seen, JavaScript is a very thorough and in some ways complex scripting language—especially for something Netscape says is designed for nonprogrammers. But with that relative complexity comes the power and flexibility to write some very useful client-side applications. Let's take a line-by-line look at a few of the core applications of JavaScript. On the way, we'll also check out a few of the leading-edge sites that hit the Web in the early days of JavaScript.

JavaScript Examples

One of the most common uses of JavaScript will be to do quick, client-side calculations. The simplest application (and an extremely simple JavaScript program to write) is a calculator. Other JavaScript-based calculating engines that made an early appearance on the Web include scripts for calculating interest (see Figure 9-10), taxes, metric conversions, background colors (as in Figure 9-7), spreadsheets, and more.

Let's try something a little different and build a script for calculating a baseball pitcher's earned run average (ERA). An ERA is the average number of earned runs a pitcher allows in a typical nine-inning game, or

(Total Earned Runs Allowed * 9) / Total Innings Pitched

The output of this script is in Figure 9-11. Following is the script and HTML tags that make this possible. (Note: In all of these examples, we include comments within the text of the script that explains what is going on.)

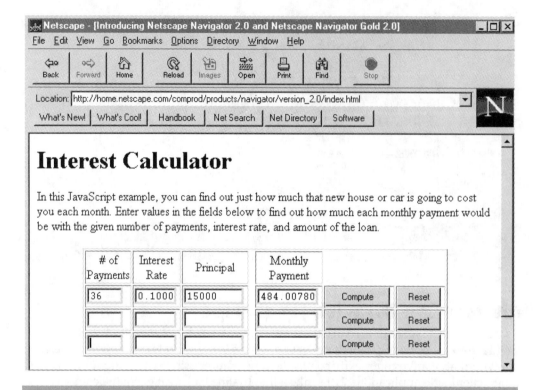

Figure 9-10. *Netscape's JavaScript interest calculator*

```
<HTML>
<HEAD>
<SCRIPT LANGUAGE="JavaScript">
< ! --  The function takes the user input and calculates the ERA.
-- >
function compute(form) {
    form.result.value = (form.EarnedRuns.value) * 9 /
(form.InningsPitched.value)
  }
</SCRIPT>
</HEAD>
<BODY>
<CENTER>Calculating Earned Run Average</CENTER>
<FORM>
```

```
<!-- Here we create a form for inputting the pitcher's
statistics-- >
Earned Runs Allowed:
<INPUT TYPE="number" NAME="EarnedRuns" SIZE=5 >
<P>
Innings Pitched:
<INPUT TYPE="number" NAME="InningsPitched" SIZE=5 >
<P>
<INPUT TYPE="button" VALUE="Compute" ONCLICK="compute(this.form)">
<BR>
<BR>
<!-- Here is the output of the calculation --
Result:
<INPUT TYPE="number" NAME="result" SIZE=4 >
<BR>
</FORM>
</BODY>
</HTML>
```

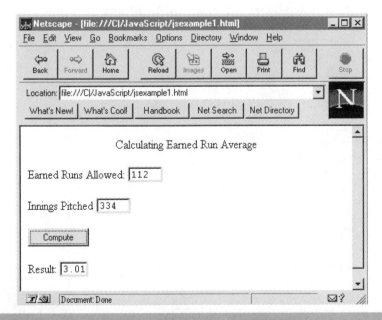

Figure 9-11.   *JavaScript calculates this pitcher's ERA (not bad!)*

Another use for JavaScript is to verify that the input in a form field is valid. For instance, if you are requesting a number, you don't want the input to be a letter. And if you require that a form field be filled in, you don't want the user to leave a form field blank. In this example, we'll ask visitors to our Web site to describe their job title. If they do not return a value between 1 and 5, we'll ask them to try again. When they are successful, we'll thank them for their input. The output of our script is in Figure 9-12. Here's the script and HTML page:

```html
<HTML>
<HEAD>
<SCRIPT LANGUAGE="JavaScript">
< ! --First, we set a function to check the form field.
The first conditional if statement makes sure the field is not
blank.
The second statement makes sure the input is a number between 1
and 5.
We call an alert—a pop-up window—if the input is invalid.
//Finally, we pop an alert thanking the user for a successful
input. -- >
function checkNum(str, min, max) {
   if (str == "") {
     alert("Enter a number in the field, please.")
     return false
   }
   var num = 0 + str
   if (num < min || num > max) {
     alert("Try a number from 1 to 5.")
     return false
   }
   return true
}
function thanks() {
   alert("Thanks for your input.")
}
</SCRIPT>
</HEAD>
<BODY>
What best describes your job title:<p>
1. Engineer<P>
2. Management<P>
3. Analyst<P>
4. Private contractor<P>
5. Something else<P>
```

```
<P>
<P>
<!--Below we send the user input to the function above ONCHANGE.
We build a submit button to encourage the user to click on the
page,
//which is required to initiate the ONCHANGE event handler --
Please enter the correct number:
<FORM>
<INPUT NAME="num" SIZE=5
  ONCHANGE="if (!checkNum(this.value, 1, 5))
    {this.focus();this.select();} else {thanks()}"
  VALUE=" ">
<INPUT TYPE="button" Value="Submit"
</FORM>
</BODY>
</HTML>
```

Figure 9-12. *JavaScript enables local forms validation*

Now, for one final example. Let's use JavaScript's date object to inform a visitor to our Web site how old a page's content is and when it is scheduled to be changed. The output will change based on the date on which the user accesses the Web site, which will obviously change day to day. It works like a countdown clock. This has become a fairly common thing to do, especially at sites such as magazines that have rotating content.

To do this, we'll need to give the script two things in advance: the date the current page was created and the date when it is scheduled to be changed. To do the comparison, JavaScript's date object will provide the current date (which will obviously change every day). The output of our script is in Figure 9-13. Here's the JavaScript code and HTML page that make this possible:

```
<HTML>
<HEAD>
<SCRIPT LANGUAGE="JavaScript">
< !--first, set the day the page is due to be changed and the day
the page was created -- >
today = new Date()
pageChange = new Date("January 20, 1996")
pageChange.setYear(today.getYear())


pageCreated = new Date("January 1, 1996")
pageCreated.setYear(today.getYear())


< ! -- next, we create a variable for the number of milliseconds
in a day -- >
msPerDay = 24 * 60 * 60 * 1000


< ! -- then we calculate the daysLeft and daysSince, -- >

< ! -- using Math.round to return a whole number -- >
daysLeft = (pageChange.getTime() - today.getTime()) / msPerDay;
daysLeft = Math.round(daysLeft)

daysSince = (today.getTime() - pageCreated.getTime()) / msPerDay
daysSince = Math.round(daysSince)


< ! -- finally we print the strings to the screen -- >
document.writeln("This page is " + daysSince + " days old.")
document.write("It will change in " + daysLeft + " days.")
</SCRIPT>
</HEAD>
</HTML>
```

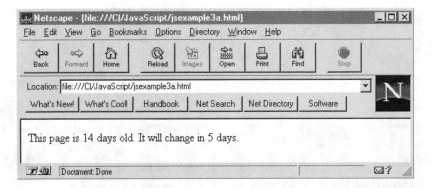

Figure 9-13. *Using JavaScript to track the freshness of pages*

The dates in this example represent a range during which this chapter was written. If you were to do this yourself, you would want to make the pageCreated and pageChange variables fit your real-world situation.

An even more interesting use of the date object is to customize your pages based on the time of day. Here's an interesting site we found on the Web, which changes based on the time of day (See Figure 9-14). We accessed the page just before noon (lunchtime!).

Plug-ins

In addition to frames and JavaScript, Navigator 2.0 also introduced what it is calling a new "plug-in" architecture, which allows third-party vendors to plug their helper applications right into Netscape, with the results displayed inline directly in the Navigator window. This new architecture means that there will be a virtually unlimited new stream of media types and applications—included virtual reality, multimedia, streaming audio and video, and interactivity—that HTML authors can now embed into their home pages (see Figure 9-15 for an example of a VRML plug-in).

Application vendors have shown great enthusiasm for Netscape's new plug-in architecture, no doubt enticed by Netscape's huge installed base of users and the chance to very easily make their desktop applications Internet-enabled. Even before Navigator 2.0 finished its beta cycle, almost a dozen plug-ins had appeared, with more appearing every week (see Table 9-3).

Note ▶ *Most of the early plug-ins today run only under Windows, though the plug-in architecture is supported across Netscape's entire browser line.*

Figure 9-14. *JavaScript lets this page change based on the time of day*

To take advantage of a plug-in as an HTML author, you will need access to the original application that fuels the plug-in. For instance, Macromedia's Shockwave player runs files generated by Macromedia Director, the company's multimedia authoring tool (see Chapter 10 for an in-depth look at Shockwave), and Adobe's Amber plug-in plays files created using Adobe Acrobat (see Chapters 1 through 3 for a look at Acrobat).

The great thing about plug-ins from a design perspective, however, is that in most cases if you already know an application, you won't need to learn anything new to build files capable of being read by a plug-in. You will, however, need to keep in mind

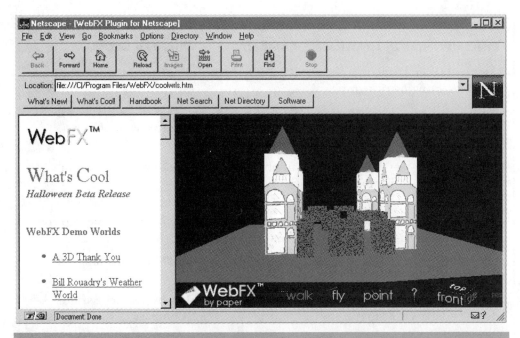

Figure 9-15.   *Paper Software's WebFX plug-in*

that you are designing for delivery over the Internet, which means you'll need to keep your files relatively small.

Clearly leading the plug-in must-have list thus far are Macromedia's Shockwave (multimedia), Adobe's Amber (Acrobat files), Paper Software's WebFX (VRML), Progressive Networks' RealAudio (streaming audio), and VDONet's VDOLive (streaming video). See the RealAudio inline plug-in shown in Figure 9-16, noting how the controls are built right into the HTML page.

Also of note are a pair of plug-ins that enable Navigator to run Object Linking and Embedding Controls, also known as OCXs. The OLE Control plug-in from NCompass and the OpenScape plug-in from Object Power bring to Navigator the same OCX support today that Microsoft has been bragging will be available in the next version of its Internet Explorer browser.

As we saw in Chapter 8, OCXs, when adapted for the Internet, can offer much of the same ability to enable downloadable, executable content as Sun's Java programming language. The drawback is that OCXs lack many of the built-in security features of Java; but they make up for it with a huge installed base of developers already familiar with working in the OLE environment. See the NCompass plug-in shown in Figure 9-17. The browser is displaying a rotating 3-D figure while playing an audio file in the background.

Product Name/Description	Company	Where to Get It
Amber Reader: Displays Acrobat PDF files, bringing rich graphical layouts to the Web	Adobe Systems Corp.	http://www.adobe.com
CMX Viewer: Displays vector graphics	Corel Corp.	http://www.corel.com
Envoy Reader: Views files in Envoy format, similar to Adobe Acrobat	TumbleWeed Software Corp.	http://www.twcorp.com
Formula One/Net: A live, Net-based spreadsheet	Visual Components Inc.	http://www.visualcomp.com
Lightning Strike: A wavelet image codec	Infinet Op	http://www.infinop.com
OLE Control: Brings downloadable OCXs to the Navigator	Ncompass	http://www.excite.sfu.ca/NCompass
OpenScape: Delivers OLE/OCX compatibility and enterprise application development tools	Object Power	http://www.opower.com
RealAudio: Streaming audio with control panel built right into Web page	Progressive Networks	http://www.realaudio.com
Shockwave: Brings multimedia and interactive files created with Macromedia Director to the Web	Macromedia Corp.	http://www.macromedia.com
VDOLive: Enables streaming video and audio	VDONet Corp.	http://www.vdolive.com
VR Scout: VRML plug-in	Chaco Communications	http://www.chaco.com
WebFX: First plug-in available, an inline VRML browser	Paper Software Inc.	http://www.paperinc.com

Table 9-3. *The First Wave of Netscape Plug-Ins*

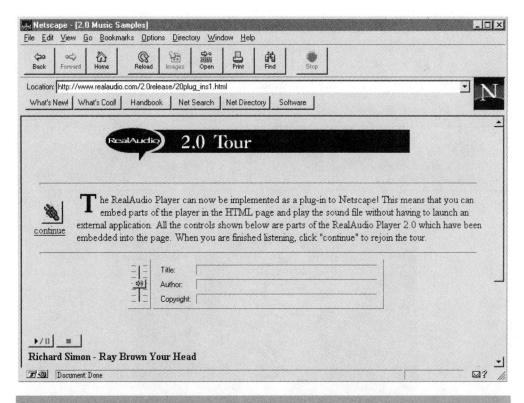

Figure 9-16.   *The RealAudio plug-in*

Plug-ins and HTML

To use plug-ins, you need to learn a new HTML tag, called EMBED. The EMBED tag lets you put documents directly into an HTML page. The default attributes for the tag are

```
<EMBED SRC="path/filename.ext" WIDTH=n HEIGHT=n>
```

You always must include the file or URL from which the plug-in will load. The WIDTH and HEIGHT parameters lets you specify the width and height of the plug-in's display space in the Netscape browser in pixels. The optional TEXTFOCUS parameter lets you tell the plug-in when to start responding from user input.

A second tag, NO EMBED, can be used to substitute text or a graphic file for a plug-in file so that visitors to your site without a plug-in-capable browser won't see a fractured page.

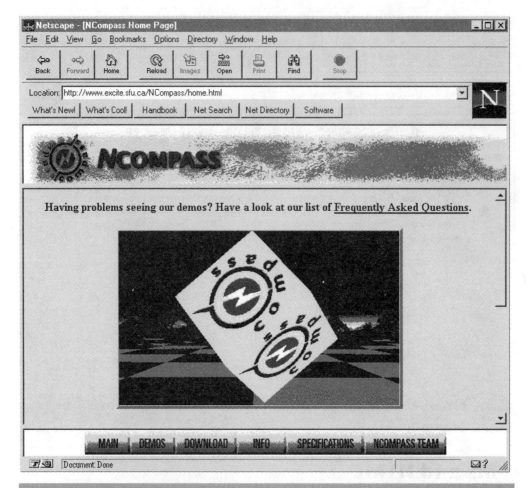

Figure 9-17. *The NCompass plug-in*

The art of plug-ins is not in the HTML but in the original applications used to create the now HTML-embeddable files.

The Future of Plug-ins

Netscape plug-ins sound great: they offer Webmasters an opportunity to add exciting new file formats to their Web site. But the catch is that users will have to go out, find, and install a plug-in before they will be able to view plug-in files on the Web. Obviously, there is no assurance that every user you want to target with a specific application or file format will make this effort.

Netscape is expected to solve this problem in part by choosing several plug-ins to be integrated directly into the Navigator browser. Standard integration into Navigator will be an important landmark for the plug-ins chosen, ensuring that they will immediately have an installed base of millions of users. Netscape faces some tough choices. It will be interesting to see, for instance, which of the many competing VRML or real-time audio applications that Netscape chooses to bless with its approval.

If we had to place a bet on the chosen few plug-ins, likely choices would be the applications that are already shipping as part of the Netscape Power Pack, a consumer-oriented CD that includes the Netscape browser and several helper applications. That would include Adobe's Acrobat, Progressive Networks' RealAudio, and Apple's QuickTime players. Other candidates would likely include Shockwave and VDOLive, both of which represent cutting-edge capabilities that have already drawn plenty of interest from Web developers.

Another drawback for Netscape plug-ins is that they have to be specifically written for each computer platform (for instance, PC or Macintosh). Also, a Netscape plug-in cannot be used with another browser, for instance, Spyglass Mosaic or Microsoft Internet Explorer. That means software companies will have to build different plug-ins for different computer platforms and different browsers—a time-consuming task. Spyglass and Microsoft have both announced plans to offer a plug-in-type browser architecture similar to Netscape's.

One possible solution to this problem may be Sun Microsystem's Java technology, which would enable application vendors to write an inline player for their media type and have that one piece of software run on every computer platform (almost every operating system is getting a Java port) and browser (most browser vendors are preparing to integrate the Java run-time engine), making the addition of new media types to a Web browser a much more seamless experience.

If Java-based media players proliferate, they may replace Netscape plug-ins. Even Netscape—which is a big Java backer—admits that. But until that day, taking advantage of Netscape's plug-in architecture may be the best way to add exciting new media types to your Web pages.

Netscape Navigator Gold

Having conquered the browser market, Netscape has now turned its attention to building a first-class HTML editor and Web site builder, Netscape Navigator Gold. Netscape is working from its strength—Gold is built directly into the Navigator browser, giving users the ability to browse the Web and author HTML pages from the same interface. Netscape will continue to build a stand-alone browser, but also will offer a separate Navigator Gold combination browser and editor.

Navigator Gold promises a lot: full What-You-See-Is-What-You-Get (WYSIWYG) HTML editing (no need to type HTML tags), the ability to drag-and-drop links and images onto HTML pages, and simplified methods for adding Netscape Live Objects—including Java applets, plug-ins, and more—to HTML pages.

The first beta of Navigator Gold, which ran only on Windows 95 and NT, appeared in early 1996. The examples we show here are from the first beta, but note that many of the features expected to be in the final version of Gold did not make it into the first beta.

For example, the first beta did not include WYSIWYG creation of tables, forms, frames, or image maps, nor did it offer a simplified way to script plug-ins or Java applets. All of these things can be done, but you must do raw HTML coding to make them work, which, of course, defeats the purpose of having a WYSIWYG HTML editor. Netscape promises many of these features will find their way into the final release, though some features, such as WYSIWYG frames support, will not. Also missing in the first beta was the ability to do one-button posting of HTML pages to a Web hosting service or Web server, an important feature, which Netscape said will be in the final version.

JavaScript authoring is supported in Gold, but only in the most basic ways. For example, if you click on Properties/Character/JavaScript from the Gold menu, you will be able to author JavaScript code directly onto your HTML document and set it off with the code displayed in a different color than the rest of the text in the Edit window.

Working with Gold

Navigator Gold adds a new button to the browser toolbar called Edit (see Figure 9-18). If you click on it, are connected to the Internet, and then view a Web page, Gold will attempt to save the page you are viewing so you can edit it. While it's unlikely you'll want to download an entire page, the integrated browsing/editing feature makes it easy to download an individual element, such as a graphic file or link, and use it on your own page.

More likely, however, you will want to begin building a new document from scratch, which you can do by clicking on the New Document button on the Gold toolbar or by choosing File/New Document from the Gold menu.

Before we check out the features of Gold, let's introduce its toolbars. Gold has three main toolbars, which provide easy access to its most important features. The toolbars are

■   The File/Edit Toolbar, which lets you open, save, and modify files:

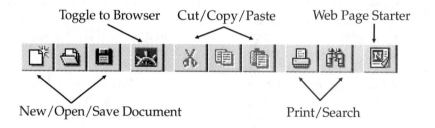

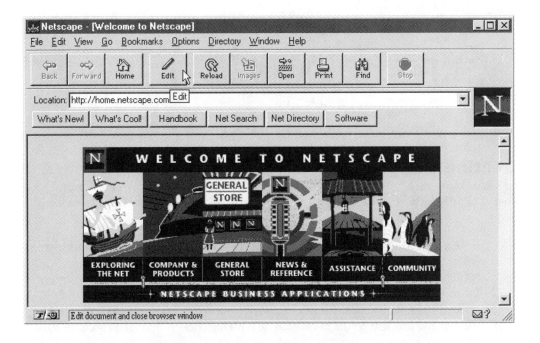

Figure 9-18. *The Edit button toggles the user from browser to edit mode*

■ The Paragraph Format Toolbar, which lets you set text and paragraph styles and create bulleted and numbered lists:

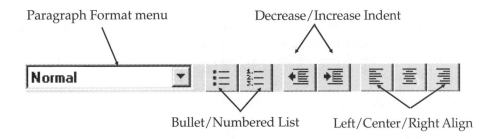

■ The Character Format Toolbar, shown next, which lets you set font size, style, and color, as well as add links and images to your page.

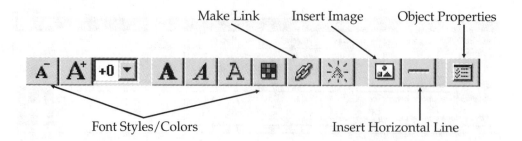

Creating a Page

Let's start building a new page in Gold from scratch. In the process, we'll examine most of Gold's authoring features. We'll begin our work in Navigator Gold browser mode:

1. First, we need to choose the background color or background image and text colors for our page. To do this, we click on Properties/Document on the Navigator Gold menu. This calls up a dialog box with two settings, Document Information and Colors/Background. We'll choose the latter setting, which presents us with a screen for adding background colors or images and setting the text and link text colors to coordinate with the background (see Figure 9-19).

2. We click OK to apply the colors. Next, still in browser mode, we click on File/New Document from the menu to create our new page. The Navigator Gold authoring environment launches, and the three tool bars sit at the top of the page while the actual authoring space displays the background color we chose. Before anything else, Gold requires that you save the file and give it a name ending with a .htm or .html extension. We'll call our page **beyond.html**. Now let's build our sample page.

3. To start, let's insert an image that will act as the banner for our page. To do so, we click on the Insert Image button on the Paragraph Format toolbar. That calls up a dialog box (see Figure 9-20) that lets us choose the image we want to add; select an alternative presentation, such as a text message in case the image doesn't load; and determine the alignment of the image and the spacing around it.

4. Next, we'll add the text subhead, "Weaving a New Web" by typing in the text, highlighting it, and applying the H1 headline code from the format window. We'll also center the headline by clicking on the Center icon on the Paragraph format toolbar.

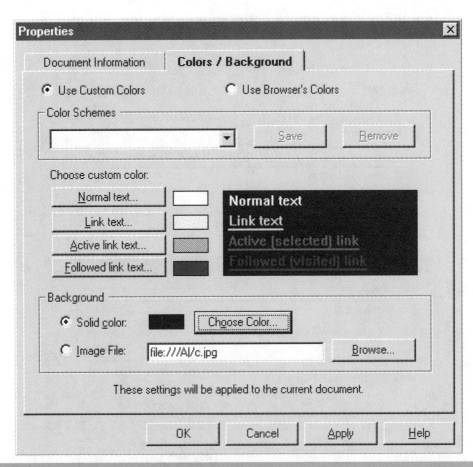

Figure 9-19.   *Colors/Background dialog box*

5. Next, we'll add a list of hotlinks. First, to create the list we'll type the names of several topics covered in this book, including Acrobat, Java, Shockwave, and VRML. Next, we'll highlight each of the names individually and then click on the Link button in the Character Format toolbar. This calls up the Create Link dialog box, which lets us associate a Uniform Resource Locator (URL) with each name on our list. The Create Link dialog box is shown in the following illustration.

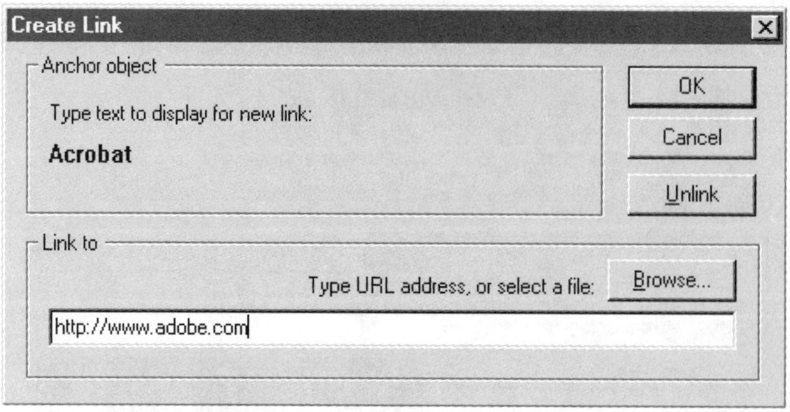

Create Link

Anchor object

Type text to display for new link:

Acrobat

OK

Cancel

Unlink

Link to

Type URL address, or select a file: Browse...

http://www.adobe.com

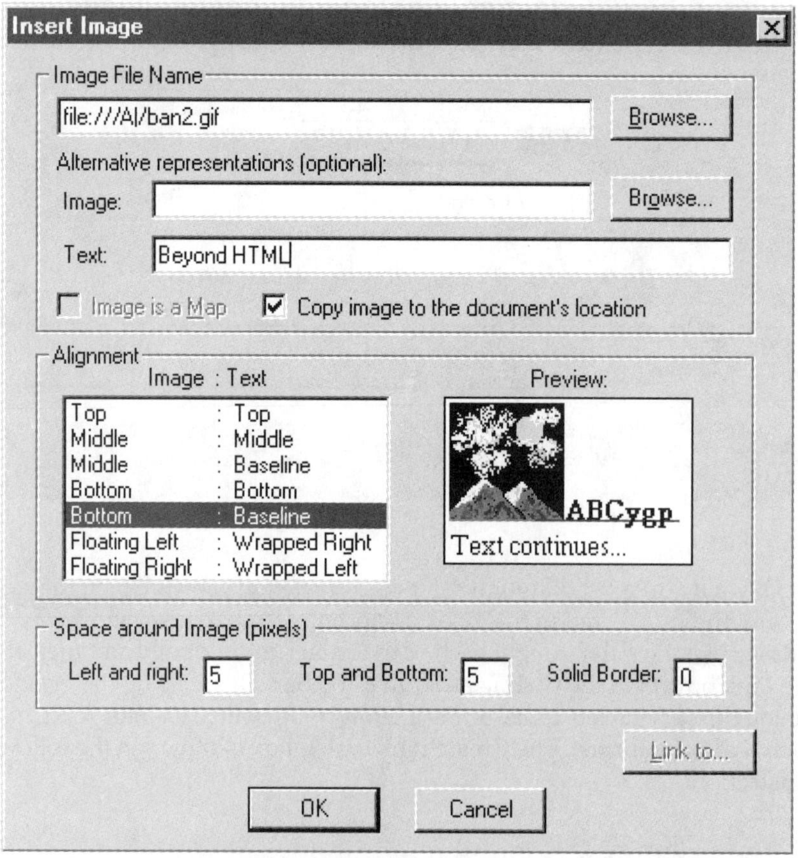

Insert Image

Image File Name

file:///A|/ban2.gif   Browse...

Alternative representations (optional):

Image: Browse...

Text: Beyond HTML

☐ Image is a Map   ☑ Copy image to the document's location

Alignment

Image : Text   Preview:

Top	: Top
Middle	: Middle
Middle	: Baseline
Bottom	: Bottom
Bottom	: Baseline
Floating Left	: Wrapped Right
Floating Right	: Wrapped Left

ABCygp

Text continues...

Space around Image (pixels)

Left and right: 5   Top and Bottom: 5   Solid Border: 0

Link to...

OK   Cancel

Figure 9-20.   *Insert Image dialog box*

In addition to using the Create Link dialog, Gold lets us drag and drop links from a browser, bookmark, mail, or news window directly into the editor window.

The page we have created, shown in Figure 9-21, is obviously a very simple HTML page, but we created it without writing a single HTML tag—something any Webmaster can appreciate. It provides a good demonstration of Gold's basic capabilities. More features will be added as the software goes through its beta cycle. But, overall, Netscape has designed Gold to be as simple as possible, sacrificing some cutting-edge authoring capabilities so as not to scare away users new to HTML editing.

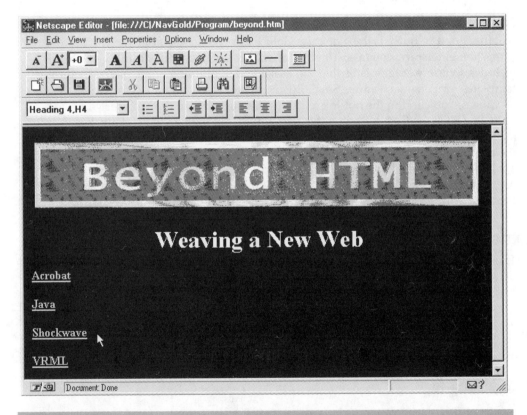

Figure 9-21.   *The page in Navigator Gold; notice the full WYSIWYG work-space*

Netscape Helper Pages

To help users create better home pages, Netscape has created several pages, accessible via the Web, with links to page templates, graphics and icon libraries, authoring guides, and more.

Netscape Page Starter Site

A good place to start is the Netscape Page Starter Site, which is accessible via Help/Web Page Starter on the Navigator Gold menu or via the URL **http://home.netscape.com/home/starter.html**. The page includes links to the Navigator Gold Data Sheet, a FAQ list, and more. It is a good place to start your Gold authoring journey.

Netscape Gold Rush Tool Chest

Another good resource is the Netscape Gold Rush Tool Chest, at **http://home.netscape.com/assist/net_sites/starter/samples/index.html**. The site includes a variety of templates that can assist you in building home pages, including templates for Personal, Family, Small Business, and Department pages. To use the templates, you click on the hotlink to call up the template in the browser window. Then you click the Edit button on the Navigator Gold toolbar, which launches Edit mode and saves the template page to your hard drive. You can then add and modify the template in Gold's WYSIWYG editing environment.

In addition to the templates, the page includes links to sites containing clip art, background images, Web design tips, copyright information, and more. It also contains a link to the Netscape Page Wizard, discussed next.

Netscape Page Wizard

The Netscape Page Wizard page offers a series of questions and choices for visitors to fill in. You can submit personal information such as your name and e-mail address. You can also choose a background image, choose your text and link colors, pick the graphical bullet type and horizontal rule you want to use, and add your favorite URLs to the page (see Figure 9-22).

When you've finished with the form, click submit, and your choices get spit back out a few moments later as a fully-designed Web page. You can then click the Edit

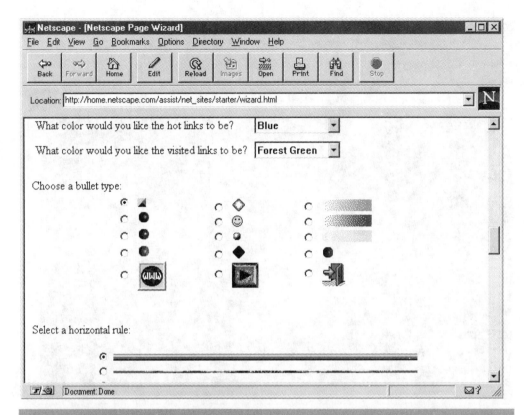

Figure 9-22. *The Netscape Page Wizard*

button to save the basic Wizard page and add to it in Gold's design window. See Figure 9-23 for an example of a page created with the Netscape Page Wizard. Notice the long **http://** address in the Location window, which shows the trick behind this. When you submit your choices, your data is sent to a Common Gateway Interface script running on the Netscape server that assembles and returns your custom Web page.

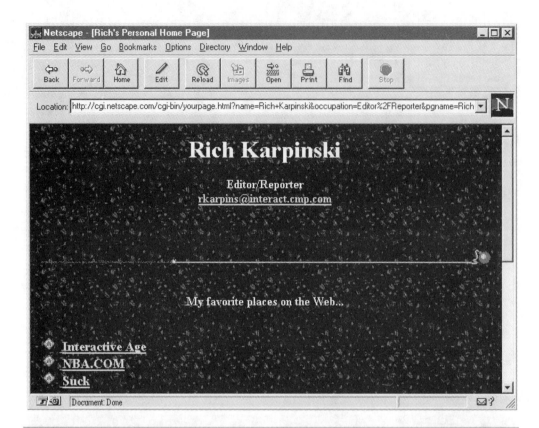

Figure 9-23. *A personal Web page built with the Wizard*

System Requirements

The following information is valid as of January, 1996. Support for more platforms is expected.

NETSCAPE NAVIGATOR 2.0
Runs on Windows 95, NT, 3.1, Mac OS, and a variety of Unix platforms.

NETSCAPE NAVIGATOR GOLD
Initially runs only on Windows 95 and NT.

Where to Find More Information about Netscape's Net Technologies

KEY NETSCAPE PAGES
Main page: **http://www.netscape.com**
Navigator 2.0 information: **http://www.netscape.com/comprod/products/ navigator/version_2.0/**
Navigator Gold information: **http://www.netscape.com/comprod/products/ navigator/gold/index.html**
Download Netscape Software: **http://www.netscape.com/comprod/mirror/ index.html**
JavaScript Resources page: **http://home.netscape.com/comprod/products/ navigator/version_2.0/script/script_info/index.html**
Frames Authoring Guide: **http://home.netscape.com/assist/net_sites/frames.html**
Navigator Gold Authoring Guide: **http://home.netscape.com/eng/mozilla/Gold/ authoring/navgold.htm**

OUTSIDE RESOURCES
Enhanced Netscape Hall of Shame: **http://www.meat.com/netscape_hos.html**
JavaScript Index: **http://www.c2.org/~andreww/javascript/**

Summary

Netscape has emerged as the company doing the most to lead the Web beyond HTML. It seems fitting, since Netscape also has stretched the limits of HTML itself with a series of innovative extensions. Netscape's Navigator 2.0 browser includes support for a number of important features, including frames, Java, JavaScript and Netscape's plug-in architecture. Netscape has also released Navigator Gold, an HTML authoring tool that should prove a great help to Webmasters. In Part Three, we'll see how Netscape is also making an impact on Virtual Reality Modeling Language (VRML). In Part Four, we'll examine their plans for delivering real-time audio and video. For Webmasters wanting to keep tabs on the next-generation of Web technology, keeping up with Netscape needs to be a priority.

Chapter Ten

Macromedia Shockwave

Of all the Netscape plug-ins we discussed in Chapter 9, the one having the biggest impact on the Web is undoubtedly Macromedia's Shockwave. If Shockwave effects on a Web site remind you of a CD-ROM title, including animations, video, sound, and interactivity, it's not surprising. What Shockwave does is bring the power of Macromedia Director, one of the leading multimedia and CD-ROM development platforms, to the World Wide Web.

Macromedia Director features an innovative user interface and powerful authoring capabilities that let multimedia developers create not only CD-ROM titles but multimedia kiosks, training titles, corporate presentations, and more. Shockwave brings those capabilities to the Web. It is made up of two parts: a compression engine called Afterburner that shrinks the size of Director titles for easier delivery over the Internet, and a Shockwave player that includes security, caching, and streaming features optimized for network playback. The result: inline Director movies that play back within a Web browser window, right within an HTML page. The Shockwave player will eventually plug into a variety of browsers, but in its early days worked only with Netscape Navigator 2.0.

Because Shockwave is not a new authoring environment but simply a new way to play back Director titles on the Web, the payoff was immediate: within days of Shockwave's release, scores of titles appeared on the Web, courtesy of an existing Director developer base that Macromedia estimates at more than 250,000 users. All of them were already experienced with Director and simply had to compress existing movies and create new movies with already familiar tools for delivery to a whole new online audience.

Shockwave can be used to create everything from small animations and effects to complete online games or movies. The only limit—though a major one still—is bandwidth. To keep visitors to your site happy, you don't want to include Shockwave files that are any larger than an average graphic file, say 50K to 100K—at least not without a warning. But you'd be surprised at the cool effects even such small titles can achieve, including a very engaging degree of interactivity, something that is missing today on most Web sites. We'll take a tour of the best "Shocked" sites later in this chapter.

Consider Shockwave a sneak preview of how the Web will eventually look when access bandwidth catches up with all the recent advances in Web software. The result will be full multimedia and engaging interactivity. Today, Shockwave sites are limited only by bandwidth constraints. It takes time to download a Director movie over a modem connection. But Macromedia is a major supporter of high-speed Net access—including a partnership with cable modem company @Home—and heralds the day when the bandwidth problem goes away and the Web becomes the standard way to deliver CD-ROM quality multimedia content.

In this chapter, we'll step through the process of using Director and Shockwave on the Web, including:

- A hands-on introduction to the Director authoring environment
- A step-by-step example of how to build Web-ready Director title
- An overview of how the Afterburner compression engine works

- A look at the Shockwave player
- A roundup of cool "Shocked" sites out on the Web

Working with Director

The simplest thing we can say about Director is that it is an *authoring tool*. To see what we mean by that, let's start our discussion by comparing Director and Java, both of which can enable multimedia and interactivity on the Web and are often viewed—mistakenly—as being somewhat interchangeable tools for creating interactive Web content.

Java, as we saw in Chapter 6, is a Web programming language. Still to emerge are solid Java development environments or authoring tools that can hide the complexity of Java from Web designers. Even as such tools emerge, the Java developer needs to do a lot of bare-bones coding to get the job done and needs to be fluent in high-end programming concepts.

Director, on the other hand, is built from the ground up as an authoring tool for multimedia designers, artists, and writers—not programmers. All of its complexity is hidden behind a rather ingenious user interface that makes it very easy to implement often complex effects. It also includes a simple programming language—the Lingo scripting language—that helps add interactivity to your work. (Macromedia has also licensed Java for inclusion in future versions of Director—more on that later.) The real strength of Director is that it makes it easy to create very powerful multimedia content, yet it also has the powerful features that will let high-end developers build extremely sophisticated titles.

This is not to say one of these technologies—Java or Director—is better than the other. They're just very different. As we take a closer look at Director, you'll see what a different experience it is from using Java, even though in some cases we can accomplish very similar effects.

One final note: all of this power does not come cheap. Macromedia Director carries a list price of about $1,200 (though the street price is almost half of that if you hunt around), which is quite a penny to drop but worth it if your Web site is looking for a new jolt.

Setting the Stage

So why did Macromedia call its tool Director? The answer is that the program literally lets you be the "director" of your multimedia "talent"—including text, graphic, video, and audio files. The authoring environment is built around this "director" metaphor: you import files into the "cast," orchestrate their movements using the "score," make a dry run through their efforts on the "stage" and play back resulting "movies" on a VCR-like "control panel." The Director environment may seem a little daunting at first glance (see Figure 10-1), but it is actually quite easy to understand once you begin working with it.

To build any Director movie, no matter how simple or complex, you'll need to go through the following steps:

1. Create a Cast, and if needed make changes or adjustments to individual Cast members.

2. Place the Cast on the Stage or in the Score.

3. Create animations.

4. Add transitions.

5. Add sound effects and music.

6. Make the movie interactive using the Lingo scripting language.

Let's introduce the key concepts in each of these steps one at a time. This will give you a good overview of Director's many capabilities. Later in this chapter, we'll take a more hands-on view, building a movie from scratch to better demonstrate Director in action.

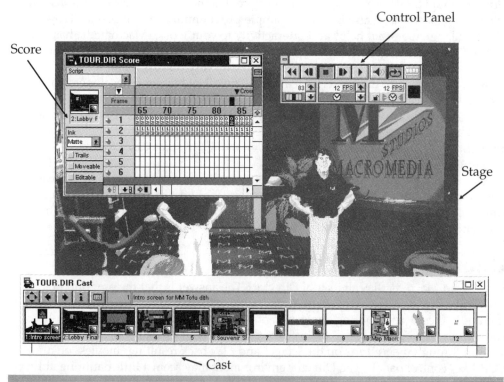

Figure 10-1. *The Director authoring environment*

Creating a Cast

The Cast shown here is a multimedia database that stores every piece of artwork in a Director movie. Anything stored in the Cast window is called a Cast member, including graphics, text, sound effects, and music, color palettes, buttons, digital video and Lingo scripts. Director supports a wide array of text, sound, graphics, and video formats. In Director 4.0 (the version we'll use here), you are able to create 32,000 different cast members.

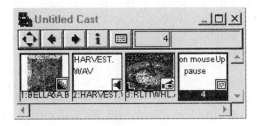

Director supports the following file types:

File Extension	File Type
.aif and .wav	Sound
.avi and .mov	Digital video movies
.bmp	Windows bitmap
.dir	Other Director movies
.eps	Encapsulated PostScript
.flc and .fli	Animator movies
.pal	Palettes
.gif	GIF files
.pcd	PhotoCD files
.pct	Macintosh PICTS
.pcx	PC PaintBrush files
.pnt	MacPaint files
.tif	TIFF files
.wmf	Windows metafiles

You can add files to the Cast window in two ways. You can create them with one of the tools, such as the Paint, Text, or Script window, that come as part of Director. More likely you'll want to create files with applications with which you are already familiar—such as PhotoShop (graphics), Premiere (video), or SoundEdit (audio)—and then import the files into the Cast. As long as you create files in a format that Director will understand, the program does not care how the files were created.

For creating simple graphic cast members or modifying existing ones, you'll likely spend significant time working with Director's Paint toolbox. The Paint toolbox includes all the usual things you'd expect, including drawing and coloring tools of all different sorts (see Figure 10-2).

One common way you'll use the Paint tools is to create a series of images for an animation. You can do this manually, but Director also includes a series of commands that make it very easy to make a series of small changes to a Cast member in order to create an animation. In many cases, you can even create the first and last images in an animation and let Director create the in-between positions itself, a powerful time-saving capability that also helps create smoother animations.

Paint also includes so-called Ink Effects, which let you modify the way colors or objects are displayed within a Director movie. For instance, you can choose which objects or colors will remain in the foreground and which will be in the background as they move about the Stage.

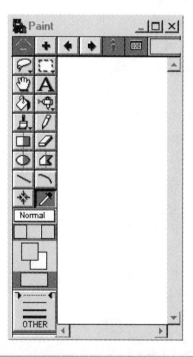

Figure 10-2. *Director's Paint toolbox*

Director also offers several options for creating text files. You can create bitmapped text in the Paint window, or use the Tools window to create straight text. Again, the environment offers lots of options and capabilities for creating just the text effects you need to spice up your movie.

Placing Cast Members on the Score and Stage

To add Cast members to a movie, you can either drag and drop them directly onto an individual cell in the Score, or you can place them on the Stage and their position will be recorded in the Score. In essence, the Score is just another view of what is happening on the Stage. But there is a difference. The Stage is a visual representation of your movie, allowing you to see how objects are assembled. The Score grid offers a much more detailed view, containing the precise details of every frame of your movie, including not only the images moving around on the Stage but details about the music, sound effects, color palettes, transitions, and interactive Lingo commands associated with each frame of the movie.

The Score is a grid made up of cells (see Figure 10-3). Each cell contains information about one Cast member at a particular moment. Each column of cells represents a frame of animation. It is the sum of everything that is happening at that moment in the movie. Each row of cells is called a *channel.* There are several different kinds of channels, including one each dedicated to tempo settings, color palettes, and scripts; two channels dedicated to sounds; and 48 sprite channels, mainly used for animations. The concepts of cells, frames, and channels will become more clear as we use Director.

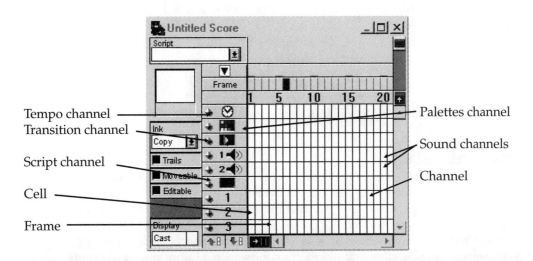

Figure 10-3. *Close-up view of the Score*

An important note: when you place a Cast member on the Stage or in the Score, you are not physically moving the file to a new spot. Instead, you are creating a new element called a sprite. In general terms, a *sprite* is an object used to create an animation. In Director, a sprite is essentially a copy of a Cast member that also includes information relating to where and how it appears in the movie. The unique information about a particular sprite is recorded in a cell, including the sprite's Cast number.

Placing individual sprites in the Score can be time-consuming, but Director has a number of time-saving techniques to help you fill the frames of a movie with the correct Cast members.

You can also place Cast members directly on the Stage (with their position automatically recorded in the Score as well). This can be useful in order to get a good visual picture of how your movie is developing. Until the process of constructing a movie begins, the Stage is a blank rectangle. But once you begin building your movie, you can see your work played back on the Stage frame by frame.

Creating Animations

Animations are the heart and soul of Director. While it does take some basic graphical skills to build the images to be used in an animation, Director also provides several powerful tools and capabilities that greatly simplify the creation of animations.

Before we take a look at Director's various animation techniques, let's also introduce the Control Panel (shown below) a key element in creating animations. The Control Panel looks and acts much like a VCR: it enables you to play, record, stop, rewind, and fast forward a movie or step through it frame by frame. You can use the Control Panel to record animations and other simple changes in your movie; then—like a VCR—you can use it to play back the movie to see if you have achieved the results you wanted.

Auto Animation

An easy way to create some simple animation effects is to use the Auto Animation command, which is found by pulling down the Score menu. It is used mainly in text- and chart-based animations; we'll use other techniques for more graphical animations. Typical uses for Auto Animation include animated banners, bar graphs, bullet charts, and credit lists. Auto Animation can also be used for text effects, such as creating text that appears to sparkle, slide into place across the screen, or appear as if it is being typewritten onto the screen.

All of these effects are created using simple, menu-driven templates. As an example, let's create an animated bar chart. The dialog box in Figure 10-4 shows our options.

We'll input a title and labels (both of which will remain stationary on the screen) as well as values for the bar chart (which will animate themselves into place). The results of our effort appear in Figure 10-5. The coins animate themselves into place, rising up from the bottom of the screen. As you can see, Auto Animation offers an extremely simple way to add some nice animated effects to our movie.

Real-Time Recording

Another very simple way to build an animation is to use real-time recording. Here, we get to see the Control Panel's VCR abilities in action. To do a real-time recording, you turn on the Control Panel's record button and grab a sprite and drag it across the Stage. The Control Panel records the motion, saving the placement of the sprite as it moved across the screen in the appropriate frames in the Score.

A common example of this sort of animation is a rising sun. First, with Director's Paint tool, we'll create a yellow circle. Then we'll add the file to the cast and select it. We initiate the real-time recording by holding down the CTRL key and the SPACEBAR

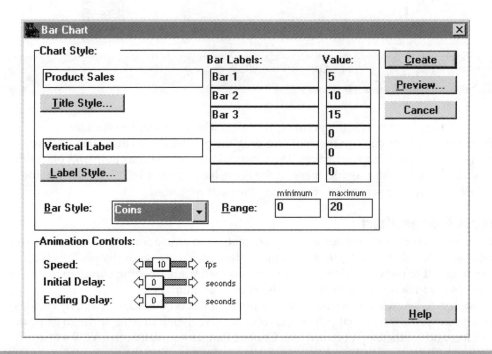

Figure 10-4. *The Bar Chart dialog box*

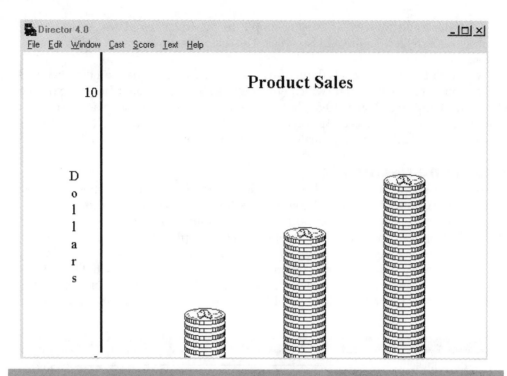

Figure 10-5.   *The output of the animated bar chart*

and pointing our mouse at the point on the Stage where we want to start the animation. Then we click on the spot and drag the pointer across the screen, releasing the mouse button to stop recording. The Control Panel records our path and places the information about our moving sprite in the Score (see Figure 10-6). On playback, the yellow sun will trail across the Stage along the path we traced.

Step Recording

A more tedious but often necessary way of creating an animation is to take a series of successive snapshots of a sprite as you manually move it across the Stage. This is a good method to use when there are multiple animations happening simultaneously, or when you want a certain degree of precision in your animation.

To step record, we'll place our sun cast member out on the Stage again. By clicking on the sun sprite, its original position is recorded. We then move the sprite to its next position, and hit the Step Forward (the Control Panel's equivalent to a VCR's fast forward button) to record the next frame. We continue moving the sprite and recording its placement frame by frame until our animation is complete. The movements on the Stage are duly recorded in the Score.

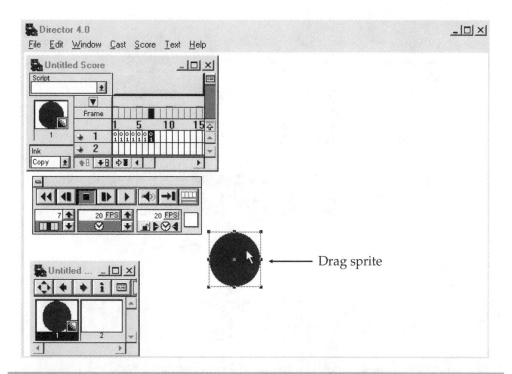

Figure 10-6. *For real-time recording, we turn the "VCR" on and drag a sprite; for step recording, we move and record the sprite one frame at a time*

Director has several tricks that make step recording easier, including a Cast to Time command that automatically arranges a series of cast members on the Stage to form an animation and a Paste Relative command that lets you repeat a sequence of images—for instance, a bird flying or person walking—while also automatically positioning the beginning of one sequence precisely at the position the previous sequence ended.

In-Betweening

The final animation command in Director is called in-betweening. This lets you indicate the starting and ending spots for an animation and have Director fill in the "in-between" images, either in a straight line or in a user-defined special path, such as a zigzag or arc. To use in-betweening, you place two sprites on the Score—one indicating the initial location and one representing the final location (see Figure 10-7). Highlight the space between the two sprites on the score, choose In-Between Linear or In-Between Special from the Score menu, and Director automatically fills in the in-between sprites to complete the animation.

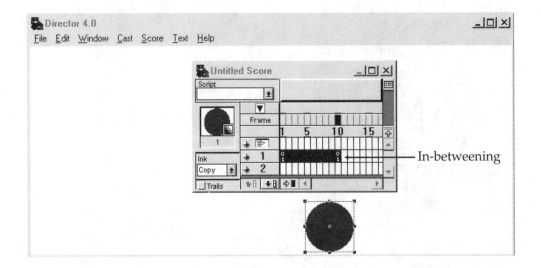

Figure 10-7. In-betweening an animation

In addition to creating simple animations, the In-Between command lets you quickly add background images to a movie. For instance, say you want a constant background through the first 100 frames of your movie. You can drag the background Cast member to cell 1, select the next 100 cells, and use the In-Between command to fill in the rest of the cells with the background Cast member.

Although we've just scratched the surface here, it's clear that Director's basic animation techniques and commands seem simple enough. It's how you use them that counts. With the ability to drag Cast members out on Stage and control the position of each and every sprite in the Score on a precise frame-by-frame basis, you can create literally any sort of animated effect you could possibly desire. The only limit is your creativity.

Adding Effects: Transitions and Sound

It's often said a movie is truly created not out on location but in the editing room. That's where the raw footage is assembled and pieced together into the final product, with a lot of magic added in the process. In Director, editing is done through the use of transitions. The program comes with over 50 built-in transitions offering a wide range of effects. For instance, you can dissolve from one scene to the next, wipe across a screen revealing a new scene as you go, or display a new scene strip by strip.

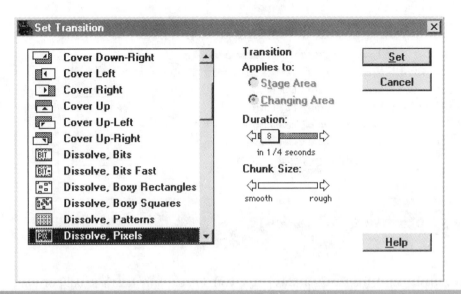

Figure 10-8. *The Set Transition dialog box*

As we noted earlier, there's a special channel in the Score just for transitions. To create a transition, you select the exact cell in the score where you want the transition to begin. Then you choose Set Transition from Director's Score menu, calling up the Set Transition dialog box (see Figure 10-8). Now you can choose the style of transition you want to employ. In addition, you can set how long the transition takes and whether it changes the whole Stage or just a portion of it.

Adding Sound Effects and Music

What's a movie without a soundtrack, right? Director offers two channels dedicated to sound effects, which makes it possible to have a score (background music) and a voice-over narration simultaneously, among other effects. Director also provides capabilities for controlling the playback of sounds, including in-betweening sounds to match them to movie events; repeating a short sound over and over, for instance, simulating a galloping horse or a knock on a door; controlling how sounds relate to other events on Stage; and controlling a sound file with a Lingo script, enabling effects such as an audio fade-out.

Director supports two audio formats: AIF and WAV. Since sounds cannot be created or recorded within Director, you'll need to import them into the Cast from other applications. To add sound to a movie, you drag the sound Cast member from the Cast window to the appropriate cells in the Score.

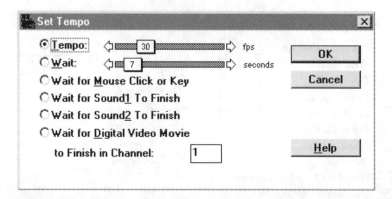

Figure 10-9. *The Set Tempo command*

If you play back the movie at this point, you'll likely only hear a small portion of the sound played back, because individual sounds usually need to take up more space than a single cell. To achieve better control of how sounds play back within a movie, you can use the Score's Set Tempo command (see Figure 10-9). This feature lets you slow down individual parts of a movie, or even better, ensure that a movie doesn't continue until a specific event finishes (in any channel you specify), for instance, the playback of a sound or a digital movie. Because different computers play back sounds at different rates (due to different processing speeds or sound card quirks), this method ensures your movie remains in sync.

Adding Interactivity with Lingo

Underlying all of Director's graphics tools and layout commands is a fully functional scripting language called Lingo. Lingo lets you add interactive elements to a Director movie. As you'll see later in this chapter, Shockwave movies—even small ones—can be quite complex. And obviously, full CD-ROM titles created in Director offer a great degree of interactivity and complexity. Driving such capabilities is Lingo, which lets you:

- Create navigation features that let users travel through a movie in the way that suits them best
- Interact with users by accepting user input and having it affect the playback of a movie
- Combine animation and sound in ways the Score can't do alone
- Have pinpoint control over text, sound, and digital video

As we saw earlier, Lingo scripts get their own channel in the Score. Director also provides a special window for writing Scripts, shown here. The first and last lines of the script are provided for you.

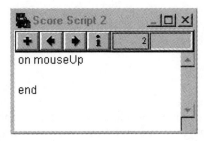

Lingo is a fully featured scripting language, and we'll just scratch its surface here. Perhaps the most common form of Director interactivity is navigation. So what we will do is show how easy it is to use Lingo to do some of the most common navigation effects, such as creating clickable buttons and hypertext links for navigating between scenes of a movie.

Navigating with Lingo Scripts

Creating navigation buttons is simple using Director. The Tools window (accessible via the menu) has tools for creating standard buttons, radio buttons, and checkboxes, as shown below. For navigation purposes, you'll most likely use a standard button, which a user will click to initiate an action such as jumping to another scene in a movie. That jump is enabled by a Lingo script.

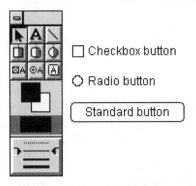

In addition to using buttons for navigation, you can also highlight individual text blocks or images and have them act as hotlinks (much like a Web URL). The trick to do this is to lay a transparent box over the word or image you want to link. The box—which won't be seen on Stage once it is made transparent—can have the script attached to it. Thus when you click on the word or image, you'll also be clicking on the transparent box with a script attached.

We'll need to introduce one more concept before we write some sample navigation scripts: markers. With a navigation script, you will be telling Director to jump to a specific frame in a movie. You could use the Lingo command:

```
go to frame 13
```

The problem is that if you delete or add a frame, the numbering of individual frames could change, ruining your script. Frame 13 will no longer contain the context you intended. Director addresses this by letting you attach a marker to a frame and giving it a name, as shown here. To create a marker, you grab one from the Marker Well and drag it above the frame you want to mark.

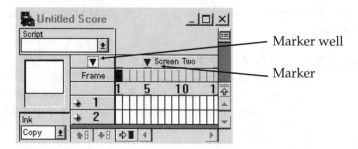

Then use the following Lingo command:

```
go to frame "Screen Two"
```

If the frame number changes, that's ok. You can still jump to the frame's marker name.

Writing Lingo Scripts

Whether you want to navigate using buttons or text-based hotlinks, you'll need to write a Lingo script to create the actual navigation logic. There are three main types of script when it comes to navigation: cast member scripts, sprite scripts, and frame scripts.

CAST MEMBER SCRIPTS When you attach a script to a cast member, the script stays with the cast member every time it is used in a movie. The most common use of cast member scripts is the creation of the navigation buttons themselves. For instance, you might want to create a button that always returns a user to the first screen of a title—a "Home" button. Set a marker called "Home" on the frame containing the first screen. Create a button using the Director toolbar, and then attach the following script to it:

```
on mouseUp
  go to frame "Home"
end
```

INSIDE Spin

What Macromedia Has to Say About Shockwave

Shockwave is most exciting when viewed through the eyes of Macromedia Director developers, says Joe Dunn, Macromedia's vice president of product management.

"Our user base is incredibly enthusiastic about Shockwave," says Dunn. "They all know Director and they have their movies ready to go [to the Web]. A large percentage of these people will just go berserk. In the first wave we'll see simple animations and preexisting titles being put on the Web. Then as these people get more fluid in this new medium, we'll see all kinds of innovative, new stuff."

Dunn believes that once Web surfers see Shockwave in action, they will "go berserk" as well. "Shockwave changes people's perception of the Web immediately. Once you've seen a page like this you don't want to go back," Dunn said.

Dunn adds that while Macromedia is a big backer of cable modems and other emerging high-bandwidth alternatives, "there all kinds of authoring tricks to generate nice-looking, small movies. Because we compress the movies with Afterburner, you can get a decent animation in less size than the original graphic."

Macromedia is already hard at work on the next version of Shockwave, which will include support for streaming audio, media-specific compression, and the ability to download a large Shockwave movie in pieces rather than all at once. Macromedia will also introduce new capabilities that will let Director-built CD-ROM titles be extended with dynamic Internet content via Shockwave, according to Dunn.

Macromedia has also forged a close relationship with Sun Microsystems, working together to build new multimedia object classes for Java as well as integrate Java applets into Director. While Java's hype machine has that programming language being used for everything from small-scale animations to large-scale networking applications, Dunn says he envisions Java mainly being used to add more sophisticated networking capabilities to Macromedia Director.

That will be especially important as greater amounts of bandwidth become available via cable modems and other technologies, says Dunn. Macromedia is working with Sunnyvale, California–based @Home to build a new generation of interactive multimedia applications that can be run over 10Mb/s-plus–capable cable modems, Dunn says, an effort that should begin to bear fruit this year as @Home rolls out its first trials. "With cable modems in place, very highly interactive and dynamic titles suddenly become possible."

Since the button and script are associated in the cast, you can use the same Home button at many different places within your movie and achieve the same effect: a trip back to the opening screen.

SPRITE SCRIPTS   Alternatively, you might want to add a script to a sprite (the individual instance of a Cast member on Stage and in the Score). A text hyperlink is a good example of this. Say you want to make a particular onscreen image "hot." You can create a script for the particular sprite, without having it attach it to the cast member from which the sprite was created. Thus the image will have a script attached to it only at one specific appearance on Stage. The Cast member that is that image can then be used elsewhere in a movie, and the script will not be attached.

FRAME SCRIPTS   You might also want to attach a script to a frame in a movie. A common use of this is a "pause" script, which uses Lingo to momentarily pause the movie at a certain frame. Perhaps the simplest Frame script is one that pauses and then continues a movie based on user input. To pause the movie, use the script:

```
on exitFrame
  pause
end
```

This will hold the movie up at the frame that contains this script. To get the movie playing again, create a Standard button and attach a Cast script to it:

```
on mouseUp
  continue
end
```

When the user hits the button, the movie will continue.

More Lingo

There's obviously much more you can do with Lingo than we have shown so far. Table 10-1 offers a view of some of the more useful features. We'll also try some new Lingo tricks in the next section, including using Lingo commands introduced with Shockwave that target the Web specifically.

Building a Shockwave Movie

Now let's have some fun with the new skills we've learned. Our goal: create a graphical, interactive table of contents for a potential Web site supporting this book.

To Achieve This Effect	Use This Command
Make a sprite highlight or change when a user clicks on it	puppetSprite
Make a sound play when a user clicks on a button or image	puppetSound
Have something happen when the user holds the mouse button down	on mouseDown
Have something happen when the user moves the pointer over an element	on rollOver
Have a movie make a decision based on user input	if then else

Table 10-1. *Some Lingo Commands*

Our Cast members will include a several small logos representing the different sections of the book. We'll strike up the band for some background music, use some autoanimate text effects and animation techniques to dance the logos out on the Stage, and then set them up in an interactive fashion as live hotlinks to related pages on the Web.

That may not seem simple, but it is. As we'll see with this example and in our tour later in the chapter of "Shocked" sites, many sites use a very small range of Director features to create very compelling effects on a Web page. The addition of even a small dose of animation and sounds is really quite a shock to the system when you are accustomed to static Web pages.

In addition to applying our newly learned Director skills in a hands-on environment, this exercise will also let us examine what's needed to turn a Director movie into a Shockwave file. We'll examine and use the Afterburner compression engine and look at the HTML tags and server tricks you'll need to serve up Shockwave titles.

Beyond HTML: the Shocked Version

We won't go through the building of our movie step by step—we'll just hit the highlights (especially where they introduce new concepts).

First, we'll import the logos we plan to use in our movie into the Cast window. Some of the logos are in JPG format, others in GIF (we stole them from Web pages), but the Cast accepts both, as you can see here.

To start the movie, we'll use an autoanimate effect that types the word "Introducing…." across the screen one letter at a time. To do this, we'll access the Auto Animate option of the Score's menu. The Auto Animate dialog box to achieve this effect is shown in Figure 10-10. Once we hit OK, Director automatically does everything necessary to create the effect, filling up a long series of cells in the score with the data needed to achieve this effect.

Next, we'll use a combination of another Auto Animate feature and some simple animation techniques to bring our logos (representing several of the major sections of this book) out onto the Stage.

First, we'll use the Auto Animate effect Zoom Text to flash the name of a section on the Stage. The Zoom Text dialog box (Figure 10-11) lets us very easily create this text effect. Next, we'll replace the Zoom Text on the Stage with the appropriate logo by dragging the appropriate logo out of the Cast window and into the Score precisely at the Zoom Text effect ends.

Finally, we'll use the in-betweening animation techniques we learned earlier in the chapter. We'll drag another version of the same logo Cast member into the Score,

Figure 10-10. *The Text Effects dialog box*

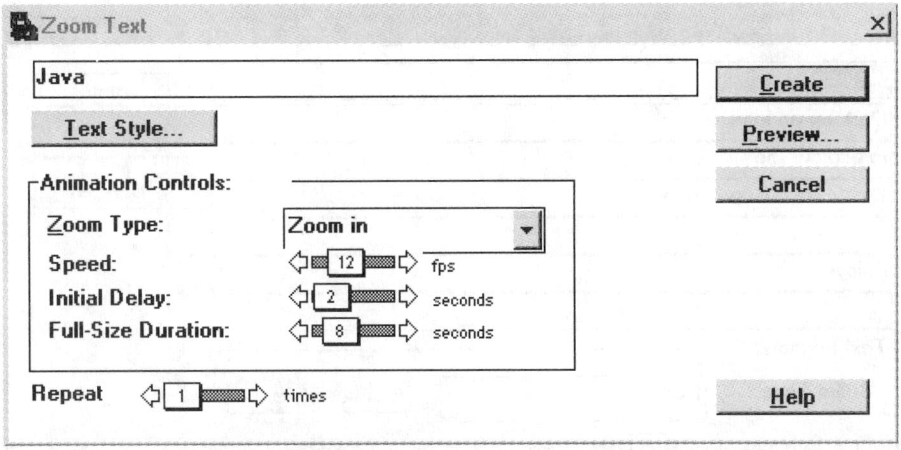

Figure 10-11. *The Zoom Text dialog box*

about 20 frames ahead of the logo already there. Then we highlight the frames between the two cells, and click on the In Between Linear option of the Score menu. This automatically creates the animation to move the logo from its starting place across the screen to its final resting place. One by one, like a puzzle, we'll introduce each section in the book with a Zoom Text effect and then animate the section's logo across the screen.

With all of the logos in place, we'll use another Auto Animate effect, Bullet Chart, to introduce some additional text welcoming visitors to our site. The Bullet Chart effect will let us bring the text out onto the Stage like a text marquee. The dialog box enabling the Bullet Chart is in Figure 10-12.

Next, although you obviously won't hear it in print, we'll add a small, looped WAV audio file that plays behind the movie as it runs. To add the sound, we'll import the WAV file into the cast. Double-clicking on the sound Cast member calls up a dialog box (see Figure 10-13) that shows the details of the sound file and lets us preview it and check a box that causes the sound to loop. With that, the main animation for our movie is complete.

Now, let's add an interactive element to our movie. The main thing we want to do is make each of the logos a hotlink to a Web URL containing more information on that section. To do that, first we'll add a transparent button covering each of the logos' final sprite position on the Stage, as we demonstrated earlier in the chapter (see "Navigating with Lingo Scripts"). Then, we'll associate a short Lingo script with each of the Cast member boxes:

```
on mouseUp
 GotoNetPage "http://www.beyond.html/sectionname.html"
end
```

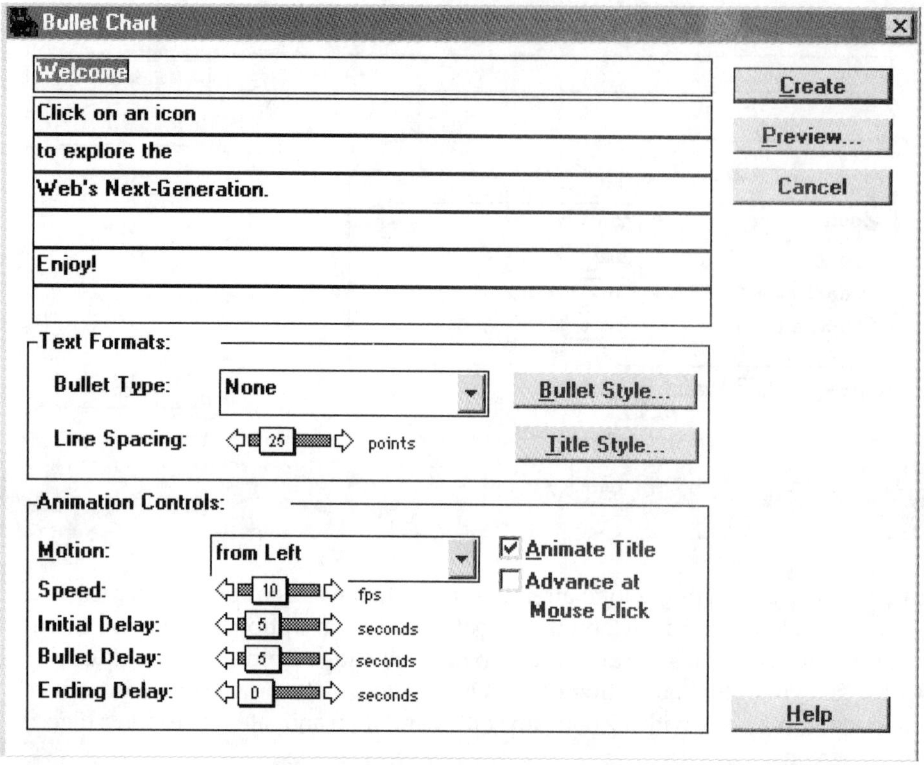

Figure 10-12. *The Bullet Chart dialog box*

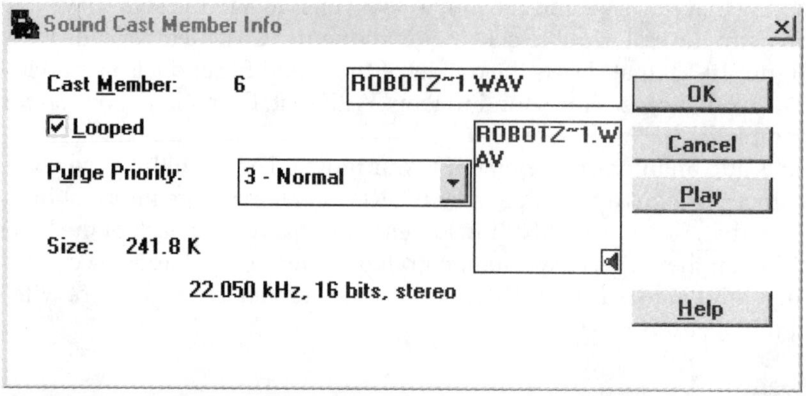

Figure 10-13. *The Sound Cast Member Info dialog box*

This Lingo script will send the Web browser out to get a new HTML page and display it within the browser window. It is one of a series of new Lingo commands introduced with Shockwave, all of which help Director deal with network resources (see Table 10-2).

And with that, we're done creating our Director movie, and now we're set to get it ready for delivery over the Web.

Preparing a Movie for the Web

The next step in getting our Director movie ready for the Web is to run it through the Afterburner compression engine, available from the Macromedia Web site at **http://www.macromedia.com**. Afterburner is available for free on the Macromedia Web site, and it will be included as part of future versions of Director. You can download the software and then run it on your local PC. To compress a movie with the Windows version, you double-click on the Afterburner icon to display the Open dialog box. Select the movie (with a .dir extension) you want to convert. Afterburner compresses the title to reduce download time and converts it to .dcr format (see Figure 10-14). The conversion doesn't change the appearance of the movie—it simply compresses it.

That's all there is to Afterburner. It simply converts a .dir file to a .dcr format, compressing it in the process. In theory, Macromedia says Afterburner can make

Use This Shockwave Lingo Command	To Achieve This Effect
GetNetText URL	Retrieve an HTTP item that is read by Lingo as text. URL is a parameter that specifies the HTTP item to retrieve. At present, only HTTP URLS are supported as valid uri parameters.
PreloadNetThing URL	Preload an HTTP item into the local file cache. The HTTP item can be anything, including a Director movie, an HTML page, a graphic, etc. At present, only HTTP URLS are supported as valid uri parameters.
GotoNetMovie URL	Retrieves a new Director movie from the network and plays it in the same display space as the calling movie.
GotoNetPage URL	Opens a URL, whether it's a Director movie or some other MIME type. Using GotoNetPage opens a new page within the net browser.

Table 10-2. *New Shockwave Lingo Commands*

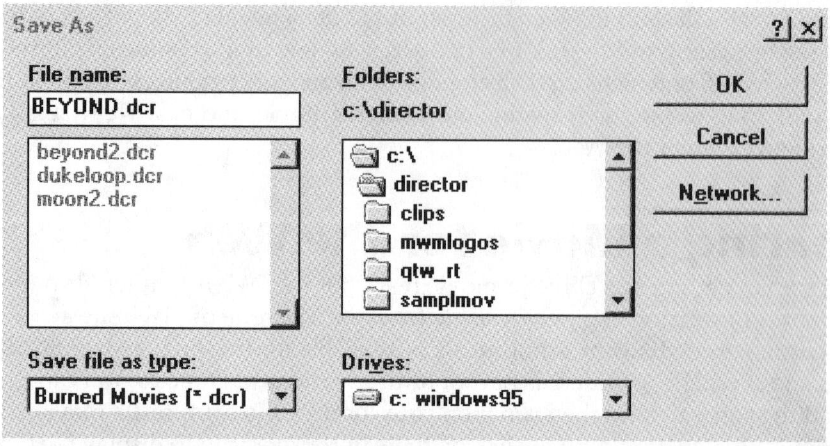

Figure 10-14. *The Afterburner dialog box*

Director movies as much as six times smaller. The sample movie we created started out at 146K and shrunk down to 42K, a compression of almost 4:1 (a typical level we found in our testing of Afterburner).

You also need to set your HTTP server to handle Shockwave content. Set the MIME type for .dcr files to application/x-director.

The final step is to create an HTML page that serves up the Shockwave movie. A new HTML tag—EMBED—allows you to put documents directly into an HTML page. The syntax for the tag is this:

```
<EMBED SRC="path/filename.ext" WIDTH=n HEIGHT=n TEXTFOCUS=focus>
```

The WIDTH and HEIGHT parameters let you specify the width and height of the Shockwave title display space in the Netscape browser in pixels. The optional TEXTFOCUS parameter lets you tell the Shockwave plug-in when to start responding from user input. The parameters include onStart, onMouse, and never.

A second tag—<NOEMBED>—can be used to substitute text or a graphic file for a Shockwave movie so that visitors to your site without a Shockwave-capable browser won't see a fractured page.

The HTML page for our sample Shockwave movie looks like this:

```
<HTML>
<HEAD>
<TITLE>Shockwave</TITLE>
</HEAD>
```

```
<BODY BGCOLOR="#FFFFFF">
<H1>Beyond HTML: Weaving a New Web</H1>
<EMBED SRC="Beyond2.dcr" Height= 450 width=750>
</BODY>
</HTML>
```

Shockwave Player: Viewing the Movie

To play back our movie within the Netscape browser, we'll need the Shockwave plug-in, also available for free download at **http://www.macromedia.com**. For our work in this chapter, we used the beta version 1.0b1 of the Shockwave plug-in for Windows 95. To use the plug-in, you download the executable file from the Macromedia Web site and install it. Shockwave does not exist as a stand-alone application; it only works in conjunction with the Netscape browser. It does so seamlessly. You won't even know it's there until Navigator hits a "Shocked" Web site.

By the time this book hits the stores, version 1.0 of Shockwave should be available for both Windows and Macintosh platforms. Shockwave won't end with version 1.0; Macromedia is already working on new features for the next generation of Shockwave (see "The Inside Spin" for details). Macromedia promises to always have the Shockwave plug-in available for free download over the Net.

The first version of the Shockwave plug-in works only with Netscape Navigator, but Macromedia promises to have versions available for browsers from Microsoft, Silicon Graphics, CompuServe, and America Online's Navisoft browsers as well.

As a final step in creating our sample "Beyond HTML" movie, let's play it back in the Netscape browser. First, the logos animate themselves into place. Then the welcoming text animates itself into place (see Figure 10-15). When complete, the logos in the movie can be clicked on to hotlink to other HTML pages on the site.

A "Shocked" Tour of the Web

The best way to get a sense of the power of Shockwave is to head out onto the Web for a tour of "Shocked" sites. Within a month of Shockwave's release, literally hundreds of Shockwave movies appeared on the Web. Let's take a look at a few of the more innovative sites on the Web to get an idea of just how far you can take Shockwave with a little creativity.

One popular and fairly simple use of Shockwave is to create an animated logo or banner. It may not sound like much, but again, it makes a major difference to Web surfers to see an animated logo and hear a background sound track. And because it is a fairly small file, animated logos can be integrated seamlessly into a Web page. The Yahoo search engine animated its logo, which was already a funky graphic—suiting the company's image—that became even funkier with a bouncy sound track and an

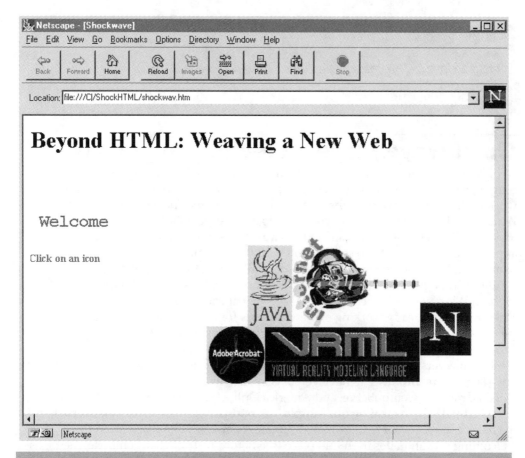

Figure 10-15. *With the logos assembled, the final text, Welcome," enters, stage left*

animation that caused the logo's letters to dance around (see Figure 10-16). See the movie at **http://shock.yahoo.com/shock/**.

   An even better use of Shockwave is to create a multimedia, interactive user interface. One of the major things lacking in HTML user interfaces is any sort of feedback. Typically, a user will click on an image map and then check out the Netscape

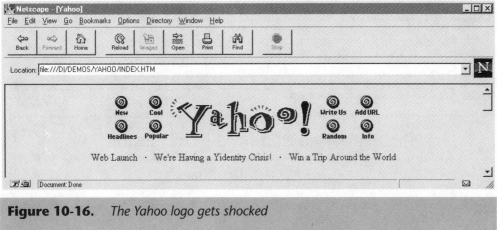

Figure 10-16. *The Yahoo logo gets shocked*

logo to make sure the new page is being fetched. With Shockwave, you can build user feedback right into your interfaces, for instance, by adding a click or having a button change colors when clicked on.

Speaking of feedback, one of our favorite Shockwave sites is this Beavis and Butthead site by Patrick Joiner (see Figure 10-17), which can be found at **http://www.worldramp.net/~pjoiner/bandb**. Click on one of the buttons, and the guys spring to life with animation and sound. A simple but entertaining use of Shockwave.

All of these examples so far add interesting inline elements to HTML pages, serving to "accessorize," so to speak, a Web page. But Shockwave can also be used to create more elaborate movies. Games are an especially hot area. The site supporting the movie *Toy Story*, for instance, includes a Concentration-style game that lets the user turn over pieces of a puzzle to find matches of *Toy Story* characters (Figure 10-18). Find the site on the Web at **http://www.toystory.com/toybox/shock.htm**.

Design house MB/Interactive, meanwhile, has created a new sort of animal—sort of a Shockwave animated music video called Deep Forest—that includes cool animations and a pulsing sound track (see Figure 10-19). This very large file can be downloaded from **http://www.mbinter.com/deepforest/deepforest.html**.

These examples are just a start. And don't believe that just because many of these sites are run by large companies or design firms that the average user can't tap into Shockwave. There are plenty of personal home pages sporting Shockwave movies, including animations, games, and even multimedia, interactive resumes. The possibilities are endless.

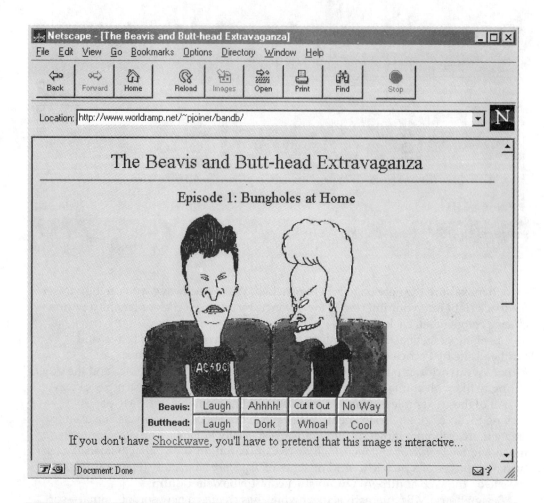

Figure 10-17. *Beavis and Butthead get Shocked*

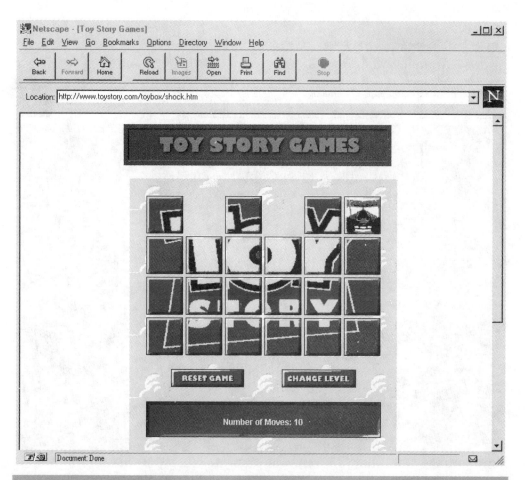

Figure 10-18. *The Toy Story site includes a Shockwave game*

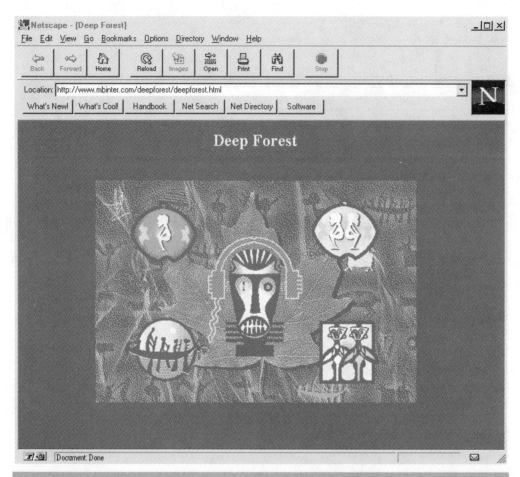

Figure 10-19. *Deep Forest offers a Shockwave animated music video*

System Requirements for Shockwave

SHOCKWAVE PLAYER
Available for Windows 3.1, Windows 95, and Mac OS.

AFTERBURNER COMPRESSION ENGINE
Available for Windows 3.1 and Mac OS.

Where to Find More Information on Shockwave

SHOCKWAVE MAIN WEB PAGE
http://www.macromedia.com/Tools/Shockwave/

SHOCKWAVE DEVELOPERS CENTER
http://www.macromedia.com/Tools/Shockwave/sdc/Dev/index2.htm

Finding Shockwave Titles on the Web

Shockwave Gallery: **http://www.macromedia.com/Tools/Shockwave/Gallery/index.html**
The Vanguard Gallery: **http://www.macromedia.com/Tools/Shockwave/Gallery/Vanguard/index.html**
Shockwave Epicenter: **http://www.macromedia.com/Tools/Shockwave/Gallery/epicenter.html**

Other Web Sites Devoted to Shockwave

Marc Canter/Mediaband: **http://mediaband.com/shockwave.html**
The Director Web: **http://www.mcli.dist.maricopa.edu/director/**

Summary

In this chapter, we took a look at the hottest plug-in on the Web, Macromedia's Shockwave. Forget static Web pages—Shockwave brings a new wave of animations, graphics, sound, and interactivity to the Internet. And because it is based on Macromedia's popular and well-established Director authoring tool, you can begin working with Shockwave today.

We demonstrated how easy it is to begin authoring compelling multimedia titles using Director, while at the same time showing Director's power features for creating more sophisticated content, such as online games or CD-ROM-like titles. Finally, we examined the Shockwave player and the Afterburner compression engine, the tools that make Director on the Internet a reality.

Shockwave makes it easy to add multimedia to your Web pages. The price tag may be high, but the learning curve is low—"Shock" your Web site today.

PART THREE

VRML: Virtual Reality Meets the Web

In Part Three we will take a hands-on look at the Virtual Reality Modeling Language (VRML), which can be used to create 3-D worlds on the Web. In Chapter 11, we'll examine the history of VRML and introduce the language itself. Chapter 12 provides a hands-on tutorial of several of the most exciting authoring tools—Caligari's Fountain, Virtus' WalkThrough, and ParaGraph's Virtual Home Space Builder—and gets you started building your own 3-D worlds. Finally, in Chapter 13, we'll take a guided tour of emerging VRML worlds.

Chapter Eleven

Introduction to VRML

The Internet and the World Wide Web are often described as representing the "leading edge of cyberspace," a phrase first popularized by science fiction writer William Gibson to describe a non-physical world of pure information. But where's the "space" in the current Web's version of cyberspace? While Web surfing can often feel like a three-dimensional experience, as you envision yourself bouncing from server to server across the globe, what you are really interacting with is a flat, 2-D page filled with mostly flat, 2-D information. There's no "there" there. The Virtual Reality Modeling Language (VRML) promises to change all that.

VRML is a language that can be used to create three-dimensional worlds on the Web. By taking advantage of easy-to-use authoring tools based on the VRML 1.0 standard, Web authors can build virtual representations of almost any space in the real world—houses, museums, even the inside of an Intel microprocessor (see Figure 11-1).

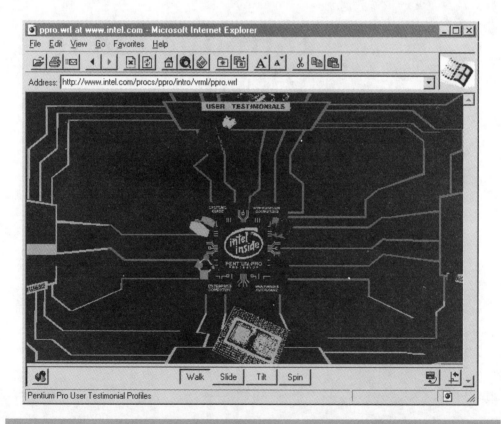

Figure 11-1. *Inside an Intel Pentium processor (viewed with Microsoft Explorer 2.0 VRML add-on)*

Web authors can deliver entirely new virtual environments, sprung full-blown from their imaginations. These worlds can then be delivered from standard Web servers and navigated in three dimensions by site visitors.

3-D worlds are not stand-alone islands. VRML is completely linked to the Web and any pages built using HTML. To reach a VRML world on the Web, click on a hotlink or type in a URL. 3-D worlds are downloaded over the Net and displayed in a VRML viewer. The viewer is run either as a helper application or a plug-in. Once inside a 3-D world, you can move around and click on hotlinked objects that will transport you to another VRML site, or even out to an HTML page. VRML does not replace the 2-D Web; it complements it.

Why is VRML important? In other words, why build a 3-D site rather than a flat HTML page? VRML offers a way to represent and organize information that is more intuitive than the Web's now-comfortable paradigm of interlinked "pages." We navigate a 3-D world every day—the real world we live in. We respond instinctively to visual and spatial cues such as the texture of an object, the location of light sources, or the speed of an approaching object. We process, learn from, and form opinions about this information without even thinking.

Virtual reality also offers a more compelling way to organize information. It is very natural in the real world to describe something by specifying its relationship to something else: "I live in the last house on the right;" "The book is in the library, on the top shelf." Wouldn't it be better to point a visitor to information on your site visually—"it's near the front gate," for instance—than offering them a cryptic URL? As we all travel the wide expanses of the Web, wouldn't it be nice to navigate a consistent, interconnected, virtual world rather than a series of pages filled with unrelated text and graphics? This vision can become a reality thanks to VRML.

Let's say you want to set up a virtual "home" on the Web. What would be more welcoming to your visitors, a page with graphics, text, and links; or a 3-D world complete with comfortable chairs, a blazing fireplace, and a view of a lake through a large picture window? A successful VRML world invites the user to come on in, look around, and make themselves at home.

As with most of the technologies discussed in this book, VRML is still in its early stages, but it has evolved quickly, becoming a viable alternative to HTML for some important Web applications. Even in their early phases, VRML and VRML-based tools were used to create some extremely interesting 3-D spaces on the Web. Future versions of VRML will have new capabilities, making 3-D worlds even more realistic and interactive than before.

In this chapter, we'll discuss some of the fascinating background details of how VRML was created, tour a handful of 3-D worlds, and provide a downloader's guide to the best VRML viewers and authoring tools on the Web. We'll also introduce some key concepts from the world of 3-D graphics and give an introductory look at the bare-bones VRML 1.0 scene description language.

VRML vs HTML

ADVANTAGES

- VRML offers a richer, more immersive experience than HTML, a familiar way of presenting and organizing information, and the ability to experience a space first-hand or view an object in three dimensions.

- VRML can help Web surfers better navigate your site—or the entire Web. Remembering URLs or waiting for new HTML pages to download can in no way compare to moving through a fully three-dimensional space.

- VRML provides authoring tools that hide the complexity of the language from Web authors, allowing them to create sophisticated 3-D worlds with little fuss.

DISADVANTAGES

- VRML is more complex than HTML for both Web authors and surfers. Designing a space requires visualization skills that even experienced page layout artists may lack. Like Java, Webmasters may have to hire VRML experts from the outside. For Web surfers, meanwhile, working with a keyboard and mouse, navigating a VRML world can at times be a dizzying, frustrating experience.

- VRML works best on high-end computers with relatively fast modems. There is no way to view VRML on low-end machines, and if you are running a slow modem some worlds will take a long time to download.

- There is a danger that VRML will splinter as industry giants battle over the direction of VRML 2.0.

The Sixty-Second History of VRML

VRML has an interesting history—and, as with all Web technologies, a relatively recent one. Mark Pesce and Tony Parisi are the two individuals credited with pushing the early vision of a virtual reality interface for the Web. Jazzed by the notion of linking 3-D graphics with the interconnectivity of the Web, they built the first prototype virtual reality browser, dubbed Labyrinth, in February of 1994. Labyrinth displayed a 3-D banana that, when clicked on, jumped out to the HTML-based Web.

The next step in the evolution of Web-based virtual reality came later that May at the First International Conference on the World Wide Web in Geneva. There, led by Web pioneers Tim Berners-Lee and Dave Raggett, the seeds of a new 3-D Web language were planted. Back then, VRML meant Virtual Reality *Markup* Language, to mirror HyperText Markup Language. Later, the VRML acronym changed to Virtual Reality Modeling Language.

Then, Brian Behlendorf, VRML pioneer and Webmaster at HotWired, started up a mailing list to encourage contributions to the development of VRML. The list soon became a vibrant sounding board for 3-D enthusiasts pitching 3-D graphics formats as the best solution for VRML. The mailing list is still a vital source of information. (See the "Tech Resources" section in the next chapter subscription information.)

The ultimate winner in 3-D graphics formats, which eventually became the standard for VRML 1.0, came from a subset of Silicon Graphics' Open Inventor 3-D programming library with a scene description language the group thought could serve as the foundation for VRML. Open Inventor's principal designers were Gavin Bell and Rikk Carey. Silicon Graphics, Inc. (SGI) placed the subset of Open Inventor into the public domain. With some additional networking extensions, the subset eventually became VRML 1.0. SGI, Bell, and Carey also wrote a VRML parser, called QvLib, which takes in VRML files and spits out 3-D objects.

The draft specification for VRML 1.0 made its maiden appearance at the Second International Conference on the Web in Chicago in October of 1994, a little less than half a year after the first seeds of VRML were planted in Geneva. VRML was made "official"—a strange phrase, given all of the openly public development that had already come to pass—in April of 1995, when SGI announced the existence of VRML to the world, and its own plans to build (along with its partner, Template Graphics Software) a VRML browser called WebSpace.

From its launch, VRML has exploded. Hundreds of VRML worlds are already available for touring on the Web. A growing group of companies have built VRML browsers and authoring tools. In addition, the VRML file format has become a standard feature in most 3-D graphics tools.

In less than two years, the dream of a virtual reality interface into the World Wide Web moved from vision to reality.

What's Possible with VRML?

A textual history of VRML is nice, but before we move on let's see a few more VRML worlds in action. (For a more in-depth tour of VRML worlds, see Chapter 13.)

One of the most ambitious early VRML projects was a complete 3-D rendering of San Francisco's SOMA neighborhood, an area that includes many of the pioneering companies and individuals working with 3-D graphics and the Web. Visitors to Virtual SOMA can tour the neighborhood and click on buildings to enter additional 3-D worlds and Web pages from the companies in the neighborhood (see Figure 11-2). VR SOMA was built by Planet 9 Studios and can be found at **http://www.planet9.com/ vrsoma.htm**.

While the VR SOMA project is notable for its size and ambition, another early site, Duke's Diner, gets points for combining two next-generation Web technologies—VRML and RealAudio streaming sound (see Figure 11-3). Created by SteelStudios and MarketCentral, the Duke's Diner site offers a sharp, three-dimensional diner and includes audio clues that help you hunt down Duke. The site can be found at **http://www.marketcentral.com/vrml/vrml.html**.

These two worlds will get your imagination flowing about how you might want to use VRML. Almost anything is possible, but some natural VRML applications include three-dimensional engineering and medical visualizations, commercial applications such as navigable shopping malls and virtual offices, as well as virtual museums and art galleries.

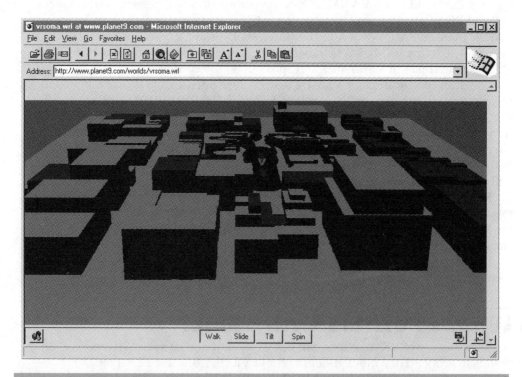

Figure 11-2.   *VR SOMA (viewed with Internet Explorer VRML plug-in)*

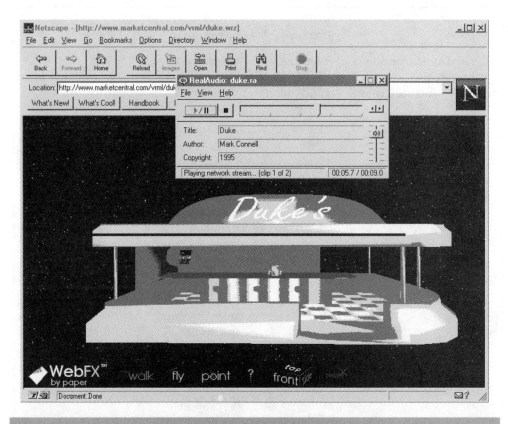

Figure 11-3. *Duke's Diner combines VRML and RealAudio (viewed with Paper Software's WebFX plug-in for Netscape Navigator)*

Where to Find VRML Viewers

By now, you probably want to get out on the Web and view these and other cool VRML worlds for yourself. To do that, you'll need a VRML viewer. VRML viewing tools come in a wide variety these days. Some run only as helper applications to Web browsers, others run as stand-alone applications, and others work as plug-ins to browsers such as Netscape Navigator (see Table 11-1).

Since our discussion here is more about VRML authoring than browsing, we won't go into great detail about how to obtain and run each VRML browser. Instead, for each VRML screen shown in Part Three, we'll note which browser is used. That way, you'll get a good feel for the different VRML viewer user interfaces and their approach to basic navigation.

Viewer	Platform	Comments	Price
Chaco Communications VR Scout http://www.chaco.com	All Windows platforms Stand-alone (1.1) or Netscape plug-in (X)	*Upstart contender for best viewer *Full VRML 1.0 support.	$49 Free evaluation
Caligari Corp. Fountain http://www.caligari.com	All Windows platforms	*Browser/authoring tool *Lets user edit worlds downloaded from Net	Free beta/ evaluation
Integrated Data Systems/ Portable Graphics V-Realm http://www.portable.com	Win 95 and NT	*VRML 1.0 support, plus extensions for gravity, collision detection, integrated animation, audio, and video	Free beta/ evaluation
Template Graphics WebSpace Navigator http://www.sd.tgs.com	SGI, Sun Solaris, IBM AIX, Win32, Windows 95, NT. In development: Win 3.1, Mac, OS/2, and more	*SGI distribution partner, releases WebSpace for non-SGI platforms *Unique navigation scheme *A key browser for its link to SGI/Open Inventor	Free beta/ evaluation $49 for support
Paper Software WebFX http://www.paperinc.com	All Windows Netscape plug-in Promised: Mac, Unix, and Win 95-Explorer versions	*Very strong Netscape plug-in, gets lots of support among VRML users as viewer of choice	Free beta/ evaluation

Table 11-1. *VRML Viewers (as of January 1996)*

Viewer	Platform	Comments	Price
InterVista Software WorldView http://www.intervista.com	All Windows Mac promised	*From VRML pioneer, Tony Parisi	Free beta/ evaluation
Virtus Corp. Voyager http://www.virtus.com	Windows 95, Mac	*One of the first Mac viewers. *VRML 1.0 support, plus planned support for Virtus' own file format *Runs stand-alone or as helper application	Free alpha/ evaluation
Sony CyberPassage http://vs.sony.co.jp/VS-E/vs top.html	Windows 95	*Supports VRML 1.0 plus series of interactive extensions from Sony	Free beta/ evaluation
Microsoft VRML add-on http://www.microsoft.com/ windows/ie/vrml.htm	Windows 95	*Plug-in VRML viewer for Internet Explorer 2.0	Free, in beta
Vream WIRL http://www.vream.com	Windows 95, NT Netscape plug-in Other ports planned	*Plug-in viewer for Netscape, featuring more than 100 WIRL extensions enabling interactivity and behaviors	Free beta/ evaluation Subscription: $29

Table 11-1. *VRML Viewers (as of January 1996) (continued)*

What Is VRML and How Does It Work?

The great irony of VRML is that all of the virtual worlds and 3-D representations are created using a text-based language. VRML code consists of text descriptions of 3-D objects and scenes—such as an object's coordinates and surfaces—as well as the expected behavior of those objects based on the actions of the user. The code itself is written in plain ASCII format. When a Web browser encounters a VRML world (specified by the .wrl extension), it accepts the downloaded VRML code and hands it off to a VRML viewer, which parses (interprets) the text-based instructions and displays the 3-D scene onscreen.

Typical download time for a VRML file can last from a few seconds to several minutes. Once a VRML world is downloaded, almost all user interaction—such as zooming in and out of a space or turning a 3-D object around on its axis—is handled locally. That makes the navigation of VRML worlds very fast and smooth.

There are some advantages to this approach to 3-D graphics. For starters, while a VRML world may look like a high-bandwidth file when it is displayed—having colors, shapes, and textures that resemble large graphic files—what is actually transmitted over the Internet is the text describing that world. In many cases, a very small text file can describe a very complex 3-D world.

In general, the typical VRML world can be viewed with a 486-class computer and a 14.4 kb/s modem. Most new computers shipped today have faster processors (for example, the Pentium and the PowerPC), faster modems (28.8 kb/s), and even built-in 3-D acceleration chips—all of which greatly aid the performance of VRML.

Worlds built to the VRML 1.0 standard offer limited interactivity. A click on an object may call a link to another world or to an HTML page. It is also possible to add audio and video downloads to a VRML world, just as you would to an HTML page. In each case, the VRML viewer reaches back out over the Net and pulls down the necessary data. In VRML 1.0, audio and video clips are played via an external helper application. VRML 2.0, discussed later in this chapter, will add the ability to insert audio, video animations, and more, directly to a VRML world.

Close-Up on VRML

We are not going to spend a lot of time here examining the details of the VRML scene description language. Frankly, the average Webmaster is not going to wade through the language, and more specifically, emerging VRML authoring tools make it less necessary to have to craft a VRML object or scene by hand. It is not difficult to create a simple 3-D object by writing it out by hand (as we'll see later in this chapter). But to build a more complex 3-D world, you will want to use a graphical tool. Many VRML authoring tools are now available, and we'll examine them in more detail in Chapter 12.

Still, there are some important concepts of 3-D graphics in general and of VRML in particular that you should know before you try to author a VRML world.

Understanding 3-D Graphics

While navigating through a 3-D world may be intuitive, many Webmasters probably are not acquainted with the basic terms and concepts of 3-D graphics. A basic understanding will help you as you begin to author VRML worlds.

For starters, what does it mean for an object to be "three-dimensional"? The answer is actually quite obvious. It means the object has three dimensions: height, width, and depth. For a computer to render a 3-D object, it must know the width (represented by the x variable), height (y variable), and depth (z variable) of its individual points. The plotting of these three variables gives the size and position of a single point in 3-D space.

A collection of points is called a point cloud. By linking together all the points in a cloud, the computer creates a wire-frame rendering of an object. As an example, think of a piece of chicken wire stretched between two posts: it establishes a skeletal structure. Once a wire frame is created, the computer wraps a surface over the frame. The surface adheres to the contours of the wire frame and makes the object seem solid. Think of a surface as wallpaper draped over the wire frame. Like wallpaper in the real world, computer-generated surfaces can be smooth or have a texture. In VRML, there are built-in capabilities for adding plain color surfaces to an object, or more complex surfaces via standard graphic files, including .gif, .jpg, and .bmp files.

Another key concept in 3-D graphics is a polygon. The surfaces of all 3-D objects are made up of polygons. If you remember back to basic geometry, a polygon can have any number of points (three points is a triangle, four is a rectangle, and so on), but it must have an area inside of it. In computer-generated graphics, there are methods to determine how light is reflected off a polygon surface.

The computer's ability to calculate the way light is reflected off an object is known as *shading*. To figure shading, the computer needs a light source. In the real world, every object either emits or reflects light. The same is true in virtual worlds. In order to make objects in a virtual world realistic, the computer needs to light the object using a computer-generated light source. There are several different kinds of lights in 3-D graphics, including *point lights*, which radiate out uniformly in all directions; *directional lights*, which direct light at a particular object; and *spot lights*, which act like laser beams by shining streams of light on particular spots on an object.

Writing VRML

If we wanted to, we could build an entire VRML world by hand, intricately figuring out the position, size, and lighting of every object in our scene. Early VRML worlds were built just this way, and VRML authoring tools output their worlds into code as well. You can open up a .wrl file you've downloaded from the Web in any text editor to see the VRML code that is used to render the world—the intricacy and length of VRML code needed to create a complex scene can be staggering.

Yet even as we examine the language, it is important to recognize that 3-D worlds—the most intensely visual of all the graphics arts—are not meant to be built by hand. It's simply not very intuitive to build a 3-D object by writing out all its points individually. And with the growing availability of a good variety of VRML authoring tools, you may never have to code in VRML.

That caveat aside, let's briefly review the VRML 1.0 specification to give you some idea of the code behind the VRML worlds you see on the Web.

Note ▶ *A complete online version of the VRML 1.0 specification—which contains all the details of the text-based scene description language—is available at http://vrml.wired.com/vrml.tech/.*

VRML 1.0   VRML 1.0 is based on the Open Inventor ASCII File Format from Silicon Graphics. The Inventor File Format supports complete descriptions of 3-D scenes with polygonally rendered objects, lighting, materials, ambient properties, and realism effects. A subset of the Inventor File Format, with extensions to support networking, forms the basis of VRML.

Every VRML file must begin with the characters (with no spaces or other characters preceding):

```
#VRML V1.0 ascii
```

This defines the file as a VRML, or .wrl file, to be parsed by the VRML viewer. You can use the "#" character to write comments anywhere within a VRML program.

After the header, a VRML file contains descriptions of objects, which in VRML syntax are known as nodes. Nodes are arranged hierarchically within a VRML file, and the entire list of nodes is called a scene graph.

A node has the following characteristics:

■ What kind of object it is, such as a cube, a sphere, a texture map, etc. VRML defines 36 different types of nodes. There are three different categories of nodes: shape, property, or group. Shape nodes define the basic geometric shapes in the scene. Property nodes affect the way shapes are drawn, for instance, how an object is textured or lighted. Group nodes gather other nodes together, allowing collections of nodes to be treated as a single object. (See Table 11-2 for a complete list of node types.)

■ The parameters that distinguish this node from other nodes of the same type, such as the radius of a sphere or the specific image used to make up a texture map. In VRML, these parameters are called fields. The VRML specification has a complete list of the 36 nodes and each of the nodes' acceptable fields.

■ A name to identify the node. Nodes do not have to be named, but if they are, they can be more easily referred to elsewhere in the file.

Creating a simple object in VRML is extremely easy. For instance, let's create an object called Ball. The file to do this looks like this:

```
#VRML V1.0 ascii
        DEF Ball Sphere {
                radius 5
        }
```

Write that code into a text editor, save it as ball.wrl, and open the file in a VRML viewer. You'll see a 3-D sphere, as shown in Figure 11-4. All we did was call on the Sphere node and give the radius variable a value. That's all there is to creating a simple VRML object. In part, it is this kind of immediate feedback that makes VRML so much fun to play with.

Let's expand on this example to show off some of the other key concepts of the VRML language. Here's our mission: create three differently colored objects, each with an embedded link out to one of the Web's search engines: a red sphere (Yahoo), a green cube (Excite), and a yellow cone (Lycos). To do this, we'll need to learn a few more VRML basics.

Shape Nodes	**Property Nodes**	**Group Nodes**
AsciiText, Cone, Cube, Cylinder, IndexedFaceSet, IndexedLineSet, PointSet, Sphere	Coordinate3, FontStyle, Info, Level-of-Detail, Material, MaterialBinding, Normal, NormalBinding, Texture2, Texture2Transform, TextureCoordinate2, ShapeHints, MatrixTransform, Rotation, Scale, Transform, Translation, OrthographicCamera, PerspectiveCamera, DirectionalLight, PointLight, SpotLight	Group, Separator, Switch, TransformSeparator, WWWAnchor

Table 11-2. *The Nodes Supported in VRML 1.0*

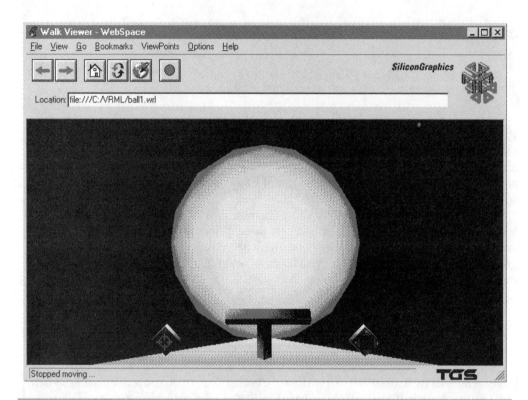

Figure 11-4. *A simple sphere in VRML (displayed in TGS' WebSpace viewer)*

The first new concept is the Separator node, one of the group nodes. Think of the Separator node as a box. All of the objects within that box are given the same attributes. For instance, if we place our three objects within a single "master" box, we can very easily place them in our 3-D world by defining their position relative to one another. Obviously you don't want to give every object in your world the same attributes. To give objects different attributes (for instance, different colors or lighting), you can nest one Separator node within another (one box inside another).

To give an object a color, we use the Material node. For the material to "attach" to an object, the Material node must precede the Shape node. The field within this node to set color is called diffuseColor, and must be a number between 0 and 1. The numbers refer to the intensity of red, green, and blue in the object. Examine the following code to see how we set different colors for each of our objects.

To set the different objects in our scene, we'll need to use the Transform node to place each object in relation to one another. In VRML, the first object in your scene graph is established as a point of reference. When you build additional objects, you use the Transform node to set each object in space in relation to the first reference object. The Transform node uses the Translation field with values X Y Z. So, for instance, a Translation node with Translation 5 5 5 would move an object 5 units on the x axis, 5 units on the y axis, and 5 units on the z axis away from the initial object.

Finally, we'll associate a URL with each of the objects. This will let our 3-D world serve as an interface out onto the rest of the Web. The node to accomplish this is WWWAnchor, which takes as its field the Web URL.

Here's the code (with comments describing the action) to create our example:

```
#VRML V1.0 ascii
Separator { # this separator groups all of our objects
        Material {
                diffuseColor 1 0 0 # the color red
        }
        WWWAnchor {
                name "http://www.yahoo.com" # assign URL
                        DEF Yahoo Sphere {
                                radius 5 # create a sphere
                }
        }
        Separator { # another separator
                Transform {
                        translation 5 5 5 # arrange objects
                }
                Material {
                        diffuseColor 0 1 0 # the color green
                }
                WWWAnchor {
                        name "http://www.excite.com"
                                DEF Excite Cube {
                                        width 5
                                        height 5
                                        depth 5
                                }
                }
        }
        Separator { # we've seen most of this earlier
                Transform {
                        translation -5 5 5
                }
                Material {
                        diffuseColor 1 1 0 # the color yellow
                }
                WWWAnchor {
```

```
                              name "http://www.lycos.com"
                                   DEF Lycos Cone {
                                            parts ALL
                                            bottomRadius 2
                                            height 5

                         }
                    }
               }
          }
```

Type this code into a text editor, save it with a .wrl extension, and load it into a VRML viewer. The results can be seen in Figure 11-5. In addition to the three objects, notice that when we move the pointer over one of the objects, the target URL is displayed in the browser window. Some viewers also display the text-based DEF Name you give to an object—in our case "Yahoo," "Excite," or "Lycos"—which lets you provide additional information to the user about a particular object.

The examples should give you a good idea of how the VRML text description works. If you want to explore the language further, you can move onto parts of the VRML 1.0 specification that enable some of the more complex 3-D concepts we discussed earlier:

■ Add a texture rather than a mere color to an object's surface. Textures can be defined within VRML or imported as a graphic file, using the Texture2 node and its image and file name fields.

■ Link an object to other MIME types, such as an audio file, using the WWWAnchor tag, with the target URL holding the MIME file.

■ Add lighting and shading to an object, by placing light sources in your scene, using the PointLight, SpotLight, and DirectionalLight nodes.

■ You can also learn to place cameras in a scene, defining the visitor's point of view of your world. (Use the OrthographicCamera and Perspective Camera nodes.)

■ Import objects into your world from all around the Web, on-the-fly, using the WWWInline mode. There are several repositories of VRML objects on the Web, and you can literally pull these objects straight into your VRML scene.

■ Define an object's Level-of-Detail, a node that gives you greater flexibility in designing how an object will look when it is far away and then moves closer to the viewer. Smart use of this node can help a viewer render a VRML world more quickly.

■ For the very ambitious, you can move beyond the built-in geometrics of VRML to define any shape you can imagine. Using the Coordinate3 and

IndexedFaceSet nodes you can build all sorts of shapes—if you have the patience to define series of variables that can literally stretch pages in length. These long series of variables are used to define the point clouds we introduced earlier.

We'll leave those explorations for your own time, if you feel the need. As we've seen, VRML 1.0 is not difficult to pick up, although it is a bit tedious—and at times downright maddening—if you are trying to build very complex worlds by hand. To build a complete scene or world, beginners are better off working with a visually oriented VRML authoring tool.

VRML Authoring Tools

As we have seen, building a VRML world by hand can be a time-consuming task. Luckily, there's really no need to work with the bare-bones language. Sophisticated VRML authoring tools, in many cases built by the same 3-D graphics vendors that provide high-end tools to Hollywood and the video game industry, are already available on the Web.

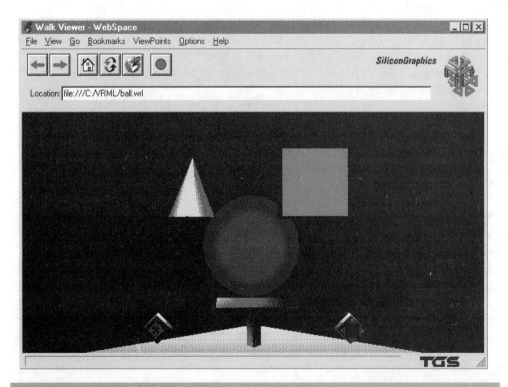

Figure 11-5. *Our VRML world, with hotlinks out to the Web (viewed in TGS' WebSpace)*

Most tools today fall into one of two categories: 3-D object modeling packages or VRML authoring tools.

Three-dimensional modeling software has been around since long before VRML appeared, and will continue to be used for a variety of other purposes even as VRML proliferates. Packages such as Microsoft's Softimage 3D, AutoDesk's 3D Studio, Strata's Studio Pro, and Caligari's trueSpace provide very sophisticated modeling tools for the creation of 3-D objects. Most, if not all, of these tools now output VRML files. Those that don't, offer conversion utilities for changing proprietary files into the VRML format. These tools are, in general, fairly expensive and often are optimized for high-end computers. But if you can get your hands on one, you can build very sophisticated objects that can then be imported into a VRML space builder. We won't delve into these high-end packages here, but you can hunt them down on the Web to learn more about them if you'd like.

VRML-specific authoring tools, on the other hand, are designed from the ground up for building 3-D worlds on the Internet. They are often built with the new user in mind, and are optimized for creating 3-D worlds designed to work over low-bandwidth modem connections. Some of the most popular tools for building full-fledged VRML worlds include Paragraph's Home Space Builder, Caligari's Fountain, and Virtus' Walkthrough Pro, all of which are reviewed in-depth in Chapter 12. These tools and others not only let you build 3-D spaces, they include many of the VRML 1.0 capabilities—such as adding a link or inlining an object—that you can add to a VRML world with the simple click of a button.

For information on VRML authoring tools—many of which are still under development—see Table 11-3.

While a lot of graphics and design work in the 2-D world is done on Apple Macintosh machines, 3-D rendering seems centered mainly on two platforms. Silicon Graphics boxes are used for very high-end 3-D modeling and Windows platforms are used for more mass-market-oriented, but still very capable, applications. As this book was written, there were only two VRML browsers for the Mac and few VRML authoring tools.

Where Is VRML Headed Next?

One of the major reasons that VRML is a major success is the early decision to limit the capabilities of VRML 1.0. In doing so, the VRML community was able to get a quick consensus on the VRML standard in little more than five months, clearly record time. But that just put the tough decisions off until later. The VRML 1.0 specification recognized the looming battles ahead:

"Design of a language for describing interactive behaviors is a big job, especially when the language needs to express behaviors of objects communicating on a network. Such languages do exist; if we had chosen one of them, we would have risked getting into a 'language war.' People don't get excited about the syntax of a

Tool	Platform	Key Features	Price
Caligari Corp. Fountain http://www.caligari.com	Windows	Real-time 3-D shape creation tools such as 3-D primitives, 2-D polygons, face editing, lathing, sweeping, and interactive lighting. Supports wide object import.	Not set Free beta
Caligari Corp. TrueSpace 2	Windows	Popular modeling, raytracing, and animation package. Once a complex object is created in TrueSpace, it can be converted to VRML.	Free demo Commercial: about $500
Portable Graphics V-Realm Builder http://www.portable.com	PC, Mac, Unix	Advanced authoring tool, outputs VRML and Open Inventor. Planned 1996 release.	NA
Radiance Software EZ3D http://www.webcom.com/ radiance	SGI, Sun Soon: Win 95	Full line of cross-platform VRML authoring tools	Free demos available
ParaGraph International Virtual Home Space Builder http://www.paragraph.com	Windows	Easy-to-use authoring tool for creating rooms, buildings in VRML.	Beta: $49.95 Commercial release: $495
Virtus Corp. WalkThrough Pro http://www.virtus.com	Windows and Mac	Powerful modeling software with focus on creating virtual spaces. Can output to VRML.	$495

Table 11-3. *VRML Authoring Tools*

Tool	Platform	Key Features	Price
Virtus Corp. Virtus VR http://www.virtus.com	Windows and Mac	Scaled down version of WalkThrough Pro, targeted at entry level users.	$99
Sony CyberPassage Conductor http://vs.sony.co.jp/VS-E/vstop.html	Windows 95	Basic VRML authoring plus access to Sony multimedia extensions, including TCL scripting. Files best viewed with Sony CyberPassage viewer.	Free beta/evaluation
Vream VRCreator http://www.vream.com	All Windows platforms	Can author VRML as well as interactive extensions based on Vream's VreamScript language.	Pre-release program: $449
Silicon Graphics WebSpace Author http://webspace.sgi.com/WebSpaceAuthor/index.html	SGI platforms	SGI's high-end graphics software can output VRML and Open Inventor.	$995

Table 11-3.   *VRML Authoring Tools* (continued)

language for describing polygonal objects; people get very excited about the syntax of real languages for writing programs. Religious wars can extend the design process by months or years."

That's a pretty good description of the state of VRML at the beginning of 1996. A draft specification for VRML 1.1, which will add some incremental features such as collision detection, spatial sound, and user-defined backgrounds, was put on the table at the end of 1995. It has languished as the VRML Architecture Group (VAG), a team of ten VRML pioneers; and the VRML Mailing List, which is made up of individuals interested in the development of VRML, has debated whether to skip VRML 1.1 and go directly to VRML 2.0. This would likely mean a new architecture and scripting language for VRML that would enable animations, interactivity, and other advanced capabilities.

As this book was written, the VRML community seemed ready to abandon VRML 1.1 and move straight on to VRML 2.0, because many features of 1.1 were already supported by viewer vendors as VRML 1.0 extensions. A Request for Proposals for VRML 2.0 went out in early January, and proposals were due by February.

The front-runners include the following:

- "Moving Worlds," from Silicon Graphics and partners WorldMaker, Sony, OnLive, Black Sun Interactive, Visual Software, and Paper Software. Moving Worlds is designed to enhance static worlds with more realistic geometry, enable interaction with objects in a world, and support animation through the addition of scripting languages (most likely Sun's Java). Given SGI's position in the VRML community, Moving Worlds is clearly the leading contender.

- Microsoft's ActiveVRML, which supports the animation of 3-D images and establishes relationships between media types in both space and time. For instance, a sound can be attached to a moving 3-D airplane. ActiveVRML has fewer ties to VRML 1.0 than does "Moving Worlds," but the VAG recognizes the Microsoft contribution as a serious option.

- A proposal from Apple Computer called Out of this World, based on the company's 3-D Meta File, a file format for 3-D graphics applications that make use of the QuickDraw 3-D graphics library. Apple, in a pitch to gain standing on the Internet, has proposed to place a portion of 3DMF in the public domain if it would aid the VRML 2.0 process.

- A proposal from Sun Microsystems, based on its Java programming language augmented with new virtual reality object classes it is building with SGI and others.

Incorporating behaviors and interactivity into VRML 2.0 is the highest priority for the VRML community. There is a great deal of concern that what began as a cooperative process could splinter as mega-companies like Microsoft, SGI, Sony, IBM, and others battle over the future standard 3-D interface for the Internet, a development that is arguably more important than even the battle of Java versus Visual Basic. It will be interesting to see if the VRML community can stay together and craft a VRML 2.0 standard.

At stake is the future of cyberspace.

INSIDE *Spin*

Tony Parisi on the Future of VRML

Tony Parisi is chief technology officer of Intervista Software, member of the VRML Architecture Group (which is defining VRML 2.0 standards) and, along with Mark Pesce, one of the original pioneers of the VRML community. This interview was conducted during a milestone week for VRML 2.0. Companies including Silicon Graphics, Microsoft, Apple, and Sun had submitted VRML 2.0 proposals. In a surprise move, SGI rounded up 50 companies including Netscape to back its Moving Worlds proposal, a major coup for SGI. To fuel its VRML ambitions, Netscape acquired VRML vendor Paper Software and released a beta plug-in of Moving Worlds. In all, a landmark, yet somewhat controversial, week in the history of VRML.

Q: Playing devil's advocate, many in the VRML community might say that the major display of industry support behind Moving Worlds subverts the open VRML 2.0 decision-making process.

Parisi: It's a valid point, absolutely. I could see where people could say, "gee, the industry has now come in and made some decisions." There's always an interaction, a tension between the [VRML] community and industry. One could say this is really forcing the community in a certain direction. I'm not sure that's a bad thing. It has pluses and minuses. If it helps us coalesce around one standard quickly, that's a good thing. I'm tired of the internecine battling. SGI has done a lot of good work, and they've done it the right way.

Q: Will we see several VRML 2.0 proposals combined into a single effort?

Parisi: This is my opinion, but I don't believe it works to make a patchwork proposal. That is not to say we won't work with people to incorporate certain features of other specs. But we won't do [something like] take the syntax from one proposal and the API from another.

Q: Which features will definitely make it into VRML 2.0, and which features won't?

Parisi: We'll definitely have animation-style behaviors such as canned animations; integrated multimedia, and richer interactivity, where you can drag and drop objects, such as dropping a cereal box into a shopping cart. What we won't have in the basic VRML 2.0 standard is support for multi-user spaces.

Q: What is your reaction—as a browser vendor—to Netscape's acquisition of Paper Software?

Parisi: There's a definite tension there. Innovators hustle to create new technology and [the favored ones] get bought out. The thing is, the companies that wind up not being purchased still have a lot of technology and understanding of the key issues. There's always room to build new servers, clients, and tools.

Summary

We've learned a lot in this chapter. We pointed you to places to download the latest VRML viewers and authoring tools. We also learned some key basic concepts of 3-D graphics. It may take some time to understand some of the concepts of computer-generated graphics. But it is worth the work—only that way can you gain the strong design sense that will help you in building your own 3-D worlds. We also examined the conception, birth, and somewhat troubled adolescence of the VRML language itself, and worked through some introductory VRML code. Luckily, you won't need to hand-code your worlds. This is a very complex task as worlds become more sophisticated. Instead, you can use any one of a number of very intuitive VRML authoring tools that have hit the market. We'll take a hands-on look at several of them in Chapter 12.

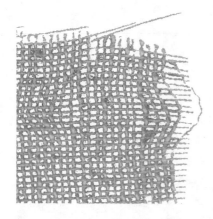

Chapter Twelve

Building Worlds
with VRML Tools

It is very meaningful that the pioneers who led the way with virtual reality on the Web often call themselves the "VRML community." The creation of VRML 1.0 was a cooperative, grassroots process driven by individuals, not faceless corporations. And it was driven not by the smell of money but by the vision of virtual space where people could gather to work, play, and interact—in other words, a virtual community. The idea of community means all individuals—and not just experts in 3-D graphics—can not only navigate VRML sites on the Web but build and share their own 3-D worlds as well.

Clearly, the average Webmaster is not going to wade through the VRML 1.0 spec and hand-write a virtual world. The good news is—you won't have to. A variety of easy-to-use and relatively inexpensive tools have emerged that let even novices build 3-D worlds for the Web. VRML vendors can't give non-artists an overnight, flawless, aesthetic feel for 3-D design, but they can provide tools that make it easy to begin building and populating 3-D worlds.

We'll provide a hands-on look at three VRML editors in this chapter: ParaGraph International's Virtual Home Space Builder, Virtus' WalkThrough Pro, and Caligari's Fountain. All three output VRML files, and offer a variety of built-in tricks and shortcuts to get you started building VRML worlds. They are focused on building virtual spaces—not just objects—and thus are perfect for VRML authors. While the tools have similarities, it will also be instructive to see the differences between the three tools—this will let you know which tool is best for your needs.

By the time you finish this chapter, you will have all the skills you need to build worlds every bit as engaging as most of the VRML sites you see on the Web today.

ParaGraph's Virtual Home Space Builder

Perhaps the easiest VRML authoring tool to start with is ParaGraph's Virtual Home Space Builder (VHSB). This has something to do with its roots—the product was originally envisioned as children's software, but with the explosion in the Web and online publishing, it was revamped as an entry-level VR building tool. VHSB comes bundled with a variety of features that make it easy to get started building 3-D worlds, including scene templates and textures. You can also import your own 3-D models directly into VHSB.

VHSB 1.0 runs on all Windows platforms and outputs both ParaGraph's proprietary .mus files and standard VRML 1.0. Authors work and build files in .mus, then convert them to VRML at the end. VRML authors must be careful—some advanced capabilities of VHSB such as sound, video, animation and guided tours are not supported in VRML 1.0. Thus you can build a world with these features in the .mus format, but when you output it to VRML, all will be lost in the translation.

The basic concept behind VHSB is that you build a structure using two main elements—walls and boxes. You can then hang "pictures" on the walls, which can have Web URLs associated with them. That's really all there is to it. But you can build some very sophisticated environments with only those tools (see Figure 12-1).

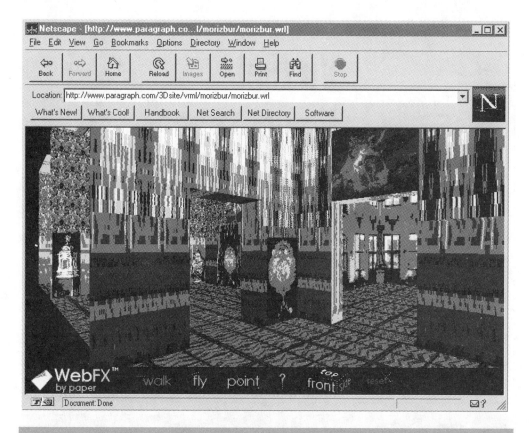

Figure 12-1. *A "virtual art gallery" created with VHSB*

You can download or order copies of VHSB at http://www.paragraph.com. For download, there is a free evaluation version of VHSB 1.0, though saving files is disabled. For $49, you can purchase a supported beta version of VHSB, and for $495 you can purchase the supported version of VHSB 1.0. Both the beta and 1.0 versions come on a CD-ROM that includes the program plus tutorials and an extensive supply of example worlds, templates, and textures. ParaGraph's home page has some additional freebies, including free textures for decorating your home spaces, and templates for speeding up the design process.

Using VHSB

Upon starting VHSB, you'll be greeted with a startup screen (see Figure 12-2) that provides you with your work options. VHSB's View mode lets you view .mus files included on the program's CD-ROM or downloaded from the Web. The New mode

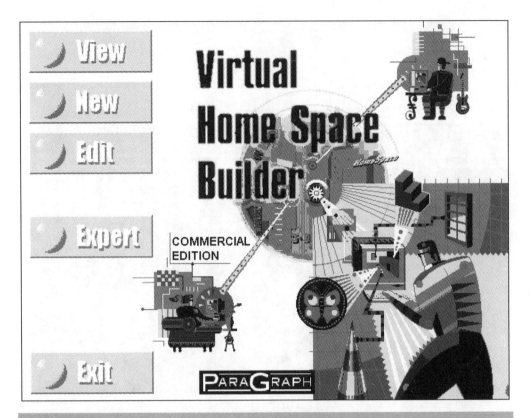

Figure 12-2. *The Virtual Home Space Builder startup screen*

lets you build 3-D spaces from scratch, Edit mode lets you modify existing 3-D worlds, and Expert mode lets you switch between the View and New mode on-the-fly and contains some expert settings for advanced users.

The VHSB User Interface

For our purposes, we'll enter the New mode, which will let us create new 3-D worlds. The VHSB interface consists of five separate elements (clockwise from the top left): the 3-D Space window, the Plane Builder window, the Builder toolbox, the Walker toolbox, and the Chooser window (see Figure 12-3). You will use each of these five elements to build a 3-D world. Let's briefly examine each of these work spaces to better acquaint you with the VHSB interface.

The 3D Space Window

VHSB offers a representation of the world you are building in the 3D Space window. This is very convenient, because though you will be doing your work in the 2-D Plane

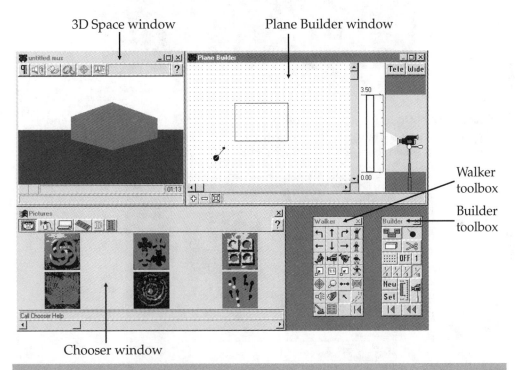

Figure 12-3. *The VHSB user interface*

Builder window, you will be able to instantly see and navigate through the output in the 3-D Space window, as shown here.

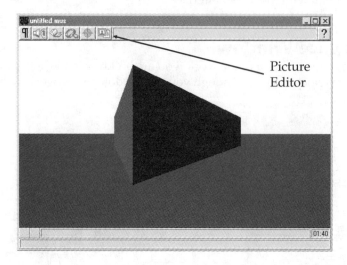

The row of buttons across the top of the 3-D Space window lets you access and manipulate pictures hanging on the walls of your 3-D objects. The last button, the picture editor as shown here, lets you attach elements to a picture, including Web URLs.

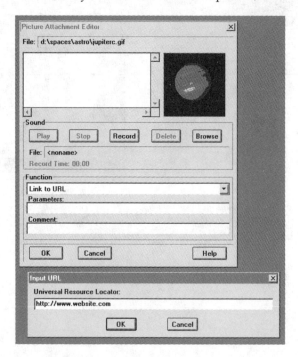

The Plane Builder Window

The Plane Builder window is where the actual construction of your 3-D world takes place. The window includes three elements: a top view of the workspace, a Height Indicator, and a Viewing Camera (see Figure 12-4).

To build an object in VHSB, click your mouse in the Plane Builder workspace, drag to form a box or wall, then release the mouse button to create the object. You will do all the work to create your 3-D world in the Plane Builder.

The Height Indicator is used to determine the height of the objects—walls or boxes—that you construct in the Plane Builder. This is a vital tool. It not only sets the height of an object, it can be used to set one object on top of another. And more importantly, it can be used to cut "holes" into the boxes you construct—creating interior spaces, doors, and windows. We'll demonstrate this in more detail when we build a sample world.

The Viewing Camera works just like a real camera, and can be used to set the viewer's point of view in a scene. The Walker window has icons to control the Viewing Camera, but you can also control it manually. You can raise and lower the point of view by grabbing the circle where the camera meets the tripod and moving it

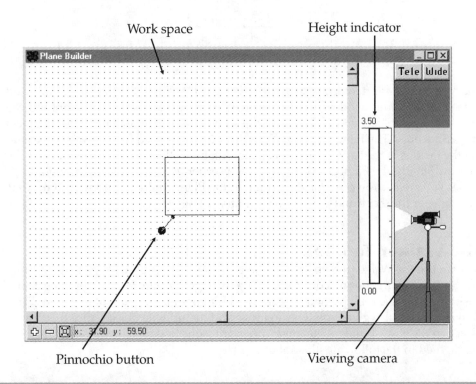

Figure 12-4. *The Plane Builder window*

up and down. You can tilt the camera using the handle behind the camera. And you can use the Tele button and Wide button to zoom the camera in and out on a scene.

The Builder Toolbox

The Builder toolbox has all the construction tools you'll need to create objects, as shown in the following illustration:

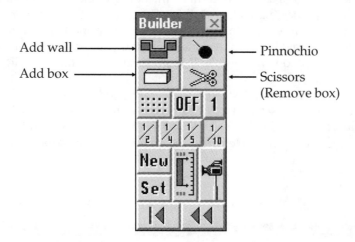

The four most important icons are on top. The Add Wall tool lets you add solid walls to the Plane Builder window. Control the height of the wall using the Height Indicator. The Add Box tool lets you add a box to the scene. Boxes are the main building blocks of VHSB scenes. The Remove Box tool, or the scissors, is used to cut away or excavate out the insides of the solid boxes you create. Again, we'll take a hands-on look at this later on. Finally, the Pinnochio button offers a second way to navigate through the scenes you create. You can grab the button in the Plane Builder window and move it to anywhere in the scene and point it to view at any angle.

The Walker Toolbox

You can use the Walker toolbox to maneuver through the 3-D space you are building. The toolbox has a series of icons for moving through a scene, for changing the camera position and angle for a particular scene, and for zooming in and out of a scene. The Walker toolbox also gives you tools to move and manipulate objects once they are placed in the scene builder. The most important icons in the Walker toolbox are highlighted in the following illustration:

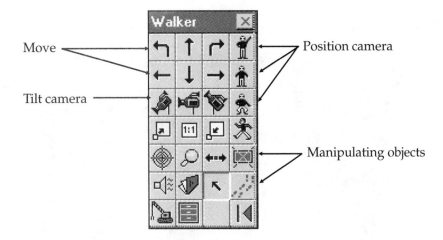

The Chooser Window

The Chooser lets you add colors, textures, and pictures to the surfaces of the walls, ceilings, and floors you create. The Chooser offers four options: Wallpapers, or images that will cover a large surface such as a wall or floor; Airbrush, which lets you add a solid color to a surface; Pictures, which lets you "hang" an image on a wall, and later link it out to the Web or a MIME file; and Movies, which are supported in ParaGraph's .mus file format but not in VRML (see Figure 12-5).

The Select Directory icon brings up a file directory dialog box that lets you navigate through the VHSB CD-ROM or your local hard drive looking for the files to add. Once you find a file, it is shown in Thumbnail mode in the Chooser window. You can then drag and drop the images or textures directly onto an object in the 3-D Space window.

Building VRML Worlds in VHSB

Since Virtual Home Space Builder is designed to build rooms with pictures hanging on the walls, let's build a simple virtual art gallery to show off how VHSB works in practice. Our art gallery will consist of a room, a bench, and two "paintings" hanging on the wall, each with an embedded link out to the Web. We'll also add a door and a window.

We start our project by building a box, the way most projects in VHSB start. The box will eventually represent the four walls of our virtual gallery. To build our box, select the Add Box tool in the Builder toolbox. Then drag the mouse in the Plane Builder window to create the box. Our first step is shown completed in Figure 12-6.

Picture mask   Airbrush mode   Wallpaper mode   Select directory

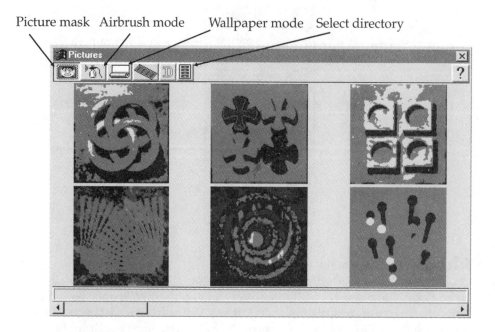

Figure 12-5. *The Chooser window*

To create the interior of the room we'll need to "scoop" out the inside of our cube. Think of the cube as being solid. If we go in and cut away the inside, we then have a space we can move around in, complete with four walls, a ceiling and a roof. To remove the inside of our cube, we use the Scissors tool and the Height Indicator bar. To make sure we don't cut the entire cube away, we'll adjust the Height Indicator bar to leave about .10 units (meters) from the top and from the bottom. That will leave a sliver of the cube for the ceiling and floor. With that set, click on the Scissors tool and drag a box *inside* the box we created earlier. This will create the four walls of our room. The entire operation is shown in Figure 12-7. Notice that we've placed the Pinnochio button *inside* our newly created interior space—the view in the 3-D Space window represents the inside of our gallery.

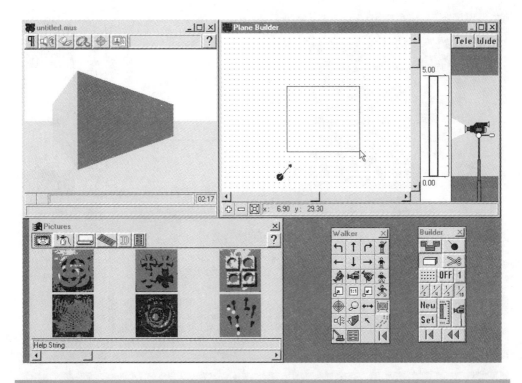

Figure 12-6. *First, we build a box—it will become our room*

Now let's cut out a doorway and a window. Again, we'll need to make use of the Height Indicator, because we want the door to cut from the bottom of our room about halfway up to the ceiling, while the window needs to be cut out from the middle of the wall. We use the scissors in the Plane Builder space to cut the door and windows into the walls of our box. See Figure 12-8 for a demonstration of how we cut out the window. (The door in this picture is already cut out.)

Next, we move inside our art gallery. We promised a bench, the building of which will show off the use of the Height Indicator again. To build a bench, we create and stack boxes on top of one another. To do this, we simply make accurate use of the Height Indicator to make sure the bottom of one box sits directly on the top of another. You can see our bench, complete with wood textures, in Figure 12-9.

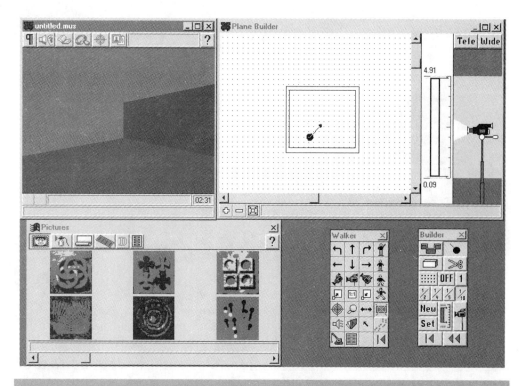

Figure 12-7. *We scooped out the box to create the interior of our room*

While working with textures on the bench, let's paint the walls and put a carpet on the floor. To include surface textures, we click on the Wallpaper icon in the Chooser window. VHSB includes many types of textures, including bricks, marble, and many funky textures. Once you call up the texture you want in the Chooser window, we can simply drag and drop the texture onto the object you want to cover. The Spray Paint icon works in much the same way. Click on the icon and a pallete of colors appears. Click on a color, drag it to the surface you want to paint, release, and the surface is painted.

Finally, we'll hang two "pictures" on the wall. To do this, we click on the Picture icon in the Chooser window. Again, we can choose images from the VHSB CD or from our hard drive. VHSB supports twelve different graphic formats, including the Web's popular GIF and JPEG files. We'll hang a pair of pictures on our gallery wall; again its a simple matter of drag and drop.

If we want to, we can attach Web URLs to the pictures. The dialog box to accomplish this, shown previously, is accessed from the 3-D Space menu. To add a URL,

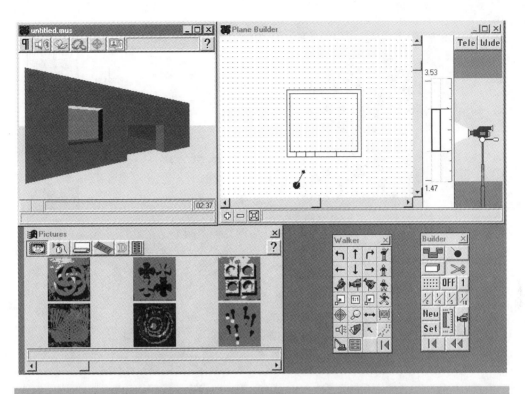

Figure 12-8. *The room now has a door and window to see inside and out*

first we click on the picture to activate it and then click on the picture editor icon to retrieve the dialog box. Next, we select the function Link to URL and type in a URL. Click OK and the URL is attached.

Check out our completed art gallery in Figure 12-9, shown in the VHSB workspace.

We are now only a few steps away from completing our world and posting it on the Web. The final step is to save the scene as a VRML file with a .wrl extension. (It is also a good idea to save a version with the .mus extension, since VHSB cannot import or read .wrl files.) If you don't save your room as a .mus file, you won't be able to edit it later.

In addition to .mus and .wrl file options, VHSB offers two save options: Save 3-D space and Copy All. If you are only going to view your world on your own local computer, choose Save 3-D Space. But if you want to post the world to the Web, choose

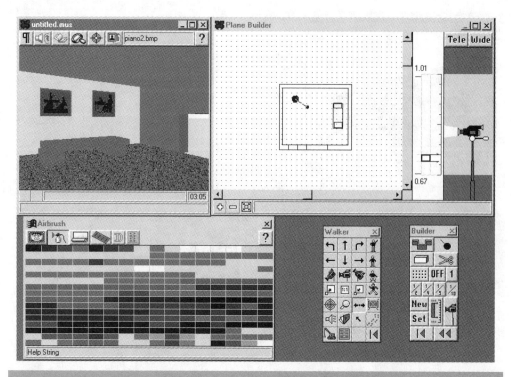

Figure 12-9. *The finished art gallery, viewed in the VHSB workspace*

Copy All. What this does is save not only the VRML code needed to render our art gallery, but also the textures and pictures we used to brighten up the room.

All of the files will be saved to a single directory, which we can then post to our Web server. Our finished product, viewed locally in a VRML viewer, can be seen in Figure 12-10.

One final note: we had a very mixed experience with our VHSB VRML file in how VRML viewers handled it. The Chaco VR Scout plug-in for Netscape (as shown in Figure 12-10) handled the file perfectly, displaying the wall colors and picture and texture files as expected. The Microsoft plug-in also performed well, though it rendered most of the colors much darker than designed. The WebFX plug-in for Netscape handled the picture files and textures, but displayed all the walls as black. WebSpace displayed the correct wall colors, but none of the picture or texture files. The problem: WebSpace only displays files in the .rgb texture format. To fix this, we would have to change the files in an image editor from their current format (.bmp, in this case, to .rgb). In addition, VHSB offers a setting that automatically changes the file extensions in your .wrl file to .rgb, relieving you of the need to go into the .wrl file and change those extensions by hand.

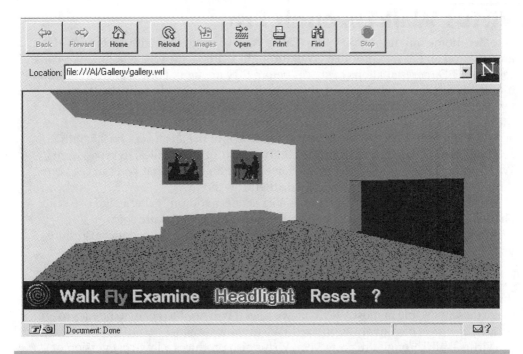

Location: file:///A|/Gallery/gallery.wrl

Walk Fly Examine Headlight Reset ?

Document: Done

Figure 12-10. *The finished gallery in a VRML viewer (the Chaco VR Scout plug-in for Netscape)*

The lesson—no two VRML viewers work exactly alike. Best to check your VRML worlds on as many viewers as possible.

Exit Thoughts: Virtual Home Space Builder

ParaGraph's Virtual Home Space Builder is incredibly easy to use, yet at the same time enables the creation of very complex, textured worlds. All it takes is a lot of imaginative, patient work with the Add Wall, Add Box, and Scissors tools. Not only can you create rooms, with a little creativity you can build rudimentary furniture (ie., our bench) and other objects, such as pillars or beams to complement your rooms. For first-time users, or any level user looking for an easy way to build spaces—be they houses, museums, or whatever—VHSB could be the tool choice.

The tool is limited, however, by its inability to import .wrl files and the lack of advanced 3-D sculpting tools for creating more sophisticated objects. It also lacks support for some advanced VRML features, such as Level-of-Detail, that sophisticated authors might want to optimize their 3-D worlds. For those capabilities, you'll need a more full-featured tool.

Virtus WalkThrough Pro

Another "home-building" type tool is Virtus WalkThrough Pro, with roots as a 3-D architectural and design product. "Walkthrough" refers to the idea of allowing people to see the 3-D representations of spaces before they are built. For instance, a common interior design use might be to let people walk through a newly-furnished virtual living room to get an idea if what looks good on paper (in 2-D) has the same feel in the 3-D world.

WalkThrough Pro has been around since 1990, but the latest version 2.5 of the product, released last year, gained the ability to output VRML files. In broad terms, WalkThrough Pro is similar to Virtual Home Space Builder in that you can see your 3-D models rendered in 3-D as you create them, on-the-fly.

To help in the creation of 3-D spaces, Virtus offers add-on "galleries" of pre-built objects such as furniture, appliances, and more. These galleries are sold separately—including home, office, and science fiction—but the product also ships with a good selection of pre-built objects.

Like VHSB, Virtus models are first built in a proprietary file format, .wtp, and then exported to VRML. Like VHSB, it also contains some features that don't translate directly to the Internet. Most importantly, it uses .pict and .bmp files for textures. To make these viewable in most VRML viewers, you will need to change the files to .gif or .jpeg, the most commonly supported Web graphic formats.

Virtus WalkThrough Pro costs $495. Virtus also produces a low-cost version of WalkThrough Pro called Virtus VRML. Today, the $40 product ships on a CD-ROM and comes with a book called Virtus VRML Toolkit. The company also is planning to release a boxed version of the software sometime this year, at a cost of less than $100. Feature-disabled demo versions of both Virtus WalkThrough Pro and VirtusVRML can be downloaded from the Virtus Web site, **http://www.virtus.com**.

Using WalkThrough Pro

Virtus WalkThrough Pro is a very sophisticated product, and we'll only cover a subset of its features here—enough to build a simple VRML scene. In particular, the product offers a very realistic view of 3-D space, and a relatively complex scheme for navigating within the 3-D spaces you build. You need to master these skills before you can master the product itself.

WalkThrough Pro can be used to build very detailed views of the interior of an entire home—or even an entire neighborhood. For most users looking to build a VRML world, this is more than you'll need. But it's good to know you've got that sort of power under the hood for when you feel more ambitious.

WalkThrough Pro's User Interface

To start, let's get familiar with the environment we'll be working in. Because WalkThrough Pro is a relatively complex tool, we won't be able to run through all its features. Instead, we'll just highlight the main interface elements and then, as we build a sample world below, we'll provide more details and examine how to use and work with the most important elements and tools we mention here.

The WalkThrough Pro workspace has two main views: the Design View where you draw, drop and drag 2-D objects, and the Walk View where the same objects are rendered in a three-dimensional view. We do most of our editing, coloring, and building in the Design View (in 2-D). The Walk View is for viewing only. When you draw a 2-D object in the Design View, it is instantly rendered in 3-D in the Walk Window.

The Design View is actually made up of six sub-views—top, bottom, front, back, left, and right—that give you great flexibility in positioning objects. You can toggle back and forth between these views from the pull-down Views menu. The Design View also includes three editors that perform specific operations on objects you create: a Surface Editor, a Tumble Editor, and a Lighting Editor. Access the editors via the Design toolbar.

WalkThrough Pro has five separate icon toolbars, one for each of the two main views—Design and Walk—as well as each of the three Editors.

Another key element to mention is the Observer, the small circle at the center of the Design View. The Observer represents where you are in the virtual world. The line in the middle of the Observer represents the direction of the Observer's view. You can drag the observer around the Design View. It also moves as you navigate about in the Walk View.

You can see the basic workspace and most of the elements we have discussed so far in Figure 12-11.

There is one more important element of WalkThrough Pro we haven't discussed yet—the Library. This is where the product's built-in objects are stored. You can access it by selecting Library from the File menu and located the object you want to import. For instance, WalkThrough Pro includes built-in objects including home and office furniture (see Figure 12-12).

Building a World in WalkThrough Pro

Before we examine WalkThrough Pro, there are a few caveats. Of the three tools we tested, WalkThrough Pro had the greatest difference between files created in its proprietary formats and the files it could export to VRML. A common model built in WalkThrough Pro consists of a 3-D room or building with a textured exterior and an interior laden with pre-built furniture objects imported from the Library. In the tool's

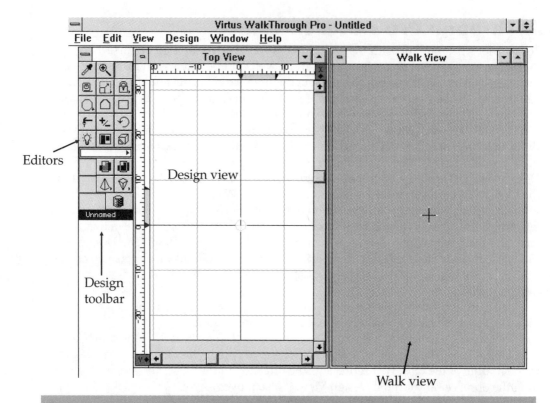

Figure 12-11. *The WalkThrough Pro workspace*

.wpt format, you can explore the exterior of the house and then go through a door or opening and navigate the interior (see Figure 12-13).

Such sophisticated models cannot be exported to VRML; they simply won't work. The inside-outside nature of the .wtp models does not translate well to VRML. This doesn't cancel out WalkThrough Pro as a VRML tool, however. There are two ways to use the software as a VRML tool.

First, you can use the basic polygon building tools to create 3-D objects by hand, arranging them in a way that creates an interesting scene.

Or you can use the program's extensive library of built-in objects, arranging them in the design space to create a 3-D room that users can navigate.

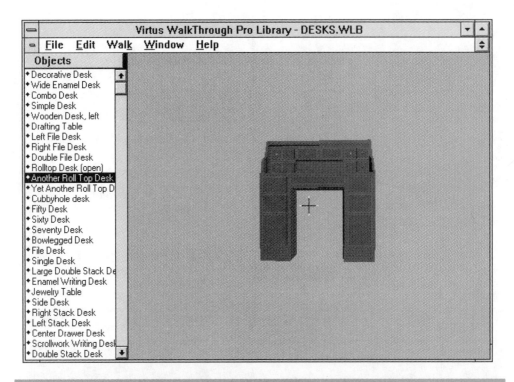

Figure 12-12. *A desk in the Library*

We'll explore both of these approaches in brief: building a 3-D house model, and creating a virtual office space using WalkThrough Pro's built-in objects.

Building a 3-D House

This lesson introduces us to WalkThrough Pro's object building tools, and demonstrates how to add textures to an object.

To start, we'll need to build the cube that represents our house. Click on the Design View to call up the Design toolbar. WalkThrough Pro offers five basic polygon building icons (shown next), that will let you build most of the shapes you will need in your world-building.

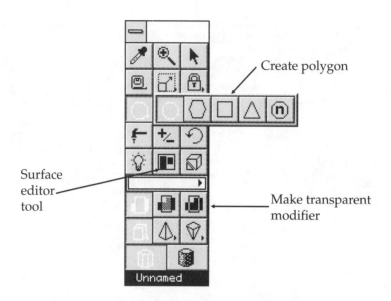

Create polygon

Surface
editor
tool

Make transparent
modifier

Unnamed

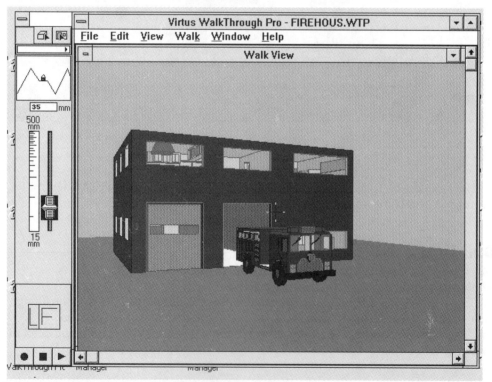

Figure 12-13. *A complex WTP model*

First, we click on the four-sided polygon tool and move onto the Design View space. Then we drag a square that is 20 ft. by 20 ft. The cube this square represents is automatically rendered in the Walk View. If we position the Observer outside of the square in the Design View, we'll see the outside of the cube (as shown in Figure 12-14). If we move the Observer inside, we'll see the interior space, ceiling, floor, and walls.

Let's work on the exterior of our structure. The first thing we'll want to do is cut open a door. In doing this, we'll learn a little more about WalkThrough Pro's tools for dealing with objects and object surfaces.

To start, we click on the Surface Edit tool in the main Design View toolbar. With this tool activated, we click the cursor on the bottom line in the square where we drew in Design View. This line represents the front surface of our home. When we click on it, a new window is created called Surface:Outside. This displays the front surface of our cube.

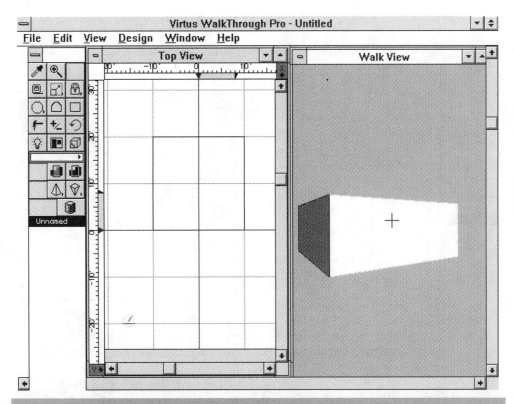

Figure 12-14.   *The cube laid out in Design View and rendered in Walk View*

Our next step will be to cut our door into this surface. On the Design View toolbar, first we click on the Make Transparent Modifier icon, then click the same four-sided polygon tool we used earlier. We will use these tools to draw a transparent, four-sided polygon on the front surface of the cube—in other words, cut out a door. Move to the surface in the Design View and drag a rectangle in the shape of a door. See the results of this process in both the Design View and Walk View windows in Figure 12-15.

Next, let's add a roof to our house. The first thing we need to do is make sure the room covers the entire upper surface of our cube. To do this, we'll need to change the Depth Control Gauge, located along the left-hand side of the Design View. Drag the end-points of the gauge so they extend slightly beyond the width of the square in the Design View.

With that done, we change the view from Top View to Front View. Then, using the Create Irregular Object tool from the toolbar drag a triangular roof onto the cube. See the results of this process in Figure 12-16.

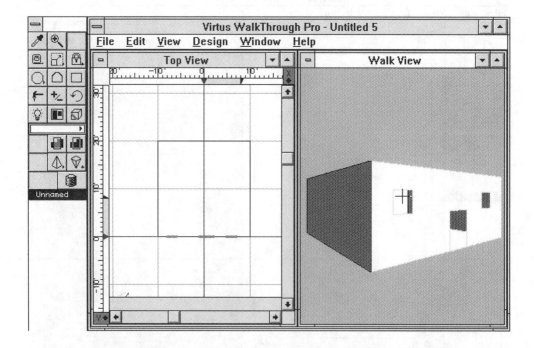

Figure 12-15.   *A door and two windows cut into the front surface of our house*

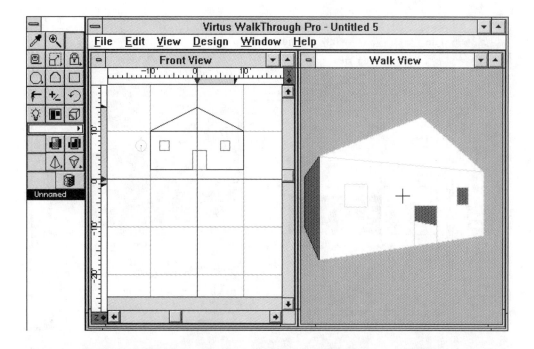

Figure 12-16.   *A roof is added to the house*

We introduced the Textures window earlier. Now let's put it to use. What we'd like to do is add a brick texture to the front view of our house. To start, we access the Textures Window from the Windows menu. The Textures Window lets us dig down into our hard drive or disk drives to retrieve texture files. WalkThrough Pro accepts .pict and .bmp files only (a problem we'll deal with shortly). When we call up a file, it is displayed in Preview mode in the Textures Window.

To add a texture to the front of our house, first use the Surface Editor tool and call up the front surface as before when we cut the door and windows of our structure. The texture is then applied by clicking on the front wall to activate it and then double-clicking on the texture to apply it (see Figure 12-17).

In order to have a VRML viewer display the texture we created, we must include the graphic file in the same directory as our .wrl file. Getting it there is easy enough. But if you remember, the file in its current form is either a .pict or .bmp file, neither of which is a common graphic file format on the Web. To work around this, we'll need to do two things.

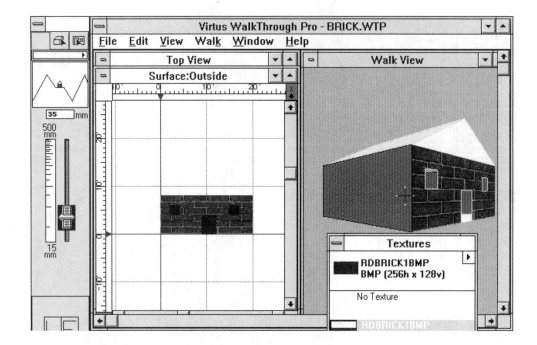

Figure 12-17. *A brick texture added to the front surface of our house*

First, we'll export the file to VRML. The file is now in the .wtp format. From the File menu, we access the Export option, and choose Export to VRML from the sub-menu. We'll be greeted with a dialog box asking if we would like to include textures with our files. It also gives us the opportunity to change the *internal* file extensions on our graphics files. The default option is a .jpg extension. Understand: this does not change the extensions of the actual graphics files. What it does is uniformly change the extensions in the .wrl file itself. This is handy because then we do not have to go into the file and change the extensions by hand.

We will also have to change the file extensions on the graphic files themselves. To do this, open the textures in a graphics converter or paint program like Adobe PhotoShop and save a copy of them with a new extension: the best choices are .jpg or .gif.

Now when a VRML viewer loads the .wrl file, the file extensions within the VRML code and the file extensions of the graphics files will be in sync and in a format that can be read and rendered by the VRML viewer.

Note ▶ *We often ran into a problem trying to attach textures to objects in WalkThrough Pro. We would receive an error: Expected '}' got "".*

Using the WalkThrough Pro Library

Building a scene by hand is relatively simple, but assembling a scene from pre-built objects is even easier. We introduced the Library window earlier. Virtus WalkThrough Pro ships with a good supply of objects, including office and home furnishings. For our example, we'll build a virtual office. One by one, we call up the furniture elements we desire in the Library window, copy them to the Windows clipboard, then paste them onto the Design View workspace (see Figure 12-18).

As noted earlier, when working in native .wtp file formats, you build a structure first, then furnish its interior. But for creating a simple VRML scene, we can drop the objects directly onto the design space. When viewed in a VRML viewer, the office seen will "float" in mid-air, but be fully navigable in three dimensions (see Figure 12-19).

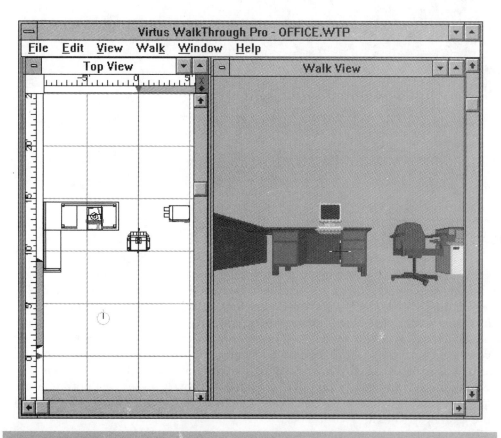

Figure 12-18.   *Office scene in WalkThrough Pro workspace*

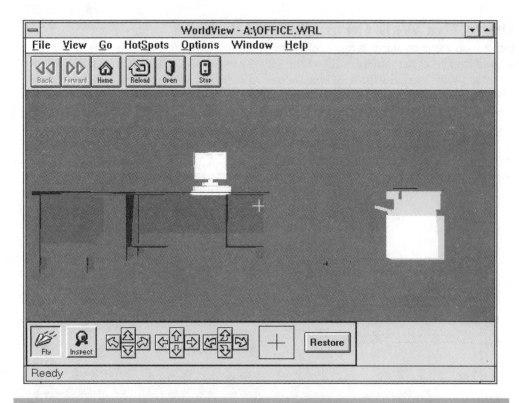

Figure 12-19. *The office scene in a VRML viewer (InterVista WorldView)*

Exit Thoughts: Virtus WalkThrough Pro

Based on our experiences, WalkThrough Pro is still a work-in-progress when it comes to exporting VRML files. Perhaps its greatest liability—and of course this isn't all its own fault—is that the VRML files you can create with the tool are a far cry from the files you can create using its proprietary .wtp format. The problem is that the tool offers a very sophisticated, real-time rendered workspace. But most of the subtle shading of the .wtp environment is lost in the output to VRML. We also ran into several situations where VRML files contained internal errors and would not open in a VRML viewer, or would open in one flavor of viewer but not another. This again speaks as much to the state of the VRML 1.0 spec and how browser vendors are implementing it as it does to the quality of WalkThrough Pro. Such inconsistencies can cause great headaches for Webmasters.

That said, the tool scores big points for including a variety of built-in scenes and objects. Virtus engineers tell us they are working to improve the tools ability to export high-quality VRML files, and avoid the limitations presented by the VRML 1.0

specification. It is a tool worth watching, and in its low-cost Virtus VRML version worth trying out if you can get your hands on it.

Caligari's Fountain

An interesting and relatively inexpensive VRML authoring tool is Caligari's Fountain. It is expected to cost less than $100 when released in commercial form. Fountain is based on Caligari's TrueSpace 3-D sculpture studio, but it is built from the ground up with advanced VRML world-building in mind. While Virtual Home Space Builder and Virtus WalkThrough Pro are focused on building virtual homes and spaces, Fountain is more of a free-form tool. You can use it to create almost any kind of object or structure you can imagine.

The most unique feature of Fountain—a code-name that likely will change when it is released—is that it is both a browsing tool and an authoring tool. While such a setup is obviously convenient, it also lets us do some interesting things. The most obvious advantage is that it lets you build a VRML world and then instantly test it in the integrated viewer.

But that's only the start. It will also let you download a VRML world and edit the world in real-time, changing colors or textures and adding or subtracting 3-D objects. We can also "steal" objects out of the scene, cutting and pasting them into the Fountain authoring space for use in our own VRML worlds. In an interesting twist on browser bookmarks, Fountain has a feature that lets you add VRML objects you find on the Web to a "Virtual Neighborhood," a 3-D version of bookmarks. Later you can browse the neighborhood, click on an object, and be transported out to the site on the Web (see Figure 12-20). The idea behind Fountain's integrated browsing/authoring paradigm is that virtual worlds should be a shared, community experience, with users not only visiting but making contributions to cyberspace.

In addition to offering both browsing and authoring modes, Fountain offers 3-D modeling tools and VRML space creation tools. The 3-D modeling tools are based on Caligari's TrueSpace tool, and offer a variety of features that are often only available in high-end 3-D tools. Since it was built from the ground up as a VRML tool, the VRML space creation tools support features such as Level-of-Detail and Inlining that help you build more efficient, compact 3-D worlds.

You can download a free beta/evaluation version of Fountain from **http://www.caligari.com**.

Fountain's Browsing Mode

Since browsing is an integral part of Fountain, let's take a brief look at the tool's browsing environment. Fountain includes many advanced browsing features, such as support for textures, levels of detail, and inlining. It can work as a stand-alone browser—you would need to know the exact URL of the .wrl files or access them from your Virtual Neighborhood—as well as a helper application that works in conjunction with a standard Web browser.

Figure 12-20. *The Virtual Neighborhood 3-D bookmarks*

Navigation is kept simple. You can move in Walk or Fly mode, and all navigation options are accessed through the two mouse buttons, such as spin and tilt. You can also access the main view and the perspective view simultaneously (see Figure 12-21).

Note ▶ *In both browsing and authoring modes, you can get access to all of a button's functions by clicking and holding on the button with the left mouse button. You can move any of a buttons features onto the main toolbar, and can always switch back and forth between them.*

Fountain's Building Mode

The power of Fountain is that it enables browsing and authoring, all within an integrated workspace. To access the world-building mode, click on the first button on the browser toolbar to switch to Builder mode. You'll see the same scene you were viewing in the browser. The toolbar, meanwhile, expands to give you access to the

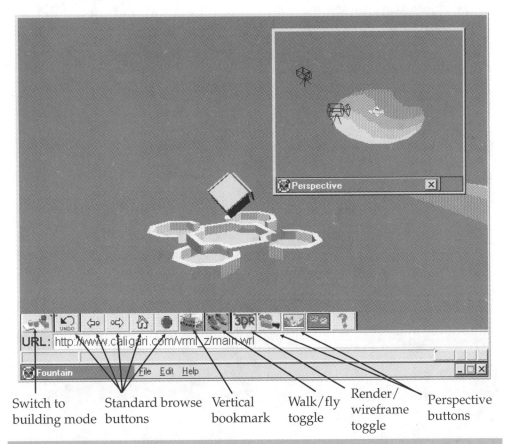

Switch to building mode Standard browse buttons Vertical bookmark Walk/fly toggle Render/ wireframe toggle Perspective buttons

Figure 12-21. *Fountain in browsing mode, showing two perspectives at once*

tools you'll need to edit existing worlds and create new 3-D objects from scratch (see Figure 12-22). We'll examine the toolbar icons one at a time as we demonstrate what Fountain can do.

3-D Modeling

Like many high-end 3-D studios—and unlike Virtual Home Space Builder—Fountain gives you access to a toolset for building complex geometric shapes. The features are similar to those found in Caligari's flagship product, TrueSpace.

Fountain includes 3-D shape creation tools such as 3-D primitives, 2-D polygons, face editing, lathing, sweeping and tips, all of which we will examine in greater detail. In addition, you'll be able to add light sources to your models, and paint individual faces on your models. All of the sculpting work is done directly on texture-mapped

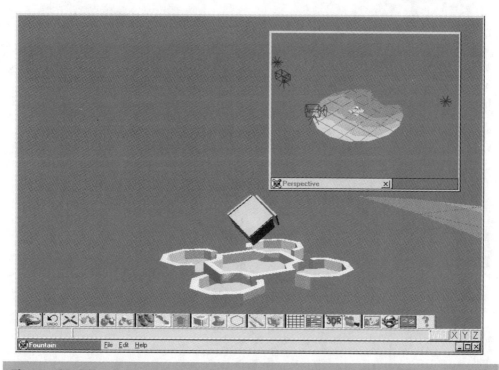

Figure 12-22. *Fountain shifts the same scene from browsing to building mode*

objects, not on wire frames as with some 3-D tools. That makes the creation of 3-D objects much easier for 3-D novices.

In addition to creating new objects, Fountain can import 3-D objects in WRL (VRML) format as well as in the proprietary formats of most high-end 3-D modelers. It also allows the import of 2-D formats in .bmp and .jpg form.

THE PRIMITIVES PANEL   To access, click on the Primitives Panel icon in the toolbar, as shown in Figure 12-23. The panel gives us access to the following:

- **Six built-in geometrics**   Plane, Cube, Cylinder, Cone, Sphere, and Torus. Adjust the size of each of these objects by right-clicking on the object's icon. Using large values for resolution, latitude, or longitude will make the object more complex—that means it will take longer to render in a VRML viewer. To add an object to the scene, simply click on it.

- **Cameras**   Fountain lets you add up to five cameras to a scene. Adding cameras to a scene will allow you to control the point of view of a scene in a VRML viewer. In our example we set a single camera pointed at our objects.

■ **Lights**   Fountain supports two types of lights: infinite light, which covers the
scene uniformly, and local light, which radiates from a point source and
illuminates outward like a star. You can also control the color of your lights and
their intensity. The features can be accessed by right-clicking on the Light icon.
Our example has three light sources, each of a different color and intensity.

■ **Text**   The text tool is used to create vertical 2-D text objects. In Browse
mode, you can maneuver in and around the text like any other object in 3-D
space. Fountain lets you use any TrueType font style and size installed on
your system.

Let's take a look at the objects you can create using the Primitives panel.
Figure 12-23 shows the objects in our workspace, including the Primitives and
lighting panels.

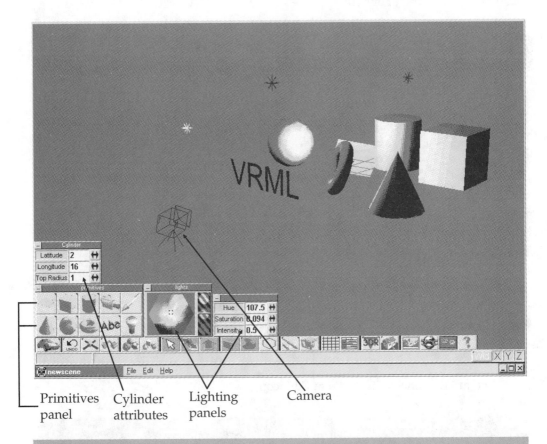

Primitives   Cylinder   Lighting   Camera
panel   attributes   panels

Figure 12-23.   *The Primitives scene in the building workspace*

MANIPULATING 3-D OBJECTS   Building primitive geometric shapes is just the start of what you can do with Fountain. The program also offers a full set of tools for manipulating existing objects, including extrusion, tip, and lathe tools. These terms are new to many readers so let's explore the tools and how to use them. They enable the creation of literally any sort of 3-D object.

We'll examine these tools one by one. To set the stage for our work, we'll create a simple cube object using the Primitives Panel.

The first tool to explore is the Point Edit tool. This lets us select and manipulate individual faces on our objects. First we click on the Point Edit icon, which turns the cursor into a small "p." Then, we click on a face on our cube. This opens up a Point Edit control panel, which includes tools for moving, scaling, and rotating faces. Each tool changes our cube in a different way, creating an altogether new shape. When we click on a tool in the control panel, then click on the face of our cube, we can drag the face into all sorts of new shapes. For instance, in Figure 12-24, we use all three tools to create a new object out of our cube.

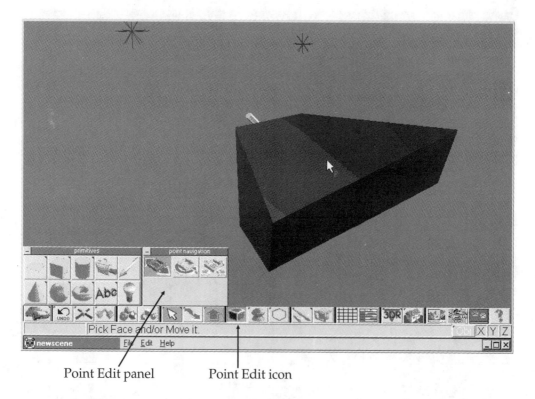

Point Edit panel   Point Edit icon

Figure 12-24.   *A new shape using the Point Edit tool*

The Point Edit tool is good for twisting standard shapes into new forms. Fountain has additional tools that can let you take a simple shape and build it into a more complex one.

The Tip tool lets us take any polygon or object face and extend it out to a three-dimensional point—or a tip. Click on the face you want to extend, click on the Tip icon and you can "pull" the face to a new point.

The Sweep tool lets us extrude—a common term in 3-D graphics, meaning to force out or protrude—an object to create an entirely new shape. By making a number of small extrusions one after another, and using the Point Edit tool to manipulate each new shape, we can create very sophisticated, multi-dimensional objects. To use the Sweep tool, we click on the face we want to extrude, click on the Sweep tool and "pull" the face away from its original position. Each sweep operation extends the object in a new direction.

Finally, we can use the Lathe tool to sweep a shape along a circular or spiral path. This tool provides an axis and path that can be changed and fine-tuned. We click on the Lathe icon to start the process and set the path, click the icon again and the object is created automatically.

In Figure 12-25, we show objects created using the Tip, Sweep, and Lathe tools. We also point out where to find the tools on the Fountain toolbar.

In addition to these tools to manipulate 3-D images, Fountain provides tools to create 2-D polygons. Once a polygon is created, you can use the Point Edit, Sweep, and other tools to extend and form it into a 3-D object. With these object modeling tools in hand, it is possible to create practically any 3-D object in your imagination. The tools may take a little practice, but they are not difficult to use.

PAINT AND TEXTURES   Once you build a 3-D object in Fountain, you'll want to decorate it. Fountain gives you a choice of painting and texture tools to add color to your objects (refer to Figure 12-26 for this discussion).

To paint, select the Paint icon on the toolbar. It will expand to offer five choices: Paint Face, Paint Vertices, Inspect, Paint Over, and Paint Object. Clicking on one of these icons also calls up the Material Color panel, a "color cube" that lets you pick the color you want to use by clicking on it. A separate panel called Shader Attributes let's you control a color's texture, shininess, ambient glow and transparency using a sliding bar.

To add a color to an object, choose from the color cube and pick a paint tool. For instance, when you choose the Paint Face icon, the cursor turns into a paint brush. Click the paint brush on an object's surface and it will instantly change color.

You can also add more complex materials to a surface. Click on the Materials library button on the toolbar. This calls up a panel that displays the Materials library that ships with Fountain, called basic.mlb. You apply materials the same way you apply paints. Click on a material in the panel window and a red line will appear underneath it. You can then use any of the paint tools to apply the material to the object.

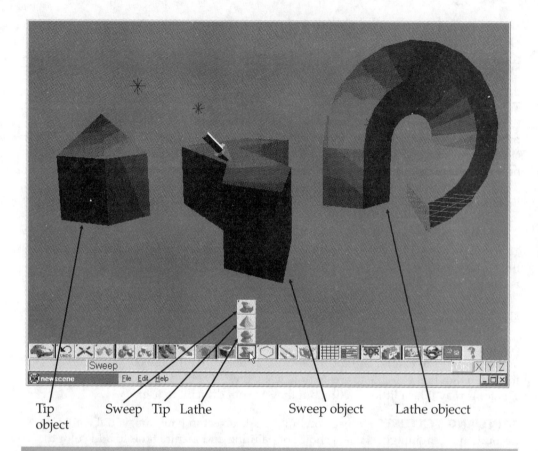

Tip
object

Sweep Tip Lathe

Sweep object

Lathe objecct

Figure 12-25. *Three objects created using the Sweep, Tip, and Lathe tools*

The combination of all of these tools—and the ability to paint and shade individual faces and polygons—makes it possible to create extremely realistic 3-D objects in Fountain.

HYPERLINKS   The final thing you may want to do to a 3-D object is attach a hyperlink to it. Fountain lets you attach URLs targeting HTML pages or VRML worlds. Simply click on an object to activate it, click on the Hyperlink icon in the toolbar (see Figure 12-26), then enter a URL into the dialog box field.

Fountain's VRML Tricks

So far, we've seen Fountain offer very powerful 3-D modeling tools that let you build your own 3-D objects. The tools also offer some VRML-specific authoring capabilities that smart designers will incorporate to make it easier for users to navigate through

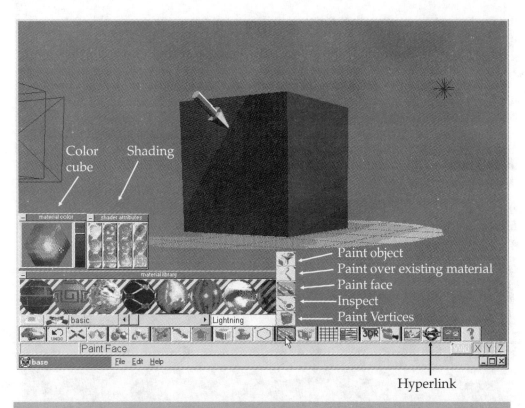

Color cube

Shading

Paint object
Paint over existing material
Paint face
Inspect
Paint Vertices

Hyperlink

Figure 12-26. *Tools and panels for adding textures and colors*

their worlds. We'll look at two key capabilities—Level-of-Detail and Inlining—that are part of the VRML 1.0 spec, but not widely deployed in first-generation VRML authoring tools. These capabilities, which are finding their way into more advanced VRML viewers, greatly improve the perceived performance as users load and navigate through VRML worlds.

LEVEL-OF-DETAIL   Levels of detail (LOD) lets VRML viewers render complex VRML objects more quickly by representing them at lower resolutions when they are farther away from the viewer. For instance, a castle that is set deep in the background of a complex scene can be represented as a simple cube. Then, as the viewer flies closer to the castle, it will slowly gain new features; first its general shape, then finer details and textures until it is rendered in its final form. All of this is done on-the-fly and is relatively seamless to the viewer. LOD makes it possible to render scenes more quickly by minimizing the total number of polygons to be rendered in real-time.

To create an LOD group, separately create each of the objects in the group as you want them to appear. Click on the LOD Group tool on the toolbar and then click on the final object—the one with the most detail, also known as the parent object (see Figure 12-27).

The group of objects in the workspace will collapse into a single object. When viewed in a VRML viewer, the object we created will appear in its simple form when it is far away and in its more complex form as the viewer gets closer to it. For example, we created a simple house that looks like a cube far away (see Figure 12-28, left screen) but springs a new detail (a roof) when the viewer gets closer to it (right).

LOD works best with extremely complex VRML worlds, where highly detailed and textured 3-D objects stretch over a large space. In such a scene, the viewer can see an object off in a distance, but doesn't see the fine details until they get close to it. Just like in the real world.

INLINING Inlining lets you break up large VRML scenes into a bunch of separate files that can be loaded one at a time. That allows a viewer to begin to see a scene right away rather than wait for an entire large file to download. In some cases, if inlining is

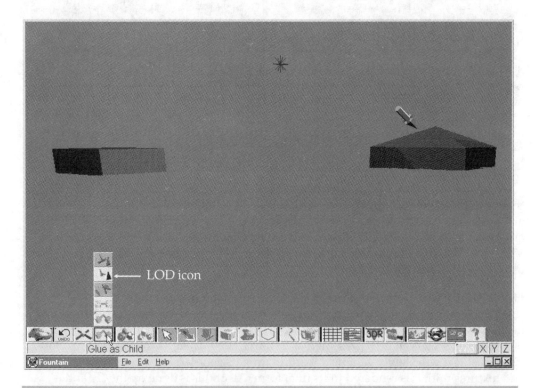

Figure 12-27. *The LOD Group tool lets you group objects*

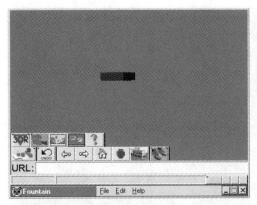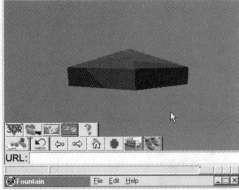

Figure 12-28. *Here is our LOD object in faraway (left), and then close-in (right) view*

used in conjunction with Level-of-Detail, the VRML viewer will choose which files to download based on the viewers position in the scene.

To mark an object for inlining, you select the Inline option in the Object Info panel. This panel displays the basic information about an object (see Figure 12-29).

To complete the job, you must be certain the different inlined objects get saved as separate (but related) files. You do this when you save the scene. If you don't choose a particular directory to store the inline objects—and any separate textures you have used—Fountain will place them in the same directory as the main file, as shown in the following Save VRML dialog box:

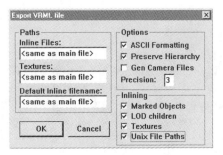

Exit Thoughts: Fountain

Fountain gets very high points for its low price and high functionality. It offers many of the same 3-D sculpting tools available only in much higher-priced products. It also gets good marks for the integrated browsing and authoring functions. This capability

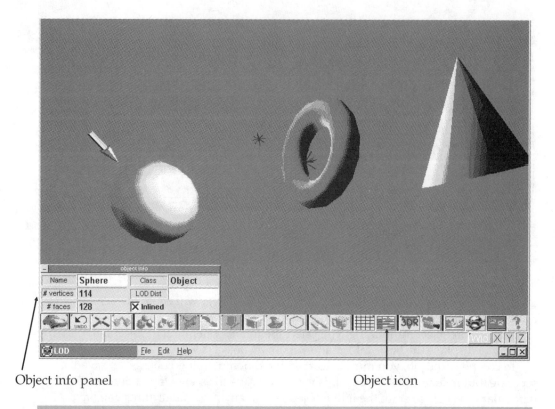

Object info panel   Object icon

Figure 12-29. *Click on the Inlined box to inline an object*

has become standard in HTML editors because for every page you build, you also need to be aware of how it will be viewed. The same is true with 3-D worlds.

If there is any downside to Fountain, it is its relative sophistication. Sculpting and shading 3-D objects, moving around a real-time 3-D workspace, and setting up cameras and lighting for a scene may be tricky for newcomers. The tradeoff for having freedom to build complex shapes and scenes is that Fountain definitely has a steeper learning curve than a tool like Virtual Home Space Builder. The extra effort offers a reward: freedom to build almost any 3-D object or scene you can imagine.

Where to Find More Information About VRML

KEY VENDOR WEB PAGES
See Chapter 11 for URLs of VRML viewer and authoring tool vendors.

VRML RESOURCES
VRML Forum: **http://vrml.wired.com**
VRML Architecture Group: **http://vrml.wired.com/VAG**
VRML FAQ: **http://www.oki.com/vrml/VRML_FAQ.html**
VRML Repository: **http://rosebud.sdsc.edu/vrml**
MeshMart: **http://cedar.cic.net/~rtilmann/mm/vrml.htm**
Terra Virtua: **http://www.terravirtua.com**
Grafman's VRML Tools Review: **http://www.graphcomp.com/vrml/review.html**

VRML SPECIFICATIONS
VRML 1.0 Specification: **http://vrml.wired.com/vrml.tech/vrml10-3.html**
VRML 2.0 Information: **http://vag.vrml.org/vrml20info.html**
SGI's Moving Worlds: **http://webspace.sgi.com/moving-worlds/index.html**
Microsoft's ActiveVRML: **http://www.microsoft.com/intdev/avr**
GMD's Dynamic Worlds: **http://wintermute.gmd.de:8000/vrml/dynamicWorlds.html**
Sun Microsystem's HoloWeb: **http://www.sunlabs.com/research/tcm/holoweb.ps**
Apple Computer's Out of this World: **http://product.info.apple.com/qd3d/**
VRML20/Out_Of_This_World

NEWSGROUPS AND MAILING LISTS
VRML Mailing List: To join the VRML standards discussion, please subscribe to the
www-vrml mailing list.
Send mail to **majordomo@wired.com.**
In the message body type: **subscribe www-vrml**
Web Hyperarchive of the VRML Mailing List: **http://vrml.wired.com/arch/**
NewsGroup: **alt.lang.vrml**

Summary

We must admit we began our exploration of VRML authoring tools with high expectations, and were a little disappointed. All three tools worked to a degree, yet all had shortcomings.

ParaGraph's Virtual Home Space Builder was a breeze to use. We built a model in less than five minutes relying on very sparse documentation. Its capabilities are somewhat limited, but it is a very good first effort at a user-friendly VRML world-building tool.

Virtus' WalkThrough Pro was a more frustrating experience. In its native mode, the tool was relatively simple to use and created very realistic, well-furnished 3-D scenes. There were some idiosyncrasies in how the tool exported to VRML. WalkThrough Pro is in its first-generation of support for VRML export, and a version due in mid-1996 will offer more capabilities.

Finally, Caligari's Fountain offers a different sort of tool, one more focused on object building with a lot of capabilities for 3-D object sculpting. With that power comes a complexity that may perplex newcomers to 3-D design tools. The tool's browsing and authoring capabilities combined with its full suite of design capabilities makes Fountain a good tool for the serious VRML world builder. It will only get better as it moves out of the beta version we tested and into full commercial release.

Chapter Thirteen

A Virtual Tour
of the 3-D Web

The extremely rapid evolution of the first generation of VRML has been mainly about one thing: getting tools and technologies into the hands of ordinary folks so they can begin building cyberspace. And build it they have. There is already a good supply of innovative VRML 1.0 worlds on the Web, built mainly by small design firms and jazzed-up VRML pioneers wanting to homestead their own piece of virtual cyberspace. More mainstream companies are getting into the VRML act as well, including chip maker Intel Corp. and technology publisher Ziff-Davis, both of which have sponsored some of the coolest VRML sites on the Internet. As you've learned in the last two chapters, VRML lets Webmasters build three-dimensional spaces that users can enter and navigate, and it offers an alternative to text-based HTML for the delivery of information and content on the Web.

This chapter takes a virtual tour of some of the best 3-D sites on the Web, exploring the themes and design tricks behind these leading-edge worlds by talking with a few of their creators. It also discusses the future of VRML tools with some of the people making them, takes a peak at AlphaWorld, a (non-VRML) 3-D world that is being populated by ordinary Web surfers, and shows you what to expect with VRML 2.0, courtesy of Netscape and its Live3D beta plug-in.

So before you begin building your own VRML worlds, you may want to see what these trendsetters have been working on. It will give you a good idea of what is possible and launch you on your own voyage into building cyberspace.

Finding VRML Worlds

Before we begin our tour, let's take a look at the best places to find VRML worlds. Here are a few of our favorite spots:

- Paper Software Inc.'s Worlds Page (**http://www.paperinc.com/wrls.html**) is a good listing of innovative VRML worlds. If you're using Netscape and the Paper Software plug-in, you also get a nice frames-based interface that makes it easy to tour the Web's best 3-D worlds.

- The VRML Object SuperMarket (**http://www.dcs.ed.ac.uk/generated/ package-links/objects/vrml.html**). Grab a shopping cart and take home some objects to use as a foundation for your own VRML worlds.

- Aereal Serch (**http://www.virtpark.com/theme/cgi-bin/serch.html**) is a comprehensive listing of 3-D worlds from Aereal, which builds VRML worlds and makes VRML tools. You can add your own worlds to the list as well.

- ProteinMan's Top Ten (**http://www.virtpark.com/theme/proteinman/ home.wrl**). Also from Aereal, this is a 3-D top ten list. In Figure 13-1, the holiday version of the list includes ten stockings, each linked to a different URL.

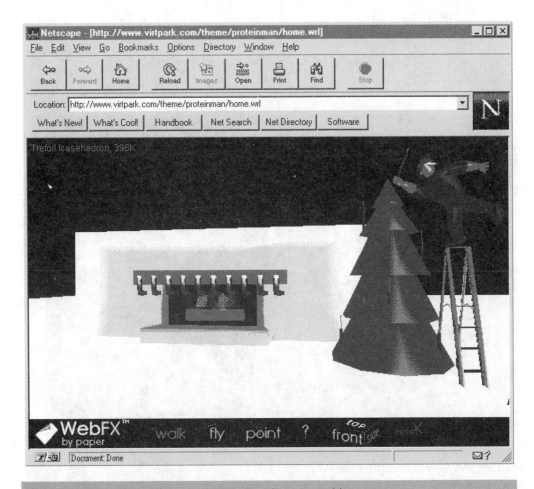

Figure 13-1.   *ProteinMan's Top Ten list of VRML worlds*

Cybertown

One of the most comprehensive efforts to build a fully navigable VRML world is Cybertown (**http://www.cybertown.com**). The site, built by Web design firm Multimedia Magic, began its life as a fancified HTML site, with graphical depictions of a futuristic world serving as image-mapped guides to other sites on the Web (see Figure 13-2). Cybertown is an attempt to organize the Web around the metaphor of a city, with a variety of sites representing the city's information center, entertainment complex, spaceport, library, shopping mall, health center, town hall, and more. City "residents" can also add content of their own in the Colony site.

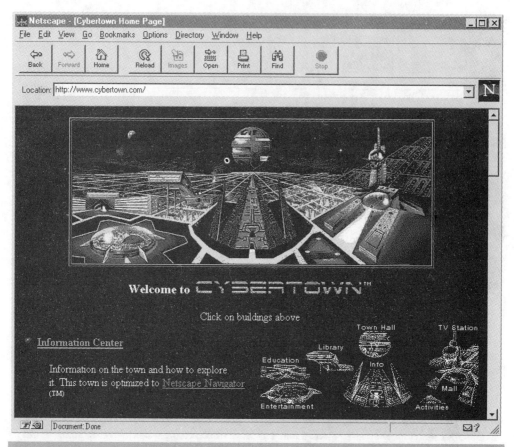

Figure 13-2. *The HTML version of Cybertown*

But Cybertown is undergoing a major transformation into a completely VRML-based 3-D space. The main city is being modeled in VRML; the first world built was the Cybertown Campus (see Figure 13-3). Multimedia Magic also lets its residents download and reuse virtual apartments built using Virtus WalkThrough Pro and ParaGraph Virtual Home Space Builder.

The ultimate vision is for all of Cybertown to be modeled using VRML, according to Tony Rockliff, producer with Multimedia Magic. "Cybertown started out when a couple of our artists fell in love with the Net. They saw it as a wonderful international canvas on which to create something. We were thinking of putting together a magazine, but found a better metaphor for cyberspace would be to create a virtual city. Now, we're working toward making the whole site 3-D. Eventually, we want to build in avatars [graphical representations of users in a 3-D environment] and add motions and behaviors."

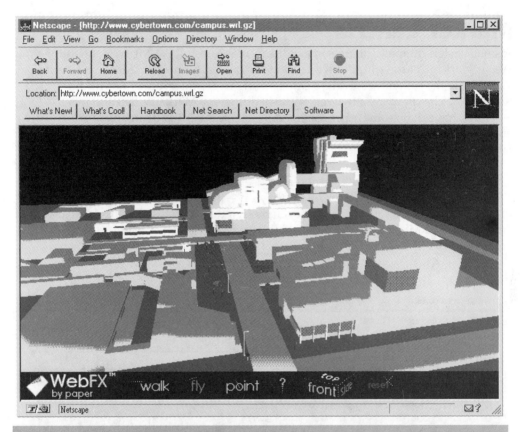

Figure 13-3. *The VRML version of Cybertown*

Multimedia Magic uses all three of the tools that were reviewed in Chapter 12: Virtus WalkThrough Pro, ParaGraph Virtual Home Space Builder, and Caligari's Fountain. "Home Space Builder is easy to use, good for textures, but limited in terms of polygons," Rockliff said. "Virtus is very good for modeling; it's fast and effective. But it's not good for textures. A lot of times we'll do stuff in Virtus, import it into Fountain, add textures and then put it out on the Net."

Pascal Baudar, Cybertown's creative director, said the VRML tools have proved very helpful in building the VRML version of Cybertown. The only reason to go in and tweak the VRML files by hand is to add lighting to the scenes, according to Baudar.

Baudar said that the main thing he has learned is that "as you build a VRML world, you have to learn not only to be an architect but an engineer, an artist, and an interior designer as well. All those professions have to come together all at once."

Market Central

A small design company doing some of the most interesting VRML work on the Web is Market Central (**http://www.marketcentral.com/vrml/vrml.html**). In Chapter 11, you saw the company's "Duke's Diner," a 3-D world integrating VRML and RealAudio. The company's two main VRML designers, Mark Connell and Joel Stephens, have done some other cool models, including a 3-D depiction of the Super Bowl stadium and a baseball stadium that includes RealAudio clips of famous baseball moments (see Figure 13-4).

The Market Central designers say they work mainly using AutoDesk's 3-D Studio, a high-end 3-D modeling package and then use a converter to turn the files into VRML. The converter works fairly well, they say—the only hand-tweaking required is to fix or add some camera angles. Yet even though they've been able to add RealAudio links to their VRML worlds, Connell said the pair has been frustrated by the limitations of VRML 1.0.

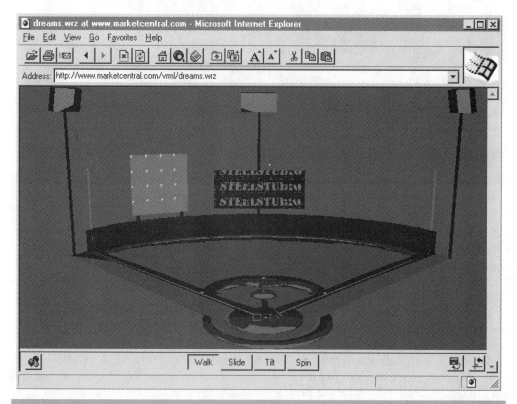

Figure 13-4. *Market Central's VRML ballpark*

"We think right now it's difficult to take VRML 1.0 and do a lot of business applications with it," Connell said. "But the next generation of VRML, plus an increase in access speeds, will give us a lot more that we can work with."

Stephens, a 3-D Studio veteran, says he recommends using high-end modeling tools for VRML—if you can afford it. "VRML-specific tools just don't have the same modeling capabilities," he says. Stephens also recommends thinking creatively about how to keep VRML file sizes small. For instance, he has started using transparent image maps to add interesting textures to 3-D objects while keeping the overall file size small.

Planet 9 Studios

Perhaps the leading VRML design house is Planet 9 Studios (**http://www.planet9.com**), which has done leading-edge VRML sites for Intel, Ziff-Davis, and its own models of San Francisco's SOMA neighborhood (as shown in Chapter 11). It also has built a VRML model of San Francisco and is rolling out VRML representations of other U.S. cities on its Web site.

Ziff-Davis' Terminal Reality is one of the most realistic-looking and easily navigable 3-D worlds. A visit to Terminal Reality begins on the exterior of the model (see Figure 13-5), which includes a virtual blimp (with links to Intervista Software's home page), a battleship (links to Intel), a rocket ship (links to Microsoft), and a plane (links to Planet 9 Studios). When you click on the terminal, you are transported inside, where there are gates that transport you to various spots on the Internet and a magazine stand that includes links to various Ziff-Davis publications.

Planet 9 Studios has also helped build several worlds for Intel, which has a major interest in forwarding VRML to help sell high-powered Pentium chips. Intel's most innovative 3-D world has been VRML Volunteer, a four-part series that takes the user through a series of virtual spaces and in the process tells an interactive story.

In the first installment, you volunteer to help out at the Museum of Digital Art. Some of the scenes are written in HTML, such as in Figure 13-6, which shows your online guide pointing you to the entrance of the VRML world and asking you to retrieve his blueprints. Once inside the world, as shown in Figure 13-7, you find the blueprint and click on it to display it. The blueprint helps you work through the second episode.

Interview with Planet 9's David Colleen

David Colleen, principal of Planet 9 Studios and formerly a renowned San Francisco-area architect, is one of the VRML's most-respected practitioners. "Planet 9 Studio's background is in architecture and planning. We used to design these great big buildings in the city using computer animation. We were the first all-digital shop in the Bay area," says Colleen. "When we'd work on a building, we'd also design the neighborhoods around [it]. One day we realized we had the largest [3-D graphical] database of the Bay area and San Francisco that existed."

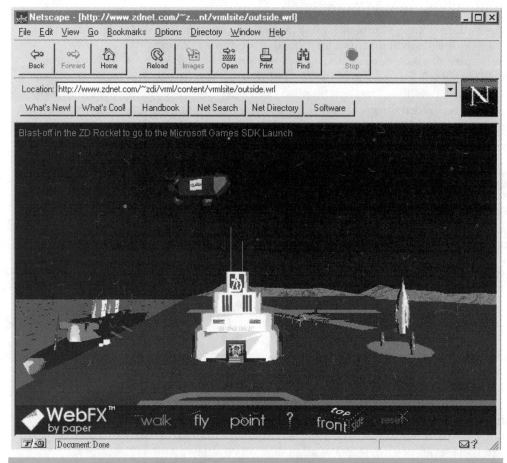

Figure 13-5. *The exterior of Ziff-Davis' Terminal Reality*

In early 1995, VRML pioneer Mark Pesce contacted Colleen, described his early work with VRML, and asked Colleen to put part of his San Francisco models onto the Web to demonstrate the potential of VRML. In August of 1995, Planet 9 Studios launched VR Soma, the first VRML world on the Internet. Planet 9 is planning to eventually post VRML representations of all of San Francisco—divided into 16 separate neighborhoods—up on the Web.

"Most of us are used to finding things by visual means," says Colleen, adding that the complete virtual representation of San Francisco will be used for business, advertising, shopping, and community-related happenings. "For instance, San Francisco is debating whether or not to build a new baseball stadium, and Planet 9 has created a VRML representation of the ballpark in its neighborhood surroundings to give the community an idea of how the new stadium will affect the area."

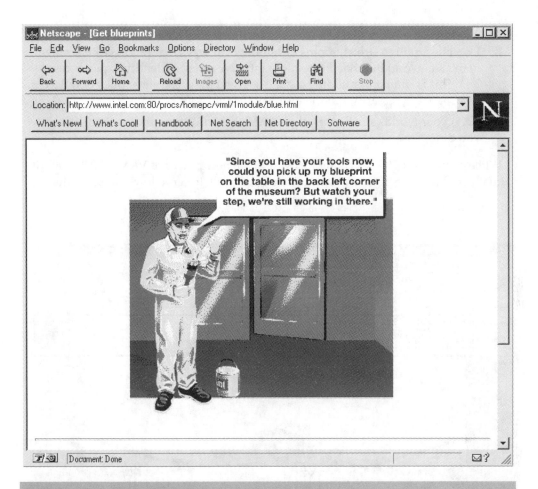

Figure 13-6.   *The HTML portion of VRML Volunteer*

Planet 9 Studios does most of its work with high-end authoring tools such as 3-D Studio. They then use conversion tools to convert to VRML, but they also do a lot of hand-coding, a time-consuming process that explains "why you're not seeing more VRML content out there," said Colleen. He has taken a look at VRML-specific authoring tools, but says they "mostly output dumb VRML files with no functionality. If you want to make extremely sophisticated 3-D worlds like we do here, you are going to have to do a lot of it by hand."

Colleen offers several tips for would-be VRML authors:

■ Begin with a strong idea of what you want to do. As you build, always keep in mind that the most important aspect of a world is how people move through a space—this is even more important in a VRML world than the real world.

- Try to tell a story in 3-D; this will add to the VRML experience.

- Don't be afraid to stretch rooms or buildings in ways that might seem strange in the real world but that create more intuitive or user-friendly experiences in 3-D. This is similar to building a stage-set for a play. The stage doesn't reflect real spaces, necessarily, but the needs of the play.

- Keep your worlds small, typically 2,000-3,000 polygons and less than 100K, if you can.

While Colleen says he is looking forward to the new power of VRML 2.0, he says it is equally important to have a VRML 1.0 site up as well, to serve low-end users that

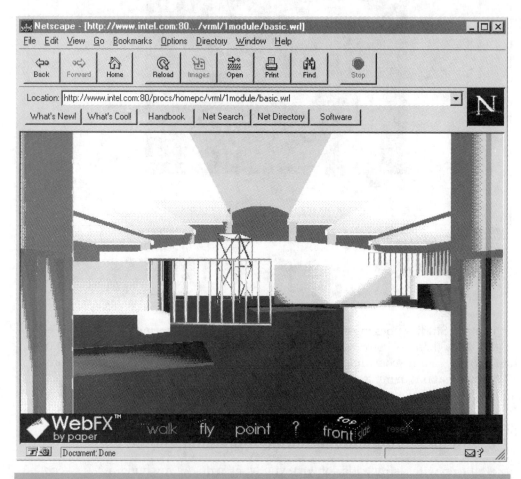

Figure 13-7.   *Entering a VRML world in VRML Volunteer*

don't have the Java capabilities required of VRML 2.0 worlds. "The installed base of Netscape 2.0 [the main browser supporting Java as this book was written] is not that great now. We are telling clients to do something in VRML 1.0 that everyone can see right now, and then add VRML 2.0 functionalities later."

VRML 2.0—Moving Worlds Beta

As this book was being written, the VRML community was just beginning to debate the eventual form of VRML 2.0. Netscape, however, made the debate a little more lopsided by endorsing—along with about 50 other companies—Silicon Graphics Inc.'s Moving Worlds proposal for adding interactivity and behaviors to VRML worlds. Moving Worlds enables VRML worlds to spring alive with animations, integrated sound, interactivity, and more. By combining VRML modeling with a scripting language such as Sun's Java, Moving Worlds scenes can contain interactivity and behaviors that were sorely lacking in VRML 1.0, enabling the creation of much more engaging and intuitive 3-D environments. To fuel the adoption of Moving Worlds, Netscape released a beta version of a plug-in that demonstrates what is possible with VRML 2.0 and Moving Worlds.

"Until now, VRML has really just been a toy. With Moving Worlds, it becomes practical to build real 3-D worlds," says Alex Edlestein, senior product manager for Netscape Navigator.

"VRML 2.0 brings 3-D to life on the Net," says John McCrea, manager of Silicon Graphics' WebForce unit, which delivers Web and VRML authoring tools. "It makes Web pages come to life, you get spinning corporate logos, animated cartoon characters. And for the first time you'll have scaleable virtual worlds, where people can enter and interact with other people. It's the movement from hypertext to hypermedia. VRML will change the notion of entertainment, education, and business on the Web."

Netscape's new Live3D makes these new capabilities possible. In Figure 13-8, a standard 3-D, VRML world adds animation, as all of the letters and objects spin and rotate on their own.

AlphaWorld

While the VRML community debates the future of VRML 2.0, Worlds Inc. (**http://www.worlds.net**) has been delivering multiuser, interactive 3-D worlds on the Internet since the spring of 1995. The company builds virtual worlds using its own proprietary technology but also has put forward VRML+ as a proposed VRML extension and is supporting SGI's Moving Worlds proposal. Worlds Inc.'s first Web project was WorldsChat, a 3-D spaceport that let users adopt an avatar, or graphical persona, and communicate via text-based chat technology with other people in a multiuser environment.

Figure 13-8. *Live3D enables animated logos*

WorldsChat was great, but Worlds Inc.'s next project, AlphaWorld, takes 3-D on the Web to a whole new level. AlphaWorld combines 3-D graphics, virtual reality, Internet chat, and multiuser avatar technology to create a fully functioning online world (see Figure 13-9). Users not only navigate through the world, they can help build it as well. Worlds Inc. provides its users with a toolkit for homesteading AlphaWorld, including the ability to create virtual buildings, parks, and cyber-newspapers. The latest versions of AlphaWorld also include a TelePortation system to help users zoom in and around AlphaWorld.

AlphaWorld includes a level of interactivity that even VRML 2.0 will be unable to attain. Users pick an avatar and are able to communicate with one another. When a

Figure 13-9.   *Worlds Inc.'s AlphaWorld*

person "speaks," his or her message is displayed in a bubble over the avatar's head, allowing communication between users via the Internet.

"Through AlphaWorld, Worlds Inc. is helping to create the first online society," says Rob Schmults, Worlds Inc.'s marketing director. "I deliberately avoid the word 'community' because it has become a bit tired and trite, and AlphaWorld is definitely not the same old thing. I also say we are 'helping to create' rather than 'creating,' because we certainly are not doing it alone. The users are already taking this thing and driving it even faster than we anticipated."

Schmults says AlphaWorld offers a good glimpse of the true power of 3-D on the Web—it's not just about virtual spaces, its about virtual interaction. "Think about all the interactions that make up our lives in the physical world: socializing, shopping, entertainment, education—you name it. We do it with other people. Virtual spaces allow you to have environments accessible from anywhere in the world that are not tied by time and place the way real spaces are. Now put people in them, and you have some pretty powerful functionality: social computing."

Summary

As you've seen in this chapter, VRML 1.0 has at last brought the concept of "space" to cyberspace. Innovative 3-D worlds like Intel's VRML Volunteer and ZD Net's Terminal Reality have taken VRML 1.0 to its limits. But there are more capabilities coming around the corner with VRML 2.0 and proprietary 3-D technologies such as Worlds Inc.'s AlphaWorld. Just beyond the horizon is a 3-D Web that offers not only virtual spaces but user interaction, animations, multimedia, and more.

PART FOUR

Real-Time Multimedia

Roadmap ▶

Part 4 examines real-time audio and video Web technologies. We'll focus closely on streaming audio technologies, but also examine some video systems. Chapter 14 provides an overview of the challenges of delivering real-time media over the Web, and it introduces the major players and their products. Chapter 15 looks at four Internet streaming audio technologies— VoxWare's ToolVox, DSP Group's TrueSpeech, VocalTec's Internet Wave, and Progressive Networks' RealAudio. Finally, Chapter 16, examines some cutting-edge sites using real-time technology on the Web.

Chapter Fourteen

Introduction to the Real-Time Web

C an the Web become what interactive TV always promised to be: an instantly accessible and customizable delivery vehicle for voice, data, and video? In typical Internet fashion, a variety of companies are riding the Web's leading edge and providing tools to deliver good-quality audio and, in some cases, video streams over the Web, all downloaded in "real time." This means the first bits of audio or video begin playing almost as soon as the user calls for the file, so users don't have to wait for entire files to download. (Due to the massive bandwidth requirements for audio and video, downloading files can often take several minutes or more.)

What does this mean for Webmasters? Almost overnight, audio has become a more usable file format on the Web. There have always been .wav and other audio format files available for download on the Web, but users were forced to completely download very large files—often megabytes in size—before they could play them back locally. For instance, a one-minute .wav file sampled at 22 kHz, 16 bits (a very high-quality sound file) is approximately 2.6MB in size. The compression technologies discussed in this chapter can reduce the file to 100K or less.

With the new real-time audio technologies, playback comes in an instant. High-end systems, like RealAudio and StreamWorks, use a server separate from the Web server to link with a player on the user's desktop to deliver an uninterrupted stream of audio data. Playback begins not long after the first few bytes of data reach the player. Other systems, such as ToolVox, Internet Wave, and TrueSpeech do not require a separate server but deliver similar functionality. The audio files are delivered directly from a standard Web server and the player begins to play the files moments after the first bytes arrive.

Though clearly limited by a lack of end-user bandwidth, streaming video technologies such as VDOLive offer the same instant satisfaction as real-time audio. When accessed via a 28.8 kb/s modem, VDOLive delivers somewhat fuzzy, clipped video streams. When accessed via ISDN lines or other high-speed methods, the system delivers fairly good-quality video.

Radio stations, news organizations, and record companies are now becoming big users of real-time audio technologies. But that's just the start. Since much of the software is free, individual users can take the technology and use it in a variety of creative ways. In Chapter 15, we'll demonstrate how to use real-time audio technologies. In the rest of this chapter, we'll introduce the major streaming audio and video technologies, and we'll provide directions for downloading players for those readers more interested in surfing the Web than creating it.

The Streaming Audio Technology Leaders

A variety of companies have emerged with real-time tools and players. The best-known is Progressive Networks' RealAudio, a client-server technology that has grown to deliver even live events over the Internet in real time. Technologies, such as DSP Group's TrueSpeech, VoxWare's ToolVox, and VocalTec's Internet Wave, have emerged to fill in the low end and free end of the market. Meanwhile, Xing Technology's StreamWorks, and VDONet's VDOLive, discussed later in the chapter, have introduced platforms that deliver video over the Internet—even over 28.8 kb/s modems.

VoxWare's ToolVox

Though a relative latecomer to the audio-on-the-Web marketplace, VoxWare has a major ally that should ensure its success—Netscape. The browser giant has licensed VoxWare's ToolVox technology to integrate into its Netscape Navigator browser and Netscape's new LiveMedia architecture.

What makes VoxWare's technology so appealing to Netscape? How about 53:1 voice compression. The compression—designed to work with voice files only—enables the delivery of high-quality audio over the Web with low-bandwidth connections of 14.4 kb/s and lower. ToolVox does not require a server to deliver its real-time files—they are simply embedded in a Web page and delivered from a Web server like any other MIME type. The files are delivered using standard HTTP and TCP/IP protocols.

ToolVox consists of two elements, both free and available for download from **http://www.voxware.com**:

■ The ToolVox Web player is available as a browser helper application and as a Netscape 2.0 plug-in. VoxWare offers Windows 3.1, Windows 95 (32-bit), Macintosh, and PowerPC versions of the player. At its launch, ToolVox enabled "streaming" playback with the Netscape plug-in and eventually with a Microsoft Internet Explorer plug-in. With other browsers, the file must be completely downloaded first. Because ToolVox files are so small, this is not a big problem. (See the ToolVox player embedded in a Web page in Figure 14-1.)

■ The ToolVox Web encoder compresses any input speech file (.wav or .aiff formats) to 8 kHz, 2400 bits per second. Source files at other sampling rates are downsampled to 8 kHz before compression. VoxWare promises a VoxWare Pro Encoder with extra bells and whistles.

Because ToolVox makes files so small, in many cases they download completely before the user starts to play them. This avoids clipped audio, since the file is essentially playing back locally. Yet in the case of large audio files, the player begins to play back the file as it is received, achieving a streaming effect. Because ToolVox audio is delivered using standard HTTP and TCP/IP protocols, the files pass through standard firewalls with no problems, something RealAudio streams cannot do. RealAudio is carried by the UDP protocol, which in some cases will not be allowed through corporate firewalls.

ToolVox does have has some limitations. Files cannot be played in the background like a RealAudio file, and it does not have rewind, fast forward, or pause features. (However, you can stop, start, speed up, or slow down the rate of playback.) It is not suited for music or other complex audio files—only voice. And it cannot do live Internet broadcasts.

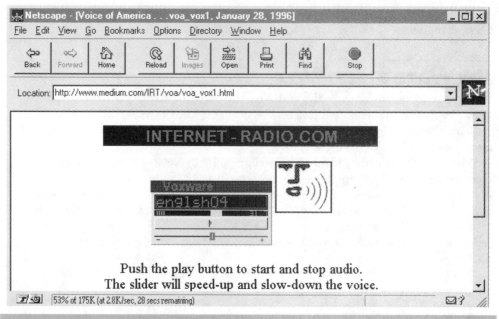

Figure 14-1. *The ToolVox player*

VoxWare admits all of these shortcomings but plays up the positive features. ToolVox is a totally free solution that delivers highly compressed voice files over the Net, eventually to a player embedded in Netscape's industry-leading Web browser. That makes VoxWare a strong niche player in the audio-on-the-Net marketplace, and it gives Webmasters serious reason to consider the technology for the delivery of basic voice files.

DSP Group's TrueSpeech

DSP Group comes to the streaming audio market on the Web from an interesting background. This company specializes in digital signal processing chips and software for speech compression. Its technology is used in a variety of devices, including digital answering machines and computer modems. In addition, TrueSpeech compression encoding technology is embedded as part of Windows 95, making it accessible at no charge to millions of users.

To leverage its work onto the Internet, DSP Group has released a free TrueSpeech player for the Internet, available for all Windows platforms, Macintosh, and PowerPC. The players are available at **http://www.dspg.com/allplyr.htm**. (See Figure 14-2 for a look at the TrueSpeech player.)

DSP Group is relying on the free Windows 95 encoder and a free Windows 3.1 conversion utility offered from its Web site to spur TrueSpeech content development.

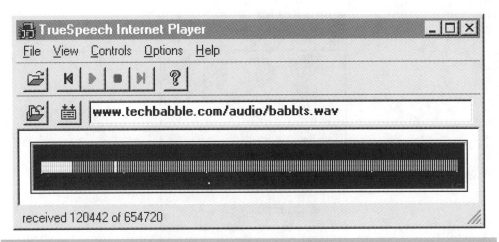

Figure 14-2. *The TrueSpeech Internet player*

The version of the encoder available in Windows 95 offers 15:1 compression. This makes it possible to simply place the files on your server and call them from an HTML page. TrueSpeech delivers voice and music files over the Internet. Like VoxWare, TrueSpeech does not require a server but has the same limitations as VoxWare: no live capabilities and somewhat limited control over the playback of the files.

So far, the response to TrueSpeech among Web authors has been strong. The number of sites offering True Speech-encoded content is quickly growing (see **http://www.dspg.com/cool.htm**).

DSP Group is working on an advanced version of its system that will have a higher-quality encoder as well as a server component to offer RealAudio-style streaming. As of the beginning of 1996, however, the product had not been released.

VocalTec's Internet Wave

VocalTec is best known for its InternetPhone product, which lets users conduct the equivalent of international "telephone" calls over the Internet. VocalTec has tried to leverage its voice-on-the-Net experience with InternetPhone by creating Internet Wave, a streaming, real-time audio system. Internet Wave is a free player that lets users hear Internet Wave files over the Web, and a free encoder/Web server extension that lets Webmasters create and post Internet Wave audio files. Both are available for download from **http://www.vocaltec.com**.

Like TrueSpeech and ToolVox, Internet Wave does not require a special server—it works with any standard Web server. The files are carried by standard TCP/IP protocols and can be played through a firewall. The standard free encoder compresses Windows .wav files and Unix .au files. This player runs only on Windows platforms (see Figure 14-3).

Figure 14-3. *The Internet Wave player*

One advantage of Internet Wave is that it offers Webmasters a choice of recording four different levels of audio files. They range from a low-bandwidth (9.6 kb/s) voice-only option to a high-bandwidth (28.8 kb/s or better) option for recording music or other complex sounds. The challenge for Webmasters, of course, is that not all listeners will have high-speed modems. You should label your files to inform the reader of the minimum bandwidth requirements. Also consider posting two sets of files: one for low-bandwidth and one for high-bandwidth users. (More on this in the next chapter.)

Finally, Internet Wave also enables random access to audio files, including fast forward and rewind. Only a Common Gateway Interface (CGI) script that comes as part of the free encoder is required—not a separate server.

Internet Wave's limitations are fewer than those of VoxWare and TrueSpeech—the platform offers the ability to deliver higher-quality files and lets the user have some random access to the playback stream. The system, however, does not permit multicasting and live encoding. Though promised, they had not yet been delivered as this book was written. In all, InternetWave offers a very viable option for high-quality file delivery, including recorded music to RealAudio, for free.

Internet Wave files are proliferating quickly on the Web—hear examples at
http://www.vocaltec.com/sites.htm.

Progressive Networks' RealAudio

The best-known brand name for real-time audio on the Web is RealAudio, Progressive
Networks' client-server system. RealAudio was the first streaming audio system
available, and in many ways it remains the most advanced. Its players and servers run
on a variety of platforms—including Mac and Unix—a big advantage in a market that
generally favors Windows. RealAudio comes in two flavors: a 1.0 version offering
basic, low-bandwidth streaming, and a 2.0 version offering higher-quality audio and
live net-casting. RealAudio 1.0 players are available for Windows 3.1, Windows 95,
Macintosh, and Power Macintosh and require a minimum 14.4 kb/s connection. (See
the 1.0 player in Figure 14-4.) Unlike the systems we've examined so far, RealAudio
requires a special server to deliver audio streams over the Internet. All of the software
discussed in this section can be downloaded from **http://www.realaudio.com**.

Progressive Networks has also launched RealAudio version 2.0, which requires a
separate player. The 2.0 player is slated to be available on all Windows platforms, Mac,
PowerMac, and several flavors of Unix (including SGI/Irix, Solaris, SunOS, and
Linux). RealAudio plug-ins are available for Windows and Macintosh, which allow
the RealAudio player and controls to be embedded right into an HTML page.
RealAudio 2.0 also enables authors to embed URLs in the audio stream. In addition to
delivering better quality music (over 28.8 kb/s links) and live events, RealAudio 2.0
lets you create multimedia "slideshows" with RealAudio audio clips synchronized
with the delivery of new URLs to your browser. Here, HotWired takes a virtual tour of

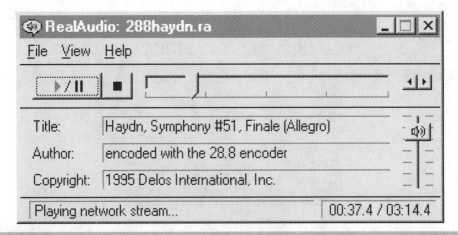

Figure 14-4.   *RealAudio 1.0 player*

the Doonesbury Web site. The HotWired server automatically "pushes" new HTML pages to the browser. RealAudio commentary is synchronized with page delivery. You can access the tour from the HotWired archives at **http://www.hotwired.com/surf/95/52/index5a.html**.

For Web authors, RealAudio offers free encoders (1.0 and 2.0 versions) for a wide variety of platforms. (For more on the encoder, see Chapter 15.)

The RealAudio system includes a separate server used to stream audio files down to the client. The RealAudio server sets up a direct connection with the RealAudio player. The server supports the Internet's UDP protocol, which is better suited than TCP/IP for delivering real-time streams. TCP/IP guarantees all of a file's packets are delivered even if it means delays, yet UDP delivers a nonstop stream of audio packets

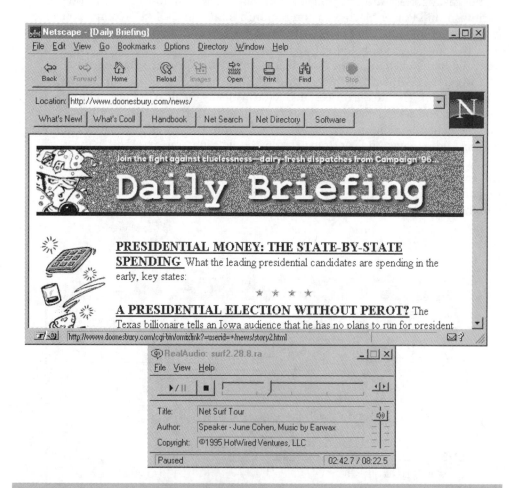

Figure 14-5. *A RealAudio-enabled Web tour*

without delay. The problem with UDP, however, is that occasionally packets will be dropped. To remedy this, the RealAudio client has the ability to "re-create" missing pieces of the signal, in most cases delivering to users a seamless audio experience. If you surf the Web with a RealAudio player, you'll realize this strategy is not flawless. Occasionally, an audio stream will suffer a clip or distortion caused by lost packets.

RealAudio stands behind UDP as its choice for streaming protocol and the need for a stand-alone server. Progressive Networks says the advantages include

- Support for a higher number of concurrent users
- Client/server feedback for user control of the audio stream
- Real-time correction of packet loss
- Large-scale live Net-casts and synchronized multimedia presentations
- Audio file plays in the background as the user continues to Web surf.

Like the RealAudio player, the RealAudio server is available in 1.0 and 2.0 flavors. Progressive Networks offers free trials of the servers. The 1.0 server runs on Windows NT, Macintosh, and a number of Unix platforms. Costs range from approximately $2500 for a 10-stream server to $14,000 for a 100-stream server. The RealAudio 2.0 server was in beta testing as this book was written, so prices were not available. Progressive Networks also offers a free personal RealAudio server, limited to delivering two streams.

The RealAudio system is a good choice for serious-minded Webmasters, who want to offer good-quality audio and with the new 2.0 version, live events and high-quality streaming music. RealAudio players are the most-used streaming audio application on the Web, with more than 1.5 million players downloaded. Progressive Networks also has deals for distribution of the player with most of the leading browser vendors—including Netscape and Microsoft. That represents a large audience of Web surfers that is looking for compelling content. Already, hundreds of Web sites have deployed the RealAudio content. You can find links to both 1.0 and 2.0 RealAudio-encoded content at **http://www.realaudio.com**.

As this book was written, Progressive Networks revealed plans to open up the underpinnings of its RealAudio system to the Internet and to work with Netscape to develop open, next-generation streaming audio technologies for the Internet as part of Netscape's LiveMedia framework.

The Next Wave: High-Quality Audio and Video

RealAudio 2.0 takes audio-on-the-Web to a new level, supporting high-quality music files, live events, and more. As RealAudio moves up-market, it runs into two competitors that focus on high-end streaming media systems, enabling not only high-quality audio, but video as well.

Xing StreamWorks

Xing Technology is the creator of StreamWorks, a platform for delivering live and on-demand audio and video over the Internet. The StreamWorks technology began as a system for delivering video streams to the desks of financial professionals over high-speed private networks. Xing scaled down the technology, based on MPEG video standards, to work over the Internet. It can deliver low-frame-rate video streams over slow modem connections. The system uses standard TCP/IP protocols to deliver its audio and video streams.

StreamWorks consists of four components: server software, client software, a video/video compression engine, and an audio-only compression engine. The system doesn't come cheap. The server software is $3500 for a T1 or lower Internet connection and $6500 and up for a higher-speed connection. StreamWorks servers run on Unix and Windows NT platforms. The high-end MPEG audio/video encoder is $6500. An encoder that enables MPEG and low bit rate audio encoding is $2500. Both encoder packages include hardware and software but not monitors.

For Web surfers, Xing offers free StreamWorks players for Windows, Macintosh, and Unix platforms. The StreamWorks player can work in stand-alone mode (it has a built-in menu of StreamWorks servers) or in conjunction with a Web browser. The same player runs audio clips (see Figure 14-6) as well as video streams, such as

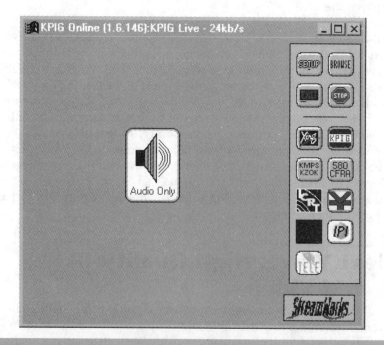

Figure 14-6. *Radio station KPIG broadcasts live over the Internet with StreamWorks*

Bloomberg Television (see Figure 14-7). It is shown running at 24 kb/s—which provides only a frame or two per second.

To see and hear the best StreamWorks has to offer, you'll need an ISDN (128 kb/s) connection or better. At ISDN rates, StreamWorks promises it can deliver 30 frames per second, quarter screen video, or 44 kHz stereo (almost CD-quality) audio. StreamWorks also delivers low-end video (one or two frames per second) to users with a 14.4 kb/s or 28.8 kb/s modem connection. For audio, the system delivers CD-quality sound to ISDN users, and near-FM quality sound to lower-bandwidth users.

The relatively expensive equipment and StreamWorks' capability to deliver good quality, live audio signals, have limited Xing technology to large companies, especially radio stations. While StreamWorks promises high-quality bandwidth over high-speed links, in reality the Internet is often congested and StreamWorks will not reach the throughput promised. In addition, the decision to use MPEG-encoding preserves the audio and video quality, but overall, StreamWorks lags behind some of its competitors when it comes to compressing large files.

Radio stations that broadcast using Xing include: KPIG—Santa Cruz (**http://www.kpig.com**), KMPS Country—Seattle (**http://www.kmps.com**), KZOK 70s Rock—Seattle (**http://www.kzok.com**), and iRock Radio (**http://www.irock.com**). On

Figure 14-7. *Bloomberg Television broadcasts live with StreamWorks*

the video side, NBC Pro Financial News Channel delivers live video streams over the Internet using StreamWorks.

StreamWorks is intriguing technology that for most users is a bit out on the Web's leading edge, both in capabilities and cost. For live audio it favors comparably to RealAudio. The high-bandwidth requirements for good-quality video, however, make the video portion of the system more suitable for corporate Intranets than for use over the public Internet until end users access more bandwidth.

For information about Xing authoring and player software, and for links to the latest Xing Net-casters, go to **http://www.xingtech.com**/.

VDONet's VDOLive

The best solution for low-bit-rate video is undoubtedly VDONet's VDOLive technology. Even over 28.8 kb/s connections, VDOLive claims it can offer as high as 10 frames per second playback with synchronized sound, making it possible to deliver streaming video over the Net to modem users. The system is scaleable, meaning a single encoded video stream can adapt itself to a user's network connection, whether it is a high-speed dedicated line, an ISDN line, or a low-speed modem link. This way Web page authors need to encode only a single file to serve every visitor's needs. VDONet can be found on the Web at **http://www.vdolive.com**.

VDOLive is based on proprietary compression technologies and communications protocols, optimized together to deliver streaming video over low-bandwidth Internet connections. VDONet offers two flavors of servers: a professional version that runs on Unix or NT machines and costs approximately $100 per stream delivered, and a free personal server that is limited to 2 streams delivered at rates under 28.8 kb/s. The servers have built-in editing and encoding tools that run on Windows 95.

Also available is the free VDOLive player, which comes in two flavors: a stand-alone helper application for Windows 3.1 and Windows 95, and a Netscape plug-in, which enables in-line streaming video on an HTML page. (Figure 14-8 shows a video running in the VDOLive player.) Like Xing, VDOLive is used primarily by large news and entertainment companies, including CBS News, Paramount Digital Entertainment, Grolier Interactive, and a number of local TV stations.

VDOLive's technology represents a true breakthrough. Though not all Web surfers may be turned on by 10 frames per second video, the technology breakthroughs for this are nothing short of amazing. If you are a Web surfer, you owe it to yourself to check out the VDOLive player. If you are a Webmaster, you'll need to weigh the value of delivering low-bit-rate video to your users versus the cost.

Figure 14-8.   *A video played back in the VDOLive player*

The Netscape Wild Card

As this chapter was written, Netscape checked in with its own real-time audio and video strategy, which it calls LiveMedia. Netscape said it will support industry standards including emerging Internet standard Real Time Protocol, MPEG video, H.261 video conferencing and GSM voice compression. To fuel its strategy, it acquired InSoft Inc. (**http://www.insoft.com**) and licensed VoxWare's ToolVox audio technology.

LiveMedia won't begin to find its way into Netscape products until late 1996 at the earliest. But its impact has been felt immediately. Every streaming audio and video company will have to decide whether it wants to follow Netscape or compete with it. Some companies—including RealAudio and VoxWare—appear to have jumped on the Netscape wagon; others, such as VDONet, say they have better technology and are ready to compete.

In Chapter 16, we'll talk with Netscape co-founder and Mosaic creator Marc Andreessen about the future of real-time audio and video on the Netscape platform.

Summary

Real-time audio and video adds a new dimension to the World Wide Web. Web surfers no longer have to download an audio or sound file and play it back later. Now it's simply a click, and within seconds an audio or video stream starts playing. Prerecorded files are spreading rapidly, including speeches, news reports, and music. Even more exciting is the advent of live Web events, including sporting events, concerts, trade show keynotes, and more.

Chapter Fifteen

Hands-on
Real-Time Audio

Learning to deliver audio from your Web site is equal parts science and art. You'll need to learn some audio technology basics to get started. But in the end, the tools you'll count on most are your own two ears. If a file sounds good to you as an author, it will sound good to your listeners.

It's very easy to get started with digital audio recording. Most computers today—including almost all Macs and PCs—come with built-in sound cards, microphones, and sound editing software. You can begin making your first basic recordings within minutes. The process of using a real-time encoder is no more complicated than importing a source file and clicking a button to start the compression.

Yet as with any science, there are intricacies revealed as you become conversant in the basics. As you delve deeper into real-time audio technologies, you'll pick up what works best for you—the best audio recording equipment, the best file compression tricks, and more. This chapter will get you started delivering real-time audio files from your home page, but you'll learn more with your ears than we can ever show you on a printed page.

Here we'll take a hands-on look at four streaming audio technologies—VoxWare's ToolVox, DSP Group's TrueSpeech, VocalTec's Internet Wave, and Progressive Networks Real Audio—progressing from the simplest and cheapest solutions to the more complex and expensive.

You'll be surprised at how easy it is to add this exciting new capability to your Web site.

Audio-on-the-Web Primer

Before we examine the streaming audio tools, let's take a moment to address some basic audio concepts we'll encounter as we move through this chapter. The two most common audio file formats streaming audio encoders accept are .wav for Windows and .aiff for Macintosh. Most of the real-time applications are biased toward Windows platforms and .wav files, but some deal with .aiff as well. If you have files in formats other than these, you can use a sound editor or conversion utility to convert the file into the format you need.

All audio data is characterized by the following parameters:

- *Sampling rate* In kilohertz per second, typically ranging from 8 khz to 44.1 khz. The higher the number, the greater the fidelity.

- *Number of bits per sample* 8 bits or 16 bits. Most sound cards and computers today are equipped to handle 16-bit audio.

- *Number of channels* 1 for mono and 2 for stereo.

As computers become increasingly capable for multimedia, there is very little you have to do to equip yourself to record basic audio files. Macintosh systems have long had built-in audio support, and most Windows PCs today ship with built-in sound cards that let you playback and record sound. Most computers today offer at least 16-bit audio, but some older systems deliver lower-fidelity 8-bit sound. Most ship with a sound board and often have built-in sound recording and editing software. And if all else fails, and you're running Windows 95, it has a decent built-in sound recorder, including support for DSP Group's TrueSpeech format.

If you need sound recording/editing software, there are a number of good shareware audio editors available on the Web. Windows-based editors include GoldWave, which can be downloaded from **http://web.cs.mun.ca/~chris3/goldwave**, and CoolEdit, downloaded from **http://www.netzone.com/syntrillium**/. On the Mac side, good places to start are the Mac Sound Utilities page at **http://www.wavenet.com/~axgrindr/ quimby4.html**, and the University of Texas Macintosh freeware and shareware archive, at **http://wwwhost.ots.utexas.edu/mac/pub-mac-sound.html**.

Sound Effects is a popular shareware Mac editor.

For general resources regarding audio on the Web, check out the audio library at **http://www.comlab.ox.ac.uk/archive/audio.html** and a copy of the Usenet audio FAQs at **http://www.cis.ohio-state.edu/hypertext/faq/usenet/audio-fmts**/.

Recording Tips

A high-quality audio source is probably the most important variable in determining your final audio quality. This includes the quality of the source audio file—an audio CD or digital audio tape (DAT) works better than a hissy cassette tape—and the quality of your audio equipment, notably the microphone.

If you are recording voice files, most computers and sound cards today offer built-in microphone jacks. The quality of your voice recording depends on the quality of the microphone. Most PCs and sound cards include a simple microphone for recording voice files. If you want better quality recordings, you can buy a higher quality microphone from an audio shop.

When recording from a microphone, be certain you are working in a quiet environment. Do not talk directly into the microphone—hold it several inches away and slightly below your mouth to avoid "pops" when you say "p" words like "perfect." Make a trial run. The level indicator on your sound recorder should reach the maximum scale when the input is loud, but settle in the middle for normal speech. If the level is set too low the recording won't be heard, if it is too high, it will be distorted. Most audio recorders have a "mixer" that displays how much sound is coming in. Make sure the peaks do not exceed the maximum levels, and the range of the audio is not too flat.

In addition to microphone recording, it is also possible to record from your computer's built-in CD drive. Just pop a CD into the drive and play it as usual. Use your sound recording software to record the playback. Set it at a higher sampling rate (though this is not necessary) and record in stereo to get the full range of sound. Finally, you can attach external sources—such as a CD or DAT player or a tape machine—directly to the sound card line input. Once connected, the recording is the same as if the CD drive was internal.

Hands-on: ToolVox, TrueSpeech, Iwave, and RealAudio

Now let's take a hands-on look at four of the most popular streaming audio applications on the Web. All of these let you add audio to your home page. Pick the one that best fits your needs.

Using VoxWare's ToolVox

VoxWare's ToolVox for the Web lets you take standard voice—no music or complicated sound—files in .wav or .aiff format and compress them at rates up to 53:1. The ToolVox encoder, which compresses files to 8 khz-2400 bits per second, is available for free download at **http://www.voxware.com**. VoxWare promised a Gold version with more capabilities, but it was not available when this book was written. The Encoder is available in Windows 3.1, Windows 95, and Macintosh versions.

In addition to the high rate of compression, the great advantage of ToolVox is that .vox files can be embedded into any HTML document and delivered from any Web server with very little effort. No separate server is required. The system works with existing Web servers and delivers the files via standard TCP/IP protocols.

ToolVox Hands-On

To begin, we must create a source audio file. ToolVox works only with mono-speech files, not with stereo files. VoxWare recommends sampling your source file at 8khz. If it is sampled at a higher rate, the ToolVox encoder will down-sample it to 8khz before compressing it.

For this example, record the following voice file using CoolEdit, sampled at 8 khz (see Figure 15-1). Save this file as hi.wav:

"Hello, this is Rich Karpinski, author of *Beyond HTML*, a book detailing the hottest technologies on the Web's leading edge."

Note ▶   *Since ToolVox doesn't handle music or background effects well, make sure the room is quiet when you record your voice file. Also, avoid static or other distortions in your original file. Because of the high level of compression in ToolVox, these distortions will be greatly magnified in the final compressed .vox file.*

Next, we'll run this .wav file through the ToolVox encoder (as shown in Figure 15-2). The original audio file, which runs just 9.25 seconds, is 144 kb. To open in it the encoder, pull down the File menu and click on Open Wave file. The encoder automatically opens the Wave File and readies for the conversion by giving the file a new .vox extension. We click on the Compress button in the center of the encoder screen and the file is compressed to .vox format. The original 144 kb file is compressed to just 2.9 kb.

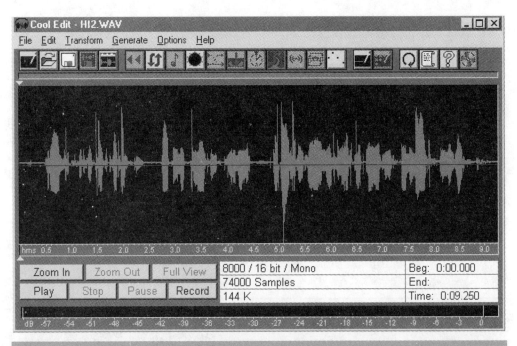

Figure 15-1. *Audio recording sampled in CoolEdit*

The ToolVox encoder offers some additional functions. Once you open a .wav file in the encoder, you can play it back by clicking the play button. You can also speed up or slow down the playback speed of the original file or the compressed .vox file. You can also use the encoder as a basic audio recorder by pressing the record button and speaking into the microphone.

The next step is to embed the compressed file in our HTML page. For standard browsers, use the usual A HREF tag to create a link that calls the .vox file (see Figure 15-3):

<A HREF="www.home.com/audio/hi.vox"> <IMG SRC=vox.gif> Click here for a ToolVox welcome </A> (2.9)

We can also optimizing the file for playback by the Netscape plug-in. This approach adds the benefit of enabling users to hear files as soon as they are accessed. The ToolVox player for Netscape does this by creating a small buffer out of the first bits of the file as it is downloaded. This streaming feature is only available for the Netscape plug-in. You can also take advantage of some special parameters of the EMBED tag for calling plug-ins. (Figure 15-4 shows a ToolVox viewer embedded in an HTML page.)

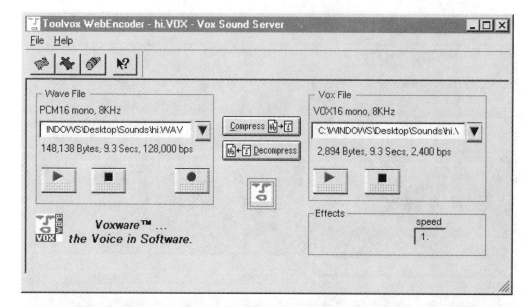

Figure 15-2. *The ToolVox encoder*

The HTML tags and parameters that make this possible are

<EMBED SRC=intro.vox playmode=auto visualmode=embed height=75 width=158 vspace=10>

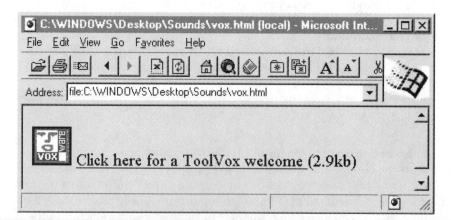

Figure 15-3. *A standard hotlink for a ToolVox file*

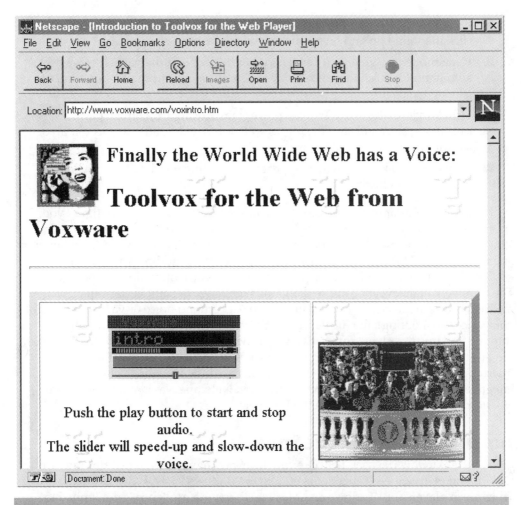

Figure 15-4. *The embedded ToolVox player*

Notice that the EMBED tag has two parameters, playmode and visualmode, that offer a variety of different display options:

- playmode=*user* The user must click either on the Vox icon or the player window's Start button to begin playback.

- playmode=*auto* The file begins to play automatically when the Web page is opened.

- playmode=*cache* The browser stores the entire file (without playing it) for later playback.

- visualmode=*icon*   A VoxWare face icon appears on the Web page. Users may click the sound off and on by clicking on the icon.

- visualmode=*background*   There is no user interface on the page. It plays back automatically. Also, there is no way to stop the sound from playing, short of leaving the page.

- visualmode=*embed*   The ToolVox player window appears on the page. Users can click to start and stop the file, as well as move the slider to speed it up or slow it down.

- visualmode=*float*   The player appears as a floating window that can be minimized or closed.

Finally, to use compressed .vox files on your Web page, you must configure your existing server to handle the VoxWare MIME type. This procedure varies by server (check your server's documentation), but generally you will need to add the following line to the MIME.TYPES file in the configuration directory: audio/voxware vox.

ToolVox is a good solution for highly compressed voice-only files. But be careful. The extremely high level of compression limits the range of sounds you can record. A monotone speech file is fine. But if you include background noise or vary the sound of your voice (ie, shouting), the file degrades. You can't record music at all. The high compression rate does have some advantages. Because they are so small, ToolVox files can be attached to e-mail or newsgroup messages to add a new element to these Internet communications. Since Netscape has licensed the VoxWare technology to integrate into its new LiveMedia architecture and Netscape Navigator browser, .vox will be a widely used file format on the Internet.

Using DSP Group's TrueSpeech

If you are a Windows 95 user, DSP Group's TrueSpeech may be the real-time authoring tool for you. A TrueSpeech encoder is built in to Windows 95. DSP Group offers TrueSpeech players for Windows and Macintosh, so your audience is not limited to Windows users.

The process for creating TrueSpeech files and preparing to deliver them from a Web server is relatively simple. You don't need a separate audio editor and can do all your work right within Windows 95. TrueSpeech is an especially good choice for newcomers to real-time audio technologies.

TrueSpeech Hands-On

The first step is to create a PCM-encoded .wav file as your source file. It will later be converted and compressed into a much smaller TrueSpeech-encoded file. Create the file in Windows 95's Sound Recorder, which is accessed from the Accessories menu. It is a simpler recorder than the full-featured audio editors we mentioned earlier, but it will do the job fine (see Figure 15-5).

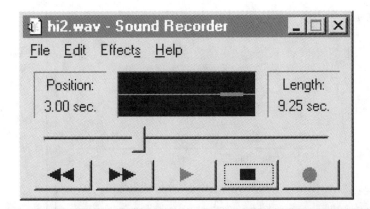

Figure 15-5. *The Windows 95 sound recorder*

First, we'll need to set the Sound Recorder to capture the recording at 8khz, 16 bits. This is the rate recommended by DSP Group, optimized for the TrueSpeech compression algorithm. Change the capture settings under the Edit menu by clicking on Audio Properties. This calls up a dialog box where we change the settings (see Figure 15-6).

Once the settings are correct, record the same simple voice file as we did with ToolVox and save the file as hello.wav:

> "Hello, this is Rich Karpinski, author of *Beyond HTML*, a book detailing the hottest technologies on the Web's leading edge."

This simple sentence, lasting 9.875 seconds, is 154 kb—rather large to be sending over the Internet. To shrink the file, convert the PCM-encoded .wav file to TrueSpeech Format. To do this, stay inside the Windows 95 Sound Editor, with the hello.wav file open, click on Save As. The Save As dialog box lets us save the audio file format (as shown in Figure 15-7). Choose the TrueSpeech format. The file keeps its .wav extension even after it is converted. Therefore, we'll rename the second file hellodsp.wav so we can compare the two files when we're done. Click on Save and the file will be converted.

How do the two files compare? The PCM .wav encoded file (8khz, 16-bits) came in at 154 kb. The TrueSpeech encoded file came in at 10.3 kb. Once it is converted, the TrueSpeech file is sampled at 8 khz, 1 bit-mono.

DSP Group also offers a PCM-to-TrueSpeech conversion utility for Windows 3.1 users. You can download it from their home page. The utility will only accept .wav files sampled at 8khz-16-bit PCM format.

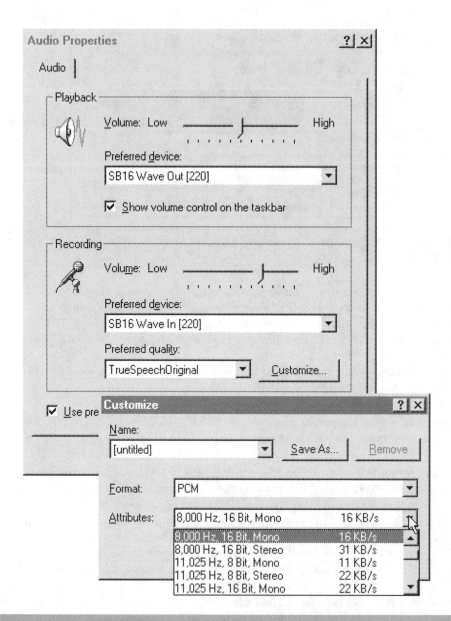

Figure 15-6. *The Audio Settings dialog box*

Now that we have a TrueSpeech file, we need to take a few final steps. The first is to create a .tsp file that is associated with the .wav file (hellodsp.wav) we created. When you click on a Web hotlink to call up a TrueSpeech clip, this is the file you will

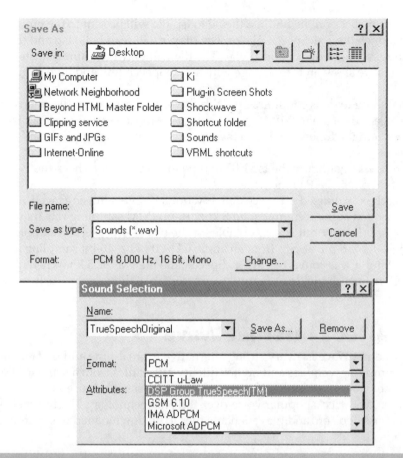

Figure 15-7. *Converting the .wav file to True Speech format*

access. It tells the browser to spawn the TrueSpeech player, and send the player the TrueSpeech-encoded .wav file.

To continue with our example, we'll use Notepad to create a file called hello.tsp. This file will be placed in the same directory on our Web server that holds hellodsp.wav. It will contain only one line, providing the URL for our .wav file:

TSIP>>www.home.com/audio/hellodsp.wav.

The next step is to reference this .tsp file from an HTML page by adding the following HTML tag:

<A HREF="www.home.com/audio/hello.tsp"> <IMG SRC=TS.GIF> Click here for a TrueSpeech welcome </A> (10.3kb)

When a user clicks on the hotlink, the hello.tsp file will be sent to the browser, which will launch the TrueSpeech player. The player will read hello.tsp and then find and play the associated file, hellodsp.wav. The file will play back almost instantly. In Figure 15-8, we show an HTML page with a TrueSpeech link and logo identifying our file.

The final thing to do is configure our Web server to accept a .tsp file extension. To do this, we need to set a new MIME type—dsptype—for the server to recognize. On Unix servers, add the following line to the server configuration: application/ dsptype.tsp.

To learn how to configure the tsp MIME type for your server, check the documentation on the DSP home page.

TrueSpeech is optimized for voice delivery, but it delivers music as well. Music originally encoded at the recommended 8 khz, 16-bit PCM sampling rate may not have the highest fidelity, but it is acceptable for the price—free. As an example, we recorded a 60-second music clip from an audio CD. At 8khz, 16-bit sampling it was a 937 kb file. After it was converted to TrueSpeech, the file was 62.5 kb. When played back in the TrueSpeech player the sound was acceptable, though obviously not crystal-clear.

Using VocalTec's Internet Wave

VocalTec's Internet Wave is a very strong alternative for real-time audio. It enables the delivery of simple speech files and higher-fidelity music files from a standard Web server. Internet Wave's compression technnology is the same one used for InternetPhone, VocalTec's popular voice-over-the-Net technology. The Internet Wave encoder, server extension, and player enable files to be downloaded in streaming

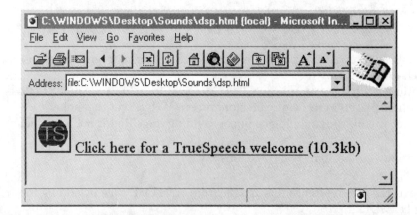

Figure 15-8.   *A hotlink for a TrueSpeech file*

fashion and let users rewind or fast forward the files on-the-fly. With a 28.8 kb/s modem and the proper file encoding, you can deliver fairly high-quality pre-recorded music over the Web in streaming fashion.

Internet Wave Hands-On

The first question to address when using Internet Wave is what quality of files do you want to deliver. Internet Wave lets you deliver four different audio formats, targeted at the low end at 9.6 kb/s modems and at the high end at 28.8 kb/s or better connections. It is a good idea to offer users an option—one file for low-speed and one for high-speed connections (see Figure 15-9). But if you don't want to offer a choice, pick an audio format that suits most users. Internet Wave's compression options are shown in Table 15-1.

The sampling rates in Table 15-1 represent the final rates after compression. Use at least that rate or higher for your source files. For our purposes here, we can reuse the 9-second speech file (144 kb, 8 khz-16 bits, mono) we used in the VoxWare example for our low-end Internet Wave compression. To demonstrate Internet Wave's ability to deliver music, we'll encode a sixty-second music clip recorded from the computer's internal CD-drive (3.63 mb, 16 khz-16 bits, stereo).

The Internet Wave encoder is similar to the other encoders we've discussed (see Figure 15-10). In the Encoder dialog box, you can

- Provide the location of the source file you want to compress.
- Provide the location of the destination file.
- Choose between four compression options.
- Designate whether it is a music or voice source file.
- Provide the URL where the compressed file will be located on the server (more details on this to follow).
- Attach information about the sound file to be provided to the end user when downloaded with the Internet Wave player.

Once you have made your inputs, click the Create button in the dialog box and the encoder goes to work. Two files are created. The file that holds the audio clip is called the media file and has a .vmf extension. A second file, used to activate the client player, is called the stub file and has the extension .vmd. This is similar to the .tsp file we created by hand with TrueSpeech. Internet Wave creates the stub file automatically. The file is placed on the Web server along with the audio file. When a user clicks on a hotlink for an Internet Wave file, the stub file launches the Internet Wave player on the client side and initiates the download on the server side.

We ran both our speech and music source files through the encoder. The speech file was compressed from 144 kb to 12.6 kb, and the music clip from 3.63MB to 162K. Both files will play back within a few seconds when downloaded over the Internet by an Internet Wave player.

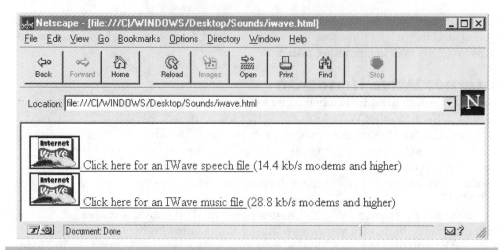

Figure 15-9. *Referencing several Internet Wave files from your home page*

Format Name	Sampling Rate	Download Requirements	Description
VSC77	5.5khz	9.6 kb	Format for speech-only. Can be used by almost all users because of low-bandwidth requirements.
VSC112	8khz	14.4 kb	Format offers excellent speech recording and reasonable music quality, yet can still be used by most modem users.
VSC154	11khz	28.8 kb	Format offers excellent speech and good music quality. Only for users with 28.8 kb/s connections or higher.
VSC224	16khz	28.8 kb	Format offers excellent speech and music quality. For use only with 28.8 kb/s connections and higher. Choose this if you want better quality and don't mind slightly larger source files.

Table 15-1. *Internet Wave Audio Files (Source: VocalTec)*

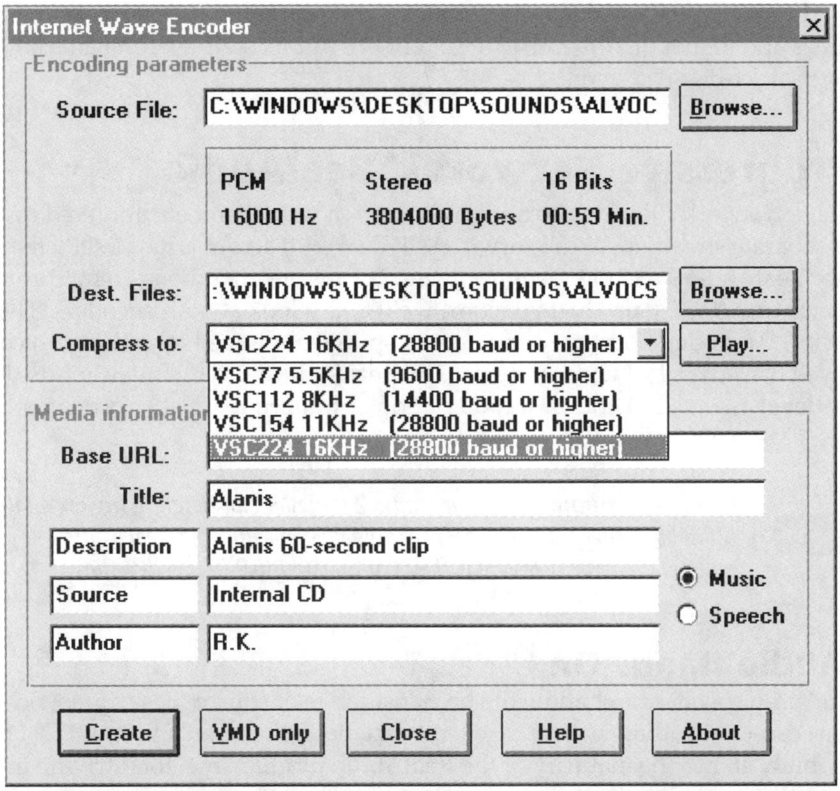

Figure 15-10. *The Internet Wave encoder*

There are two steps to setting up your Web server with Internet Wave. Step one, as with the other systems, is to configure your Web server to recognize the following MIME types:

- /application/vocaltec-media-desc vmd
- /application/vocaltec-media-file vmf

Step two regards the installation of a CGI script. Internet Wave offers a CGI script (iwpos) that will let Internet Wave players have rewind and fast-forward control of audio file downloads. Precise details of how to install the CGI script are provided in the Internet Wave documentation. In general, the script sets up a way for the client player to interact with the Web server and enables the end user to have control over how the audio file is delivered, including features such as rewind and fast forward.

In all, Internet Wave is a flexible technology with the ability to encode both basic speech files and higher quality music files. It offers Webmasters a strong alternative to expensive server-based systems.

Using Progressive Networks' RealAudio

Progressive Network's RealAudio adds a dimension we haven't encountered until now—a separate streaming audio server. We'll deal with server issues later. First, we'll introduce RealAudio's encoding environment. Because RealAudio is going through a transition from 1.0 to 2.0 product versions, we'll take a look at both encoders. The RealAudio 1.0 encoder offers only one output option, optimized for mainly voice-only files played back over 14.4 kb/s modems. The RealAudio 2.0 versions supports this 14.4 kb/s level as well, but adds a second option optimized for 28.8 kb/s delivery, including FM-quality music.

Note ▶ *Only users running the RealAudio 2.0 player can listen to higher quality (28.8 kb/s) files. Users with 14.4 kb/s modems and the RealAudio 1.0 player will get an error message if they try to listen to 2.0-encoded files.*

RealAudio Hands-On

The RealAudio encoder can handle the broadest range of source files of any encoder we've discussed, including .wav and several varieties of both .au and raw PCM files. This flexibility shows the maturity of the RealAudio product line. It is striving in its server, encoder, and player products to operate on all platforms.

The RealAudio 1.0 encoder presents a very simple interface. To open a source file in the encoder, click on the File Menu and then click Encode to choose your source file. A dialog box pops up letting you provide the name, author, and copyright information for the file. Click OK and the file is compressed into .ra format (see Figure 15-11).

We compressed the same (144 kb, 8 khz-16 bits, mono) speech file from the previous examples. The file compresses to 9.07 kb using RealAudio.

To demonstrate the features of the RealAudio 2.0 encoder, we'll encode the same music file (3.63 mb, 16 khz-16 bits, stereo) as earlier with Internet Wave. The RealAudio 2.0 encoder offers a little busier interface, with additional options including the choice between 14.4 kb/s and 28.8 kb/s compression and between an audio file and a live source. RealAudio 2.0 encoder also lets you hear the file played back as it is encoding (see Figure 15-12).

Despite these new twists, the encoding process itself is as simple as in 1.0. Hit the Browse button to call up the file we want to encode, then access Start Encoding under the Encode menu or click on the Encode icon. The compression begins and the new .ra file is automatically created. The 3.63 mb music file is compressed to just 112 kb using RealAudio 2.0 at 28.8 kb/s compression.

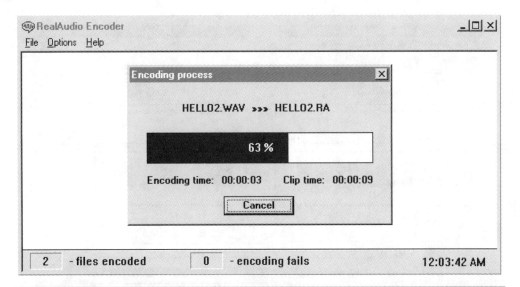

Figure 15-11.   *The RealAudio 1.0 encoder in action*

Finally, the RealAudio 2.0 encoder also has an option for live encoding. This option requires a RealAudio 2.0 server. As the encoder compresses the incoming live source feed, it sends the encoded signals directly to the RealAudio server for immediate delivery. As this book was written, Progressive Networks and its customers were beginning to experiment with Net-casting live audio events. For example, AudioNet **(http://www.audionet.com)** features live content from more than a dozen radio stations. AudioNet is discussed in more detail in Chapter 16. When it comes to RealAudio, "live" is a relative term. If you listen to a radio station and its RealAudio live Net-cast, there is typically a 10-15 second delay for encoding and delivery over the Internet.

RealAudio Server Issues

RealAudio is a client-server system. When a user clicks on a URL to download a Real Audio file, the client sets up a separate communications path between the RealAudio server and the player.

As we did with the other platforms, we need to create a separate file that spawns the RealAudio player. When a user clicks on the RealAudio link, they activate a metafile (with a .ram extension), which sends the location of the RealAudio file (with a .ra extension) to the player. The player then sends a signal to the RealAudio Server requesting that file. The file is sent to the player and played as it is received. The entire process is completed within a few seconds.

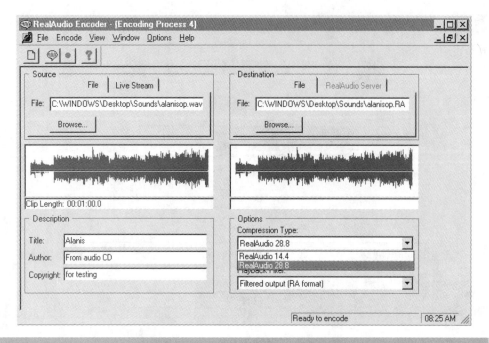

Figure 15-12. *The RealAudio 2.0 encoder*

To create a metafile for our hello.ra file, open a file in a text editor and save the following as hello.ram:

pnm://www.home.com/audio/hello.ra

Then, in your HTML document, reference the metafile in a hyperlink as follows (and as shown in Figure 15-13):

<A HREF="http://www.home.com/audio/hello.ram"> <IMG SRC=ra.gif.> Click here for a RealAudio Welcome</A> (14.4 kb/s)

Once you place a metafile on your Web server, you need to configure the server to recognize the .ra and .ram extensions as the MIME types audio/x-pn-realaudio ram and audio/x-pn-realaudio ra. The exact configuration depends on which Web server you use.

It is also possible to deliver RealAudio files from a Web server without a RealAudio server. All you do is configure the server to recognize the .ra MIME type. The files won't stream and must be completely downloaded and played back locally by the user.

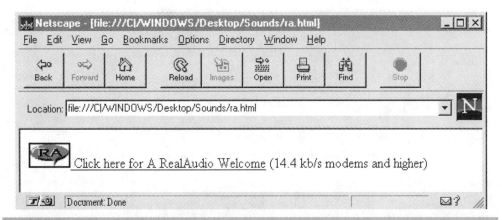

Figure 15-13. *A RealAudio file called from an HTML page*

RealAudio 2.0 adds a new twist. The RealAudio player and controls can be embedded directly in a Web page (but only for users with a RealAudio Netscape plug-in). The basic HTML tags to accomplish this are

```
<EMBED SRC="audio.rpm" WIDTH=220 HEIGHT=38
CONTROLS=ControlPanel>
```

RealAudio 2.0 has a new file extension, .rpm, designed to avoid confusion with RealAudio 1.0 files using the .ram extension. In this example, the parameter CONTROLS is set to ControlPanel, which will embed the Play/ Pause button, the Stop button, and the Position slider only (see Figure 15-14).

The CONTROLS parameter has several additional settings, including

- CONTROLS=*All* This embeds a full Player view including the ControlPanel, InfoVolumePanel, and StatusBar. This is the default view if no CONTROLS attribute is specified.

- CONTROLS=*InfoVolumePanel* This embeds the information area showing the title, author, and copyright with a Volume Slider on the right-hand side.

- CONTROLS=*StatusBar* Embeds the Status Bar showing informational messages, current time position, and clip length.

- CONTROLS=*PlayButton* Embeds the Play/Pause button only.

- CONTROLS=*StopButton* Embeds the Stop button only.

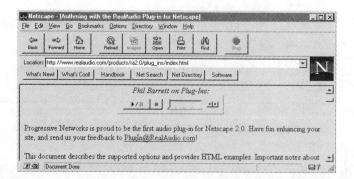

Figure 15-14. *An embedded RealAudio control panel*

One final attribute worth noting is AUTOSTART=TRUE. This tells the RealAudio plug-in to automatically begin playing when the page is visited. When using this tag, you'll probably also want to embed some control panel features—at minimum a StopButton—to give the user some control over playback.

TCP/IP vs. UDP

There are two major differences between the streaming audio systems we looked at earlier and RealAudio:

- RealAudio includes a separate server to handle audio streaming.
- RealAudio uses the Internet's UDP protocol rather than TCP/IP as its communications protocol.

According to Progressive Networks, these two factors result in quicker, more efficient file delivery. UDP is a better solution for streaming audio. Although it does not guarantee that every packet in a file is delivered, it does create an guaranteed line of communication to ensure most packets arrive without significant delay. The result is a small number of lost packets, which the RealAudio system makes up for through intelligent signal processing. However, UDP delivery ensures that RealAudio files will be delivered as quickly as possible in an uninterrupted stream.

UDP delivery and, more importantly, dedicated client-server communications are necessary to give the user complete random access to an audio file. For instance, if a user tries to access a 30-minute RealAudio file, the system will let the player communicate back to the server that you want to start with the twentieth minute. The server begins streaming the file from that point.

The key underlying technology supporting RealAudio is a new protocol for time-based media that supports bi-directional communication between clients and servers. Progressive Networks says it will openly publish this protocol in 1996 and work with Netscape to define open streaming audio protocols for the Internet, based on the RealAudio protocols and the emerging Internet standard Real Time Protocol. A discussion of RTP can be found on the Web at **http://www.fokus.gmd.de/step/rtp**.

The RealAudio 2.0 server brings new capabilities to the RealAudio line. These include: support for live events, FM-quality audio over 28.8 kb/s modems, delivery of Web pages synchronized to the RealAudio stream, multi-casting technology to deliver events to large audiences, and an open API to allow third parties to develop customized RealAudio applications.

TECH
RESOURCES

Where to Find More Information About Real-Time Audio and Video

VENDOR WEB PAGES
Progressive Networks' RealAudio: **http://www.realaudio.com**
Xing Technologies' StreamWorks: **http://www.xingtech.com**
DSP Group's TrueSpeech: **http://www.dspg.com**
Vocaltec Internet Wave: **http://www.vocaltec.com**
VoxWare's ToolVox: **http://www.voxware.com**
VDONet's VDOLive: **http://www.vdolive.com**

OTHER WEB SITES DEVOTED TO REAL-TIME MULTIMEDIA
NetWatch: **http://www.pulver.com/netwatch/**
Voice-on-the-Net Page: **http://www.von.com/**
Internet Engineering Task Force (IETF) Voice Standards:
http://www.fokus.gmd.de/step/rtp/

WEB SITES DEVOTED TO AUDIO TECHNOLOGY ON THE WEB
Center for Innovative Computer Applications Audio Tutorial:
http://www.cica.indiana.edu/cica/faq/audio/audio.html
Audio Formats FAQ: **http://www.cis.ohio-state.edu/hypertext/faq/usenet/audio-fmts/part1/faq.html**
World Wide Web Virtual Library's Audio Page:
http://www.comlab.ox.ac.uk/archive/audio.html

VON MAILING LIST
Send e-mail to **majordomo@pulver.com**, leave the subject blank and in the body write: **subscribe von-digest**

Summary

We took a hands-on look in this chapter at four of the leading streaming audio solutions on the market. These range from voice-only solutions to more powerful products that deliver high quality, live audio streams over the Internet. Delivering real-time audio from your home page can be as simple or as complex as you want it to be. On the low-end, you can get a streaming voice-only or music file up on your site in less than a day, and at almost no cost. If you set your sights higher and are willing to spend money on a dedicated server, you can deliver high quality music and live events using a system like RealAudio. The choice is up to you. Either way it is a very easy process to add this powerful new dimension to your Web site— today.

Chapter Sixteen

A Real-Time Tour of the Web

s we've seen in the last two chapters, getting real-time audio technologies up and running on your Web site is a relatively simple matter. The technology is easy to use and, in many cases, is free. As we'll see in this chapter, literally hundreds of Web sites—run by individual Web-heads to major media conglomerates—are already offering real-time audio (and in some cases video) content from their Web sites. If you'd like, you can join their ranks today with a little effort.

Before we take a tour of the real-time Web, let's address an intriguing question: can the Web replace radio? It sounds ridiculous at first. Radio is a simple, yet powerful technology. Turn it on and you can tune in any sort of music, commentary, news, or sports you want. There's a radio in your house, in your car, and on your hip (your Walkman). Why would you want the equivalent of radio on your PC?

The reason is that while your radio is tuned into local stations, the Web is tuned into the world. Moved to California but miss the University of Illinois football games? Live, real-time audio on the Web is your answer. Traveling overseas and want to keep up with the news back home? Turn to the Web. The possibilities are endless. The local becomes global and the global becomes local. Local news, local sports, and local personalities become accessible anywhere in the world. Programming no longer needs to be aimed at the masses. Niche interests can be served. Because it costs next to nothing to broadcast audio across the Internet, anyone can become the equivalent of a global radio station. There are no licenses to apply for, no radio towers to erect, no expensive equipment to buy.

This raises an important point. The Web both is and is not a mass medium. It's a mass medium because you can reach the masses of Internet users. It's not a mass medium because the masses must *choose* to tune in to you and your program, which is just one of thousands they can pick from.

The same thing can happen with video. One company, VDONet, is promoting the idea of desktop broadcasting so that everyone who owns a camcorder and a PC can broadcast their visions—or more likely their grandchildren—over the Internet. VDONet's VDOLive technology is a major breakthrough, offering 5 to 10 frames per second of real-time video over 28.8 kb/s. All that's needed to make this vision a reality is more bandwidth. ISDN speeds (128 kb/s) will do, but cable modem speeds (10 mb/s and up) would change the game completely. With the availability of those access speeds, live, full-screen, full-motion video over the Internet becomes a reality. Suddenly the same dynamics that we have already seen with audio come into play. Anyone can post a video file and anyone, anywhere in the world, can access it. Unlimited choice, limitless variety.

This may all sound like a pipe dream, similar to the never-fulfilled promises of interactive TV. But these promises are already becoming a reality. Real-time audio is here today. Real-time video is here in rudimentary form, awaiting the bandwidth explosion. Telecom deregulation could fuel the boom. Netscape, the Web leader, feels the wave coming and has committed itself to adding the LiveMedia architecture to Netscape Navigator by the end of 1996. In this chapter, we get the "inside spin" from Netscape co-founder and Mosaic creator Marc Andreessen about Netscape's real-time vision.

INSIDE Spin

Marc Andreessen: Netscape Co-founder and Mosaic Creator

Netscape has taken to real-time audio and video in a big way—a situation that promises to catapult the market to even greater heights.

To fuel its efforts, Netscape acquired InSoft Inc., a maker of TCP/IP-based audio and video conferencing technology, and cut a licensing deal with VoxWare Inc., which has unveiled speech-compression technology for the Internet.

Netscape uses these technologies to create the Netscape LiveMedia architecture, expected to be deployed by the end of 1996. LiveMedia will add the ability to deliver real-time, streaming audio and video files to Netscape's client and server product line. It also will eventually make it possible to have audio and video two-way communications from within the browser.

Never shy with its ambitions, Netscape sees LiveMedia and the Web competing with radio and TV stations and local and long-distance telephone companies, according to Netscape co-founder Marc Andreessen.

Indeed, Andreessen sees the day when Navigator will have a button with a telephone icon on it that will let users instantly place calls not only to other Internet users, but to users of the public telephone network as well.

"How to bridge into the plain old telephone system is interesting. It should be possible to bridge the Internet to the POPs (points of presence) of interexchange carriers and offer free long-distance telephony," notes Andreessen, pointing to an ongoing Net project called FreeWorld Dial-Up (**http://www.pulver.com/fwd/**) that is trying to do just that.

According to Andreessen, "The issues that need to be solved to make this vision a reality include the creation of directory services, better user interfaces, and new, compelling multiperson environments."

Andreessen admits that he has "been a skeptic for quite awhile" about the Net's ability to deliver real-time media, but says "I think its on its way now." He says the new telecom deregulation bill, passed the same day Netscape unveiled its new strategy, could put Internet service providers into the telephony business. "All it takes is some more modems," says Andreessen, "to make the ISP networks two-way."

Andreessen is also closely tracking the progress of @Home, which is promising to deliver high-speed cable modem-based services beginning spring 1996 in Sunnyvale, California. "Cable modems could make streaming video over the Net a much better experience," according to Andreessen.

"With audio and video contending for precious Internet bandwidth, a new model of usage-based Net pricing will have to emerge, with bandwidth hogs paying a premium. At the end of the day, it is an economic question. Either it will be worth the additional money (for end users) or it won't. Prices will be adjusted to reflect that reality."

Open technology has become Netscape's calling card, and Andreessen indicates that his company's approach to real-time media is "standards, standards, standards." The company will support the emerging Internet standard Real Time Protocol (RTP), for delivering real-time streams over the Internet, and existing audio and video standards such as MPEG (video), GSM (voice telephony), and H.261 (video conferencing).

With real-time audio and video capabilities built in to the Netscape browser, content providers will have a huge new base of users to target with the next generation of Web-based streaming multimedia content.

Later in this chapter, we'll talk with Jeff Pulver, one of the Web's true pioneers in real-time media, to solicit his opinions on the future of this medium. We'll also have an in-depth discussion with two Web businesses taking advantage of these new streaming technologies: AudioNet, which is positioning itself as a global radio station, and CBS Up to the Minute, a traditional TV news show experimenting with untraditional ways of reaching its audience.

But for starters, whet your appetite with a tour of the real-time Web, circa 1996.

Where to Find the Real-Time Pioneers

If you want to find real-time audio and video on the Internet, the best places to turn are the home pages of the vendors producing real-time platforms. (We'll leave out VDONet and VoxWare, which are newer platforms that don't yet have many listings up.) Each vendor provides up-to-date listings of sites using their technology, usually broken down into categories such as music, sports, business, and so on.

RealAudio

The RealAudio home page can be found at **http://www.realaudio.com**. Its listings site can be accessed at **http://www.realaudio.com/raguide.cgi** (see Figure 16-1). The site includes a directory of the growing ranks of RealAudio sites, as well as a search engine to pick a needle out of the audio haystack. There are literally hundreds of RealAudio sites out on the Web today, with some of the best, most polished real-time content available, including

- 1-800-Music-Now, MCI's new site selling CDs over the Internet, at **http://www.1800musicnow.mci.com**.

- ABC RadioNet, featuring news and features from ABC Radio, at **http://www.abcradionet.com**.

- C/Net Radio, audio news from the computer-oriented Web site, at **http://www.cnet.com/Content/Radio/index.html**.

- ESPN SportsZone, featuring daily Net-casts of news and sporting events, at **http://espnet.sportszone.com**.

- National Public Radio (NPR), with daily news features including All Things Considered, Morning Edition, and Talk of the Nation, at **http://www.realaudio.com/contentp/npr**.

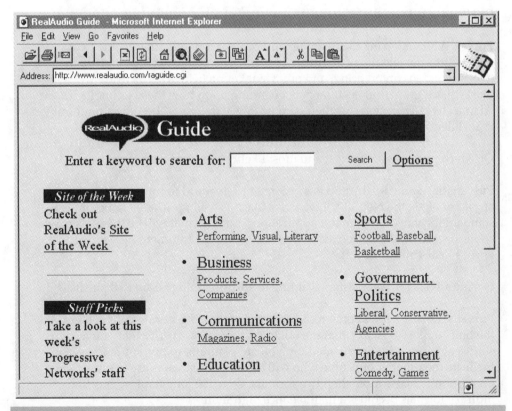

Figure 16-1.   *MCI's 1-800-Music-Now site features RealAudio*

INSIDE Spin

Jeff Pulver: Real-Time Media Pioneer

Jeff Pulver has become synonymous with voice-on-the-Net technologies. He runs NetWatch, a Web site devoted to real-time Web technologies (see Figure 16-2), moderates the Voice on the Internet and Internet Phone mailing lists, and has sponsored FreeWorld Dialup, a volunteer project that links Net phone products to the public telephone network. We asked Jeff for his thoughts on the emerging real-time Web marketplace.

Q: How would you describe the current state of the streaming audio market?

Pulver: When referring to streaming audio, at least two markets come to mind—Internet telephony audio on demand. Then there is video on demand, two-way video conferencing, and other smaller niche markets. We are watching a marketplace grow from its infancy. Depending upon how these technologies are adapted by corporations for their own IntraNet, this could become a multimillion, if not billion dollar industry within the next five to ten years.

Q: Which products are hottest and most likely to succeed long term?

Pulver: Right now RealAudio has become the standard for audio-on-demand applications on the Net. VDOLive looks like it is well positioned to become the standard for video-on-demand applications. Long term it will be the players who come together and agree on standards (including the Internet Engineering Task Force's Real Time Protocol).

Q: Any advice for Webmasters wanting to add streaming audio to their sites?

Pulver: One: use professional recording equipment to generate your content. Take the time to filter to ensure that the quality is there. Two: verify that you have sufficient bandwidth for the medium you are planning to put your message in. Estimate the number of people who will access your streams at the same time. Three: don't choose more than two formats. Over the long haul, supporting multiple formats becomes a maintenance nightmare.

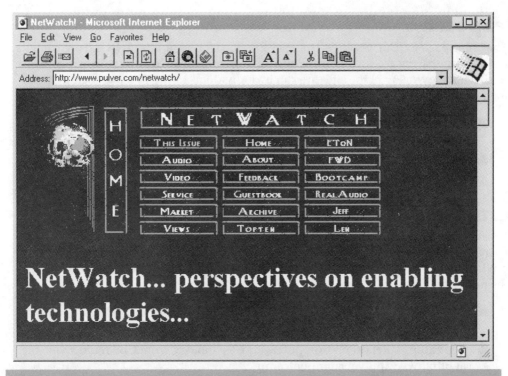

Figure 16-2. *Jeff Pulver's NetWatch site*

Xing StreamWorks

The Xing home page can be found at **http://www.xingtech.com**. Its listings page is at **http://www.xingtech.com/streams/testdrv/testdrv.html**. The site includes links—though not as many as the RealAudio site—to audio and video content, including

- Live video feeds from NBC Pro Financial Network, at **http:// www.xingtech.com/nbc.html**.

- Bloomberg Information News Radio, live from WBBR in New York City, at **http://www.bloomberg.com/cgi-bin/tdisp.sh?wbbr/index.html**.

TrueSpeech

The home page for DSP Group's TrueSpeech can be found at **http://www.dspg.com.** Its listings page can be accessed at **http://www.dspg.com/cool**. Given that TrueSpeech is a free technology, many of the sites are run by individuals trying to make their mark on the Net. A few sites that might be more interesting include

- O.J. speaks, a comprehensive site of O.J Simpson audio clips, at **http://www.socool.com/socool/oj.html**.

- TechBabble, a site featuring the latest Web technology news, at **http://www.techbabble.com**.

Internet Wave

VocalTec's Internet Wave's home page is at **http://www.vocaltec.com/iwave.htm**; a fairly extensive listings page, including a good collection of 28.8 kb/s audio clips, can be found at **http://www.vocaltec.com/sites** (see Figure 16-3), and includes the following:

- San Francisco Bay Area Underground Music, featuring audio clips from the local Bay area music scene, at **http://server.berkeley.edu/SFMusic**.

- Bootcamp...a Report on Computers and Technology, from CBS radio, available at **http://www.pulver.com/bootcamp**.

Real-Time Closeup

Running a business based on real-time Internet technologies is proving a challenge for Webmasters. The technology is new and needs to be mastered. Even more difficult is establishing a business plan for making money delivering real-time audio and video. Web users have grown used to getting their software and content for free, so charging for real-time content can be difficult. In addition, users get TV and radio programming for free today, so why should they pay on the Web?

Webmasters are tackling these technology and business challenges in some interesting ways. We'll take a look at two leading-edge users of real-time technology on the Web: AudioNet, which is building a Net-based audio and video network delivering sports, music and more; and CBS Up to the Minute, a network TV news show that is using the Web to augment its traditional coverage.

AudioNet

We talked earlier in this chapter about the Web replacing—or more realistically, augmenting—traditional radio stations. You need look no further than AudioNet (**http://www.audionet.com**) to see this vision becoming a reality. AudioNet,

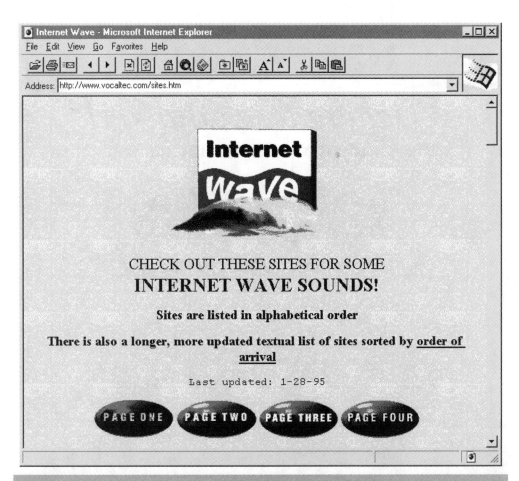

Figure 16-3. *The Internet Wave listings page*

headquartered in Dallas but with T3 (45 mb/s) connections and RealAudio servers networked across the country, it is perhaps the Net's most comprehensive real-time audio site (see Figure 16-4). You want it, they've got it including

- Live Net-casts of radio stations, including major stations in Dallas, Chicago, Washington D.C., Miami, New York, and more.
- CD Jukebox—entire CDs for the sampling.
- Live sporting events, including pre-Super Bowl coverage, college basketball, football games, and more.
- Live coverage of the 1996 presidential race.

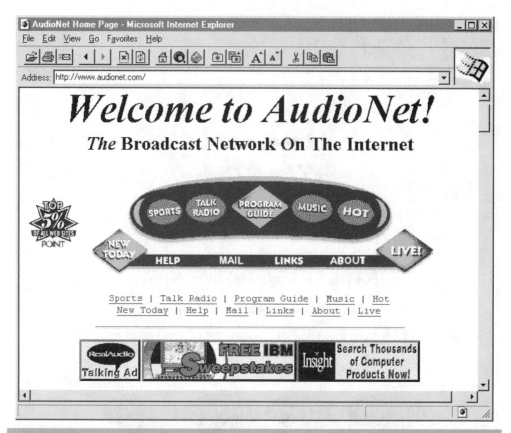

Figure 16-4. *The AudioNet home page*

AudioNet president Mark Cuban founded the company with a background in computer systems integration and a love of college sports. "The early goals we had for the company was to bring up maybe 12 colleges within six months," says Cuban's marketing director, Susan Plonka. "We've surpassed that and we keep on growing. We want to be recognized as the broadcast network for the Internet. As technology changes and throughput improves, we'll move to multimedia content. In the future, we'll more likely be competing with the Turner Network (cable TV) than with radio stations."

Cuban himself says AudioNet took an exhaustive look at audio-on-the-Net technologies—including Xing StreamWorks, VocalTec Internet Wave and DSP Group's TrueSpeech—before choosing Progressive Networks' RealAudio as its technology. For Cuban, the issue wasn't so much file compression and encoding quality as it was the ability of the technology to be networked and scaled across large-scale networks. Even from the start, Cuban had major ambitions. "We knew we were going to build

AudioNet out on a scale to handle hundreds of servers," Cuban says. "RealAudio can handle that. We felt comfortable with the company, the finances behind, and most importantly, we liked their marketing," Cuban says, referring to RealAudio's now well-recognized Web brand name. "We knew we had to get players into people's hands, people who were using 14.4 kb/s and 28.8 kb/s modems. Progressive Networks has done a good job in doing that."

The AudioNet network is set up with a data center in Dallas that is part recording studio, part computer network. Audio is distributed from this central point to regional hubs where it is delivered via RealAudio servers. The distribution of bandwidth lets AudioNet serve large numbers of users. Cuban says AudioNet runs 60 RealAudio servers (as of early 1996) capable of delivering 10,000 simultaneous audio streams.

AudioNet makes some money from bringing radio stations up onto the Internet, and some additional revenues from advertising. Live event broadcasting offers another source of potential revenues. Even more interesting is Cuban's vision to link the delivery of free audio with selling products over the Internet. For instance, if you are listening to an Indiana University football game, says Cuban, AudioNet will eventually ask you if you'd like to buy an IU sweatshirt or cap as well. An even bigger potential revenue source for AudioNet is in selling its audio-on-the-Net expertise to other companies, said Cuban. "This has been a home run for us so far," he says. "We hope it will eventually be a grand slam."

It's no surprise that Cuban resorts to sports metaphors when describing his business. After all, AudioNet began as a cure for college sports fans trying to keep up with their old alma maters. As Cuban puts it, "We're kind of a cure for homesickness."

AudioNet
Make sure you know the legal aspects of audio on the Web. Licensing rights are very important to understand.

If a company has aspirations of expanding its real-time audio offerings, the job becomes a systems integration challenge (networking computers together) rather than an audio quality or encoding challenge.

If you are going to do live events, you need to constantly monitor performance. There are many spots where a live Net-cast can break down.

CBS Up to the Minute

One of the most aggressive news organizations on the Web is CBS Up to the Minute, the overnight news show. For a while, the company had three different audio formats up on the Web before eventually signing a contract with RealAudio. But even more interesting, the site **http://uttm.com** has begun broadcasting video reports on the

Internet using VDONet's VDOLive technology (see Figure 16-5). "We are an aggressive news organization, so we feel like we also need to run an aggressive Web site," says Tom Bradford, executive producer of CBS Up to the Minute.

"We are delighted by the prospect of video on the Internet," Bradford says. "But it's very much the wild west out there. I can remember as a child in the late 1940s sitting on my grandfather's knee watching a television screen not much bigger than your fist. That was perfectly acceptable at the time. We're in the same place now with video on the Internet."

Bradford has found VDOLive's compression to be amazing. "We captured a [video file] of about eight or nine minutes in length. The original file was 450MB. VDOLive compressed it down to 1.5MB. It played just fine over the Internet [in streaming fashion]."

The CBS Up to the Minute crew tries to put one video file up on the Internet on a daily basis. The footage is the same that goes on the TV broadcast. An engineer

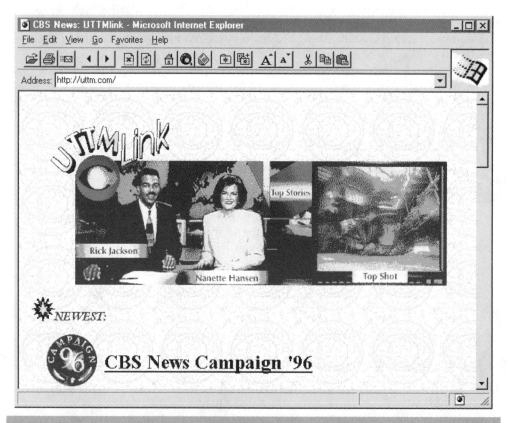

Figure 16-5. *The CBS Up to the Minute site*

schooled in VDOLive does the compression, Bradford says. But overall, the Web obligations are spread around the fairly small Up to the Minute staff.

Summary

In this chapter, we saw that real-time audio via the Internet is here today. Literally hundreds of sites have sprung up offering everything from the latest singles of independent bands to live broadcasts of major sporting events. Sites like AudioNet are already positioning themselves as the radio stations—and ultimately the multimedia stations—of the future. And just around the corner is real-time video and video conferencing. In short, the real-time Web is here today, and it will only get better and more entertaining as bandwidth increases.

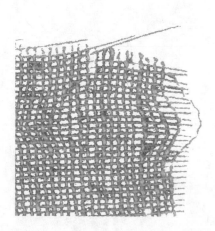

Appendix A

Web Resource Guide

One of the best places to learn about the Web is on the Web itself. This comprehensive guide to Web resources and downloadable software provides you with the ultimate bookmark list for finding the technologies that will take the Web beyond HTML. In addition to including resources for all of the major technologies in the book, it provides pointers to the latest developments that were just appearing as this book headed out the door.

With each listing, we'll provide a detailed description of what you can expect to find on the site, as well as a rating of the site's usefulness. Any rating of Web content is of course arbitrary, but here are our general guidelines:

- *Four stars*   Indispensable. Go to this page now. Learn it, live it.

- *Three stars*   A quality source of information. If you are interested in the topic the site covers, this is worth your time.

- *Two stars*   Not bad, but can find it done better elsewhere. If you must see *everything* on the Web about a particular topic, check it out.

- *One star*   Most likely a time-waster. We won't bother to even rank many one-star sites here. If we do, its because the site falls well short of expectations.

 *This appendix is organized in roughly the same way the book is organized, but some deviations and additions have been made to make this downloader's guide to the Web as comprehensive as possible.*

Enjoy, and happy Web surfing.

HTML Alternatives: Adobe and More

Adobe (***)

http://www.adobe.com

Home of Adobe Systems Inc. Here you'll find the information you need to get started with Adobe Acrobat. The site has recently undergone a face-lift, and looks much sharper for it. In particular, Acrobat users should check out the Acrobat page, **http://w1000.mv.us.adobe.com/Acrobat/Acrobat0.html**, which provides extensive resources for Acrobat users. Two new sections of interest here include Acrobat publishing on the Web, at **http://w1000.mv.us.adobe.com/Acrobat/acroweb.html**, and a comprehensive introduction to Acrobat Amber, **http://w1000.mv.us.adobe.com/Amber/**, a new version of the Acrobat Reader optimized for the Web. Before leaving the site, Webmasters should also check out Adobe's PageMill and SiteMill, at **http://w1000.mv.us.adobe.com/Apps/SiteMill**, easy-to-use Web site publishing and management tools. See the Adobe Acrobat Web site in Figure A-1.

Envoy (*)

http://corp.novell.com/market/english/mm000086.htm

Envoy technology is in a state of flux. Novell, which has been the main force behind Envoy, sold its application software business in early 1996, greatly reducing its interest

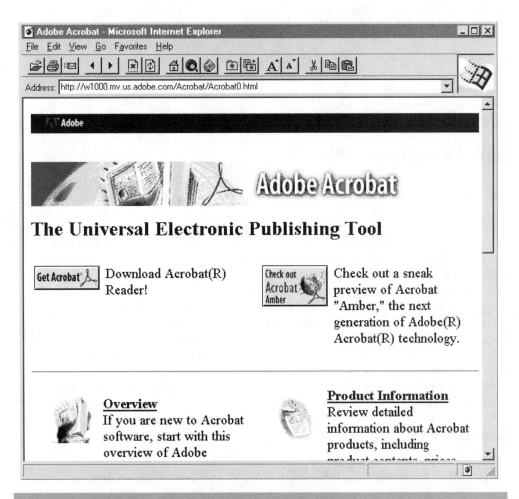

Figure A-1. *The Adobe Acrobat Web site*

in forwarding Envoy. TumbleWeed Software, at **http://www.tumbleweed.com**, which invented Envoy, is attempting to carry on the Envoy mantle, including releasing an Envoy plug-in for Netscape Navigator. But TumbleWeed is a far cry from Novell, and Envoy is more likely to fade into the woodwork than stake a major position on the Web, despite the fact that it is in many ways on a par with Acrobat.

Common Ground Software (**)

http://www.commonground.com

Another Acrobat competitor, CommonGround Software lacks the firepower to take on Adobe Acrobat. This site includes free downloads of the CommonGround mini-viewer, but is woefully lacking in examples or pointers to Web sites using CommonGround software.

Java Resources

Sun's Java Page (****)

http://java.sun.com

For Web developers, this is without a doubt one of the most oft-visited sites on the Web. As Java went from alpha to beta to 1.0 release, this was the place to find the latest, most authoritative information. A visit to the site should start at the Java overview page, **http://java.sun.com/about.html**. If you want to develop using Java, start with the Java Developers kit at **http://java.sun.com/JDK-1.0/index.html**, and then move on to the online Java developers tutorial, at **http://java.sun.com/tutorial/index.html**. If you are more interested in viewing Java applets than running them, Sun keeps a list of applets it has written at **http://java.sun.com/applets/index.html**. If you are tracking Java closely, it would be a good idea to keep tabs on Sun's main home page, at **http://www.sun.com**, as well as the SunWorld online magazine, at **http://www.sun.com/sunworldonline/index.html**, which among other features includes a column on Java development.

SunSoft (**)

http://www.sun.com/sunsoft/index.html

SunSoft is Sun's software arm, and it is delivering a suite of Java development tools. The tools were still under wraps as this book was being written, but a sneak preview is available at **http://www.sun.com/951201/feature3/feature3.html**.

Symantec (**)

http://www.symantec.com

Development tools and utilities vendor Symantec released one of the first Java development kits for Windows 95/NT, called Café, and a separate environment for Macintosh, called Caffeine. The Java Central area, at **http://www.symantec.com/lit/ dev/javaindex.html**, includes information about the two visual development environments as well as links to other Java resources. Beware, the site tends to be very slow.

Borland (**)

http://www.borland.com

Creators of the popular Delphi visual development environment and other programming tools, Borland has turned its attention to Java as well. Borland is serving the Java community with a site called JavaWorld, at **http://www.borland.com/ Product/java/java.html**, a somewhat sparse listing of Java resources and pointers. Borland has, however, released a graphical debugger for Java, available for download at **http://www.borland.com/Product/java/debugger/ bugform.html**. Borland plans to offer a complete suite of visual development tools for Java.

Metrowerks (**)

http://www.metrowerks.com

Metrowerks delivers Java development tools for the Mac as part of its Code Warrior development environment. Metrowerks Java tools and news can be found at **http://www.metrowerks.com/products/announce/java.html**. This site also includes the requisite pointers to other Java resources.

Silicon Graphics (***)

http://www.sgi.com

SGI, which is heavily involved in 3-D computing and VRML, has also released a visually-oriented development environment for Java called Cosmo. Cosmo brings together HTML, VRML and Java to let Web developers create interactive, multimedia Web applications. Learn about Cosmo, which was still under development as this

book was written, at **http://www.sgi.com/Products/cosmo/index.html**. The Cosmo
system includes Cosmo Create, Cosmo Code, Cosmo Player and Cosmo MediaBase.
See the Cosmo site in Figure A-2. The SGI site also includes a fairly extensive listing of
free tools available on the Web, at **http://www.sgi.com/Fun/free**.

Figure A-2. *SGI's Cosmo home page*

Oracle (***)

http://www.oracle.com

Database vendor Oracle is one of the industry's most aggressive backers of Web technology, including Java. Oracle's WebSystem—which includes Java-capable Web servers and browsers—have led the market in Java support. Of particular interest is the OraclePowerBrowser, which in addition to support for Java also has a Basic interpreter enabling simple client-side processing. The PowerBrowser also comes with a personal Web server and HTML editor. Check out the PowerBrowser at **http://www.oracle.com/products/websystem/powerbrowser/html/index.html**.

Natural Intelligence (**)

http://www.natural.com

Natural Intelligence has created a Mac-based Java development environment called Roaster. Available at **http://www.natural.com/pages/products/roaster/index.html**, the Roaster is a well-designed site with plenty of Roaster information and pointers to Java resources on the Web. If you are developing on a Mac, you need to check out Roaster.

IBM (**)

http://www.ibm.com

The main home for Java developments at IBM is at **http://ncc.hursley.ibm.com/ javainfo**. IBM has ported Java to OS/2 and AIX, but, more interestingly, has also said it will port Java to Windows 3.1. If they can accomplish this, IBM's Java page will become a much more important stop on our Web tour. But Win 3.1 Java is a significant technical challenge, so we'll withhold our praise until we see it.

FutureTense (***)

http://www.futuretense.com

FutureTense is an intriguing Java tool vendor that is building a product called Texture. FutureTense claims that Texture will let Webmasters build Java applets and sites without any programming. Texture promises to offer a WYSIWYG authoring environment that will let Web authors create compelling Web pages very easily and then output the results to Java code which will run in Java-enabled browsers. This could be a breakthrough product, and if history abides, FutureTense—like Vermeer Technologies and Ceneca Communications—could be acquired by a larger player.

Roguewave (**)

http://www.roguewave.com

Roguewave's JFactory is a visual interface builder for Java that automatically generates Java code. JFactory enables developers to quickly create applications by dragging-and-dropping typical controls such as buttons, list boxes, and menus. This looks like a promising tool. (It appeared just as this book was going to print.)

Sausage Software (**)

http://www.sausage.com

Creators of the popular Hot Dog HTML editor, Sausage Software also has unveiled Java animation software aimed at nonprogrammers. Named Egor, the program comes with built-in animations that you can customize, and lets you build your own animations as well. This is a good example of where Java tools are headed—development tools are vital, but Java design tools for the masses will propel Java, just as easy-to-use HTML editors have propelled HTML. See the Egor site in Figure A-3.

Dimension X (***)

http://www.dimensionx.com

Mentioned several times in the text of this book for its Java expertise, Dimension X is a company to watch. They are now building Java tools, including Liquid Reality, a Java/VRML browser; and TEA, The Easy Animator, a simple Java animation tool. Check out these tools and others at **http://www.dimensionx.com/dnx/java.html**.

Gamelan (****)

http://www.gamelan.com

This site is essential. Gamelan is the most authoritative and comprehensive source of Java applets on the Web. After developers submit their applets, Gamelan categorizes them and highlights the best ones. Categories include Arts and Entertainment,

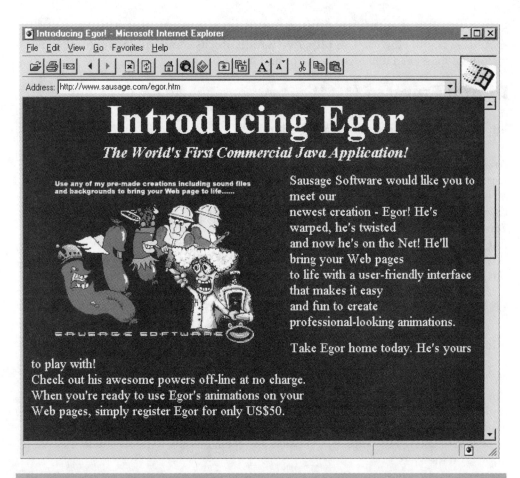

Figure A-3. *Sausage Software's Egor site*

Business and Finance, Educational, JavaScript, Miscellaneous, Multimedia, Network and Communications, News Programming in Java, Special Effects, Utilities, and Web Sites.

The Java Developer (****)

http://www.digitalfocus.com/faq

Run by Web design firm Digital Focus, The Java Developer may have the Web's most extensive listing of Java resources and pointers. Sections include Java Resources, Java

Store, Job Forum, and How Do I. This is a first-rate site. Heavy-duty developers should check-out How Do I, at **http://www.digitalfocus.com/faq/howdoi.html**, which includes a massive database of Java tips and tricks.

Digital Espresso (****)

http://www.io.org/~mentor/JavaNotes.html

Another essential site. Don't have time to keep up with the Java newsgroups? Digital Espresso summarizes (with an attitude) the main Java newsgroups and mailing lists on a weekly basis, letting you cut through the chaff and get to the good stuff. Digital Espresso's sections include Announcements, Features, Discussions, Bugs and Warnings, Comments, Queries, Class Exchange, New Applets, Services and Products, FAQ Candidates, Help Wanted, and Contract Requests. Credit goes to David Forster, Wm D. Clendening, Mike Shaver, Rehan Zaidi, R. E. Fikki, and David Robinson, who put together Digital Espresso as a labor of love and service to the Java community.

JARS (***)

http://www.surinam.net/java/jars/jars.html

JARS is the work of a group of Java developers who got together to rate Java applets. The results are uneven, but getting better as the site evolves. It includes rankings and reviews of Java applets, and tries to organize the rankings into categories such as Top Ten, Top Ten Percent, and more. Unlike Gamelan, which takes a fairly neutral approach to listing Java applets, JARS acts as a filter, helping to point you to the best applets on the Web.

JavaWorld (****)

http://www.javaworld.com

We reviewed the first issue of this Java Web-zine, which reportedly was cobbled together in less than a month, and were extremely impressed. Articles from Hot Java creator Arthur Van Hoff, news group summaries, applet reviews, and plenty of feature and news articles make JavaWorld a force to be reckoned with in the online world. See the first issue in Figure A-4.

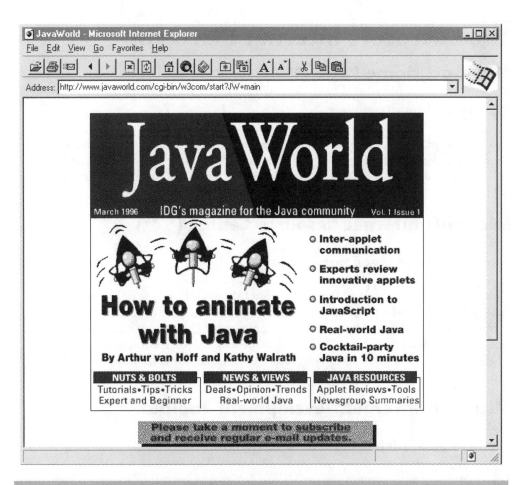

Figure A-4.   *JavaWorld online magazine*

The Microsoft Internet Platform

Microsoft Home Page (****)

http://www.microsoft.com

This is the starting point for your investigations into Microsoft's Internet plans. Microsoft is relatively new to using the Web as a major outlet for software and information, but they've taken to it in a major way. Other Microsoft pages to check out follow.

Microsoft Internet Resource Center (****)

http://www.microsoft.com/internet/irc.htm

This site includes pointers to Microsoft's main Internet efforts. Major categories include Internet Products, Development, and Authoring. The site also includes a pointer to resources from Microsoft's Internet Strategy Day, where it first laid out its ambitious Internet plans. Check back to this site to see if Microsoft can meet its goals. Also on this page are pointers to Web Tutorials, Internet Searches, Internet Central, and the Internet Services Directory.

Microsoft Internet Development Toolbox (****)

http://www.microsoft.com/IntDev/DEFAULT.HTM

This is an absolutely essential site for Microsoft Net-watchers. It includes all of the specifications and development details for its major Net technologies, including Internet Explorer browser, Internet Information Server, Internet Studio, Internet Sweeper SDK, VB Script, ActiveVRML, and more.

The Microsoft Network (***)

http://www.msn.com

MSN is evolving from a dial-up proprietary service to a fully Web-based offering. This site will be its eventual destination. The site already includes some basic content, but it has a long way to go before the evolution is complete. One interesting element is the ability to create—using a CGI script—a personalized start-up page that includes your favorite links, news feeds and more.

Netscape Internet OS

Netscape Home Page (****)

http://www.netscape.com

The home for the Web's leading software company. Millions of users dump out onto this page every day because it is the default home page for the Netscape Navigator browser. But there are many other reasons to come back as well. From the latest HTML 3.0 specifications to the JavaScript tutorial, this site has many essential resources for Web authors.

Netscape Navigator 2.0 Page (****)

http://home.netscape.com/comprod/products/navigator/version_2.0/

This page provides all the pointers and information you'll need about Netscape Navigator 2.0. It details all of the browser's major features, including support for e-mail, newsgroups, chat, FTP, Java, JavaScript, frames, plug-ins, and more.

Frames Authoring Guide (***)

http://home.netscape.com/assist/net_sites/frames.html

Everything you need to know to use frames on your site. This site takes you through a step-by-step process of creating and using frames.

Navigator Gold Page (***)

http://home.netscape.com/comprod/products/navigator/gold/index.html

Information, authoring tips, and more—everything you need to know to run Navigator Gold, Netscape's new HTML editor. Navigator Gold builds on the features of Netscape Navigator 2.0, adding an easy-to-use editor that lets you publish live, online Web pages in one integrated program.

JavaScript Resources Page (***)

http://home.netscape.com/comprod/products/navigator/version_2.0/script/script_info/index.html

Includes links to Netscape's essential JavaScript authoring guide, at **http://home.netscape.com/eng/mozilla/Gold/handbook/javascript/index.html**, plus pointers to other Web JavaScript resources and examples.

JavaScript Index (****)

http://www.c2.org/~andreww/javascript/

A very strong site that has the most up-to-date information and hotlinks for JavaScript on the Web. Set up almost like a miniversion of Gamelan, sections include JavaScript in Action, Learn About JavaScript, and Talk About JavaScript. The site itself is also JavaScript-enabled, so view the HTML source code for this page to see some good JavaScript hacks. See the site in Figure A-5.

Netscape Plug-Ins

In early 1996, Netscape claimed that more than 75 plug-ins were in development. Here are the plug-ins that were shipping at that time. For a complete list, see **http://home.netscape.com/comprod/products/navigator/version_2.0/plugins/index.html**. It's tough to rate these plug-ins because they are so new, and one measure of their success will be how widely they are adopted. We'll give four stars to essential plug-ins and three stars to plug-ins that are going to need to prove themselves before they become widely used.

Adobe's Acrobat Amber (****)

http://www.adobe.com/Amber/Index.html

The "Amber" version of the Acrobat Reader lets you view, navigate, and print Portable Document Format (PDF) files right in your Navigator window. PDF files are extremely compact, platform-independent, and easy to create. Available in pre-release form.

Figure A-5. *JavaScript Index home page*

Software Publishing's ASAP WebShow (***)

http://www.spco.com

ASAP WebShow is a Netscape Navigator 2.0 plug-in presentation viewer for viewing, downloading, and printing graphically rich reports and presentations from the Web.

The plug-in can download presentation files over the Net at a rate of three pages per second.

ASAP WebShow lets anyone view any document created by SPC's award-winning ASAP WordPower report and presentation software package.

Gold Disk's Astound Web Player (***)

http://www.golddisk.com

The Astound Web Player is a Netscape plug-in that plays dynamic multimedia documents created with Gold Disk's Astound or Studio M software. These documents can include sound, animation, graphics, video, and interactivity. The Astound Web Player features dynamic streaming; each slide is downloaded in the background while you view the current slide. See the Gold Disk home page in Figure A-6.

Corel Vector Graphics (***)

http://www.corel.com/corelcmx/

This plug-in allows smooth vector graphics to be viewed online on the Net. Download the beta of Corel's CMX Viewer along with free samples and explore the world of CMX.

LiveUpdate's Crescendo (***)

http://www.liveupdate.com/

LiveUpdate's Crescendo plug-in for Netscape Navigator enhances Web pages with MIDI-quality music. With Crescendo and Navigator running on your MPC sound card-equipped PC, you can enjoy background music as you surf the Web.

Starfish Software's EarthTime (***)

http://www.starfishsoftware.com

The EarthTime plug-in lets you tell time around the world at a glance—without leaving your browser. EarthTime displays the local time and date for eight geographic locations in your choice of more than 350 world capitals and commercial centers. Its animated worldwide map also indicates daylight and darkness.

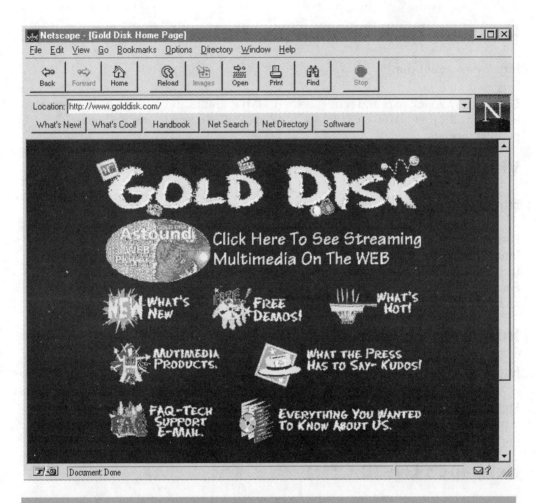

Figure A-6. *The Gold Disk home page*

Tumbleweed Software Envoy Plug-In (***)

http://www.twcorp.com

The Envoy plug-in lets users view documents on the Internet exactly as they were designed: rich with different fonts, graphics, and layouts. Download the Envoy plug-in to view embedded or entire Envoy documents from within Netscape Navigator. Tumbleweed Software offers Tumbleweed Publishing Essentials for publishing Envoy documents, and the Envoy Software Developer's Kit for creating a customized Envoy document viewer.

Electronic Book Technologies FigLeaf Inline (***)

http://www.ct.ebt.com

Dynamically zoom, pan, and scroll vector (CGM) graphics and multiple raster formats including GIF, JPEG, TIFF, CCITT GP4, BMP, WMF, EPSF, Sun Raster, and other popular formats.

Visual Components Formula One/Net (***)

http://www.visualcomp.com

Formula One/NET is the first Excel-compatible spreadsheet with built-in Internet functionality. Worksheets can include live charts, links to URLs, formatted text, and numbers, calculations, and clickable buttons and controls. Download Formula One/NET and bring the power of spreadsheets to Netscape Navigator 2.0 and the Web.

Infinit Op's Lightning Strike (***)

http://www.infinop.com

Lightning Strike is an optimized wavelet image codec ready to plug in to Netscape 2.0. It provides higher compression ratios, smaller image files, faster transmissions, and improved image quality.

Netscape's Live3D (****)

http://home.netscape.com/comprod/products/navigator/live3d/index.html

A high-performance 3-D VRML platform that lets you fly through VRML worlds on the Web and run interactive, multiuser VRML applications written in Java. Netscape Live3D features 3-D text, background images, texture animation, morphing, viewpoints, collision detection, gravity, and RealAudio streaming sound. Download Live3D and view VRML worlds available at many Web sites.

NCompass' OLE Control Plug-In (****)

http://www.excite.sfu.ca/NCompass/

This plug-in, running only under Windows 95, lets you embed OLE controls in Web pages created with standard programming languages and development tools such as Visual C++, Visual Basic, and the MS Windows Game SDK.

InterVU's PreVU (***)

www.intervu.com

PreVU provides streaming MPEG video for Netscape Navigator 2.0. It allows any MPEG video to be played on a Web page without specialized MPEG hardware or proprietary video servers. PreVU provides a first-frame view right in the Web page, streaming viewing while downloading, and full-speed cached playback off your hard drive. See the PreVU site in Figure A-7.

Business@Web's OpenScape (***)

http://www.busweb.com/

The OpenScape plug-in delivers OLE/OCX compatibility and enterprise application development to the Web. Use a visual drag-and-drop environment and Visual Basic scripting to build interactive Internet applications.

Progressive Network's RealAudio (****)

http://www.realaudio.com

RealAudio provides live and on-demand, real-time audio over 14.4 kb/s or faster connections to the Internet. RealAudio Version 2.0 is available for download now, with a powerful plug-in for Netscape that allows you to easily customize and deliver audio from your Web site.

Macromedia's Shockwave (****)

http://www.macromedia.com

The Shockwave plug-in lets users interact with Director presentations directly in a Netscape Navigator window. Animation, clickable buttons, links to URLs, digital video movies, sound, and more can be integrated within the presentation to deliver a rich multimedia experience.

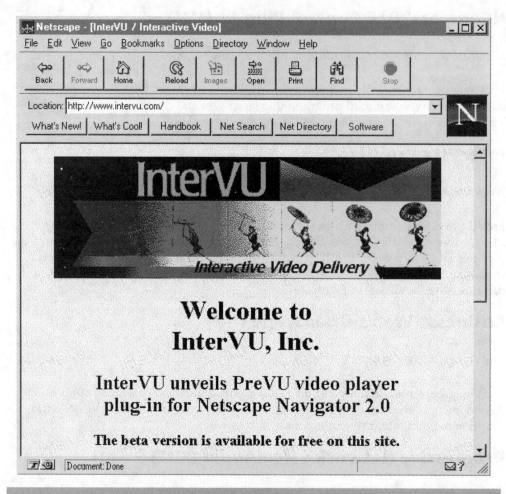

Figure A-7. *InterVu's home page*

Macromedia's Shockwave for FreeHand (***)

http://www.macromedia.com

Macromedia's Shockwave for FreeHand, in conjunction with the FreeHand application, provides the ability to integrate native FreeHand graphic files into World Wide Web pages displayed in the Netscape Navigator 2.0 browser.

MVP Solution's Talker (***)

http://www.mvpsolutions.com/

This plug-in lets Web sites talk to Macintosh users with MVP Solutions' free Talker plug-in. The Talker plug-in's speech synthesis technology uses much less bandwidth than recorded audio. You can also change the words your Web page speaks simply by editing a text file. Download the Talker plug-in and then visit one of MVP Solutions' Web pages to hear it in action.

Voxware's ToolVox (***)

http://www.toolvox.com

Add high-quality speech audio to your Web pages. With ToolVox, it's as easy as embedding a graphic: your existing HTTP server can stream audio. ToolVox delivers 53:1 compression ratios—more than three times smaller than first-generation real-time Internet voice products.

VDONet's VDOLive (****)

http://www.vdolive.com

VDOLive compresses video images without compromising quality on the receiving end. The speed of your connection determines the frame delivery rate: with a 28.8 kb/s modem, VDOLive runs in real-time at 10 to 15 frames per second.

QuickTime ViewMovie Plug-In by Ivan Cavero Belaunde (***)

http://www.well.com/~ivanski/

ViewMovie is a Netscape Navigator 2.0 plug-in that supports viewing and embedding Apple QuickTime movies in Web pages, including using movies as link anchors and image maps.

Chaco Communications' VR Scout (****)

http://www.chaco.com

Fly through 3-D graphical scenes with Chaco's VR Scout VRML plug-in. Chaco's extremely fast viewer implements the full VRML 1.0 standard. Chaco builds multiuser, multimedia software for the Internet, helping people work, play, and learn together, wherever they might be.

Integrated Data Systems' VREALM (***)

http://www.ids-net.com

VREALM, the VRML plug-in for Netscape 2.0 from Integrated Data Systems and Portable Graphics, fully supports VRML and adds features such as object behaviors, gravity, collision detection, autopilot, and multimedia.

VREAM's WIRL (***)

http://www.vream.com

WIRL brings true virtual reality to the Web. With the WIRL plug-in, you can play virtual slot machines, fly helicopters, see cybergymnasts flip, throw virtual TVs, watch business logos spin, visit exotic islands in cyberspace, and much more. WIRL fully supports VRML, and adds support for object behaviors, logical cause-and-effect relationships, multimedia capabilities, world authoring, and links to Windows applications.

Inso's Word Viewer (***)

http://www.inso.com

View any Microsoft Word 6.0 or Microsoft Word 7.0 document from inside Netscape Navigator 2.0 with Inso's Word Viewer plug-in. Based on Inso's Quick View Plus viewing technology, this plug-in also lets you copy and print Word documents with all original formatting intact.

Chemscape's Chime (***)

http://www.mdli.com/chemscape/chime/chime.html

MDL Chemscape Chime is a Netscape Navigator plug-in that allows scientists to view chemical information directly on a Netscape Navigator HTML page. Chime supports most of the popular structure display formats that scientists use, including MDL Information Systems, Inc.

GEO Interactive Media Group's Emblaze (***)

http://www.Geo.Inter.net/technology/emblaze/downloads.html

Emblaze enables real-time, online, full-motion animation with no preloading, buffering, or delay of any kind.

Totally Hip Software's Sizzler (***)

http://www.totallyhip.com/

Totally Hip's Sizzler is a multimedia software plug-in for Netscape Navigator 2.0. Sizzler enables you to create and display exciting web animation. It takes regular PICS files or QuickTime movies and converts them into sprite files that play on your Web site as they're transmitting over your modem.

PowerSoft's Media.Splash (***)

http://www.powersoft.com/media.splash/

Using media.splash, Web pages become interactive. This plug-in lets you add dancing words, flashing graphics, puzzle pieces, and visual, dynamic data—in just a matter of minutes. A companion authoring tool works as a companion to your favorite HTML editor.

VRML Resources

VRML Forum (****)

http://vrml.wired.com

An essential stop for VRML users. Includes a link to the VRML Architecture Group site, at **http://vrml.wired.com/future/**, where the future of VRML is being decided—live and online—by VRML pioneers, including Mark Pesce, Tony Parisi, and Gavin Bell. A lot of VRML work also gets done on the VRML Mailing List; a Web-based, hyperarchive version of the list is available at **http://vrml.wired.com/arch**.

VRML Repository (****)

http://sdsc.edu/vrml/

Another essential site for VRML, the VRML Repository is an impartial network resource for the dissemination of information relating to VRML. Submissions are organized by category and topic for convenient user access. The site is sponsored by San Diego Supercomputer Center, Silicon Graphics, Inc., and Template Graphics Software, Inc. Key areas on the site include Documents and Specifications, which includes pointers to the VRML 1.0 standard and VRML 2.0 contenders; and Software, which features links to VRML browsers, authoring tools, and utilities.

Grafmans VR Tools Review (***)

http://www.graphcomp.com/vrml/review.html

An interesting, independently run site that includes extensive reviews of VRML browsers. It gives the tools a star rating and provides detailed descriptions of features. It also provides .jpg screen shots of the browsers to let you get a feel for how they look and display VRML content.

Serch (****)

http://www.virtpark.com/theme/cgi-bin/serch.html

A searchable database of VRML worlds. Users submit their VRML sites to Serch, which then makes them available for searching. Also inlcudes top-ten lists and other useful information regarding VRML.

TerraVirtua (**)

http://www.terravirtua.com/

A potentially promising, independent source of VRML information. When reviewed, this site was promising more than it was delivering—including a forthcoming article on integrated Java and Shockwave. Keep an eye on it though; it could be a good resource.

Mesh Mart (***)

http://cedar.cic.net/~rtilmann/mm/index.htm

The Mesh Mart is a source of 3-D mesh object files for the growing number of 3-D modeling artist and developers. Although VRML authors may wish to design all of their own mesh objects, the rapidly increasing demand for 3-D renderings and virtual reality environments is creating a demand for reusable objects. The Mesh Mart offers a place where both users, buyers, developers, and sellers of mesh objects can get together and exchange their wares.

ZiffNet ZD3D (***)

http://www.zdnet.com/zdi/vrml/

A good source for VRML information, including a series of columns from Mark Pesce and Tony Parisi.

Chaco Communications (***)

http://www.chaco.com

Creators of the very strong VR Scout VRML plug-in and browser, the Chaco site also includes some good pointers to resources and VRML sites.

Caligari (***)

http://www.caligari.com

Caligari's Fountain VRML browser/authoring environment is one of the best new VRML tools around. The company also creates TrueSpace, a 3-D modeler. The site includes good links to VRML worlds and more. See the site in Figure A-8.

Figure A-8. *Caligari home page*

Template Graphics Software (***)

http://www.sd.tgs.com/

Home of the WebSpace browser (for non-SGI platforms), TGS is an important company in the 3-D/VRML community and their site is a good resource. For 3-D experts, the site is also notable for its focus on OpenInventor products.

InterVista Software (***)

http://www.intervista.com

Run by VRML pioneer Tony Parisi, InterVista is a key player in VRML. The site is somewhat sparse, but you can download the WorldView VRML browser here.

Virtus Corp. (***)

http://www.virtus.com

The Virtus site is noteworthy for its information on the Virtus WalkThrough Pro and Virtus VRML authoring tools and the Virtus Voyager browser. It also includes a good supply of sample objects, models, and textures.

Vream (***)

http://www.vream.com

Vream takes basic VRML and adds innovative extensions that support interactivity and behaviors. The WIRL plug-in viewer and authoring tools are available from the site.

ParaGraph International (***)

http://www.paragraph.com

Home of Virtual Home Space Builder, an easy-to-use VRML authoring tool. At this site, you can download various versions of the tool, including a free trial version.

Silicon Graphics (****)

http://webspace.sgi.com

Learn all about market leader SGI's plans for VRML, including WebSpace Navigator, WebSpace Author, and its proposed Moving Worlds specification. A necessary stop for those interested in VRML and 3-D technology.

Real-time Audio and Video

RealAudio (****)

http://www.realaudio.com

The leader in streaming audio. Come to this site to find out about Progressive Networks' RealAudio players, encoders, and servers. Also includes an extensive listings site at **http://www.realaudio.com/raguide.cgi**. This site includes a directory of the growing ranks of RealAudio sites as well as a search engine to find the "needle" in the audio "haystack."

Xing StreamWorks (***)

http://www.xingtech.com

Find out about Xing's powerful StreamWorks streaming audio and video technology. The company's listings page is at **http://www.xingtech.com/streams/ testdrv/ testdrv.html**.

DSP Group's TrueSpeech (***)

http://www.dspg.com

Check out and download DSP Group's TrueSpeech player and sample TrueSpeech content, accessible from its listings page at **http://www.dspg.com/cool**.

Vocaltec's Internet Wave (***)

http://www.vocaltec.com/iwave.htm

Come here to find out about VocalTec's InternetWave streaming audio technology. A fairly extensive listings page, including a good collection of 28.8 kb/s audio clips, can be found at **http://www.vocaltec.com/sites**. You can also check out VocalTec's InternetPhone, the market's leading voice-over-the-Internet technology.

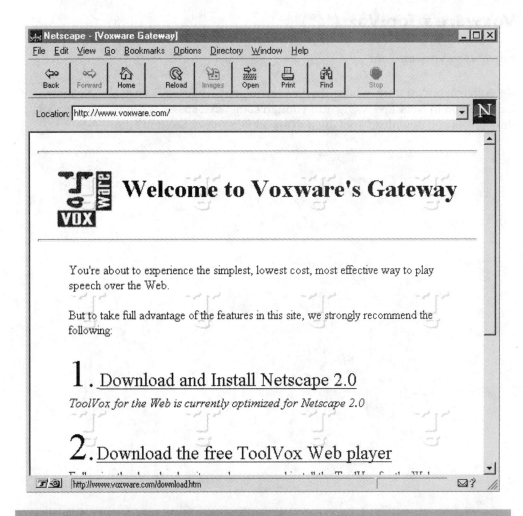

Figure A-9. *The Voxware home page*

VDONet's VDOLive (***)

http://www.vdolive.com

A strong site with downloadable viewers and personal servers for delivering
streaming audio on the Internet.

Voxware's ToolVox (***)

http://www.voxware.com

Keep an eye on Voxware, whose ToolVox technology has been licensed by Netscape for inclusion in Netscape Navigator. Though somewhat sparse when we reviewed it, the site lets you download ToolVox players and encoders. See it in Figure A-9.

Index

*, in FRAMESET tag, 200

1-800-Music-Now Net site, 399

2-D polygons, tools for creating in Fountain, 335

3-D graphics, terms and concepts of, 288

3-D house, building with WalkThrough Pro, 321-326

3-D mesh object files, source of, 433

3-D modeling in Fountain, 331-336

3-D object modeling packages, 296

3-D objects
    manipulating in Fountain, 334-335
    rendering, 289
    See also Three-dimensional objects

3D Space window, 307-308

3-D sphere, creating, 290-291, 292

3D Studio, 296

3-D VRML platform, 426

3-D worlds, 281

3Sixty, 66

A

ABC RadioNet Net site, 399

Abstract Window Toolkit. *See* AWT

Acro-Bot, 71

Acrobat. *See* Adobe Acrobat

Acrobat Amber, 410, 423
    See also Amber

Acrobat Capture, 10, 11, 50-51

Acrobat Catalog, 10

Acrobat Distiller, 9-10
    compared to PDF Writer, 31-32
    compression in, 41-42
    cost of, 7
    creating PDF files with, 38-42
    creating thumbnails in, 41
    downsampling in, 41
    fonts in, 42
    image compression in, 41-42
    options, 40-42
    user interface, 39
    uses for, 32

Acrobat Exchange, 9, 11, 42-49
    future of, 55-59

menu commands and buttons
in, 43
system requirements for, 60
viewing PDF files from, 24
Acrobat PDF Writer. *See* PDF Writer
Acrobat Reader, 10, 24-25
acquiring, 24
Amber version of, 422
Bookmarks view in, 26, 27
downloading, 24
Fit Page command, 29
Fit Width command, 29
hotlinked bookmarks in, 4
MovieLink in, 25
page-only view in, 26, 27
scrolling documents in, 26-27
scrolling pages in, 26-27
scrolling through documents
with, 26-27
Thumbnails view in, 26, 28
view option in, 26, 27
viewing documents with, 26
WebLink in, 25
Zoom In toolbar button, 30
Zoom Out toolbar button, 30
Acrobat Reader 2.1, advantages over
earlier versions, 25-26
Acrobat Search, 10
Acropolis, 71, 72
Active VRML, 299
Actual size display for PDF
documents, 29
Add Box tool in Virtual Home Space
Builder, 310
Add Wall tool in Virtual Home
Space Builder, 310
Adding machine, real-time, 79
Adobe
plans for Java, 141
support of Java, 114

Adobe Acrobat, 4, 6
advantages of, 7
applications, 64-72
compared to HTML, 7-8
components of, 9-10
current use of, 12, 14-18
design control advantages of, 13
developer tips and tricks for, 69
disadvantages of, 7-8
packaging, 11
Portable Document Format
(PDF), 8-9
pricing, 11
product family, 9-10
sources of information on, 60
and the Web, 10-12, 51-59
Adobe Acrobat Amber. *See* Acrobat
Amber; Amber
Adobe Acrobat Capture. *See* Acrobat
Capture
Adobe Acrobat Exchange. *See*
Acrobat Exchange
Adobe Acrobat Pro, 11
Adobe Acrobat Web site, 410-411
Adobe Acrobat for Workgroups, 11
Adobe PDF. *See* PDF
Adobe Systems Corp.'s plug-in, 230
Adobe Type Manager, 10
Adobe Web site, 410-411
downloading Acrobat Reader
from, 24
Aereal Serch, 344
Afterburner, 246, 267, 268
AHREF HTML tag, 377
.aif extension, 249
AIF format, 257
.aiff format, 374
compressing, 361
Airbrush mode in the Chooser
window, 311, 312
Align= attribute, 98

ALIGN HTML tag in Internet
    Explorer, 163
AlphaWorld, 353-355
Alt= attribute, 98
Amber, 13, 56-58, 59
    See also Acrobat Amber
Amber Reader plug-in, 230
Andreessen, Marc, 196, 205
    inside spin on Netscape's
        real-time vision, 396-398
Animated logos for Java, 112
Animated Web, 78-79
Animation
    controlling the speed of, 102
    creating images for in Director,
        250
Animations, creating in Director,
    252-256
Animator applet, 101-103, 104
APIs
    from Adobe, 56
    versions of Java, 93
APP HTML tag, 96
Apple Computer, Out of this World
    VRML proposal, 299
Apple Macintosh, Acrobat Exchange
    system requirements, 60
APPLET HTML tag, 96, 123
    attributes, 98
Applet portfolio, 142
Appletcode=, 102, 105
Applets, 85, 94-96
    compared to applications, 122
    downloading from the Java
        team, 100-105
    downloading public domain,
        99, 100-105
    listing of, 412
    specifying the alignment of, 98
    specifying parameters for in
        HTML, 96-98

testing newly written, 119-120
    writing simple, 122-124
    See also Java applets
appletviewer, 93, 119-120
Application Programming Interfaces.
    See APIs
Applications
    Adobe Acrobat, 64-72
    in Java, 122
Applix Inc., 81
Architecture-neutral language, 85
Arithmetic operators in JavaScript,
    212
Arrays in Java, 128, 130
ASAP WebShow presentation
    viewer, 423-424
Asteriods, 150
Astound Web Player, 424
Audio
    basic concepts, 374-375
    general resources, 375
    passing through firewalls, 361
Audio commentary, synchronizing
    with delivery of URLs, 365-366
Audio data, parameters of, 374
Audio editors, shareware, 375
Audio file formats
    for streaming audio encoders,
        374
    supported by Director, 257
Audio files, recording different
    levels of, 364
Audio Settings dialog box in Sound
    Recorder, 381, 382
Audio technologies, real-time, 360
Audio technology
    leaders in streaming, 360-361
    Web sites devoted to, 393
AudioNet, 389, 402-405
Authoring tools, 247
    for Java, 114-115

VRML, 295-298
Authoring Web sites, 174
Auto Animate dialog box in Director, 264
Auto Animation command, 252-253, 254
Autoindex plug-in, 50
Automatic Filter selection in Acrobat version 23, 42
AUTOSTART=TRUE in RealAudio, 393-394
Avatars, 346
    communicating through, 354-355
.avi extension, 249
AWT (Abstract Window Toolkit), 121
AWT class, 139, 140
Axcess magazine, 12, 14, 68-69

B

Background images, quickly adding to movies, 256
Background Sound dialog box, 166, 167
Backgrounds and Links dialog box, 165-166
Baehr, Geoffrey, 113
Bar Chart dialog box, 253
Base URL, specifying for applets, 98
Baseball stadium, 3-D depiction of, 348
basic.mlb, 335
Bauder, Pascal, 347
Bay Networks, 16
BDF (Blackbird Data Format), 158
Beavis and Butthead Shockwave site, 271, 272
Behavior of software objects, 125
Behlendorf, Brian, 283
Belaunde, Ivan Cavero, 429

Bell, Gavin, 283
Berners-Lee, Tim, 283
BGCOLOR=NAME HTML tag in Internet Explorer, 163
BGPROPERTIES=FIXED HTML tag in Internet Explorer, 161
BGSOUND HTML tag in Internet Explorer, 161
Bingham, Sanford, 71-72
Blackbird, 86, 187-188
Blitted fonts, 57
Bloomberg Information News Radio, 401
Bloomberg Television, live broadcasts with StreamWorks, 369
.bmp extension, 249
Book distribution, economics of, 71
Bookmarks, creating in Acrobat Exchange, 45-46
Bookmarks view in Acrobat Reader, 26, 27
Books, PDF versions of, 70-71
Boolean class in Java, 137
Boolean values in JavaScript, 211
Booleans in Java, 128
Bootcamp Web site, 402
Borland, plans for Java, 141
Borland Web site, 413
Bots, 182
Boxes in Virtual Home Space Builder, 304, 311, 313
Bradford, Tom, 406
Branching in Java, 131
break statement in JavaScript, 214
Browser Application option in the WebLink Preferences dialog box, 53
Browsers
    Java-capable, 92-94
    selecting to work with Acrobat, 53

shifting intelligence to, 83
without frames support,
204-205, 206
Browsing mode of Fountain, 329-330
Builder toolbox in Virtual Home
Space Builder, 307, 310
Building mode of Fountain, 330-336
Built-in objects in JavaScript, 215-216
Bullet Chart dialog box in Director,
265, 266
BulletProof.com, 148-149
Business applications on the
programmable Web, 81-82
Business@Web's OpenScape
plug-in, 427
Buttons class in Java, 139
Bytecode for Java applets, 95
Bytecode verifier in Java, 112
Byteserving PDF files, 59

C

C and C++ languages, compared to
Java, 127
C/Net Radio Net site, 399
C/Net Web site, 149-150
Café development kit, 413
Caffeine, 413
Calculation script in VB Script, 192
Calculators, JavaScript-based, 221,
222
Caligari Corp.'s TrueSpace 2
authoring tool, 297
Caligari Web site, 433, 434
Caligari's Fountain. *See* Fountain
Cameras
in Fountain, 332
placing in a VRML scene, 294
CAPTION HTML tag in Internet
Explorer, 163
Carey, Rikk, 283

Case, 249
Case sensitivity
of Java, 123
of JavaScript, 212
Cast, creating in Director, 249-251
Cast member scripts, 260, 262
Cast members, 249
placing, 251-252
Cast to Time command in Director,
255
Cast window, 248, 249
importing logos into, 263-264
CBS Up to the Minute, 405-407
CD-Link, 66-68
Cells in the Score grid, 251
CGI scripts, 83, 183
installing for Internet Wave, 387
iwpos, 387
Chaco Communications' plug-in, 230
Chaco Communications' VR Scout
viewer, 286
Chaco Communications' VR Scout
VRML plug-in, 430
Chaco Communications Web site,
433
Chaco VR Scout plug-in for
Netscape, 316, 317
Channels
number of audio, 374
in the Score, 251
on the Web, 147
Character class in Java, 137
Character Format Toolbar in
Netscape Navigator Gold, 235-236
Characters in Java, 128
Chemscape's Chime plug-in, 431
Chooser window in Virtual Home
Space Builder, 311, 312
Clark, Jim, 196
Class definition block, 133
Class files, 95-96

Class packages in Java, 121

Classes, 125, 126, 133-135
    compared to objects, 126
    defining, 133-134
    extending, 134
    names given to, 128
    vendor support for additional, 93

ClassLoader class in Java, 137

Client, executing scripts on, 207

Clock applet, 108, 109

Cloud, 289

CMX Viewer plug-in, 230, 424

Code= attribute, 98

Codebase= attribute, 98

Coding environment of Java, 118-121

Colleen, David, interview with, 349-353

Color class in Java, 139

Color images, compressing in PDF Writer, 38

Color names in Microsoft HTML extensions, 164

Colors/Background dialog box in Netscape Navigator Gold, 236, 237

COLS (column list) attribute of FRAMESET, 199, 200

Command line argument (args) in Java, 130

Commands, writing in VRML programs, 290

Comments, adding to Java code, 128

Common Gateway Interface (CGI) scripts. *See* CGI scripts

Common Ground software, 20-21

Common Ground Software Web site, 412

Common Ground Web Publisher, 21

Companies engine from Micromedia, 267

Companies licensing Java, listing of, 141

Comparison operators in JavaScript, 212

Compatibility of Java across platforms, 112

Compiler for Java, 120

Compression
    in Acrobat Distiller, 41-42
    selecting for PDF documents, 52

Compression options, in PDF Writer, 37-38

Conditional expressions, in JavaScript, 212

Cones in Fountain, 332

Connell, Mark, 348, 349

Content documents in HTML, 203

continue statement in JavaScript, 214

Control flow of Java, 130-133

Control Panel, 248, 252

Controls class in Java, 139

CONTROLS parameter in the EMBED SRC HTML tag, 391

CoolEdit, 375
    audio recording in, 376, 377

Coordinate3 node, 294

Copy All option in Virtual Home Space Builder, 315

Corel Corp.'s plug-in, 230

Corel Vector Graphics plug-in, 424

Corel's CMX Viewer, 424

Cosmo development environment for Java, 413-414

Create Irregular Object tool in WalkThrough Pro, 324

Create Link dialog box, 43-44
    in FrontPage Editor, 180
    in Netscape Navigator Gold, 237-238

Create polygon tools in WalkThrough Pro, 322

Cuban, Mark, 404-405
Cubes
 in Fountain, 332
 scooping out the insides of,
 312, 314
CyberPassage Conductor authoring
 tool, 298
CyberPassage viewer, 287
Cybertown, 345-347
Cylinders in Fountain, 332

D

Data files in Java applets, 95
Data Format (BDF) online file
 format, 158
Data type wrappers in Java, 137
Data types in Java, 127-128
Date object in JavaScript, 215-216,
 226-227, 228
.dcr extension, 267, 268
Debugger for Java, 120
Deep Forest animated music video,
 271, 274
Depth Control Gauge in
 WalkThrough Pro, 324
Design Editor in WalkThrough Pro,
 319, 320
Design toolbar, calling up, 321-322
Design View in WalkThrough Pro,
 319, 320
Development tools, emerging for
 Java, 140-142
Dial-A-Book, 70-71
diffuseColor field, 292
Digital Expresso Web site, 418
Digital Focus, 417
DigitalPaper technology, 20
Dimension X, 99, 106-108, 151
 Java authoring tool, 114, 115
 Web site, 416

.dir extension, 249, 267
Directional lights, 289
DirectionalLight node, 294
Director, 246
 Audio Animate dialog box in,
 264
 audio formats supported by, 257
 authoring software, 78-79
 building movies in, 248
 Bullet Chart dialog box, 265, 266
 Cast to Time command, 255
 compared to Java, 247
 cost of, 247
 creating animation in, 250,
 252-256
 creating a cast in, 249-251
 creating navigation buttons
 with, 259-260
 creating text files in, 251
 editing in, 256-258
 environment of, 247-248
 file types supported by, 249
 hotlinks to Web URLs from,
 265, 267
 importing WAV files into, 265
 In-Between command, 255-256
 Ink Effects in, 250
 options for creating text files in,
 251
 Paint toolbox, 250
 Paste Relative command, 255
 Point toolbox in, 250
 Set Transition dialog box in, 257
 sound effects in, 257-258
 steps for, 248
 transitions in, 256-257
 window for writing scripts,
 258-259
Discussion Bot in FrontPage, 183
distasst.ps printer driver, 39
Distiller. *See* Acrobat Distiller

Distiller Assistant, 39
Distributed language, 85
Document Information dialog box, 34
Document object, 216
Documents
　adding features to in Acrobat Exchange, 42-49
　creating in Internet Assistant, 165-172
　HTML layout and content, 203
　planning existing, 15
　scanning into PDF format, 50
　scrolling in Acrobat Reader, 26-27
Double class in Java, 137
Download Netscape Software, 243
Downsampling
　in Acrobat Distiller, 41
　selecting for PDF documents, 52
DSP Group's TrueSpeech, 360, 362-363, 380-384, 402
　Web site, 436
Duke logo, 112
Duke's Diner, 284, 285
Dunn, Joe, 261
Dynamic binding, 209

E

EarthTime plug-in, 424
EarthWeb, 146-147
　applet registry, 109
Edit button on the Netscape Navigator Gold browser toolbar, 234, 235
Edit mode in Virtual Home Space Builder, 306
Editors in WalkThrough Pro, 319, 320
Edlestein, Alex, 353

Egor Java animation software, 416, 417
Electronic Book Technologies FigLeaf Inline, 426
Electronic forms, supported in Internet Studio, 189
Electronic paper, 4
Electronic publishing systems, 4
Ellison, Larry, 78
EMBED HTML tag, 192, 231, 268-269, 377-380
EMBED SRC HTML tag, 391
Emblaze, 431
Encapsulation of objects, 126
Endimage value=, 102
Enhanced Netscape Hall of Shame Web site, 243
Envoy plug-in, 18-20, 425
Envoy Publisher, 19, 20
Envoy Reader plug-in, 19, 230
Envoy Viewer, 19-20
Envoy Web site, 411-412
.eps extension, 249
ERA (Earned Run Average) calculator, creating, 221-223
Errors class in Java, 137
ESPN SportsZone Net site, 399
Espresso add-on, 142
Event handlers, 211, 218-221
　list of common, 220
　placement of, 220
　syntax for, 219
Excel, 172
Exception class, in Java, 137
Exchange. *See* Acrobat Exchange
Expert mode in Virtual Home Space Builder, 306
Explorer file finder, integration with Internet Explorer, 190
Expressions in JavaScript, 212
Extracting objects in Fountain, 335

EZ3D authoring tool, 297

F

Features, adding to documents with Acrobat Exchange, 42-49
Fields in VRML, 290
File types, supported by Director, 249
File/Edit Toolbar in Netscape Navigator Gold, 234
Files, planning existing, 15
Firewalls, passing audio through, 361
Fit Page command in Acrobat Reader, 29
Fit Width command in Acrobat Reader, 29
.flc extension, 249
FLC files, 106
.fli extension, 249
Float class in Java, 137
Floating points in Java, 128
Floating window, 47-49
Fly mode in Fountain, 330, 331
Font blitting, 57
FONT COLOR HTML tag in Internet Explorer, 162-163
Font Embedding dialog box in PDF Writer, 37
FONT FACE HTML tag in Internet Explorer, 162-163
Fonts
    in Acrobat Distiller, 42
    embedding with PDF Writer, 37
    in PDF, 8
    reproducing in PDF Writer, 36-37
    selecting for PDF documents, 52
for loop in Java, 131-132
for statement in JavaScript, 213-214

Form Properties dialog box in FrontPage, 183-184
Format toolbar in FrontPage Editor, 179
Forms
    interactive, 79
    verifying valid input with JavaScript, 224-225
    See also Electronic forms
Forms toolbar in FrontPage Editor, 179
Formula One/Net
    plug-in, 230
    spreadsheet, 426
Fountain, 296, 329
    2-D polygon tools, 335
    3-D modeling, 331-336
    advantages and disadvantages of, 339-340
    attaching URLs in, 336
    authoring tool, 297
    browsing mode, 329-330, 331
    building mode, 330-336
    cameras in, 332
    cones in, 332
    cubes in, 332
    cylinders in, 332
    extracting objects in, 335
    Fly mode in, 330, 331
    geometric objects, built-in, 332
    geometric shapes, building, 331
    Hyperlink icon in, 336
    infinite light in, 333
    inlining in, 338-339, 340
    Inspect icon in, 335, 337
    lathe tool in, 335, 336
    levels of detail (LOD) in, 337-338, 339
    lights in, 333
    LOD Group tool in, 337, 338

manipulating 3-D objects in, 334-335

Material Color panel in, 335, 337

Object info panel, 339

p cursor in, 334

paint brush cursor in, 335

Paint Face icon in, 335, 337

Paint icon in, 335, 337

Paint Object icon, 335, 337

Paint Over icon, 335, 337

Paint Vertices icon, 335, 337

plane in, 332

Point Edit tool, 334-335

Primitive panel in, 332-333

Save VRML dialog box, 339

Shader Attribute panel in, 335, 337

spheres in, 332

Sweep tool in, 333

Text tool in, 333

Tip tool in, 335, 336

torus in, 332

viewer, 286

"Virtual Neighborhood" in, 329, 330

Walk mode in, 330, 331

Fraize, Scott, 114, 151

Frame scripts, 262

FRAME tag, 198, 201

Frame-based layout environment, 86

Frames, 197-198, 199

HTML extension, 87, 88

and hyperlinks, 203-204

nesting, 202-203

in Netscape Navigator 2.0, 196

in the Score, 251

working with, 198-205

Frames Authoring Guide, 243

Web site, 421

FRAMESET tag, 198, 199-201

FreeWorld Dialup, 397, 400

FrontPage. *See* Microsoft FrontPage

FrontPage Editor, 177-182

adding horizontal lines in, 179

Format toolbar, 179

Forms toolbar, 179

Image toolbar, 178-179

in Microsoft FrontPage, 173

Standard toolbar, 178

To Do List in, 180, 181-182

toolbars in, 177-179

FrontPage Explorer, 174-177

in Microsoft FrontPage, 173

views in, 174-175

Full page display for PDF documents, 29

Function command in JavaScript, 216

Function statement, 212-213

Functions

in JavaScript, 211-212, 217-218

in JavaScript, built-in statements, 212-215

FutureTense Inc., Java-based authoring tool from, 114-115

FutureTense Web site, 415-416

G

"galleries" of pre-built WalkThrough Pro objects, 318

Gamelan Web site, 109, 110, 146, 147, 416-417

Games, 79, 81

Garbage collection in Java, 85

Gates, Bill, 78, 156

quote from, 193

remarks on Internet strategy, 157

GEO Interactive Media Group's Emblaze, 431

Geometric objects, built-in in Fountain, 332

Geometric shapes, building complex in Fountain, 331

getAttributes method, 138

getAudioData method, 139

getImages method, 138

GetNetText URL command in Lingo, 267

Gibson, William, 280

.gif extension, 249

Gold. *See* Netscape Navigator Gold

Gold Disk home page, 424, 425

Gold Disk's Astound Web Player, 424

GoldWave, 375

Gosling, James, 113

GotoNetMovie URL command in Lingo, 267

GotoNetPage URL command in Lingo, 267

Grafmans VR Tools Review, 432

Graphics, compressing in Acrobat Distiller, 41

Graphics class in Java, 139

Graphics files, changing the internal file extension on, 326

Grayscale images, compressing in PDF Writer, 38

Greenfield, Stanley, 70, 71

Group nodes, 290, 291

Groupware tool, Internet Explorer as a, 190

GSM voice compression, 371

GSM (voice telephony) standard, 398

H

H.261 (video conferencing) standard, 398

Height Indicator bar, 312

Height Indicator in Virtual Home Space Builder, 309

HelloWorld applet, 122-124

Helper applications, 10
the end of, 80
plugging into Netscape, 227

History object, 216

@Home cable modem company, 246, 261, 398

Home page
Acropolis, 71, 72
Dial-A-Book, 70-71
New York Times Fax, 64-66
Voyager CD-Link, 68

Home pages, adding audio to, 376-393

Home Space Builder, 296

Horizontal line, adding in FrontPage Editor, 179

Hot Java browser, 84
current capabilities of, 92-93
system requirements for, 143

Hotlinked bookmarks in Acrobat Reader, 26

Hotlinks
creating in Acrobat Exchange, 44
in framed documents, 198
turning text references into, 179-180
to Web URLs from Director, 265, 267

How Do I Web site for Java tips, 418

HREF HTML tag, 55, 383, 390

.htm extension, 236

HTML
compared to Adobe Acrobat, 7-8
creating an introductory document in, 54
fundamental strengths of, 83

inline scripting of pages, 191
and Java, 96, 97
and plug-ins, 231
specifying parameters for
applets, 96-98
versus VRML, 282
HTML code in Internet Assistant,
170-172
.html extension, 236
HTML extensions
in Internet Explorer 2.0, 159-164
and Microsoft, 164
Microsoft strategy on
introducing, 157
support for open, 189
HTML files
creating to deliver Java applets,
123
for feeding parameters into
Java applets, 102
PDF within, 55
HTML forms, adding in FrontPage,
183
HTML pages
compressed ToolVox files in, 377
creating with Internet
Assistant, 165
embedding JavaScript into,
209-211
putting documents directly
into, 268
HTML template, setting in Internet
Assistant, 165
HTML.dot, 165
HTTP server, setting for Shockwave
content, 268
Hyperlink icon in Fountain, 336
Hyperlinks and frames, 203-204
Hypertext, adding to PDF files, 42-45

I

IBM infoMarket Search service, 110
IBM plans for Java, 141
IBM Web site, 415
ICE, 151
Identifiers in Java, 128
if then else command in Lingo, 263
if-else flow in Java, 131
if...else conditional statement in
JavaScript, 213
Image compression in Acrobat
Distiller, 41-42
Image toolbar in FrontPage Editor,
178-179
Imagesource value=, 102
IMG DYNSRC HTML tag in Internet
Explorer, 161
In-Between command in Director,
255-256
IndexedFaceSet node, 295
Indirect nesting, 203
Infinet Op's plug-in, 230
Infinit Op's Lightning Strike, 426
Infinite light in Fountain, 333
infoMarket Search service, 110
Inheritance, 124
init() method, 138
Ink Effects in Director, 250
Inline plug-ins, 88
Inlining in Fountain, 338-339, 340
Input streams in Java, 138
INSERT HTML tag, 192
Insert Image dialog box in Netscape
Navigator Gold, 236, 238
InSoft Inc., acquisition by Netscape,
397
Inso's Word Viewer plug-in, 430
Inspect icon in Fountain, 335, 337
Instance variable, 125
Instances of classes, 126

Integer class, in Java, 137
Integers in Java, 128
Integrated Data Systems' VREALM
VRML plug-in, 430
Integrated Data Systems/Portable
Graphics V-Realm viewer, 286
Integrated editing in Netscape
Navigator 2.0, 197
Intel
Pentium flaw information, 16
VRML worlds from, 349
Interactive forms, 79
Interactive Web, 82-83
Interest calculator, 222
Internal file extensions, changing on
graphics files, 326
Internal Revenue Service forms and
publications, Web site for, 17-18
Internet
overview of Microsoft plans
for, 158-159
versus Microsoft, 156
and Windows 95, 190
Internet Assistant, 158, 164-172
building HTML templates in
templates, 165
building tables in, 163-164
creating documents in, 165-172
creating HTML pages in, 165
edit window, 168, 169
Internet Development Toolbox Web
site, 420
Internet Explorer
BGCOLOR=NAME HTML tag,
163
BGPROPERTIES=FIXED
HTML tag, 161
BGSOUND HTML tag, 161
browser window, 168, 170
CAPTION HTML tag, 163
changing type style in, 162-163

changing typeface in, 162
creating background sounds in,
161
creating watermarks in, 161
displaying video clips in, 161
displaying VRML files in, 161
Explorer file finder integration
with, 190
FONT COLOR HTML tag,
162-163
FONT FACE HTML tag,
162-163
as a groupware tool, 190
HTML extensions in, 159-164
IMG DYNSRC HTML tag, 161
integration with Explorer file
finder, 190
MARQUEE HTML tag, 161-162
table HTML tags, 163-164
Internet Explorer 2.0, 87, 159-164
HTML extensions in, 159-164
Internet Platform from Microsoft,
158
Internet Studio, 86, 158, 186-189
electonic forms supported in,
189
future promise of, 189
scripting languages supported
in, 189
secure transactions supported
in, 189
Internet telephony, 190
Internet telephony audio, 400
Internet Wave, 363-365, 384-388, 402,
403
compression options, 385, 386
configuring MIME types for,
387
encoder, 385, 387
player, 363-364
Web site, 436

InternetPhone, 363-365, 384, 436
Interpreted language, 207
Interpreter for Java, 120-121
InterVista Software, 300
    Web site, 435
    WorldView viewer, 287
InterVU's PreVU, 427, 428
Intranets, Java on, 152-153
Inventor File Format, 290
Invisible option for creating links in
  Acrobat Exchange, 45
iwpos CGI script, 387

J

Jacob, Kurt, 106
JAM (Java Animation Machine), 114,
  115
JARS (Java Applet Rating Service),
  109, 111
    Web site, 418
Java, 84-86
    advantages of, 97
    animations, 78-79
    APIs, versions of, 93
    applications, 122
    applications in, 122
    arrays in, 128, 130
    authoring tools, 114-115
    Boolean class, 137
    branching in, 131
    Buttons class, 139
    Bytecode verifier in, 112
    C and C++ languages
      compared to, 127
    case-sensitivity of, 123
    Character class, 137
    characters in, 128
    class files, 95-96
    class packages, 121, 137-139
    class packages in, 121

    classes, 93
    classes in, 133-135
    ClassLoader class, 137
    code, compiling, 122
    coding environment of, 118-121
    Color class, 139
    command line argument (args)
      in, 130
    companies licensing, 141
    compared to Director, 247
    compared to JavaScript, 208-209
    compatibility across platforms,
      112
    compiler, 120
    compiler for, 120
    control flow of, 130-133
    Controls class, 139
    Cosmo development
      environment for, 413-414
    data type wrappers, 137
    data types, 127-128
    debugger for, 120
    development tools emerging
      for, 140-142
    disadvantages of, 97
    Double class, 137
    Errors class, 137
    Exception class, 137
    Float class, 137
    floating points in, 128
    future of, 112-116
    garbage collection in, 85
    graphical debugger for, 413
    Graphics class, 139
    home page, applets available
      on, 108-109
    and HTML, 96, 97
    IBM plans for, 141
    identifiers in, 128
    if-else flow in, 131
    immediate future of, 139-140

innovative uses of, 146-153
input streams, 138
Integer class, 137
integers in, 128
interpreter, 120-121
interpreter for, 120-121
on the Intranet, 152-153
and JavaScript, 115-116
listing of licensees, 141
literal types in, 128
literals in, 128
logos for, 112
Long class, 137
for loop, 131-132
looping in, 131
Math library in, 137
naming in, 128
newsgroups, 144
newsgroups, summaries of, 418
Object class, 137
operators in, 128
output streams, 138
packages in, 133-134
program control flow, 130-133
resources on the Web, 412-419
Runtime class, 137
scripting language for, 115-116
as a secure language, 85
security precautions in, 112
separators in, 128
as a simple programming
    language, 85
source code, 95, 122
sources of information on, 143
String class, 137
StringBuffer class, 137
strings in, 128
Sun Microsystems plans for, 113
support, in Netscape 2.0, 87, 196
syntax of, 127-128
System class, 137

system requirements for, 143
technical resources listing,
    143-144
Threads group of classes in, 137
Throwable class, 137
tools emerging for, 140-142
user group Web sites, 144
users groups and training, 144
utilities for, 121
versus HTML, 97
void keyword in, 134
and VRML, 151-152
Web pages from Sun, 143
Web site, 412
Web sites devoted to, 143, 144
Webmasters needs met by, 92
Java Abstract Window Toolkit
    package, 139
Java Animation Machine (JAM), 114,
    115
Java Applet Rating Service (JARS),
    109, 111
Java applets, 94-96
    accessing from other servers,
        99-100
    compared to applications, 122
    creating, 135-136
    debugging, 120
    directory and registry of, 109,
        110
    download rules of thumb for,
        111
    downloading from Sun, 101
    feeding parameters into, 102
    files composing, 95-96
    purchasing, 105-108
    ratings of, 418
    sources of, 108-111, 143, 416-417
    testing newly written, 119-120
    See also Applets
Java-capable browsers, 92-94

Java Developer Web site, 417-418
Java Developers Kit (JDK), 118-119
    elements of, 119-121
    system requirements for, 143
Java developments, IBM Web site,
  415
.java files, 95
Java Software Development Kit. *See*
  SDK
Java team, downloading applets
  from, 100-105
java.applet class package, 121,
  138-139
java.awt class package, 121, 139, 140
java.awt.image class library, 121
java.awt.peer class library, 121
javac command, 120, 122
java.io class package, 121, 138
java.lang class package, 121, 137
java.net class package, 121, 138
JavaScript, 87, 205-211
    arithmetic operators in, 212
    Boolean values in, 211
    break statement in, 214
    building blocks of, 211
    building objects in, 216-217
    case-sensitivity of, 212
    compared to Java, 208-209
    comparison operators in, 212
    conditional expressions in, 212
    continue statement in, 214
    date object in, 215-216, 226-227,
     228
    embedding into HTML pages,
     209-211
    examples, 221-227
    expressions in operators in, 212
    Function command in, 216
    functions in, 211-212, 217-218
    if...else conditional statement
     in, 213

    and Java, 115-116
    logical operators in, 212
    loops in, 213-214
    math object in, 215
    in Netscape Navigator 2.0, 196
    new keyword in, 217
    null value in, 211
    numbers in, 211
    object model for, 215-218
    operators in, 212
    predefined objects in, 215-216
    return statement in, 214
    for statement, 213-214
    with statement, 214-215
    statements in, 212-215
    string characters in, 211
    string operators in, 212
    strings in, 211
    this keyword, 216
    tracking page freshness, 226
    tutorial on Netscape's home
     page, 211
    values in, 211-212
    var statement in, 213
    variables in, 211-212
    while loop in, 214
JavaScript Index Web site, 243,
  422-423
JavaScript programs
    capabilities of client-side, 208
    hiding from other browsers, 210
JavaScript Resources page, 243, 422
java.util class package, 121, 138
JavaWorld online magazine, 413,
  418-419
JDK. *See* Java Developers Kit
JFactory visual interface builder, 416
Job Options dialog box in Acrobat
  Distiller, 40-42

Joint Photographic Experts Group
compression. *See* JPEG
compression
J.P. Morgan home page, 15
JPEG compression in PDF Writer, 38
JPEG format, 41

K

keystroke method, 139
Keywords in Java, 128
KPIG Radio station, 368

L

Labyrinth virtual reality browser, 283
Landscape orientation, selecting in
PDF Writer, 36
Language, interpreted, 207
LANGUAGE attribute of the
SCRIPT tag, 210
Lathe tool in Fountain, 335, 336
Lava, Netscape support for, 205
Layout documents in HTML, 203
Ledge, 198
Lempel-Ziv-Welch compression. *See*
LZW compression
Level-of-Detail node, 294
Levels of detail (LOD), in Fountain,
337-338, 339
Library in WalkThrough Pro, 319,
321, 327-328
Licensees for Java, listing of, 141
Lighting Editor in WalkThrough
Pro, 319
Lightning Strike plug-in, 230, 426
Lights
in 3-D graphics, 289
in Fountain, 333
Liner notes, 67, 68

Lingo, 247
adding interactivity with,
258-260, 262, 263
commands in, 263
creating language, 258
GetNetText URL command, 267
GotoNetMovie URL command,
267
GotoNetPage URL command,
267
if then else command, 263
on mouseDown, 263
new commands in, 267
pausing movies with, 262
PreloadNetThing URL
command, 267
puppetSound command, 263
puppetSprite command, 263
on rollOver command, 263
Lingo scripts
navigating with, 259-260
writing, 260-262
Link button on the Standard toolbar
in FrontPage Editor, 180
Link Information option in the
WebLink Preferences dialog box,
52
Link Properties dialog box in
WebLink, 53
Link tool button, 43
Link View in FrontPage Explorer, 175
Links in Acrobat Exchange, 43-45
Liquid Reality Java browser, 151,
152, 416
Listservs about Adobe Acrobat, 60
Literal types in Java, 128
Literals in Java, 128
Live3D, 353, 354, 426
Live encoding in RealAudio 2.0, 389
LiveMedia, 371, 397
LiveScript, 196, 206, 207

LiveUpdate's Crescendo plug-in, 424
LiveWire, 206, 207
Local light in Fountain, 333
Location object, 216
LOD Group tool in Fountain, 337, 338
LOD groups, creating in Fountain, 337
Logical operators in JavaScript, 212
Logos for Java, 112
Long class in Java, 137
Long file names in PDF Writer, 33
Looping in Java, 131
Loops, building in JavaScript, 213-214
Loose typing, 209
LZW compression in PDF Writer, 38
LZW format, 41

M

McCrea, John, 353
Macromedia
    inside spin on Shockwave, 261
    plans for Java, 141
    plug-in, 229, 230
    relationship with Sun
      Microsystems, 261
    Shockwave for Freehand, 428
    Shockwave plug-in, 427
    Shockwave technology, 78-79
    support of Java, 114
Macromedia Director. *See* Director
Macromedia's Shockwave. *See*
    Shockwave
MacSound Utilities page, 375
Magazines about Adobe Acrobat, 60
Make Link button in Netscape
    Navigator Gold, 236
Make Transparent Modifier icon in
    WalkThrough Pro, 324

Make transparent modifier in
    WalkThrough Pro, 322
MARGINWIDTH= attribute for
    FRAMESET, 200
Marker well, 260
Markers in Lingo scripts, 260
Market Central, 348-349
Marquee dialog box, 166
MARQUEE HTML tag in Internet
    Explorer, 161-162
Mass medium, Web as a, 396
Material Color panel in Fountain, 335, 337
Material node, 292
Materials library, calling up in
    Fountain, 335
Math library in Java, 137
Math object in JavaScript, 215
Math program, creating in Java, 129-130
MDL Chemscape's Chime plug-in, 431
media.splash plug-in, 431
Mesh Mart Web site, 433
Messages, sending to objects, 126
Method overriding, 134
Methods, 125, 126
    names given to, 128
Metrowerks
    plans for Java, 141
    Web site, 413
Mew Web dialog box in FrontPage
    Explorer, 176
Microphones, recording from, 375
Microsoft
    Active VRML, 299
    demo page, 159-160
    Developer page, WWW
      address, 191
    Home Page, 420
    and HTML extensions, 164

inside spin on, 157
Internet Development Toolbox
Web site, 420
Internet Platform, sources of
information on, 193
Internet Resource Center Web
site, 420
Java support, 93
overview of Internet plans,
158-159
plans for Java, 141
plug-in, 316
versus the Internet, 156
VRML add-on, 287
Microsoft FrontPage, 86, 158, 173-186
future of, 186
WWW site for, 174
Microsoft Network (MSN), 420
Microsoft Office applications,
Internet-enabling of, 172-173
Microsoft Windows, Acrobat
Exchange system requirements, 60
Microsoft Word
documents, viewing from
inside Netscape Navigator,
430
Internet Assistant add-on to,
164
table tools, 167-168
Milener, Scott, 148
MIME types
configuring for RealAudio, 390
setting for .dcr files, 268
Mixer for audio recorders, 375
Monitor Setup plug-in, 50
Monochrome images, comparing in
PDF Writer, 38
Mortgage calculator, 79, 80
mouse method, 139
.mov extension, 249

Movie Properties dialog box in
Acrobat Exchange, 47-48
Movie tool button in Acrobat
Exchange, 43
MovieLink in Acrobat Reader, 25
MovieLink button in Acrobat
Exchange, 47
Movies
pausing with Lingo, 262
preparing for the Web, 267-269
quickly adding background
images to, 256
viewing with Shockwave
player, 269, 270
Movies option in the Chooser
window, 311
Moving Worlds, 299, 300, 353
MPEG video for Netscape
Navigator 2.0, 427
MPEG (video) standard, 398
MSN, 410
Multimedia content, delivering
inline, 80
Multimedia files, adding in Acrobat
Exchange, 43, 47-49
Multimedia Magic, builder of
Cybertown, 345
Multimedia plug-ins, 87-88
Multimedia "slideshows," creating,
365
Multiplayer games, 79
Multiple master font technology, 37
Multithreaded language, 86
.mus extension, 315
.mus files, 304
MVP Solution's Talker plug-in, 429

N

Name= attribute, 98
Naming in Java, 128

National Public Radio (NPR) Net
site, 399
National Semiconductor, 81
Natural Intelligence
plans for Java, 141
Web site, 415
Navigation button, creating with
Director, 259-260
Navigator. *See* Netscape Navigator
Navigator applet, 146, 147
Navigator Gold. *See* Netscape
Navigator Gold
Navigator objects, 216
NBC Pro Financial Network, live
video feeds from, 401
NBC Pro Financial News Channel,
video broadcasting with
StreamWorks, 370
NCompass plug-in, 229, 230, 232, 427
NeoGlyphics Media Corp., 152-153
Nervous text applet, 100
Nested frames, 202-203
Net-casting of live audio events, 389
Netscape
acquisition of InSoft, Inc., 397
Bill Gates remarks on
competing with, 157
endorsement of Moving
Worlds, 353
Gold Rush Tool Chest, 240
helper pages, 240
Home Page, 421
Live3D, 353, 354
LiveMedia, 371
plans for Java, 141
relationship with VoxWare, 361
Netscape Live3D, 353, 354, 426
Netscape LiveMedia architecture.
See LiveMedia architecture
Netscape Navigator
extension to, 197

integration of plug-ins, 233
as a Web operating system
(OS), 87
Netscape Navigator 2.0, 196
features of, 87
information page, 243
Java support in, 93
page, 421
plug-in architecture, 227
system requirements for, 143
Netscape Navigator browser home
page, 421
Netscape Navigator Gold, 233-242
Authoring Guide, 243
creating pages in, 236-240
Data Sheet, linking to, 240
features missing from first beta,
234
information page, 243
main toolbars, 234-236
page, 421
Netscape Net technologies, sources
of information, 243
Netscape Page Starter Site, 240
Netscape Page Wizard, 240-242
Netscape plug-ins, 422-431
future of, 232-233
listing of, 230
Netscape Scripting Language. *See*
JavaScript
NetWatch Web site, 400, 401
Network protocols, tools for
accessing in Java, 121
new keyword in JavaScript, 217
New mode in Virtual Home Space
Builder, 305-306
New Page dialog in FrontPage
Explorer, 176-177
New York Times Fax, 14, 64-66
Newsgroups
about Adobe Acrobat, 60

about Java, 144

Nodes
    types of, 290, 291
    in VRML syntax, 290

NOEMBED HTML tag, 231, 268

NOFRAMES HTML tag, 204-205, 206

NORESIZE attribute for
    FRAMESET, 200

Notes, creating in Acrobat
    Exchange, 46-47

Notes tool button in Acrobat
    Exchange, 43, 46

Null value in JavaScript, 211

Number of bits per sample, 374

Number of channels, 374

Numbers in JavaScript, 211

O

Oak, 84

Object class in Java, 137

Object code for sale on the Web,
    109-110

Object Info panel in Fountain, 339

Object Linking and Embedding
    Controls. *See* OCXs

Object model for JavaScript, 215-218

Object-oriented language, 85

Object-oriented programming
    (OOP), 125-127

Object Power's plug-in, 229, 230

Object Properties button in
    Netscape Navigator Gold, 236

Objects, 125
    building in JavaScript, 216-217
    built-in in JavaScript, 215-216
    compared to objects, 126
    encapsulation of, 126
    extracting in Fountain, 335
    in JavaScript, 211-212
    Navigator, 216

predefined in JavaScript,
    215-216
    sending messages to, 126
    three-dimensional, 289

Observer in WalkThrough Pro, 319,
    323

OCXs, 158
    in Blackbird, 186-188
    running, 229

Office applications,
    Internet-enabling of, 172-173

Office Scene in a VRML viewer, 328

O.J. speaks site, 402

OLE Control plug-in, 229, 230, 427

OLE Controls (OCXs). *See* OCXs

OLE Server plug-in, 50

OLEBroker Web site, 110

on mouseDown command in Lingo,
    263

on rollOver command in Lingo, 263

onBlur event handler, 220

onChange event handler, 220

onClick event handler, 220

onFocus event handler, 220

Online OS (Operating System), 85

OnLoad event handler, 220

OnMouseOver event handler, 220

onSubmit event handler, 220

OOP (Object-oriented
    programming), 125-127

Open Inventor, 283

Open Inventor ASCII File Format,
    290

OpenScape plug-in, 229, 230, 427

Operators
    in Java, 128
    in JavaScript, 212

Oracle
    plans for Java, 141
    PowerBrowser 1.0, Java
        support in, 93, 94

Web site, 415
Orientation
    selecting for PDF documents, 51
    selecting in PDF Writer, 36
OrthographicCamera, 294
Out of this World, 299
Outline View in FrontPage Explorer, 175
Output streams in Java, 138

P

p cursor in Fountain, 334
Packages in Java, 133-134
Pacman, 150
Page Editor in Blackbird, 187
Page Settings dialog box in FrontPage Editor, 177, 178
Page setup options in PDF Writer, 34-38
Page size
    selecting for PDF documents, 51
    selecting in PDF Writer, 35
Page width display for PDF documents, 29
Page-on-Demand technology of Common Ground software, 20-21
Page-only view in Acrobat Reader, 26, 27
PageMill, 410-411
Pages
    creating in Netscape Navigator Gold, 236
    customized based on time of day, 227, 228
    scrolling in Acrobat Reader, 26-27
    tracking the freshness of, 226
Paint brush cursor in Fountain, 335
Paint Face icon in Fountain, 335, 337
Paint icon in Fountain, 335, 337

paint() method, 138-139
Paint Object icon in Fountain, 335, 337
Paint Over icon in Fountain, 335, 337
Paint toolbox in Director, 250
Paint Vertices icon in Fountain, 335, 337
.pal extension, 249
Paper Software
    plug-in, 229, 230
    WebFX plug-in, 229
    WebFX viewer, 286
    Worlds Page, 344
Paragraph Format Toolbar in Netscape Navigator Gold, 235
ParaGraph International Web site, 435
ParaGraph International's Virtual Home Space Builder authoring tool, 297
ParaGraph's Virtual Home Space Builder. *See* Virtual Home Space Builder
Parameters, passing for applets, 96-98
ParamName= attribute, 98
Parisi, Tony, 282, 287, 300
    columns from, 433
Passwords, adding in Acrobat Exchange, 49
Paste Relative command in Director, 255
"pause" script, 262
Pause value=, 102
PC Scoreboard, 149-150
.pcd extension, 249
PCM-encoded .wave file, creating as a TrueSpeech source file, 380
.pct extension, 249
.pcx extension, 249
PDF, 8-9

PDF documents
  changing the display size of,
    28, 29
  compared to original, 34, 35
  creating with PDF Writer, 32-38
  designing for the Web, 51, 52
  display size of, 28, 29
  labeling and identifying, 55
  viewing on screen, 28, 29, 30, 31
  zoom commands for, 30
  See also PDF files
.pdf extension, 55
PDF files, 9, 422
  adding hypertext to, 42-45
  adding security to, 49
  byteserving, 59
  creating, 24, 31-42
  delivering on the Web, 55, 56
  as downloadable deliverables,
    67
  embedding URLs in, 12
  guiding Web users to, 54-55
  naming, 33
  navigating, 26-31
  optimizing, 59
  optimizing for the Web, 51-52
  RSA Data Security RC4
    encryption of, 71
  search criteria for tracking, 34
  viewing with Exchange, 24
  See also PDF documents
PDF format, scanning documents
  into, 50
PDF links, local, 43
PDF Writer, 9
  compared to Acrobat Distiller,
    31-32
  compressing color images in, 38
  compressing grayscale images
    in, 38
  compression options in, 37-38

creating PDF documents with,
  32-38
Font Embedding dialog box in,
  37
fonts in, 36-37
JPEG compression in, 38
long file names in, 33
LZW compression in, 38
Print Setup dialog box in, 32-33
resolution in, 36
selecting orientation in, 36
selecting page setup options,
  34-38
PDF Zone Web site, 58
Pentium processor, information on
  flaw, 16
Personal Web server in Microsoft
  FrontPage, 174
Perspective Camera node, 294
Pesce, Mark, 282, 350
  columns from, 433
Picture editor button in Virtual
  Home Space Builder, 308
Picture mask in the Chooser
  window, 311, 312
Pictures, hanging on walls in Virtual
  Home Space Builder, 314
Pinnochio button in Virtual Home
  Space Builder, 309, 310
Plane Builder window in Virtual
  Home Space Builder, 307, 309-310
Plane in Fountain, 332
Planet 9 Studios, 349-353
playmode parameter in the EMBED
  HTML tag, 379-380
Plug-in architecture in Netscape
  Navigator 2.0, 197
Plug-ins
  in Adobe Acrobat, 50
  future of, 232-233
  and HTML, 231-232

multimedia, 87-88
in Navigator 2.0, 87, 227-233
.pnt extension, 249
Point cloud, 289
Point Edit tool in Fountain, 334-335
Point lights, 289
Point Opening Edit control panel, 334
Point of reference, establishing a VRML, 292
Pointers, elimination of in Java, 112
PointLight, 294
Polese, Kim, 113
Polygons
3-D graphics, 289
creating in WalkThrough Pro, 321-323
Portable Document Format (PDF). *See* PDF
Portable Graphics's V-Realm Builder authoring tool, 297
Portable language, 85
Portrait orientation, selecting in PDF Writer, 36
Poster in MovieLink, 48, 49
PostScript files
converting into Distiller, 39-40
converting to PDF, 38
PostScript language, converting into PDF, 9
PowerBrowser from Oracle, 415
PowerPoint, 172
PowerSoft's media.splash plug-in, 431
Predefined objects in JavaScript, 215-216
PreloadNetThing URL command in Lingo, 267
PreVU, 427, 428
Primitives Panel
accessing in Fountain, 332-333

creating objects with, 333
Print Setup dialog box in PDF Writer, 32-33
Program control flow in Java, 130-133
Programmable Web, 78
possibilities for, 78-82
Progressive Networks' plug-in, 229, 230
Progressive Networks' RealAudio. *See* RealAudio
Project Editor in Blackbird, 187
Property nodes, 290, 291
ProteinMan's Top Ten, 344-345
Public key encryption technology, 112
Pulver, Jeff, 400
puppetSound command in Lingo, 263
puppetSprite command in Lingo, 263
Push Buttons, creating in FrontPage, 185

Q

QuickTime files, playing back embedded with MovieLink, 48-49
QuickTime ViewMovie plug-in, 429

R

.ra extension, 389, 390
.ra format, 388
Radiance Software's EZ3D authoring tool, 297
Radio stations, broadcasting with Xing, 369
Radio and the Web, 396
Raggett, Dave, 283
.ram extension, 389, 390

Ratings of Web resources, 410

Reader. *See* Acrobat Reader

Reader toolbar, page-turning commands on, 26

Readers, instructions for downloading, 54-55

Real-time audio files, delivering from home pages, 374

Real-Time audio technologies, 360

Real-time audio and video resources, 436-438

Real-time client and server technology, 147

Real-time multimedia, sources of information, 393

Real-time pioneers, finding on the Net, 398-399, 401-402

Real Time Protocol (RTP), 392, 398

Real-time recording, 253-254, 255

Real-time technologies, challenges for Webmasters, 402

Real-time video, promise of, 396

RealAudio, 360, 365-367, 388-393
home page, 398-399
player, 389, 391, 392, 401
plug-in, 229, 230, 231, 427
server, 366-367
sites, directory of, 398
streaming sound, 284
Web site, 436

RealAudio 1.0
encoder, 388, 389
players, 365

RealAudio 2.0, 365
encoder, 388-389, 390

Recording audio, tips on, 375

Registration Bot in FrontPage, 183

Remove Box tool in Virtual Home Space Builder, 310

Resolution in PDF Writer, 36

Restricted environment execution of Java code, 112

Resusable Software Component Market, 110

return statement in JavaScript, 214

.rgb texture format, 316

Roaster Java development environment, 415

Rockliff, Tony, 346-347

Roguewave Web site, 416

ROWS (row list) attribute of FRAMESET, 199, 200

.rpm extension, 391

RSA Data Security RC4 encryption, 71

run() method, 138

Runtime class in Java, 137

S

Sampling rate, 374

San Francisco Bay Area Underground Music Web site, 402

Sausage Software Web site, 416, 417

Save 3-D space option in Virtual Home Space Builder, 315

Save PDF File As dialog box, 34

Save Results Bot in FrontPage, 183-184

Save VRML dialog box in Fountain, 339

Scaling of printing in PDF Writer, 36

Scene graph, 290

Schmidt, Eric, 78

Schmults, Rob, 355

Scissors tool, 310, 312

Score, 248
grid, 251
placing Cast members in, 251-252

Screen size, selecting for PDF
documents, 51
SCRIPT HTML tags, 192, 210
Scripting language for Java, 115-116
Scripting languages, supported in
Internet Studio, 189
Scripts
executing on the client, 207
hiding from non-Netscape
browsers, 210
window for writing in Director,
258-259
SCROLLING= attribute for
FRAMESET, 200
Scrolling images applet, 103-105
Scrolling text box, adding in
FrontPage, 183
Scrolling Text Box Properties dialog
box in FrontPage, 183
SDK, 93
Search Bot in FrontPage, 182
Secure language, Java as, 85
Secure transactions, supported in
Internet Studio, 189
Security
adding to PDF files, 49
for BV Script applet
downloading, 191
Security dialog box in Acrobat
Exchange, 49
Security precautions in Java, 112
Select Director icon in the Chooser
window, 311, 312
Separator node, 292
Separators in Java, 128
Serch Web site, 432
Server-side scripts, enabling, 83
Servers, reconfiguring for PDF files,
55
Set Tempo command, 258

Set Transition dialog box in Director,
257
Settings for Savings Results of Form
dialog box in FrontPage, 184-185
SGI. *See* Silicon Graphics
Shader Attribute panel in Fountain,
335, 337
Shading, 289
Shape nodes, 290, 291
"Shocked" sites, tour of, 269-274
Shockwave, 246-247
for Freehand, 428
Macromedia's inside spin on, 261
movies, building, 262-267
player, 246
plug-in, 229, 230, 269, 270, 427
sources of information on, 275
system requirements for, 275
technology, 78-79
Web sites devoted to, 275
Silicon Graphics, Inc. (SGI), 283
Moving Worlds, 299
plans for Java, 141
Web site, 413-414, 435
WebSpace Author, 298
Simple applet, creating, 135-136
Simple programming language,
Java as a, 85
SiteMill, 410-411
Sizzler, 431
Slideshows, creating multimedia, 365
Softimage 3D, 296
Software objects, 125
Software Publishing's ASAP
WebShow, 423-424
SOMA neighborhood, 3-D rendering
of, 283
Sony's CyberPassage
Conductor authoring tool, 298
viewer, 287

Sound card line input, recording audio through, 375

Sound Cast Member info dialog box, 265, 266

Sound Effects, 375

Sound effects in Director, 257

Sound Recorder in Windows 95, 380-381

Sounds, creating background in Internet Explorer, 161

Sounds value=, 102

Soundsource value=, 102

Soundtrack value=, 102

Source code for Java applets, 95-96

Specialty publishing with Adobe Acrobat, 17-18

Speech audio, high-quality, 429

Speech files, compressing, 361

Sphere
creating a 3-D, 290-291, 292
in Fountain, 332

Spivack, Nova, 146-147

Sports Network, 147-148

Spot lights, 289

SpotLight, 294

Spreadsheet, with built-in Internet functionality, 426

Sprite scripts, 262

Sprites, 252

Spyglass Mosaic, Java support in, 93

Spyglass plans for Java, 141

Stage, 248
placing Cast members on, 251-252

Standard toolbar in FrontPage Editor, 178

Starfish Software's EarthTime plug-in, 424

Statements in JavaScript, 212-215

States of software objects, 125

Static binding, 209

Steaming coffee cup logo, 112

Step Forward in the Control Panel, 254

Step recording, 254

Stephens, Joel, 348

Streaming animation player applet, 99, 106-108

Streaming audio technologies, hands-on look, 376-393

Streaming audio technology, leaders in, 360-361

Streaming video technologies, 360

StreamWorks, 360, 401

StreamWorks players, 368

String characters in JavaScript, 211

String class in Java, 137

String operators in JavaScript, 212

StringBuffer class in Java, 137

Strings
in Java, 128
in JavaScript, 211

Strong typing, 209

Studio Pro, 296

Subclasses, 126-127
creating, 134

Summary View in FrontPage Explorer, 175

Sun Java Web page, applets available on, 108

Sun Microsystems
Macromedia relationship with, 261
plans for Java, 113

Sun Microsystem's Java programming language. *See* Java

Sun's Java Web pages, 143

SunSoft Web site, 412

SunSoft's Workshop Java, 142

SunWorld online magazine, 412

Super Bowl stadium, 3-D depiction of, 348

Superclass, 126

Supercrop plug-in, 50

Superprefs plug-in, 50

Surface Edit tool in WalkThrough
Pro, 322, 323

Surface Editor in WalkThrough Pro,
319

Sweep tool in Fountain, 335, 336

Symantec
plans for Java, 141
Web site, 413

Syntax of Java, 127-128

System class in Java, 137

System requirements for Java, 143

T

Table of Contents Bot in FrontPage,
182

Table HTML tags in Internet
Explorer, 163-164

Table tools in Microsoft Word, 167

Tables, building in Internet
Assistant, 163-164

Talker plug-in, 429

target keyword in Netscape, 203

Tax forms, home page for, 17

TCP/IP versus UDP, 392-393, 394

TEA, The Easy Animator, 416

TechBabble Web site, 402

Technical documentation, posting
on the Web with Acrobat, 16-17

Tele button in Virtual Home Space
Builder, 309, 310

Telephony, Internet, 190

Telephony audio, 400

TelePortation system in
AlphaWorld, 354

Template, building HTML pages in
Internet Assistant, 165

Template Graphics Software Web
site, 434

Template Graphics WebSpace
Navigator viewer, 286

Templates for building home pages,
240

Terminal Reality, 349, 350

TerrVirtua Web site, 433

Text, compressing in Acrobat
Distiller, 41

Text files, options for creating in
Director, 251

Text references, turning into
hotlinks, 179-180

Text tool in Fountain, 333

TEXTFOCUS parameter for the
EMBED tag, 231

Texture2 node, 294

Texture Java authoring product,
114-115, 415-416

Textures
adding in Virtual Home Space
Builder, 314
adding in WalkThrough Pro,
325, 326
defining in VRML, 294

this keyword in JavaScript, 216

Threads group of classes in Java, 137

Three-dimensional modeling
software, 296

Three-dimensional objects, 289
See also 3-D objects

Throwable class in Java, 137

Thumbnails
creating in Acrobat Distiller, 41
creating in Acrobat Exchange,
46

Thumbnails view in Acrobat Reader,
26, 28

Tic-Tac-Toe applet, 108, 109

.tif extension, 249

Time, taking around the world, 424

Times. *See* New York Times Fax

TimesFax, 64-66

TimeStamp Bot in FrontPage, 182

Tip tool in Fountain, 335, 336

To-Do List
    in FrontPage Editor, 180,
       181-182
    in Microsoft FrontPage, 173

Toggle Browser button in Netscape
  Navigator Gold, 234

Toolbars in FrontPage Editor, 177-179

Tools, emerging for Java, 140-142

ToolVox, 429
    encoder, 376, 377
    player, embedded in an HTML
       page, 377, 379
    Web encoder, 361
    Web player, 361, 362
    Web site, 437, 438

Torus in Fountain, 332

Totally Hip Software's Sizzler
  plug-in, 431

Toy Story site's Shockwave game,
  271, 273

Transform node, 292, 293

Transitions in Director, 256

Transparent box, laying over
  another image, 259

TrueSpace, 296

TrueSpace 2 authoring tool, 297

TrueSpace 3-D sculpture studio, 329

TrueSpeech
    compression encoding
       technology, 362
    Internet player, 362, 363
    launching player, 384

Trusted environment execution of
  Java code, 112

.tsp file, creating, 382-383

tsp MIME type, configuring, 384

Tumble Editor in WalkThrough Pro,
  319

Tumbleweed Publishing Essentials,
  20

TumbleWeed Software, 18-19
    Envoy plug-in, 425
    plug-in, 230
    Web site, 412

Tumbling Duke demo, running, 119

Type style, changing in Internet
  Explorer, 162-163

Typeface, changing the color of in
  Internet Explorer, 162

U

UDP protocol, 366-367
    advantages of, 367
    versus TCP/IP, 392-393, 394

UnderConstruction applet, 109

Unicode format, 128

Uniform Resource Locators. *See*
  URLs

University of Texas Macintosh
  freeware and shareware, for
  audio editors, 375

unLoad event handler, 220

URLs
    attaching in Fountain, 336
    attaching in Virtual Home
      Space Builder, 314-315
    embedding within PDF files, 12
    showing in WebLink hotlinks,
      52
    specifying base for applets, 98
    synchronizing audio
      commentary with delivery
      of, 365-366

User feedback, building in with
  Shockwave, 271

User interface
for Virtual Home Space
Builder, 306-311, 312
of WalkThrough Pro, 319
Users groups, Web sites for Java, 144
Utilities for Java, 121

V

V-Realm Builder authoring tool, 297
V-Realm viewer, 286
Values in JavaScript, 211-212
Vanguard Gallery, 275
var statement in JavaScript, 213
Variables, 125, 126
declaring in Java code, 129
in JavaScript, 211-212
names given to, 128
VB Script, 158, 191-192, 207
applets, security concerns, 191
calculation script in, 192
interpreter, calling, 192
invoking, 210
VDOLive, 360, 370-371, 429
player, 370, 371
plug-in, 229, 230
technology, 396
Web site, 437
Vermeer Technologies, 86, 173
Viacom New Media, 150
Video
low-bit-rate, 370
and the Web, 396
Video clips, displaying in Internet
Explorer, 161
Video on demand, 400
Video technologies, streaming, 360
View mode in Virtual Home Space
Builder, 305-306
View option in Acrobat Reader, 26,
27

Viewer. *See* Envoy Viewer
Viewing Camera in Virtual Home
Space Builder, 309
ViewMovie plug-in, 429
Views in FrontPage Explorer, 174-175
Virtual Home Space Builder
(VHSB), 304-305
Add Box tool, 310
Add Wall tool, 310
adding textures in, 314
advantages and disadvantages
of, 317
attaching URLs in, 314-315
authoring tool, 297
boxes in, 304, 311, 313
Builder toolbox, 307, 310
building VRML worlds in,
311-317
Chooser window, 311, 312
Copy All option, 315
downloading, 305
Edit mode, 306
Expert mode, 306
Height Indicator, 309
home of, 435
main elements in, 304
modes in, 305-306
New mode, 305-306
ordering, 305
Picture editor button, 308
Pinnochio button, 309, 310
Plane Builder window, 307,
309-310
Remove Box tool, 310
Save 3-D space option, 315
save options in, 315-316
Scissors tool, 310, 312
startup screen, 305-306
Tele button in, 29, 310
user interface, 306-311, 312
View mode in, 305-306

Viewing Camera in, 309
Walker toolbox, 307, 310-311
walls in, 304
Wide button in, 309, 310
Work space top view, 309
"Virtual Neighborhood" in Fountain, 329, 330
Virtual Reality Modeling Language. *See* VRML
Virtual SOMA, 283-284
Virtual spaces, 355
Virtus Corp.
    Virtus VR authoring tool, 298
    Voyager viewer, 287
    WalkThrough Pro authoring tool, 297
    Web site, 318, 435
Virtus VRML, 318
Virtus WalkThrough Pro. *See* WalkThrough Pro
Visual Basic (VB) Script, 158
Visual Components
    Formula One/Net spreadsheet, 426
    plug-in, 230
visualmode parameter in the EMBED HTML tag, 379-380
VocalTec's Internet Wave, 360, 363-365, 384-388, 402, 403
    Web site, 436
Voice compression in VoxWave, 361
Voice files, recording quality of, 375
void keyword in Java, 134
.vox extension, 376
.vox files, 376
    calling in HTML, 377, 378
.vox format, compressing to, 376
VoxWare
    MIME type, configuring services to handle, 380
    relationship with Netscape, 361

ToolVox, 360, 361-362, 376-380, 429
ToolVox Web site, 437, 438
Voyager Company, 66-68
Voyager viewer, 287
VR Scout
    plug-in, 230
    viewer, 286
    VRML plug-in, 430
VR SOMA, 284, 350
VRCreator authoring tool, 298
VREALM VRML plug-in, 430
Vream
    VRCreator authoring tool, 298
    Web site, 435
    WIRL plug-in, 430
    WIRL viewer, 287
VRML, 280-281
    add-on, 287
    advantages of, 282
    authoring tools, 295-298
    browsers, extensive reviews of, 432
    code, 287-288
    disadvantages of, 282
    establishing a point of reference, 292
    exporting .wtp format to, 326
    future of, 296, 298-300
    history of, 282-283
    and HTML, 282
    Internet resources, 341
    and Java, 151-152
    mailing lists, 341
    newsgroup, 341
    resources on the Web, 432-435
    sources of information on, 341
    specifications on the Internet, 341
    Tony Parisi on the future of, 300
    viewers, 281, 285-287

writing, 289-295
VRML 1.0
    draft specification for, 283
    specification, 290-295
VRML Architecture Group site, 432
VRML Architecture Group (VAG),
    299
VRML community, 304
VRML files, 283
    displaying in Internet Explorer,
        161
VRML Forum, 432
VRML Mailing List, 299, 432
VRML Object SuperMarket, 344
VRML Repository site, 432
VRML Volunteer, 349, 351
VRML worlds
    building in Virtual Home Space
        Builder, 311-317
    examples of, 283-285
    finding, 344-345
    navigation of, 288
    saving as VRML files, 315
    system requirements for
        viewing, 288
Vspace= attribute, 98

W

Walk mode in Fountain, 330, 331
Walk View in WalkThrough Pro,
    319, 320
Walker toolbox in Virtual Home
    Space Builder, 307, 310-311
WalkThrough Pro, 296, 318
    authoring tool, 297
    building worlds in, 319-328
    cost of, 318
    exporting VRML files from, 328
    library, 327-328
    user interface, 319

as a VRML tool, 320-321
    workspace, views in, 319, 320
Wall Street Web, 147-149
Wallpaper icon in the Chooser
    window, 314
Wallpaper mode in the Chooser
    window, 311, 312
Walls in Virtual Home Space
    Builder, 304
Watermarks, creating in Internet
    Explorer, 161
.wav extension, 249, 381
.wav file, converting to TrueSpeech
    format, 381, 383
WAV file, importing into the cast in
    Director, 265
.wav format, 257, 374
    compressing, 361
Wavelet image codec, 426
Web
    Adobe Acrobat and, 10-12,
        51-59
    animated, 78-79
    delivering PDF files on, 55, 56
    designing PDF documents for,
        51, 52
    guide to resources and
        downloadable software,
        410-438
    guiding users to PDF files, 44-45
    interactive, 82-83
    low barrier to entry, 83-84
    as a mass medium, 396
    multiplatform nature of, 83, 84
    new technologies for, 83-88
    object code for sale on, 109-110
    optimizing PDF files for, 51-52
    possibilities for programmable,
        78-82
    preparing movies for, 267-269
    programmable, 78

and radio, 396
"shocked" tour of, 269-274
video and, 396
Web browsers, selecting to work
with Acrobat, 53
Web channels, 147
Web Creations, 109
Web Page Starter button in Netscape
Navigator Gold, 234
Web pages
creating in FrontPage Editor,
177
embedding RealAudio player
into, 391, 401
Web programming languages, Bill
Gates remarks on, 157
Web Publisher, 21
Web servers, reconfiguring for PDF
files, 55
Web sites
authoring, 174
building with FrontPage
Explorer, 175-177
devoted to Java, 143, 144
tracking page freshness, 226
Web URLs, hotlinks to in Director,
265, 267
WebBots, 173, 182
WebFX
plug-in, 229, 230, 316
viewer, 286
Weblink, 12, 52-54
in Acrobat Reader, 25
Preferences dialog box, 52-53
Webmasters
challenges for, 84
challenges of real-time
technologies, 402
needs met by Java, 92
WebSpace, 316
Author, 298

browser, home of, 434
Navigator viewer, 286
WebView in Windows 95, 190
while loop in JavaScript, 214
Wide button in Virtual Home Space
Builder, 309, 310
Width= attribute, 98
Window object, 216
Windows 3.1, PCM-to-TrueSpeech
conversion utility, 381
Windows 95
as a fully integrated Internet
platform, 190
Sound Editor, Save As dialog
box, 381, 383
Sound Recorder, 380-381
TrueSpeech compression
technology in, 362
Wire-frame rendering of objects, 289
WIRL plug-in, 430
viewer, 287, 435
with statement in JavaScript, 214-215
Wizards and templates in Microsoft
FrontPage, 174
.wmf extension, 249
Word Viewer 7.1, 172
Word Viewer plug-in, 430
Work space top view in Virtual
Home Space Builder, 309
Workshop Java, 142
Worlds Inc. 3-D worlds, 353
WorldsChat 3-D spaceport, 353
WorldView viewer, 287
.wrl extension, 288, 315
.wrl file, 290
.wtp format, 318
exporting to VRML, 326
WTP. *See* WalkThrough Pro
WWW Browser Application option
in the WebLink Preferences dialog
box, 53

WWWAnchor node, 293
WWWAnchor tag, 294
WWWInline node, 294
WYSIWYG HTML editor, 177

Xing StreamWorks, 360, 368-370, 401
    Web site, 436

Yahoo search engine logo, 269-270,
    271

Z

Zane, Barry, 82
Ziff-Davis' Terminal Reality, 349, 350
ZiffNet ZD3D Web site, 433
Zoghlin, Alex, 152-153
Zoom In toolbar button in Acrobat
    Reader, 30
Zoom Out toolbar button in Acrobat
    Reader, 30
Zoom Text dialog box, 264, 265
Zoop demo, 150, 151